INSTRUMENTAL REASONING AND SYSTEMS METHODOLOGY

THEORY AND DECISION LIBRARY

AN INTERNATIONAL SERIES
IN THE PHILOSOPHY AND METHODOLOGY OF THE
SOCIAL AND BEHAVIORAL SCIENCES

VOLUME 15

INSTRUMENTAL REASONING AND SYSTEMS METHODOLOGY

An Epistemology of the Applied and Social Sciences

RICHARD MATTESSICH

University of British Columbia, Vancouver, Canada
and
Technische Universität Wien, Vienna, Austria

D. REIDEL PUBLISHING COMPANY
DORDRECHT : HOLLAND / BOSTON : U.S.A.

Library of Congress Cataloging in Publication Data

Mattessich, Richard.
Instrumental reasoning and systems methodology.

(Theory and decision library; v. 15)
Bibliography: p.
Includes indexes.
1. System theory. 2. Science – Methodology.
3. Science – Philosophy. 4. Decision-making.
5. Economics – Methodology. I. Title.
Q295.M38 003 77–26670
ISBN 90–277–0837–1

Published by D. Reidel Publishing Company,
P.O. Box 17, Dordrecht, Holland

Sold and distributed in the U.S.A., Canada and Mexico
by D. Reidel Publishing Company, Inc.
Lincoln Building, 160 Old Derby Street, Hingham,
Mass. 02043, U.S.A.

Printed in The Netherlands

Dedicated to the many Austrian Philosophers,
Mathematicians and Scientists
*who emigrated to the West,**
conquering it not with arms
but through their imagination
and brilliance of mind

* The following galaxy of names is a mere illustration of those Austrian scholars who enriched the Western hemisphere: Ludwig von Bertalanffy, Peter Drucker, Herbert Feigl, Paul Feyerabend, Sigmund Freud, Kurt Gödel, Friedrich von Hayek (NL . . . stands for "Nobel Laureate"), Hermann Heller, Viktor Hess (NL), Karl von Frisch (NL), Hans Kelsen, Richard Kuhn (NL), Karl Landsteiner (NL), Paul Lazarsfeld, Konrad Lorenz (NL), Fritz Machlup, Hermann Mark, Lise Meitner, Karl Menger, Ludwig und Richard von Mises, Oskar Morgenstern, Johann von Neumann (Austro-Hungarian), Otto Neurath, Wolfgang Pauli (NL), Max Perutz (NL), Sir Karl Popper, Isidor Rabi (NL), Kurt Rothschild, Erwin Schrödinger (NL), Wolfgang Stegmüller, Gerhard Tintner, Abraham Wald (Austro-Hungarian), Ludwig von Wittgenstein, Hans Zeisel, Richard Zsigmondi (NL).

CONTENTS

PREFACE

This book has been written primarily for the applied and social scientist and student who longs for an integrated picture of the foundations on which his research must ultimately rest; but hopefully the book may also serve philosophers interested in applied disciplines and in systems methodology. If *integration* was the major motto, the *need for a methodology*, appropriate to the teleological peculiarities of all applied sciences, was the main impetus behind the conception of the present work. This need I felt a long time ago in my own area of analytical and empirical research in accounting theory and management science; later I had the opportunity to teach, for almost a decade, graduate seminars in Methodology which offered particular insight into the methodological needs of students of such applied disciplines as business administration, education, engineering, informatics, etc. Out of this effort grew the present book which among other things tries, on one side, to illuminate the difference and relationship between methods of cognition and methods of decision and on the other, to sketch a framework suitable for depicting means–end relationships in a holistic setting. I believe that a systems methodology which incorporates recent endeavours of deontic logic, decision theory, information economics and related areas would be eminently suited to break the ground for such a future framework.

Yet systems theory has two major shortcomings which might prevent it from evolving into the desired methodology of applied science. First, systems theory is not sufficiently integrated with existing insights and conceptual tools of present-day epistemology (partly because most, but by no means all, system experts lack proficiency in philosophy, and partly because professional philosophers have ignored the systems approach for too long a time). Second, the systems approach, in spite of half a century of tradition, has not yet become rigorous enough to serve in the envisaged capacity. I am far from claiming to have overcome either of these two handicaps. It was rather my more modest ambition to offer a survey of the territory, combined with some of my own thoughts on systems and instrumental reasoning. Thus I hope to have made the first stumbling steps in the direction of a systems methodology of the applied and social sciences.

From the very beginning I have pleaded for analyzing the means–end relationship from a more comprehensive or holistic point of view than has been customary. The ultimate result of this endeavor emerges toward the end of the last chapter in the form of *five basic system principles* together with their ontological counterparts (polarity, periodicity, concrescence, formative preference and information). But the main pedagogic feature of this effort lies in its eclecticism without which a high degree of integration of fairly diverse areas would not have been possible. To explain the most important among the many logical and epistemological achievements of the last century or so, to point out the numerous cross-references, thus to hint at and illustrate relations between logic and mathematics, deductive and inductive inferences, induction and probability, probability theory and modal logic, decision theory and information economics, holism, Gestalt theory and structuralism, systems methodology and ontology, etc., is one of the major tasks of this book. In this connection I have also tried to illustrate the widely ignored fact that *typical system features are encountered in many traditional areas*, that is to say in logic, mathematics, epistemology, etc. The hinting at these dispersed system characteristics penetrates the book like a red thread, and forms a link between areas which traditionally are disregarded in system literature. Such a broad scope often enforced great conciseness (a reason why the reader must be asked to study some passages as carefully as possible); on the other side, I had to present some topics cursorily only. In both cases supplementary literature is indicated. On a general level we may recommend at this place the *Encyclopedia of Philosophy* as an excellent reference work on most, though not on all, topics, relevant to our scope. As a general supplementary reading, I may recommend the *second* volume of Stegmüller's *Hauptströmungen der Gegenwartsphilosophie* which only recently (1975) appeared (the English translation of the *first* volume was published in 1969 under the title *Main Currents in Contemporary German, British and American Philosophy*). The first volume too is recommendable, especially the last three chapters on Carnap, Analytical Philosophy, and Wittgenstein, but it is outranked in relevance and wide scope by the second volume (of which an English translation seems to be in preparation) which ranges from linguistic philosophy and modern semantics, over the many phases of modern evolutionary theory (physics and biology as well as cosmology), to the evolution of scientific thinking. Wherever it overlaps with our book, it either illuminates different aspects or applies a different method of presentation (it hardly uses symbolic presentations, tables etc. of which we made plenty of use for the sake of utmost conciseness), furthermore it varies greatly in view point and purpose, and thus constitutes a most suitable *complementary* piece of literature.

Our Chapter 1 (*Introduction*) discusses the need for, and the essence of, an epistemology of the applied sciences. It touches such problems as the design and conflict resolution of systems, the testing of instrumental hypotheses together with the characteristics distinguishing instrumental from cognitive hypotheses, as well as the economic aspects of epistemology.

Chapter 2 (*Systems Analysis as a Tool of Philosophical Investigation*) starts from the ever stronger felt need for a fundamental mathematical or logical structure capable of satisfying the normativistic and teleologic needs of instrumental reasoning. It offers a first survey of the systems approach (a topic which is taken up again in Chapter 7 where it is further elaborated), and discusses such necessary system conditions as existence, plurality of elements, relations, embedding environment, boundary determination, as well as auxiliary conditions such as openness, goal-directedness, functional capacity, adaption, sensory capacity, introspection, as well as further problems of system boundaries. However, the point of gravity is found in the second half of this chapter where some novel questions are taken up and analyzed: Is it meaningful to regard a system as normative (or alternatively, as neutral or positive)? How is it possible to incorporate (or alternatively, to exclude) norms or value judgements into (from) a system? What are the conditions for extending such sentential notions as description and prescription to system structures? A method is sketched enabling us to locate, as well as localize, the norms of a system; furthermore an attempt is made to show that the application of this method to Searle's (1964, 1969) reduction of ought-sentences to institutional is-sentences would be further clarified; above all, it could establish the system character of such institutions.

Chapter 3 (*Philosophy and Evolution of Logic from a Systems Point of View*) offers an evolutionary survey of deductive logic and semantics. In our experience, applied scientists, in general, do greatly benefit by gaining deeper insight in this fundamental area (especially in its development during the last hundred and fifty years). To look at this field from the point of view of a systems methodologist, and to integrate it with aspects of other areas (e.g. with the mind–body problem) was our foremost task (the more technical aspects, in as far as we have dealt with them, were reserved for the next chapter). But neither of these two chapters is concerned with *teaching* the rudiments of logic, the chapters were designed to offer a broad survey ranging from the contributions of Aristotle to those of such contemporary authors as Chomsky, Montague and Kripke.

Chapter 4 (*Modern Deductive Logic*) deals with the more technical aspects of deductive logic, including multi-valued and modal logic as well as imperative and deontic arguments. The Chapter begins with a discussion of the essence of sentence logic and predicate logic, and the differences between them. Thereby not only the simpler issues of sentence connectives and truth tables, but also more complex issues are discussed: e.g. the presentation of a deductive argument in "conditional form" (so crucial for understanding the *validation* of an argument and the problem of *decidability*) is explained; furthermore, such issues as axiomatization of the sentence calculus, valid formulas of predicate logic, the theory of description and opposing views (and thus the connection to semantics) are presented concisely.

More than half of this Chapter is devoted to multi-valued and modal logic, which are depicted as two versions pursuing a common or at least similar goal. Modal logic (dealing first of all with the problems of *necessity, possibility* and *impossibility*) is further expanded, but less as a foundation for probability theory (which it could easily be), than as a rapidly growing sub-area of logic, comprising also deontic inferences (dealing with the problems of *permission, forbidding* and *obligation*) as well as imperative and mixed inferences, posing special problems due to its utilization of non-propositions such as commands, recommendations, advice, etc. The relevance of these issues to instrumental reasoning is emphasized and the connection to ampliative arguments is pointed out. Rescher's notion of "task thesis" and von Wright's *T–I*-calculus are briefly discussed, but there is not enough space to go into the full pioneering efforts in this area. Thus we did neither include von Wright's first (and nowadays somewhat obsolete) formulations of deontic issues, nor such areas as epistemic logic (only shortly mentioned), temporal logic, nominalistic logic, quantum logic etc. For a general discussion of these areas, as well as further aspects of modal logic etc., we refer the reader to Stegmüller (1975a, pp. 147–220).

Chapter 5 (*The Controversy Around Inductive Logic*) presents the hitherto unresolved Humean problem of induction (unresolved with regard to explanation, justification as well as quantification), its historical perspective, as well as the great variety of its many scintillating facets. Above all, its relation to probability theory is emphasized in this and the next Chapter. The discussion of the hypothetic-deductive approach (as one attempt to face the stubborn issue of induction) leads to Sir Karl Popper's influential contributions of *falsificationism* and the variegated criticism directed against it. A discussion of Mill's *methods* of induction (presented concisely in its modern version as given by H. von Wright) offers some opportunity for explaining the difference between *necessary* and *sufficient* conditions. Then Carnap's impressive attempt to create a *theory of confirmation* is discussed with reference to Bayes' theorem and by means of some examples and illustrations. From this concern with the analytical aspects of induction, the Chapter proceeds to the empiristic *frequentists'* approach of von Mises, Reichenbach and others. In this connection an attempt is made to sketch the related issues of statistical *parameter estimation* and *hypothesis testing* (as developed by Neyman and Pearson) together with the presentation of such notions as error characteristics, type I and type II errors, confidence intervals, levels of significance, etc. B. Russell's postulational approach to induction seems to us of special significance, as it gives evidence that scientific-inductive work can be justified only by admitting a set of assumptions (e.g. quasi permanence, separable causal lines, spatio-temporal continuity, structure, and analogy) which are based on nothing but intuition. This unexpected subjective element in Russell's approach, to our mind, forshadowed the growing realization of the limitations set to an uncritical empiricism – a realization nowadays manifested in the structuralistic formalization of Thomas Kuhn's thesis, as presented by Sneed and Stegmüller (see our Section 7.32); an approach that saves the picture of science as a *rationalistic* enterprise, in spite of its subjective elements.

Modern inductivism as applied, on one side, to the cognitive act, on the other, to the instrumental act, cannot be properly understood without an analysis of the assumption about the "uniformity of the universe" and its relation to the system approach. Such an analysis is here illustrated. Goodman's paradox, not unrelated to this issue, demonstrates first that *inductive projectibility* is a matter of degree and, second, that its degree may depend on the language system (hence on an arbitrary or subjective element) used to describe the pertinent uniformity or regularity. Finally, the connection between induction and probability is explored and the major interpretations (the empirical-objective, the analytical-objective, and the empirical-subjective interpretation) of Kolmogoroff's probability calculus are discussed. The conclusion summarizes major issues and offers an additional survey of different forms and types of inductions.

Chapter 6 (*Decision Theory and the Economists' Methodological Endeavors*) is, in a way, a continuation of the preceding chapter, and forms a link between induction and probability theory, on one side, and information economics, as well as the economics of knowledge acquisition, on the other. After some further reference to Carnap's confirmation theory, the essence and history of modern decision theory is concisely presented and illustrated.

In this connection Neyman and Pearson's theory of hypothesis-testing is taken up again and presented as a decision problem whereby an extension into the issue of experimental design as a decision theoretical optimisation is undertaken. Yet more thoroughly are discussed the principles of rational choice (transitivity of preferences, willingness to accept risk, preference of certainty, continuity I and II, irrelevance of order, and decomposability), the closely connected notion of Neumann–Morgenstern utility, preference scaling by means of interpolation and complex betting situations (lottery tickets), and similar issues. After some reference to Stegmüller's decision theoretical interpretation of Carnap's *confirmation theory*, J. Marschak and Radner's *team theory*, and Arrow's *impossibility theorem* (concerned with the aggregation of preference functions and the existence of an equitable method for social decisions), the Chapter deals with *information economics* as the most recent extension of decision theory. A detailed example illustrates how the expected utility of an information system can be determined, and how a monetary value can be attributed to it. In this connection *epistemo-economics* (the economic problem of knowledge acquisition) is taken up in the next Section. Inevitably, several fundamental questions arise, e.g. "Is an information or a piece of knowledge worth acquiring if its opportunity cost is higher than its benefit?" Another question probes into the difference between information versus knowledge, and between information economics versus knowledge economics. It is then suggested to regard *information* as the mere raw material of knowledge and hence as "*evidence*" in the Carnapian sense, while knowledge comes closer to the corresponding *hypothesis* (deemed to be true) which this evidence supports. The task of epistemo-economics is ultimately found in the attempt to determine the priorities of research goals in a systematic decision theoretic way on the basis of fundamental value judgements.

The last Section reviews further major methodological endeavors of economists, and centers on such issues as: normative versus positive economics, the questionable value neutrality of economic sciences, the interaction between cognition, valuation and action. Thus we are led back to our method of neutralizing (or deneutralizing) scientific systems, as discussed in Chapter 2. However, the core of this Section pivots on Milton Friedman's notorious assertion that not the assumptions, only the economic conclusions, need to be realistic, and on the methodologic dispute (between Samuelson, Machlup and others) that ensued. Finally, some thoughts on the stochastic and holistic aspects of economics are sketched.

Chapter 7 (*Philosophy of Science and the Systems Approach*) first offers a concise survey of the so-called "Received View" (and its principles) dominating the epistemological and scientific scenery until recently, but now being seriously challenged. Then, the ideas of the major challengers are shortly discussed: e.g. Hanson's *doctrine of the theory-ladeness of facts*, Thomas Kuhn's *distinction between normal and revolutionary science* and his *paradigmatism*, Feyerabend's *theory pluralism* and *epistemological anarchism*. Above all, it offers the reader some insight into the most significant *structuralistic* (hence system-theoretical) synthesis and formalization of T. Kuhn's thesis as presented by Sneed and Stegmüller. The structuralistic–instrumentalistic definition of theory, the notions of *intended application*, of *core improvement*, of *scientific progress* and *theory dislodgement*, etc. are concisely discussed. Hopefully they will inspire the reader to concern himself at a closer range with the promising pertinent literature. Yet, so far, this literature is in no way integrated with the systems approach. Hence the next section attempts to illuminate the similarities and relationships between the normativists (or *Weltanschauungs*-philosophers) and the system theorists, and resumes the topic of systems research and theory begun in Chapter 2. The contributions of Bogdanov, von Bertalanffy, Ackoff, Churchman, Herbert Simon, and many others (e.g. Othmar Spann, the Gestalt-theorists and the linguistic structuralists) are briefly discussed or at least pointed out.

The last Section tries to establish the systems approach as a holistic or, perhaps I should say, a *relatively* holistic methodology. This not only requires reference to Hegel, Whitehead, Georgescu-Roegen and others, but also an understanding of the reaction of our time to positivism and the traditional epistemological approach, with its disregard for value judgements. Above all, systems methodology cannot be based on mere technical notions, but must go back to fundamental ontological assumptions. These are finally formulated in a dual fashion (as ontological postulates as well as systems principles – as listed in the beginning of this Preface). I can only hope that these principles do not merely stand at the end of this book, but also at the beginning of a new Chapter in methodology. The reason for this hope lies in my optimistic belief that sooner or later system theorists will cease to be dazzled by the great variety of peripheral novelties that emerge almost daily in this field. Then they will recognize the need for erecting their systems on the firm ground of basic principles available for a world-view which is, if not utterly holistic, at least, as holistic as possible.

Finally I should like to express my thanks to all those who contributed, in one form or the other, to the publication of this book. First, I feel bound to express gratitude to my Ph.D.-students, auditors and assistants who – through discussions, ideas, queries, criticism as well as the occasional collection of material, and the reading of proofs – helped in shaping the manuscript. In this connection the following persons deserve special mentioning: Dr. habil Janos Ács, Mr. Ken Allen, B.Sc., M.B.A., Mr. Terry Brown, B.A.(Hons.), B.Com., C.A., Dr. Bevan Clarke (Professor and Chairman of Accounting and Management Information Systems at the University of Canterbury, Christchurch N.Z.), Dr. Giuseppe Galassi (Professor of Business Administration at the University of Parma, Italy), Dr. rer.soc.oec. Paul Jankowitsch, Dr. Ernst Offermann, Dr. Sudhir Saha, Dipl.Ing. Berndt Sigloch, M.B.A., Dr. Karl Stroetmann, Mr. Dennis Van Westerborg, B.Com.M.B.A., Dr. Baba Vishvanath, Mr. Frank Wolf, B.A. For typing various portions of the manuscript my thanks go to Mrs. Marlies Adamo, Miss Theresa Fong, Frau Frieda Lackner, Miss Marianne Leischner, Miss Nancy Shell, and Frau Elfriede Weigl. For support in financing the services of assistants, secretaries etc., I owe special gratitude to the Canada Council, The Fonds zur Förderung der wissenschaftlichen Forschung (Austria), the Faculty of Commerce and Business Administration of the University of British Columbia, Vancouver, B.C., The Technische Universität Wien, The Österreichische Industrieverwaltungs-A.G. and its Generaldirektor, Dipl. Ing. Dr. Franz Geist, as well as the "Fachverband für Stahl- und Maschinenbau der Bundeswirtschaftskammer" of Austria. A particular kind of gratitude goes to my wife Hermi whose life, for many years, would have been much easier, were it not for the book in front of you. Finally I should like to express my thanks to the D. Reidel Publishing Company as well as to both editors of the *Theory and Decision Library*, especially to Professor Werner Leinfellner.

Vancouver, B.C.,
November 1977 R.M.

ACKNOWLEDGEMENTS

The author wishes to thank the following authors, editors and publishers for the use of short passages as well as for permission (designated by P) to reprint from articles and books of which they hold the copyright:

Addison–Wesley Publishing Company (Reading, Mass.) for H. Raiffa, *Decision Analysis*, 1968 (P).

George Allen & Unwin Ltd. (London) for B. Russell, *Autobiography of Bertrand Russell*, quotations from the Bantam Books edition, Toronto, 1968 (P); B. Russell, *A History of Western Philosophy*, New York, 1945 (P) exclusive USA; B. Russell, *Human Knowledge, Its Scope and Limits*, New York, 1949 (P) exclusive USA; B. Russell, *Mysticism and Logic*, London, 1929 (P) exclusive USA.

Cornell University Press (Ithaca, N.Y.) for S. F. Barker, *Induction and Hypothesis*, © 1957 by Cornell University (P).

Dell Publishing Company (New York, N.Y.) for C. W. Churchman, *The Systems Approach*, 1968.

Dickenson Publishing Company (Belmont, Ca.) for B. Skyrms, *Choice and Chance*, 1966 (P).

Doubleday & Company, Inc. (New York, N.Y.) for I. Assimov, *Biographical Encyclopedia of Science and Technology*, 1964.

The editors of *General Systems* (Ann Harbour, Mich.) for R. L. Ackoff, 'General Systems Theory and Systems Research Contrasting Conceptions of Systems Science', *General Systems* 8, 1963 (P).

Gordon & Breach Science Publishers Ltd. (London) for E. Laszlo, *Introduction to Systems Philosophy*, New York, 1972 (P).

Harcourt Brace Jovanovich, Inc. (New York) for K. Lorenz, *Behind the Mirror*, English version of *Die Rückseite der Spiegels*, München/Zürich, 1973 (P for USA, its dependencies and the Philippine Islands).

Harper & Row, Publishers, Inc. (New York) for R. B. Braithwaite, *Scientific Explanation*, 1960 (P); H. L. Dreyfuss, *What Computers Can't Do*, 1972 (P); B. Russell, *Mysticism and Logic*, London 1929, quotations from the Doubleday 1957 edition (P for USA, its dependencies and the Philippine Islands).

Harvard University Press (Cambridge, Mass.) for N. Georgescu-Roegen, *The Entropy Law and the Economic Process*, 1971 (P); G. Myrdal, *The Political Element in the Development of Economic Theory*, 1954 (P for USA, its dependencies and the Philippine Islands).

Richard D. Irwin, Inc. (Homewood, Ill.) for W. Fellner, *Probability and Profit*, 1965 (P).

The editors of the *Journal of Philosophy* (New York, N.Y.) for P. Suppes, 'The Philosophical Relevance of Decision', *Journal of Philosophy* 58, 1961 (P).

Macmillan Publishing Co., Inc. (New York, N.Y.) for C. G. Hempel, *Aspects of Scientific Explanations and Other Essays*, 1965 (P); J. C. Emery, *Organizational Planning and Control Systems*, London, 1969; H. E. Kyburg, Jr, *Probability and Inductive Logic*, 1970 (P); for the articles 'Meaning' by W. P. Alston, Vol. 5; 'Induction' by M. Black, Vol. 4; 'Logic, Modern' by A. E. Blumberg, Vol. 5; 'Decision Theory' by P. Suppes, Vol. 2 of *Encyclopedia of Philosophy*, ed. Paul Edwards, 1967 (P).

McGraw-Hill Book Company (New York, N.Y.) for C. W. Churchman, *Challenge to Reason*, 1968 (P).

The editors of *Management Science* (New York, N.Y.) for R. L. Ackoff, Towards a System of System Concepts', in *Management Science* 17, 1971; R. Mattessich, 'The Incorporation and Reduction of Value Judgements in Systems', *Management Science* 21, 1974 (P).

M.I.T. Press (Cambridge, Mass.) for H. A. Simon, *The Sciences of the Artificial*, 1969 (P).

The editors of *Organization and Administrative Sciences* (Kent, Ohio) for A. J. Melcher, 'Theory and Application of Systems Theory: Its Promises, Problems and Realizations,' in *Organization and Administrative Sciences* 6, 1975 (P).

Oxford University Press (Oxford) for J. R. Searle, *The Philosophy of Language*, 1971 (P).

The editors of the *Philosophical Review* (Ithaca, N.Y.) for J. R. Searle, 'How to Derive "Ought" from "Is" ', in *Philosophical Review* 73, 1964 (P).

The editors of *Philosophy of Science* (East Lansing, Mich.) for N. Maxwell, 'A Critique of Popper's Views on Scientific Method', *Philosophy of Science* 30, 1972 (P).

R. Piper and Co. (München/Zürich) for K. Lorenz, *Die Rückseite des Spiegels*, 1973 (P).

Pitman Publishing Ltd. (London) for J. Robinson, *Economic Philosophy*, 1962, quotations from the Penguin 1973 edition (P).

Sir Karl Popper (Penn) for his book *Conjectures and Refutations*, New York, Basic Books 1962, 1965; Harper Torchbooks, New York, 1968; Routledge and Kegan Paul, London 1963; 5th edition 1974. Quotations from Basic Books edition, 1962 (P).

Prentice-Hall, Inc. (Englewood Cliffs) for B. Brody, *Readings in the Philosophy of Science*, 1970.

Random House, Inc. (New York, N.Y.) for J. J. Smart, *Between Science and Philosophy*, 1968 (P).

D. Reidel Publishing Company (Dordrecht) for I. M. Bochenski, *The Method of Contemporary Thought*, 1965 (P); W. Stegmüller, *Main Currents in Contemporary German, British and American Philosophy*, 1969 (P); G. Menges, 'On Subjective Probability and Related Problems', in *Theory and Decision* 1, 1970 (P).

Routledge and Kegan Paul, Ltd. (Henley on Thames) for G. Myrdal, *The Political Element in the Development of Economic Theory*, Cambridge, Mass. 1954 (P).

The editors of *Scientific American* (New York, N.Y.) for D. Layzer, 'The Arrow of Time', *Scientific American*, December, 1975.

J. R. Searle (Berkeley, Cal.) for his article 'How to Derive "Ought" from "Is" ' in the *Philosophical Review* 73, 1964 (P).

Simon & Schuster (New York, N.Y.) for B. Russell, *A History of Western Philosophy*, 1945 (P for USA, its dependencies and the Philippine Islands); B. Russell, *Human Knowledge, Its Scope and Limits*, 1949 (P for USA, its dependencies and the Philippine Islands).

Springer Verlag, Inc. (New York, N.Y.) for M. Bunge, *Scientific Research*, Vols I and II, 1967 (P).

P. Suppes (Stanford, Cal.) for his article 'The Philosophical Relevance of Decision Theory', *Journal of Philosophy,* 58, 1961 (P).

University of Chicago Press (Chicago, Ill.) for R. Carnap, *Meaning and Necessity: a Study in Semantics and Modal Logic*, 1947, enlarged ed. 1956 (P); T. Kuhn, *The Structure of Scientific Revolutions*, 1962 (P); M. Friedman, *Essays in Positive Economics*, 1953 (P).

The Board of Trustees of the University of Illinois (Urbana, Ill.) for F. Suppe (ed.), *The Structure of Scientific Theories*, 1974 (P).

University of Pittsburgh Press (Pittsburgh, Pa.) for W. C. Salmon, *The Foundations of Scientific Inference*, © 1967 (P).

J. Wiley & Sons, Inc. (New York, N.Y.) for S. S. Stevens, 'Measurement Psychophysics and Utility', in *Measurement, Definitions and Theories*, ed. by C. W. Churchman and P. Ratoosh, 1959 (P); C. W. Churchman,

'An Approach to General Systems Theory', in *Views on General Systems Theory,* ed. by M. D. Mesarovic, 1964; R. D. Luce and H. Raiffa, *Games and Decisions*, 1957 (P).

Yale University Press (New Haven, Conn.) for J. Marschak and R. Radner, *Economic Theory of Teams*, 1972 (P).

CHAPTER 1

INTRODUCTION

This book aspires to meet a dual task: on one side, there is the call *to initiate a philosophy of applied science* (see Chapters 1 and 2, as well as 6 and 7), on the other, there is the need *to acquaint the adepts of those applied fields with major problems of the philosophy of science (epistemology) in general* (see Chapters 3–5). A philosophy of the applied or instrumental sciences, no doubt, ought to be of interest to students of philosophy; but it would hardly fulfill its objective were it not comprehensible to applied scientists. As the philosophy of (pure) science has served many natural and social scientists, a future *philosophy of instrumental science* must, primarily and ultimately, serve a large array of professionally oriented experts: the administrative and management scientist, the economist and systems engineer, the medical specialist and researcher, the forestry and agricultural scientist, the space scientist and meteorologist, the education expert and ecologist, the political scientist as well as the disciples of newly emerging instrumental disciplines. But then, a major obstacle has to be mastered. Students no less than professors of most applied fields have traditionally been trained in modes of thinking that show little affinity to philosophical analysis. Whoever tried to teach epistemology to students of applied disciplines, will admit the initial difficulty of getting them started in an entirely novel and very different manner of thinking. But once they are acquainted with the previously unfamiliar conceptual apparatus, with the profundity of probing questions, the subtlety of many answers and the difference in ultimate goals, then this subject and its significance is readily appreciated. Of course some persons, by dint of disposition, will be unable to grasp the philosophical mode of analysis. Occasionally this anti-disposition seems to derive from a fixation on those acts and things that are *immediately* useful. Such people fail to recognize that acts useful in the short-run are not necessarily useful in the long-run, and that contemplation apparently useless at the moment, may ultimately prove to be most beneficial. The excessive worship of short-run needs and the failure to see that in the long-run the theoretical is the most practical, is symptomatic for the mood of our immediate past. Such an attitude falls hardly short of killing the proverbial goose that lays the golden eggs. Only slowly are we willing to face the overwhelming evidence that long-run thinking is more urgently needed today than ever before. And the study of philosophy is eminently suited to promote the prerequisite attitude. It provides sufficient draught to keep us from shallow reasoning, it reveals implied value judgements, helps to disentangle the goals to be envisaged from the goals actually pursued, and makes us see the limitations of our conceptual tools and methods.

1.1 Do Scientists Need Epistemology?

To ask why a scientist should be familiar with the theory of knowledge, and thus with the philosophy of science, seems to be a preposterous question. Is it at all possible to become a man of science without being aware of the foundations on which it rests? As much as we would wish to negate this question, it cannot be done. Scientists, even very successful ones, who care little and know nothing about epistemology are legions; and there is no use pretending that this, or any other area of philosophy, is a necessary condition for a successful scientific career. Whether one needs epistemology or not will rather depend on what kind of scientist he wants to be. If he resolves to utilize all his resources in concentrating on a narrow but significant area, perhaps to satisfy a specific purpose or ambition, the study of philosophy of science may occasionally be dispensable. But even if the enterprise of knowledge creation advances by *particular* insights, few of them are gained in isolation, and most require a broad vision. The majority of truly eminent scientists do not seem to be of the narrow type. They rather devote considerable time to the exploration of connections between their own efforts and the overall scheme of scientific endeavor. *Where and how does my own research fit into a large pattern? By means of which criteria do I determine whether my hypothesis or theory is tenable? Within which bounds is this theory valid? From these and related queries there is hardly an escape for any serious scientist.* To brush off these questions, as for example the second one, by citing some statistical rules of acceptance (the limitations of which are often enough insufficiently understood) would be grossly superficial. *Occasionally even the choice of a particular research project is prompted by philosophical contemplations and by discovering new gaps in this overall pattern of available, coherent truths*. Whoever chooses any scientific calling out of *genuine curiosity*, will find it difficult to stop his inquiry at the threshold of his own discipline. His inquisitiveness will lead him at least to a rough understanding of neighboring as well as foundational areas.

Continuation of the accelerating growth of knowledge might require ever increasing specialization. Apart from ultimate limits set to such a trend, it is obvious that the division of labor in science harbors no lesser danger than in industry. An elite of scholars, one-sidedly trained and conditioned by a narrow outlook, constitutes a threat to society which easily matches that of an army of workers bored by mind-numbing assembly lines. In both cases the balance has to be restored not by abandoning the division of labor but by introducing a counterweight. In the case of science such a countermeasure is found in a philosophic examination which offers the expert a broad and deep glance beyond the blinkers of specialization. Alas, the educational trend during the past decades did not favor this kind of equilibrium. Research activity during this time was geared more toward the generation of peripheral bits of knowledge than toward the integration of these bits to an overall view. Not even in Europe, the cradle of epistemology, was it possible to maintain completely the great interest paid by the majority of scholars to philosophy during the nineteenth and first part of the twentieth century. But philosophy is no passing fad, it is a well-weathered and most profound human endeavor. Its neglect creates reaction and counterforces. Indeed, there are tokens assuring us that the pendulum of academic fashion is reversing its course in direction of greater and broader receptiveness by the scientific community. An increasing number of philosophic topics (often under disguise) are nowadays being dealt with, in courses of ecology, systems theory and various social sciences. Beyond that the question was seriously raised whether cybernetics (which we regard as synonymous with "systems analysis") is not becoming a substitute for philosophy in general (see H. G. Frank, 1966, pp. 12–17). Some scholars, as for example K. Steinbuch (1961) even regard cybernetics as the only "valid" philosophy of our time. Although the monopolization of philosophy seems to be too ambitious an undertaking, one important fact must be recognized: *systems analysis is about to play the same stimulating role for the philosophy of the second half of the 20th century as evolution theory did for the philosophy of the second half of the 19th century*. And it matters little in which courses or under what label this philosophy is promulgated. Important, however, is that such a system of philosophic analysis is presented, not under the pretense of an empirical science and that it is comprehensive enough, hence not consisting of mere bits and pieces or some isolated ideas. The fractionalization of the piecemeal approach, usually encountered, is more harmful to a philosophy of science than to an empirical discipline. Major aims of the former are (1) *disclosure of inconsistencies* (i.e. of the limits of the prevailing knowledge) and (2) *insight into the interdependencies of relevant variables*; to accomplish these tasks a comprehensive over-all picture is required.

To understand fully the need for epistemology, one must realize that *empirical science as a system of information and knowledge creation is still in a suspended state, it literally hovers above its foundation without being sufficiently tied to it.* The strongest justification for science has always been its rationality or consistency. But where does this consistency begin and where does it end? Whoever pretends that science is consistent from alpha to omega behaves no different than a bank clerk counting a bundle of bills supposedly worth five thousand dollars, but stopping short at three thousand with the following argument: "Since it was correct that far, the rest will be correct too". This trite analogy should not be disparaged. It vividly drives home the insight that the most accurate procedure is inadequate if not consistently carried out to the very end. "Meaningful knowledge is based on experience only". This is not merely the battle cry of positivism but the foundation stone of every empirical science. Yet this sentence in parenthesis, is it itself based on experience? The fact that it is not, forces us to admit the present foundational dilemma, or at least incompleteness, of the entire enterprise of science. Is it not the task of epistemology to overcome this puzzling inconsistency and to look at science not as an isolated body of sentences, but as an entity embedded in the total environment of human values and actions? If it is, then *the search for the sources, criteria, structure and limitations of knowledge* is still highly acute. But can it be accomplished without participation of the applied scientist? As long as science is tied by nothing but threads to its foundation and value matrix, there will be good reason to have both the epistemologist as well as the applied scientist participate in the business of reinforcing these ties. The impressive achievements of modern science deceive easily about the shaky foundations on which it rests. *Too many of us are satisfied with the pragmatic criterion that science is true because it works*. Works for how long? Until Mother Earth has become uninhabitable thanks to this working? How can we be sure the expedient of today is not the impediment of tomorrow? Could the pragmatic answer not become the death certificate of science and mankind alike? Indeed, truth and knowledge deserve a firmer foundation than short-run usefulness.

All sciences are afflicted with foundational difficulties, yet increasingly so when moving from the physical over the biological to the social and finally the administrative sciences. In this ascent the teleological and normative aspects become more and more significant, and the positivistic attempt to banish them only aggravates the dilemma. A good deal of research in the social and administrative sciences is intricately interwoven with value judgements and thus belongs to the border area of science and philosophy. Often the accommodation of these philosophic problems constitutes a prerequisite for further progress in these sciences. But as long as these problems of value judgements are suppressed, further insight is grossly inhibited. The attempt to banish value judgements from the realm of science, especially from the administrative and other applied sciences, may ultimately turn out to have been a curse rather than a boon to mankind.

Among the innumerable instances demonstrating the neglect to consider basic value judgements and long-run effects, the repeated damming and ultimate diversion of the waters of the lower Colorado river is outstanding. Here is an example on a grand scale where shortsighted planners built one dam after another until this magnificent river salinated valuable crop land, dissipated into porous rocks, evaporated in big lakes and literally petered out in the desert instead of serving present and future generations to the fullest extent possible. It is not likely that the politicians, administrators and engineers responsible for those decisions had a good grounding in the philosophy of applied sciences; otherwise their decisions would have been very different.

Were they aware for whose benefit and at whose damage they built? In other words, were they aware of the value judgements involved? Was it not *blindness toward value judgements* rather than a deliberate choice to damage the economic base of future generations? Perhaps only a critical holistic view is rich enough to impart a full picture of the preferences entailed in our actions.

The basic epistemological problems are the same for all empirical sciences, but some aspects, as for example methods of testing and verification, acceptance and truth criteria, boundaries of universal statements, degrees of involvement in value judgements, etc., vary greatly from discipline to discipline. Hence there is justification for teaching epistemology in *various* academic faculties, or at least for arranging within one department, philosophy of science courses for different areas (e.g. natural sciences, social sciences, administrative and other applied sciences). After all epistemology has been advanced by philosophers and empirical scientists alike. As Stegmüller (1969a, p.8) asserts, "... the separate sciences which in the first flush of independence sought to draw farther and farther away from philosophy, have themselves been compelled on internal grounds to engage in philosophical reflections. In doing so they have at the same time given a fresh impetus to philosophic research." The communication between philosopher and scientist is no one-way street; the more intensive this interchange becomes, the more significant will be the common endeavor.

The increasing predominance of the *instrumental sciences* seem to require special attention. These applied disciplines, on one side, have much in common with the pure sciences; on the other, deviate in fundamental aspects from them. But epistemology paid little attention to these differences and hardly any to the closely related problem of the *economics of knowledge creation.* Yet the mood of our super-technologic age cannot be comprehended without the particular value judgements and points of emphasis characteristic for the applied sciences. The hydrogen bomb and nuclear reactor, the computer and information revolution, the supersonic jet plane and lunar space craft are only a few of the spectacular and direct achievements of the *applied* sciences. No less important are the consequences, such as overpopulation and overarmament, potential energy and raw material shortages, unemployment and inflation, multi-dimensional contamination of the environment and mental pollution through mass media and behavioral propaganda techniques. For which ends shall we employ scientific means? This question concerns the applied scientist no less than the businessman, government administrator, politician or statesman. But these remarks may easily be misunderstood. In this book we are not concerned with suggestions of a moral code appropriate for our time; nevertheless we cannot escape the fact that value judgements, so obvious in politics, business, law and other practical areas are embedded in a *hierarchy of norms* penetrating right down to the applied sciences. Yet not these norms shall here be investigated, merely *the principles governing them*. A further task of this book, to which some space will be devoted, deals with the *difference in truth claims between hypotheses of the pure and those of the applied sciences.* And finally the *interrelations between norm and truth, value and belief, utility and probability* cannot be overlooked in a treatise on the philosophy of applied science.

1.2 Towards a Philosophy of Applied Science

The philosophy of applied science, although never systematically elaborated, has an ancestry that can be traced from Aristotle's *Nicomachean Ethics* over Kant's *Critique of Practical Reason* (1788) and *Critique of Judgement* (1790), to Bogdanov's *Tectologia* (1912), Hostelet's *L'investigations scientifique des faites d'activité humaine* (1960) and Kotarbiński's

Praxiology (1955/65). But none of these pioneering efforts is sufficiently integrated with, and focused specifically upon, a philosophy of applied science. Only in the most recent past have attempts in this particular direction been made: Bunge in the second volume of his monumental work on *Scientific Research* (1967) devoted the entire Chapter II (Vol. 2) to the philosophy of applied science. And much of Churchman's writings (e.g. 1961, 1968a, 1968b) is penetrated with thoughts closer to applied than pure science. Furthermore some of his disciples, for instance Mason (e.g. 1969) and Mitroff (e.g. 1973) as well as other management science philosophers such as Helmer and Rescher (e.g. 1959) seem to share this special orientation of epistemology. Occasionally one encounters similar interests in areas beyond management science; the magazine *Technology and Culture,* for instance devoted an entire issue (Vol. VII, No. 3, 1966) to this topic under the title "Toward a Philosophy of Technology". See also Rapp (1974).

Both, pure and applied sciences fulfill a cognitive as well as an instrumental task, but in each branch these two ingredients are mixed in different proportions. Roughly speaking one might say that the *cognitive element* dominates pure science: All of its statements have a sufficiently high degree of reliability as to be *assumed* true, but their specific usefulness may not be established. Whereas the *instrumental element* dominates applied science: All of its statements are *assumed* to be useful but their degree of reliability is not necessarily high enough to regard them as true in the conventional sense. Thus the applied sciences use the same methods as the pure ones (observation and measurement, induction and deduction, interpretation and testing, etc.) but with *a fairly specific purpose* in mind, and under consideration of an economic or *cost–benefit criterion*. The distinction between pure and applied science is not simply that between "knowing" and "doing", but rather that between "believing for the sake of knowing" and "believing for the sake of doing". And since epistemology cannot restrict its concern to *knowing* but must be equally concerned with *believing*, the philosophy of both pure as well as applied science belongs to it.

Obviously there exists neither an absolute nor a generally accepted line of demarcation between pure and applied science. And Figure 1-1 offers nothing but a crude categorization of science in general. The distinction between analytical and empirical science is one of the most favored categorizations of our time. But it was not always accepted, nor is it certain that it will survive in future. Quine (1953), for instance, tried to exploit Gödel's incompletability theorem to express doubt that the distinction between analytical and empirical propositions is justified. However, as long as the counterevidence

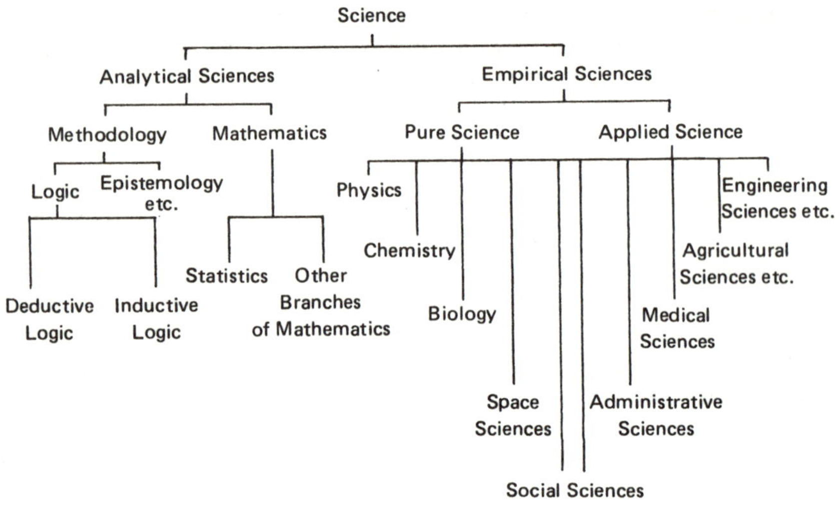

Fig. 1-1

supplied by Quine and others is not more conclusive, we might accept these two categories, at least provisionally, as mutually exclusive and exhaustive. The *analytical sciences* deal with statements *irrefutable by experience*. Their most important branches are logic and mathematics, both consisting of nothing but tautologies. Whether logic is a branch of methodology or *vice versa* is still disputed (the same holds for methodology vs. epistemology) – even worse, there is not even a concensus as to the nature of the statements generated by methodology, epistemology and philosophy in general.

The *empirical sciences* deal with statements which, in principle at least, are *refutable by experience*. Such statements are not true by necessity and thus are never completely reliable. Their truth is a provisional one and based on the strength of the pertinent evidence. If such statements are unrefuted and, in addition, sufficiently corroborated or confirmed or grounded, then they are *assumed* to be true. But when is a statement *sufficiently* verified? This is one of the most puzzling questions of epistemology and its discussion has to be postponed to Chapter 5.

At the beginning of the empirical spectrum (right-hand side of Figure 1-1) there are the "purest" sciences such as physics, chemistry etc., as well as the less pure space sciences (geography, astronomy etc.) and social sciences (psychology, etc.), further down are more or less applied sciences, the foundational research of which may be close to or even transgress into the area of pure science (economics, management science, systems science etc.), and finally there are the extreme applied sciences such as agricultural science, engineering, etc. The boundary between pure and applied sciences is fairly arbitrary and the distinction between both is an issue of semantics. In this book we merely rely on the criterion outlined above for distinguishing one from the other.

But there is another distinction frequently encountered, that between applied science and technology (invention). Some authors (Hatfield, 1933; Agassi, 1966; Skolimowski, 1966; and Wisdom, 1966) try to separate these closely related notions, yet when it comes to the definition of each area there seems to be little common ground. Others regard the spectrum from pure science over applied science to technology as consisting of many discontinuities, but none large enough to find articulate thresholds of demarcation. In this regard we share Bunge's view, and his words hold no less for the present work than for his own contribution: "The terms 'technology' and 'applied science' will be taken here as synonymous, although neither is adequate: In fact, 'technology' suggests the study of practical arts rather than a scientific discipline and 'applied science' suggests the application of scientific ideas rather than that of the scientific method. Since 'technique' is ambiguous and 'epistechnique' unborn, we shall adopt the current lack of respect for etymology and go over to more serious matters." Mario Bunge (1966, p. 329).[1] Yet this view must not be identified with the pragmatic notion which regards any science – whether pure, applied or technological –

[1] But Bunge distinguishes among the applied sciences (technological theories) between *substantive theories* (e.g. electrical and mechanical engineering) and *operative theories* (e.g. operations research and other administrative sciences):

> On the other hand the theories of value, decisions, games, and operations research deal directly with valuation, decision making, planning and doing . . . These theories are technological in respect of aim, which is practical rather than cognitive, but apart from this they do not differ markedly from the theories of science. In fact all good operative theories will have at least the following traits characteristic of scientific theories: (i) they do not refer directly to chunks of reality but to more or less idealized models of them . . . (ii) as a consequence they employ theoretical concepts . . . (iii) they can absorb empirical information and can in turn enrich experience by providing predictions or retrodictions, and (iv) consequently they are empirically testable. Bunge, *Scientific Research II, The Search for Truth*, 1967.

With regard to subdividing applied sciences and distinguishing them from pure sciences we find ourselves in accord with not only the view expressed by Bunge, but also with the writing of Ackoff, Churchman and other management scientists.

as exclusively instrumental. Such a notion forces the pragmatist either to negate the cognitive function of science or to identify truth with usefulness. The opposite philosophic extreme is encountered in rationalism which rejects the truth notions of pragmatists and empiricists alike and tends, at least in its undiluted version, to accept only analytical insights as truly cognitive. We shall defend neither of these extremes and follow a line of *critical empiricism* which is broad enough to recognize *introspection* as experience and thorough enough to admit the *speculative* nature of its own foundation. This early hint of our philosophic bias is offered in order to dispel the misconception that a philosophy of applied science by its very nature must surrender to the premises of pragmatism.

1.3 Management Science and the Philosophy of Applied Science

One bias freely admitted by us is a strong emphasis of the economic, administrative and systems science, in short of the "management sciences". The reason for this is by no means a disregard of other applied disciplines; it is rather the belief that management science is in a position to contribute more than any other instrumental field to the philosophical analysis of *all* applied areas. This is neither a novel view, nor is it merely due to the author's background. Even a logician like Kotarbinski (1965), pointed out that "It is only of late, perhaps only in the last seventy years, that something like a general praxiology has emerged. I refer to certain works by individuals working on the theory of business management. They include numerous very general observations, so general that in many instances the idea of a rationalizing engineer coincides with a philosopher's methodological idea . . . This is by no means a problem specific to business management" (Kotarbinski, 1965, p. 7).

This trend has been reinforced by the metamorphoses which the administrative sciences underwent since the second World War. Not only did this lead to more rigorous research methods but also to contributions preparatory for a philosophic analysis of applied science. We think primarily of the Systems Approach but shall reserve its discussion for Chapter 2. As to the general methodology in these fields, a point has to be made that is rarely sufficiently emphasized. Predominantly descriptive presentations gave way to analytical–empirical approaches; and the experts of business, industrial and public administration, political science, systems analysis, economics and management science, succeeded in adapting scientific methods to their applied disciplines. The deployment of modern mathematical tools in these areas led to more rigorous ways of thinking as well as to a host of theories and models of various degrees of generality. Indeed, administrative scientists nowadays are engaged in a continuous process of theory construction to a greater extent than are natural scientists. A good deal of the latter are rather concerned with what the well-known historian of philosophy of science, Thomas Kuhn, calls: "mopping-up operations", i.e. with the elaboration and strengthening of existing theories.

> Mopping-up operations are what engages most [natural] scientists throughout their careers. They constitute what I am here calling normal science. Closely examined, whether historically or in the contemporary laboratory, that enterprise seems an attempt to force nature into the performed and relatively inflexible box that the paradigm supplies. No part of the aim of normal science is to call forth new sorts of phenomena; indeed those that will not fit the box are often not seen at all. Nor do [natural] scientists normally aim to invent new theories, and they are often intolerant of those invented by others. Instead, normal-scientific research is directed to the articulation of those phenomena and theories that the paradigm already supplies.[2]

Our remark is by no means meant to be derogatory of natural science. On the contrary, the mere fact that pure scientists are dealing with deeper, more general and perhaps more permanent theories than applied scientists, requires the former to devote more time and energy to consolidating their theoretical structures. Applied scientists in contrast are less concerned with *cognitive* than with *instrumental* theories, less with general than with fairly specific paradigms which are directed toward particular goals. It is this difference in activity and orientation which keeps the administrative scientist busy with theory and systems construction, making him the model builder *par excellence.* But such intensive concern with the construction of theories, models and systems puts a heavy and, in a way, new responsibility on the administrative scientist. *None of his innumerable models is of much use unless to be tested; to be tested not so much as to its truth, but as to the degree of accomplishing its purpose.* Yet, this is a highly complex issue and plunges him head on into philosophic reflections presently dealt with in management science. This aspect arouses problems of many branches of methodology (logic, epistemology, praxiology, ethics, mathematics, systems theory, etc.) and the recent infatuation of many administrative scientists with mathematics might give way to a greater concern with philosophic issues. Indeed,

[2] Kuhn, *The Structure of Scientific Revolutions,* 1962, p. 24.

there exist tokens that the mathematical emphasis in management science is shifting away from purely technical considerations to those of fundamental and structural significance. Above all, management scientists have adopted a philosophic framework that enables them to reconcile the goals of a specific system with the goals of the super-systems in which the former is embedded. Or in Churchman's words:

> For the applied scientist, scientific method must include a philosophy of the whole system, however vague, however inadequate, however difficult to defend . . . The pure scientist believes he can discover truth in a piece of reality without disturbing the whole . . . The more heroic applied scientist tries to bear the burden of the enormous risk and vagueness of his Weltanschauung . . . The applied scientist is – or struggles to be – both a humanist and a scientist. For him science is an art, an ethic, a comedy, and tragedy.[3]

Thus the applied scientist must be acquainted with the major issues of up-to-date scientific and philosophic thinking. To construct proper theories he will do better when aware of the revolutionary reorganization of *deductive logic* since George Boole made his contribution. To test theories and systems an acquaintance with recent issues of *inductive logic* will make him more advertent. To adjust the tools of pure science for applied purposes he may even need insight into praxiology and analytical ethics. The fate of the future lies in the hands of the applied scientist; if we train him to become a narrow-minded technocrat, his skills may not benefit but terrorize mankind.

1.4 Conclusion

We are now in a position to conclude that the *philosophy of instrumental science investigates the validity and reliability of generalized knowledge about purposeful actions*. By necessity it comprises traditional epistemology but must go beyond it to lay the foundations for the supplementary problems listed subsequently. But actions are usually prepared within more or less complex decision systems, and the pertinent problems must be conceived in terms of such systems.

(1) *The Problem of Design*: The optimal or satisfactory matching of a system structure to the specific *goal* pursued by the system. This problem

[3] Churchman, *A Challenge to Reason*, 1968, pp. 133–134.

is obviously related to the classical problem of theory construction. But the task of a theory is to represent reality at a degree of approximation considered to be satisfactory (whatever "satisfactory" may mean), whereas the task of a system is to fulfill a more specific and often non-cognitive purpose. The latter includes not only the mere attainment of a task but its attainment under certain constraints among which economic efficiency constraints assume a prime position. Hence, considerations of the *cost–benefit criterion* play a decisive role in the problem of system design.

(2) *The Problem of Conflict and Resolution*: The conflict between the goals of different systems and the resolution of such a conflict constitutes a typical *dialectical problem* and plays an eminent role in every applied science. Whether the decision involves a conflict between keeping too large a quantity of merchandising stocks, safeguarding good customer service, versus too low stocks, avoiding excessive storage costs, or whether it refers to the conflict between administering too high a dosage of diphtheria serum, securing an effective reaction in the patient, versus too low a dosage, avoiding fatal overreaction, or whether it concerns any other kind of goal conflict, *a resolution in form of an optimal, quasi-optimal, or at least satisfactory decision is needed.* Often a conflict exists between the goals of two or more subsystems to be resolved within the goal of the main system, or alternatively the conflict between the goal of a sub-system and the goal of the main system to be resolved in the goal of a supersystem. Therefore this issue involves two further subproblems (i) that of the hierarchy of systems and (ii) the *cybernetic problem* of feedback and interdependence of elements as well as of systems. The classical analogue to this problem complex is more difficult to discern; it might be found, on one side, in *reductionism* (which conceives of a hierarchy of scientific disciplines claimed to be ultimately reducible to the primitive notions of physics) and, on the other side, in the *theory of coherence* (which emphasizes the complementarity and thus interdependence of all scientific truths).

(3) *The Problem of Testing, Rejecting, and Accepting*: How can a decision system be tested as to its goal fulfillment and efficiency? Does the system fulfill its purpose at a reasonable degree? Does it satisfy the minimal criteria set for it? Shall it be accepted, revised or rejected? These questions resemble closely those of hypotheses and theory verification encountered in traditional epistemology. But there exist marked differences between the testing of cognitive hypotheses and theories on one side, and the testing of

TABLE 1-1

Some characteristics distinguishing cognitive from instrumental hypotheses

	Cognitive hypotheses	Instrumental hypotheses
(i)	Structure of the general form: "All *A* are *B*" and variations.	Structure of the general form: "To attain *A* do *B*" and variations.
(ii)	Non-teleologic.	Goal oriented.
(iii)	Efficiency irresponsive.	Highly efficiency responsive.
(iv)	Rigorous criteria of acceptance based on truth assumption.	Relaxed criteria of acceptance based on assumption of better goal attainment.
(v)	High degree of generality.	Limited degree of generality.
(vi)	Not behaviorally limited.	Predominantly oriented toward decision behavior.
(vii)	Oriented toward cause and effect relations.	Oriented also toward reason and action relations.
(viii)	Serving the inference of statements within assertorial (declarative) arguments.	Serving the inference of imperatives, etc., within deontic (normative) arguments.

instrumental hypotheses and systems, on the other. Table 1-1 indicates in rough strokes some major differences between cognitive and instrumental hypotheses influencing their testing procedures.

The difference between cognitive and instrumental hypotheses shall be illustrated by the following two versions of a proposition frequently encountered in microeconomics and the administrative sciences:

(CH) "The maximum net return of an enterprise is attained at that production (or sales) volume at which the cost increment (marginal revenue) equals the revenue increment (marginal revenue)."

(IH) "In order to maximize the net return of an enterprise, attain a production (or sales) volume at which the cost increment equals the revenue increment."

Sentence (CH) constitutes either an analytical or empirical cognitive hypothesis. It is analytical if certain mathematical conditions are implied or stipulated, in such a way that the sentence becomes a tautology and thus its truth a matter of logical necessity (e.g., if it shall refer only to situations where the cost curve is either a linear function, or a cubic hyperbola, etc., and the revenue curve is either a linear function or a quadratic hyperbola, etc.). If, however, nothing is known about the shape of cost and revenue functions, this same proposition becomes an empirical hypothesis, because it then is open to refutation by experience (e.g. in some situations of discontinuous cost or revenue functions (CH) would not hold). In this case the sentence (CH) actually is a refutable hence empirical hypothesis about the cost behavior of all firms within a certain universe. Ideally this universe is assumed to be unbound. But this assumption is always precarious; in the physical sciences it may nevertheless be permissible, but is less so in biology (e.g. different biological laws may hold for extra-terrestrial organisms), even less so in the social sciences and least permissible in the administrative and other applied sciences. For this very reason sentence (CH) and similar propositions of economics are frequently regarded as idealistic or unrealistic hypotheses. Obviously the more narrowly the universe is defined, the less law-like becomes the character of this "universal" sentence. If, on the other hand, the universe is defined too broadly (as it is frequently the case in the social sciences), instances of refutations can easily be found. And even if one argues that a single instance of refutation need not necessarily falsify an empirical hypothesis (since the refutation may be due to measurement, observation or experimentation errors), it would be too tenuous to apply this argument to hypotheses of the type mentioned above.

A solution to this dilemma is found by interpreting our proposition in the form of an instrumental hypothesis (IH). Imagine the naive situation in which a management consultant, Mr. *X*, gives advice on the basis of this hypothesis, since his experience has shown that (i) it holds in more than 80% of the cases of his consulting business and (ii) a failure rate of not more than 20% does not prove too harmful for his practice. In this case the instrumental hypothesis (IH) has a *truth value* expressible on a probability scale and is *even considered acceptable*; but in view of the relatively high rate of negative outcomes one cannot pretend it constitutes an absolute truth (because no longer can one argue that the negative outcomes are due to observational or similar errors). *Thus an instrumental hypothesis is acceptable because the assumption that it is "goal attaining" is supported by stronger evidence than that of any alternative available,* whereas a cognitive hypothesis is acceptable because the assumption that it is "true" is supported by sufficiently strong evidence (according to rigorous but arbitrary acceptance criteria set in such processes as verification or corroboration or coherence testing, etc.).

This raises the question whether *instrumental* reasoning is at all concerned with truth and belief (as is *cognitive* reasoning and traditional epistemology) or merely with usefulness. Or can one argue that an instrumental hypothesis is useful only by virtue of the fact that *it possesses a truth value* (i.e., a probability)[4] which, in relation to other factors, determines its acceptability and preference over other instrumental hypotheses? To answer this question we have to explore further aspects contained in Ch. 2. In spite of the crude example here offered, we hope that it has illustrated that instrumental reasoning harbors unexplored philosophical aspects and may constitute an economic extension of traditional epistemology.

(4) *The Problem of Epistemo-Economics:* Closely related to item 3 is the question whether the creation of knowledge has an economic aspect. If it has one, this can hardly be discerned from the conventional theory of knowledge. Only recently, under the impact of game and decision theory, have epistemologists like Carnap (1962, p. 269) and Hempel (1965, pp. 75–76) begun to employ a notion which Hempel calls "epistemic utility". Thus philosophers can no longer ignore the fact that information and knowledge systems are costly, nor can one continue to accept the time-worn assumption that any creation of knowledge is worth its cost. Thus one may suspect that epistemology possesses a long neglected economic dimension, which creates the need for a border discipline in which economics and philosophy of science intersect. This sub-area is closely related to information economics but is not identical with it (just as the notions of information and knowledge are not synonymous). For lack of a better expression we christen this embryonic sub-discipline *epistemo-economics* (for details see Chapter 6).

At a superficial glance it might appear that this idea promotes a pragmatic philosophy. But there is a fundamental distinction between pragmatism and epistemo-economics. The pragmatic view that something is true because it is useful, must not be confused with the belief that truth in the long-run may prove useful, and that the relation between truth and usefulness requires further exploration.

[4] This, of course, assumes that a multivalued truth scale is permissible.

CHAPTER 2

SYSTEMS ANALYSIS AS A TOOL OF PHILOSOPHICAL INVESTIGATION

This chapter might be regarded by some readers as the weakest, by others, hopefully, as the most important one of the entire book. If it proves controversial, it would be due to our experimentation (in Sections 2.3 to 2.8) with a novel and somewhat daring approach. First of all, we share with Leibniz, Whitehead and Teilhard de Chardin the view that *every entity or system possesses not only an outer or material aspect but also an inner or reflective one* (in the case of human beings and animals of higher order one would say a *"mental" aspect*, though in the case of entities of lower order the term "mental" is easily misunderstood). According to Leibniz the "monade", to be identified with the reflective aspect of a system, is *"windowless"*. That is to say, the reflective aspect of one entity remains unknown to all the others, as there is no opening through which other entities can explore it. In the case of human beings this seems to be obvious, since we all know that no one can peep into the mind of one's spouse, one's neighbor, or one's fellow-being. But if a system can be identified with some goal, and thus be looked at from a teleologic point of view, we might be able to catch a glimpse of the norms which determine or dominate this goal. We might also discover that some of these norms are, more or less permanently, incorporated into the system structure while others are, more or less temporarily, imposed from the environment. In other words, the notions of goal, prescription, norm, value judgement, reflection, mind, consciousness and those of related terms, belong to one category, serving to represent the specifically reflective or *mental facet* of *every* system; whereas the notions of datum, fact, description, assertion, empirical judgement etc. belong to an entirely different category, serving to represent the specifically material facet of every system. Such a dual representation might hopefully lead to further clarification of the perennial problem of "ought" versus "is".

Thus we have two possibilities or modes (either the normative or the factual mode) of representing one and the same system, and it will depend on the purpose of analysis which of the two should be applied. The factual or material representation of a system causes hardly any difficulty. On the other side, the major precondition for exhibiting an entity in the normative mode, revealing its reflective aspects, is the availability of an approach for *attributing norms not only to sentences, but to systems as well*. To explore the possibility of such an approach and to initiate it, is the ultimate task of this chapter. In this way we aim at *the representation of the material as well as the reflective facet of reality*. Linguistic configurations do not seem to offer satisfactory means for reproducing the interconnection of both of these aspects. We have to search for another approach, for one which exploits *structural analogies* (of both aspects) *between reality as a natural and theory as an artificial system*. Although the linguistic or sentential approach enables the distinction between descriptive and prescriptive sentences, these sentences are like two-dimensional sheets, one beside the other. But they should be envisaged as two opposite facets of a multi-dimensional form, connected to each other by further planes in new dimensions. It seems that mathematical structures, systems, or institutions reveal much better than sentences the multi-dimensional and dynamic nature of these two aspects. We must recognize that the processes of "being created" (as a system) and of "creating" (e.g. pursuing a specific goal) depict *the connection* between the normative reflective aspect and the positive-material aspect better than do traditional means of representation, because these system processes not only reveal the material aspects but also *the creation, incorporation, mutation and transfer of norms.* Those readers who disagree with such a program will hardly be hampered from benefiting from our Chapters 4 to 6, and a good deal of Chapter 7, but are likely to disagree with the two concluding Subsections 7.53 and 7.54.

2.1 In Need of an Expanded Analytical Superstructure

Modern mathematics and logic provide a vast and highly useful superstructure for empirical science. Yet the question is occasionally vented whether this analytical superstructure is not one-sidedly oriented, favoring physical sciences at the cost of biological and social as well as applied sciences. Mathematics, for example, does not provide any means to take into consideration teleological and normative arguments, and formal logic only recently is promoting attempts toward developing the new area of deontology which deals with arguments containing prescriptive premises and conclusions. There are probably many reasons why the philosophy of applied science has been neglected hitherto. But in the face of the above-stated doubt, it seems that one factor is the lack of a superstructure through which descriptive statements may be connected with normative and teleologic sentences.[1] These also would permit

[1] Ahmavaar (1969, 1975) is concerned with such problems and has advanced interesting suggestions.

a clear representation of the hierarchy of value judgements from entity to superentity and so on. Since applied science has a much stronger prescriptive orientation than pure science, these relations seem to be highly significant for our task.

This unaccommodating attitude of the traditional analytical disciplines must be comprehended in the light of two components: (1) the difficulties in overcoming a well set pattern of thinking which rejects any possible overlapping of value judgements with descriptive statements, and (2) the positivistic notion that value judgements are non-cognitive. Let us assume that you suddenly *become aware of a certain preference* of yours through *introspection*. Whether it is the preference for Dutch cheese over Swiss cheese, or that for Mozart's *Don Giovanni* over Puccini's *Tosca*, or of one managerial policy over another is here of secondary importance; what counts is the fact that not everyone would regard such an insight as an acquisition of knowledge. Although you now seem to *know* what you did not know before, namely that you prefer *A* to *B*, an uncritical empiricist or positivist would not recognize this insight as knowledge. If Mr. *X* observes your actions and notices that you choose *A* to *B* undeceptively and persistently, a behavioral positivist would admit that Mr. *X* "knows" your preference. But when do *you* know it? Only after Mr. *X* has informed you about your own preference? Or after you have *observed your own actual choosing* but not before? Perhaps an expression of the sort "I prefer *A* to *B*" is a double-faced Janus head looking in two directions. *Does it not manifest a value judgement and, simultaneously, describe the state of a system*? This possibility will have to be examined in more detail in Section 2.7–2.8. So far this aspect has been overshadowed by the positivist quest for the *value neutrality of science*. According to this any discipline broad enough to enunciate conclusions dependent on value judgements has to be regarded as non-objective, and would forfeit its status as a science. To protect itself from scientific excommunication, a discipline would have to guard its boundaries against the intrusion of value judgements. Whether and when it is possible to draw these boundaries tightly enough in order to relegate value remnants to the environment of the pertinent scientific system are precarious questions, and will be investigated in this Chapter. But it is questionable whether such requirements are not too stringent for applied science in general. Or could a discipline remain objective in spite of abandoning this positivistic ideal? Perhaps it could, if scholars would recognize that *not the elimination but the explication of value judgements is the decisive criterion for objectivity*. To reveal indubitably when a normative idea is present and where it is located, or even hidden, may open a new road to knowledge – perhaps the only one in a world beleaguered by value judgements. Their ***overt disclosure*** within a theory or discipline might be as good a guarantor of objectivity as is the *pro-forma* elimination of norms by setting artificial boundaries, and certainly a better one than the pretense of freedom from value judgements when the latter have been swept under the rug.

A further possibility for coping with this problem is to make a distinction between those value judgements that affect the outcome of a theory and those that do not. But to determine when an outcome is affected or, precisely speaking, ***substantially*** affected and when not, poses its own problems. Apart from such difficulties we believe that the objectivity of a theory is best served by disclosing all of its value judgements, and by offering a comparative analysis of their effects as far as this is reasonably possible.

It is not by accident that the failure to provide a superstructure, able to cope with teleological and normative patterns, found early reaction among experts of the life sciences. Apart from Bergson's and Driesch's doctrines, it was Bogdanov, a physician, and Bertalanffy, a biologist, who were the first to plead for a systems science which stresses such notions as purpose, preference, efficiency, information, etc. An examination of the extent to which these pioneers were successful or not must be postponed to Chapter 7. At this moment it should suffice to point out concisely the crucial shortcoming of Bogdanov's as well as Bertalanffy's approaches to systems. Both believed that their system theories sooner or later will replace the present approach to empirical science. Although they both vacillated between empirical and analytical aspects, their hearts were set toward a reconstruction of the empirical science in general, neglecting too much the need for an expanded analytical superstructure. In close connection with this major aim stood, what they must have considered, the basic idea of systems theory (or "tectologia" as Bogdanov called it): the generally acknowledged, yet still illusive, notion that ***a system is characterized by the fact that it is more than the sum of its parts.*** But neither author has succeeded in revealing what this "more" actually is or means. In this regard we find their explanations no better than the much older habit of assigning expressions like "soul" or "entelechy" or "*élan vital*" etc. to this mysterious phenomenon. Therefore we shall abstain from adopting any such ambitious brand of systems science, but prefer to rely on the following three basic requirements:

(1) Systems analysis aims at an *expansion of the analytical superstructures* serving the empirical and normative sciences.

(2) The system notion is a conceptual tool serving *man's need to categorize the universe into separate functional or goal oriented entities.*

(3) To overcome the dangers inherent in such an artificial departmentalization, system analysis insists that *every system must be analyzed within the context of its environment* in order to be more than a mere *structure.*

In our view it is the third principle, *prohibiting the analysis* of a functional or goal oriented entity *in isolation*, which constitutes the crux of the modern systems approach. Its importance might fully be understood only by contemplating the neglect which this principle has experienced in traditional science as well as philosophy. To mention only two examples: In the natural and social sciences the *confusion* regarding value judgements is *due primarily to the following practice*. First, one draws deliberately tight system boundaries, so as to exclude the pertinent value judgements; second, one then neglects the system's environment harboring those value judgements. In philosophy it is likely that such notions as "deterministic", "rational", "normative", etc. have led to confusion and paradoxes precisely because of a failure (i) to distinguish clearly between system and environment and (ii) to observe the relationship between the two. Hence a word like "deterministic" (or "free will") or "rational" or "normative" may be meaningful only within a fairly well defined system but may become meaningless when applied to an unstructured infinite universe. To give further support to our contention we mention two examples *par excellence* from mathematics and philosophy where the right kind of system thinking was applied with enormous success. The first is the distinction between object-language and meta-language. Before this distinction (and its precursor, Russell's theory of types) was known, the Russell paradox (for details see Subsection 3.35) had no solution. Only after the object-language (the system) was clearly separated but related to the meta-language (the system's environment), could this crucial paradox of set theory be solved. Although, to our knowledge no one has ever related this distinction to systems analysis, we believe that this was one of the first, if not *the* first (albeit unconscious) application of modern systems thinking which led to a major success. But it certainly is not the only application within mathematics. Without much stretch of imagination one could regard Gödel's incompletability theorem and proof another, even more fundamental, achievement of systems thinking. Nobody can deny that the sharp distinction between system and meta-system (environment), meta-system and meta-meta-system (environment of the meta-system) and so on, plays a vital role in these achievements. For us the essence of systems analysis lies in the generalization and broadening of these ideas which emerged in the first third of this century and which have revolutionized a good deal of thinking in mathematics and philosophy alike.

The application of system theory to the philosophy and evolution of science, though having precursers in Whewell, Mach, Boltzmann and Duhem (cf. Oeser, 1976, p. 19), is of most recent origin. An explicit attempt of such an application was undertaken by Laszlo (1972), another, less explicit but much more elaborate one, is found by Sneed (1971) and Stegmüller (1973a, 1976).

Laszlo (1972c) regards "science" as an open system the environment of which is "nature". He then envisages the unity of both as a closed system that moves in direction of the most probable equilibrium state through constant interchange between science and nature. But, according to Laszlo, this equilibrium state might or need not be a state of maximal entropy (disorder) because of the same ***stratified stability*** (see our Subsection 7.53 and its Principle of Concrescence) which enables the creation of even higher levels of well organized and ordered entities in a universe of increasing disorder. Thus he expects science, as a self-organizing process, to progress in direction of an equilibrium of increasing stability. Furthermore he proposes two notions which he calls "empirical adequacy" (A . . . a measure of the number of facts to be explained and the precision of science) and "integrative generality" (E . . . a measure for the internal consistency and simplicity of science) which must be in equilibrium in order to attain an optimal state of a theory. This ideal equilibrium state $(A/G)^E$ is envisaged as forming the basis for comparing different theories with each other and thus for evaluating them (cf. Oeser, 1976, S. 16–19).

A better founded and more substantiated approach is offered by Sneed (1971) and elaborated by Stegmüller (1973, 1975) – see also our Subsection 7.32. Sneed starts from the fact that among various approaches to axiomatize a theory there exists one which ***regards the theory not as a collection of propositions but as a mathematical structure*** (we could say a "system"), the set-theoretical predicate of which is defined by the set of axioms – examples of this type are found in Kolmogoroff's (1933) axiomatization of probability theory and Mattessich's (1964a, 1970) attempts to axiomatize accounting theory. Thus the axioms are neither propositions nor formulas of a specific calculus (as is the case in other types of axiomatization schemes). This ***structuralistic approach*** enables the reconstruction of essential relations of reality by structural analogues rather than by sentences (thus circumventing a puzzling question originally raised by Wittgenstein: "How is it possible to depict reality by means of words and sentences?"). Already Ramsey (1926/1931) attempted to substitute the purely *theoretical terms* through logical structures, ultimately attaining a somewhat less elegant theory, but one having the advantage of being based solely on *observational terms*. Sneed improved upon Ramsey in such a way that the emerging theory *becomes a system in a truly instrumental sense.* That this approach belongs to system theory is re-affirmed by the following words of Oeser (1976, p. 14): "With the model-theoretical explication of the notion of 'mathematical structure' emerges by Sneed a triple division – into structural frame, structural core, and expanded core – completely adequate to the systems point of view." However, Oeser (1976, p. 14), adds the following warning: "In order to be able to do justice to the problem of the dynamics of science, it is necessary to expand Sneed's approach in a dual fashion: on one side, through a broadening of the system notion, and on the other, through a thorough examination of the role which experience plays in the mutations of science." (For further details see our Sections 7.3 to 7.5.)

In view of the importance of this topic we shall, for the time being, offer a concise review of the systems approach in Section 2.2 and then present in Section 2.3 *a central theme of this book*. It pivots on the idea that *there exist important relations between a body of sentences, e.g. a theory, and a system*. One consequence of this idea rests in the quest for *an extension of the notions of "normative" and "neutral" (= "positive") from sentences to systems*. Another is the fact that *systems*, even mechanical systems, *possess patterns that in some respect resemble sentential patterns of a language*. Once these aspects are understood we shall attempt to clarify the perennial controversy of "is" versus "ought", of positive versus normative, of descriptive versus prescriptive. Our approach also offers a vehicle for incorporating value judgements into a system or, alternatively, of externalizing such value judgements from a system. To accomplish this, it will be necessary to formulate conditions under which these attributes of sentences are applicable beyond language patterns to system patterns. Furthermore we will have to justify such an extension and shall find good reason for doing so in modern neurophysiology and computer science. Otherwise we might be castigated by the disciples of "ordinary language philosophy" for abusing the term "normative" against the background of its traditional usage.

After the extension of the superstructure (in form of the systems approach) has been sketched, it should be possible to view scientific research in a somewhat different light. Indeed we shall first illuminate (in Chapters 3 and 4) deductive reasoning, and then (in Chapter 5) inductive reasoning from that new point of view which makes hidden or implicit value judgements overtly known. This concomitantly will give us opportunity to acquaint the applied scientist with many problems and recent achievements of modern methodology. It will also prepare him for the remaining chapters which deal with philosophic problems encountered specifically in the applied sciences.

2.2 The Essence of the Systems Approach

2.21 *Alternative and Complementary Attempts*

If modern mathematics and logic have shortcomings as superstructures of the biological, social as well as applied sciences, one might ask: "how should a more adequate analytical structure be constituted?" In detail this question cannot be answered because such superstructures cannot be programmed in advance, nor would they develop as scheduled; they evolve out of particular needs and over long periods of time. But during the past century and especially during the last two decades *an increasing need for generalized presentations of organic and organizational entities* made itself felt. There did not and still does not exist any analytical framework ideally suited to depict the teleological and preferential structure of such entities. This resulted in the following three endeavors:

(1) *The utilization of present-state mathematics*, as well as possible, for such novel needs. These attempts lie mainly in the realm of mathematical programming, in game-, decision- and information-theory and in a new sub-area reflected best by the journal *Mathematical Systems Theory.* Although these fields were extremely successful, their success touches only to a limited extent the peculiar need for teleological and preferential structures. But on this point opinions diverge. Herbert Simon for example argued: " . . . we may hope to find that a large part of the work has already been done for us . . . For these reasons I have found the logic used by professional decision makers an excellent starting point for inquiry into the requirements of imperative and deontic logic. Particularly useful for the task are areas of practice where the decision-making process has been imbedded in formal models . . . The central conclusion reached . . . is that there is no need for a special 'logic of imperatives' or 'logic of action'; the basis for the conclusion is that the practitioners in the fields examined, clearly get along very well without one."[1a]

[1a] Simon, 'The Logic of Heuristic Decision Making', 1966, pp. 1–2.

Others, less positivistically oriented authors, do not share this view, and are not at all convinced that the practitioners presently get along so well (for a response to H. Simon see Binkley (1966) and Belnap (1966)). Simon's optimistic attitude must certainly be respected, but only as long as it does not impede experimentation with new analytical superstructures like deontic logic. Because only *ex post*, i.e. after these new analytical tools have been created and extensively applied, will it be possible to decide who had the better foresight, H. Simon or his adversaries.

(2) *The search for a general systems theory* has been under way for more than half a century since A. Bogdanov began to publish his *Tectologia* (1912) in Russia. But his work remained neglected for a long time and only recently seemed to have found broader attention in the Soviet Union but very little attention elsewhere – for an exception see Gorelik (1974). In the West it was The Austrian biologist Ludwig von Bertalanffy who published his *Kritische Theorie der Formbildung* (1928) – this book was translated into English as early as 1933. Soon after taking up residency in Canada, Bertalanffy promulgated his ideas on the American continent under the name of "general systems theory" (1950, 1970), founded the Association for General Systems Theory and published annually from 1956 till his death in 1972 the *General Systems Yearbook.*

Systems thinking found an even more important impetus from management science. And a considerable amount of literature poured forth during the last two decades under such names as systems research, systems analysis, systems engineering, etc., in order to distinguish it from the controversial general systems theory of Bertalanffy and his disciples (for further details see Chapter 7). But neither group could resolve the problem as to the precise character of this new area. Should it be an analytical or an empirical discipline? There may well be a need for an analytical as well as for an empirical systems approach. At present the general trend seems to point into the empirical direction, and scholars like H. Simon (1969) are pleading for a behavioral study of systems. Indeed, there exist comparatively few attempts of presenting a comprehensive *analytical* framework for systems in general – e.g., Lange (1962/65) and Mesarovic (1964) and publications contained in the journal *Mathematical Systems Theory.* In the face of the need for an extended superstructure this extremely limited interest, of mathematicians and especially philosophers, in the systems approach seems regrettable.

(3) *The development of a logic of normative arguments and concepts (deontology).* This area is occasionally regarded as a branch of modal logic

which in its turn could be considered the logical backbone of probability theory. The pioneers in deontic logic were two Austrians, E. Mally (1926) and K. Menger (1934, 1939), whose works however, found little attention until the Swedish–Finnish philosopher H. von Wright incited, with his first article on "Deontic Logic" (1951), a wave of publications on this subject which has not yet abated (for details see Chapter 4).

The connection between systems analysis and deontic logic becomes more obvious through the insight that norms, value judgements and imperatives play a particularly important role in systems. We shall try to demonstrate in this Chapter that it is not possible to comprehend fully the subject matter of systems analysis without those normative notions. And since deontic logic helps us to clarify them, there is hope that it also will facilitate a better understanding of systems analysis. Indeed, Rescher (1966, pp. 43–51) has pointed at the connection between the deontic logic of commands and computer programming. This idea is about to find increasing response among experts of computers, systems and artificial intelligence.

2.22 *General Characteristics*

The hierarchy of systems is based advantageously on natural evolution which reaches from purely physical or mechanistic systems, over living systems of various stages, to self-reflecting and self-perfecting human beings and their social organizations. Ackoff (1971) supplied us with a behavioral classification of systems which offers a crude approximation to the major evolutionary steps (see Table 2-1). As valuable as this hierarchy is, it hardly touches upon the following issue crucial for the analysis pursued in this chapter: Where in this evolutionary hierarchy does a system begin to have built-in preferences and thus exercise value judgements? For a system to have preferences and exercise value judgements, is it necessary to have an inner aspect (consciousness in the broadest sense)?

The last question suggests that we might not be able to escape the perennial and often futile mind–body problem of philosophy. Of course there is some hope that the rapidly advancing field of neurophysiology together with insights gained in computer science as well as ethology will help to clarify this issue – not only its empirical but also its philosophic–semantical aspects. As the systems approach has been conceived from the very outset as a kind of superdiscipline for dealing with organs and organizations, computers and neuro-cybernetic structures, learning machines and decision-making automata, etc., we must explore the relevance of the mind–body problem

TABLE 2-1
Behavioral classification of systems[2]

Type of system	Behavior of system	Outcome of behavior
State-maintaining	Variable but determined (reactive)	Fixed
Goal-seeking	Variable and chosen (responsive)	Fixed
Multi-goal-seeking and purposive	Variable and chosen	Variable but determined
Purposeful	Variable and chosen	Variable and chosen

to those systems. First of all, one should realize that even the thinking processes, including those of electronic computers, are fraught with those two aspects, the reflective–introspective and the material–physical one. But this duality does not imply that the clarification of one aspect enforces the clarification of the other. This hiatus and *the category-difference between the reflective and the material parts of thinking* might become more obvious when we compare the impressive progress of neuro-physiology and the systems sciences in the "mechanical–chemical–electronical area of thinking", with the complete dead-lock in the area of "feeling the thoughts". In other words we have reached the stage where we can design *thinking systems*, but are far away from designing *feeling systems*. The material aspects of thinking seem to be explainable as processes creating highly complex chemical, electrical, or even mechanical patterns of an immense number of elementary events. The advantage of such or similar explanations is obvious, it can be offered solely on the physical level. But in the case of the reflective aspects (among which "feeling" is merely one among many species), it seems we are forced to an altogether different plane.[3] What happens in a human or animal when he or it feels something? How can we design a system capable of experiencing pain, pleasure and other emotions? Although such questions imply some doubt about the purely physical nature of feeling, they do not suggest that the events "causing" this feeling are not physical ones. We rather suggest that only one of their two aspects is accessible through the methods

[2] From Ackoff, 'Towards a System of Systems Concepts', 1971, p. 665. Another, though similar, systems classification is found by Boulding (1956).

[3] Our choice of the term "reflective", for characterizing the inner aspect of systems, follows the notion that the mind and all its more primitive anticedents are mirrors (cf. Leibniz; Lorenz, 1974) which reflect some aspects of reality *within an internal* (perhaps physically inaccessible) *dimension of matter*; hence the expression "introspective", here used synonymously to "reflective".

of traditional physics. The other aspect was so far accessible only through introspection, but we harbor some hope that evolutionary studies about the origin and the construction of systems, especially about the incorporation and transfer of norms in systems, might be helpful in further clarifying this second aspect.

All this, however, does not force us to subscribe to an idealistic philosophy, since we regard *the material aspects not as secondary but as simultaneous to the reflective aspects* of a system. Both are *two sides of one occurence*; thus matter is neither taken to be a prerequisite for the mind nor the mind a prerequisite for the matter. But how does this transformation of a physical event into a genuine feeling happen? Not even the neurophysiologists have the slightest idea so far. At best we may speculate that we are confronted with a double-sided phenomenon: the *outer* facet is a physical event, the *inner* facet is what you, or I, or in future perhaps an artificial system, can actually feel. To say "a feeling *is caused* by such physical events as neurophysioligical reactions" is hardly controversial, but to say "a feeling is *identical* to a physical event" is not the same. Yet if a feeling is not a physical event (or state, since states seem to be events ultimately), what then could it be? Thus we have little choice but to *assume that consciousness is merely one aspect of a physical event*, while the other is manifested by externally "observable" phenomena. Perhaps *every physical event,* be it the orbiting of electrons around the atomic nucleus or the activity of an artificial system, *has two facets,* an *inner* or *introspective* and an *outer* or observational aspect. In this case one might accept the additional assumption that the introspective aspect becomes increasingly more pronounced with progressive evolutionary sophistication of the pertinent system, until, at some stage, the critical threshold of primitive and later human consciousness is reached. To decide whether such speculations are better supported, than is, for example, the competing Cartesian duality hypothesis of the mind–body problem, must rest with the reader.[3a] He also must bear in mind that a profound analysis of systems cannot escape such kind of speculation.

Perhaps one could interpret the notion of feeling in "information theoretical" terms. If *consciousness* is regarded *as the capacity to receive information and to react to it*, this is an incomplete characterization, because linguistic habits would prohibit to address any information receptive capacity as consciousness. The latter expression seems to be restricted to

[3a] U. T. Place argues in a widely known paper (1956) that the acceptance of inner or mental processes does not entail a dualism and that the thesis that consciousness is such a brain process cannot be dismissed on logical grounds.

entities where *information is felt*. As this does not explain what "felt" means, the problem of feeling remains unsolved. Nevertheless the above reflection clarifies the situation somewhat; it confirms our previously expressed supposition that there is a common ground for organic and artificial systems, and it shows that the latter have a capacity which belongs to the same genus, though not to the same species, as the phenomenon of consciousness. In any system the interaction between the individual components seems to be guided by *information*. Thus this notion plays an indispensable role in systems analysis. Bertalanffy (1968, p. 42) even assigns to information the same central position in systems thinking which the notion of energy assumes in physics. Therefore systems analysis can disregard neither information theory nor information economics and we shall pay heed to those areas in Chapters 6 and 7.

The notion of "system" is by no means new and has been encountered in philosophy, mathematics and empirical sciences for centuries, but it has assumed a more specific meaning during the last two decades or so. Although there exist many definitions of "system", the following one summarizes widely accepted features of *a system in general*. *A system* is a set possessing the following necessary conditions:

(1) It contains two or more *elements* with specific properties.

(2) It contains *relations* (connecting the elements of the system with each other) and qualities of those which in turn lend *structure,* holistic properties, as well as possible regulators to the system enabling also its transformation.

(3) It is embedded in an *environment* containing additional inter-related elements.

(4) The *boundaries* between the system and its environment are determined by the system's elements and relations, and are sufficiently sharp and permanent to consider the system as an entity.

These may be regarded as minimal conditions[4] for a system in the broadest sense of the word. However, in applied science and in this study we are dealing mainly with *open goal-oriented decision systems*. Whenever we speak of a system, without any qualification, we shall mean such system, and may therefore add the following two conditions:

[4] Some authors (e.g. Ackoff, 1971) might even want to exclude item (3). They argue that closed systems have no environment at all. In our view however, the most essential distinction of systems thinking is that between system and environment. Without this distinction the systems approach loses a good deal, if not all, of its meaning. Thus for us *a closed system possesses an environment but no relevant or admissible relationship between any element of the system and any of the environment.*

(5) It contains at least one relation between an element of the system and an element of the environment (*open system*).

(6) It has evolved or been created to tend toward a *goal* (*goal-directed system*).

Beside these conditions one ought to state some major capacities which a system can assume. It is however difficult to address these items as necessary conditions since the capacities stated therein are a matter of degree, and range over a wide spectrum beginning at zero. The more comprehensively a system is coordinated, the more sophisticated it is, or the higher it stands on the evolutionary ladder, the more will these capacities be developed.

(7) *The functional capacity*: i.e. the ability of a system to affect the environment. In systems of higher order (e.g. teleologic systems), this capacity will result in a behavior that is purpose-oriented, goal-seeking, ideal-setting, etc.

(8) *The "sensory" capacity*: i.e. the ability of a system to be affected by some "stimulus" from the environment. While systems of lower order will have no sensory *organs* in the customary sense, those of higher order will be able to feel the effect through such organs.

(9) *The response and adaptation capacity*: i.e. the ability of a system to change its behavior, or even its structure, under the impact of the environment. This ability too is a matter of degree and spans a wide range of possibilities.

(10) *The identity and reflective capacity*: i.e. the ability of a system to identify itself and "*to observe from within*". It may sound daring to speak in the case of an artificial system of self-identification and almost absurd to speak of introspection. Nevertheless it must be admitted that every single element contributing in this direction, enhances the degree of this, or at least toward this, capacity. Thus the assumption of a gradual development, interrupted by big and small gaps or "hiatus", and ranging from the most primitive to the most complex "introspection", could become one of the most important contributions of systems analysis toward clarifying the perennial problem of consciousness (i.e. feeling pain, pleasure, emotions and thoughts).

Occasionally one encounters in the literature set-theoretical formulations of the system notion. Patzak (1976, p. 37), for example, defines a system S as consisting of a set of elements E, a set of qualities F, and a set of relations B, hence:

$$S = \{E, F, B\} .$$

As meritorious as such definitions might be, they hide, or even leave out of consideration, a most important system aspect. The new *holistic properties* – that is to say, those characteristics of a particular system that go beyond the qualities of individual system components – are not explicitly shown in formulations of the kind illustrated above. Of course, it is not easy to find a satisfactory solution to the set-theoretical representation of holistic properties, because then it would also be desirable to show the relation between the holistic properties and the components. But the causal nexus between holistic system properties and component properties is usually very much in doubt, and thus it is hardly possible to present the former as a mathematical function of the latter.

The term "system", as here envisaged expresses basically a theoretical notion which however may correspond to a "natural" or "artificial" entity. Indeed the recent popularity of the system notion has a theoretical as well as a practical root. The former lies in the growing and pervading realization that the *variables* of a system and its environment are *interdependent.*[5] The practical root is to be found in the electronic computer and its applicability for simulating or embodying an immense variety of complex systems. The system notion seems to be very promising and enables the representation of the following aspects better than any other concept:

(i) It reveals the relationship between entities of different levels (subsystems embedded in systems, the latter embedded in super-systems, and so on, generally designated as the environment).

(ii) It presents the relations between the variables (objects and their attributes) of a system.

(iii) It indicates relations between elements of a system and those of its environment.

(iv) It may reveal the relations and conflicts between the goals of a system and the goals of its super-systems, and may aid in the eventual resolution of these conflicts.

[5] The interdependence of variables is an old and highly important insight. It seems to have been gained first by Leibniz (1646–1716) and is reflected on a universal level in his *monadology*. It is also encountered with Laplace and Hegel and emerges in the coherence theory of truth. In the economic sciences, it found its first manifestation in Léon Walras' general equilibrium theory which expresses the interdependence of all prices and quantities transacted within an economy. Leontief's interindustry analysis and the (*mutatis mutandis*) models of operations research (e.g. linear and non-linear programming), as well as systems analysis, are modern and practical reflections of this basic idea of interdependence.

(v) It may indicate possibilities of adaptation or of creating new but related systems by contracting or expanding the boundaries of the original system.

Such contemplations disclose an intimate connection between systems science, the logic of norms (goals) and the administrative as well as other applied sciences. We leave it up to the reader to judge whether it is or is not premature to declare the system concept the long sought key to a philosophy of the applied sciences. But it seems to be a concept deserving greater attention than thus far paid to it by contemporary philosophers.[6]

2.23 *The System Boundaries*

The boundaries of a system are those characteristics (e.g. the system's variables, parameters and relations) which separate the structure (with its inner environment) from the (outer) environment of the pertinent system. There obviously is a ***similarity between a set, in the mathematical sense, and a system.*** While the *set* represents a collection of elements and separates them from the rest of the "universe", the *system* represents a collection of objects or variables, together with their relations, and separates them from the rest of the environment (also called "outer environment" by Herbert Simon, and plainly addressed as "environment" in the rest of this book). Ontologically the system notion may encounter the same difficulties as did the idea of a set, especially if the systems approach is conceived in an analytical sense. Those like H. Simon (1969) who envisage systems science as an empirical discipline, studying the behavior of concrete entities, will have less difficulty asserting the *existence* of a system. But those who see it as an abstract notion may be forced to assume its existence in a purely mental sense, pretty much in the same way as most modern mathematicians assume the existence of a set since Zermelo announced the axiom of choice and proved the well-ordering theorem in 1904.

The boundary characteristics of a system become particularly perspicuous when this system is converted into a different, yet similar, system;

[6] However among some philosophers there exists an increasing awareness of the significance of this concept. The following books by Churchman for example show a trend of increasing concern with the systems concept: *Prediction and Optimal Decision* (1961), *A Challenge to Reason* (1968), *The Systems Approach* (1968), *The Design of Inquiring Systems* (1971). Other professional philosophers, such as Ashby (1956, 1960, 1962, 1963, 1964), Rapoport (1953, 1966 – see also Rapoport and Horvath 1959/68), and more recently Laszlo (1972, 1973), have shown great interest in advancing the systems approach.

then the shift of boundaries is reflected by the change in variables, parameters, relations, goals, values, etc. It is this notion which enables one to circumscribe a specific system and to distinguish between its *structure* and its *environment*. Yet it is still controversial whether a system's boundary can be set arbitrarily, or whether it must be given by virtue of some more or less natural criterion of integration (e.g. *Gestalt* conditions). Most experts would agree that anything fulfilling the basic system requirements is a system, while others, especially those with extreme holistic notions, may wish to limit the designation "system" only to certain organic or organizational entities of tight coherence. To give a trivial example, the first group might be willing to regard "a person with a hacksaw destined to cut a piece of iron into two parts" as a specific system – one different from the system represented by the person alone. The second group might object to this broad-minded view of setting arbitrary boundaries (i.e. adding the hacksaw and a narrow purpose to a person and thus forming a temporary, new system), and might merely be willing to recognize the person without the tool as a system proper, because only such a "natural" entity constitutes a genuine integration of components into something "new" possessing its own characteristic properties. Pressing a hacksaw into a man's hand and ordering him to work is, according to the second group, no such genuine integration.[7]

If this latter view is accepted, the difficult task arises to find "natural" criteria of integration; if, on the other hand, this view is rejected, almost everything could be called a system, and the danger of triviality looms on the horizon. Several authors pointed at this difficulty or dilemma:

> . . . earlier it was contended that the boundaries of a system are subjective; and this is strongly supported at the philosophic level by the Hegelian axiom of internal relations – which of course makes it logically possible to equate every system with the universe itself. So the crucial scientific problem for systems research is this: how to separate a particular viable system for study from the rest of the universe without committing annihilating *divisio* . . . These are problems of desperate urgency for every nontrivial systems study.[8]

[7] The proponents of the *organismic* point of view might believe in the existence of "natural" criteria for deciding which entities are systems and which are not. We cannot share this view; to our mind any system definition is arbitrary and should not serve the identification of some organismic phenomena, but the conceptual clarification and improvement of *goal-oriented activities* in general and particular.

[8] Stafford Beer, 'Below the Twilight Arch – A Mythology of Systems', in Eckman (1961), pp. 18–19.

D. C. Phillips is even more sceptical and opposes Hall's and Fagen's recommendation[9] to freely select certain interrelated entities of relevance to one's particular investigation of forming a system. But his argument is directed against GST[10], and does not hold under the relaxed conditions of our systems approach. If the latter can be regarded as a methodological tool, then one should be able to organize purpose-oriented actions in the same way as the mathematician organizes configurations of analytical geometry within the Cartesian system of co-ordinates. The latter too is "merely" a methodological device, yet no one would deny its immense fertility. Therefore, instead of imposing too tight constraints upon the concept of *system*, we suggest a more liberal attitude. If this broad interpretation is accepted, systems thinking has a decisive advantage over traditional thinking, because (1) the former focuses on an object with well defined boundaries, whereas the latter frequently pays too little attention to the limits of its objects of conversation; and (2) system thinking not only creates awareness of these boundaries, but allows them to shift easily in one direction or the other, thus creating new systems (always under awareness of the pertinent boundaries), the properties of which may be compared to those of the original system, thus yielding illuminating differences. This insight, as trivial as it may seem at first, might prove to be of considerable power in clarifying such hotly debated and unresolved issues as the problem of "value neutrality in science", of "positive versus normative models", etc.

Shifting the boundaries of a system, may obviously be conceived as converting one system, the original one, into another, the new (extended or contracted) one. By thus extending a system, i.e. by shifting its boundaries outwards, the new system will contain elements which did not belong to the original system, but to its environment. How does this affect the goals of both systems? Does the goal of the original system change or not? If it does, how is this change governed? From experience one knows that both alternatives are possible, depending on the extent of the change caused by this shift. As yet, there does not seem to exist much generalized insight about the relation between shifts of boundaries of a system and change in goals. But, goals are not the only properties significantly affected by such shifts. *The results of Gödel's theorem and proof are an illustration par excellence of the importance and non-triviality of the boundary problem with regard to another property*. This theorem supplies a *general insight* (though not with respect to

[9] Cf. Hall and Fagen, *A Methodology for Systems Engineering*, 1962.

[10] D.C. Phillips, 'Systems Theory – A Discredited Philosophy', 1969, pp. 10–11. GST stands here for "General Systems Theory" as developed by Bertalanffy and his disciples.

goals) as to the effect of a change in boundaries (of a mathematico–logical system) upon the determinacy of some elements (propositions) contained in it (cf. Subsection 3.36). According to Gödel's theorem a complex logical system will have some propositions, the truth value of which is indeterminate; if the boundaries of this system are sufficiently extended, then the truth values of these propositions can be determined within the new system, but new propositions arise, the truth values of which again are indeterminate within this system; to determine those the boundaries have to be further extended, and the cat and mouse game goes on *ad infinitum*.

Another example (from mathematics, with various interpretations from the administrative sciences) and familiar even to the least sophisticated model builder, is the influence of changes in boundaries (of a most simple mathematical system) upon changes in the character of certain variables. The "original" system is represented in Table 2-2a by the simple linear homogenous equation $y = px$, while the "extended" system introducing the additional equation $x = a + bz$ is shown in Table 2-2b.

Interpretation: e.g. a = sales quantity at zero advertising, b = additional sales quantity per unit of z, p = sales price, x = total sales quantity, y = sales revenue, z = anticipated total advertising expenditures.

The boundaries of one of the simplest systems imaginable (Table 2-2a) have been expanded (Table 2-2b) by introducing a new exogenous variable z, and two new parameters a and b. This converted x from an exogenous (independent) variable (Table 2-2a) into an endogenous (dependent) variable (Table 2-2b), which means that x is no longer given from outside but is determined within the extended system. Other interpretations using different structures, e.g. *decision variables, non-controllable variables*, etc., of this and similar examples are possible; they would all demonstrate the effects of *boundary shifts* upon the *character* of variables or parameters.

Another related example, of a most useful application of systems thinking and the boundary notion, is Carnap's classical distinction between linguistic systems (*frameworks*) and their environment in his renowned paper "Empiricism, Semantics and Ontology".[11] There he attempts to dispel the

TABLE 2-2a

$y = p \cdot x$	
exogenous:	x
endogenous:	y
parameter:	p

TABLE 2-2b

$y = p \cdot x$;	$x = a + b \cdot z$
exogenous:	z
endogenous:	x, y
parameters:	a, b, p

[11] Carnap, 'Empiricism, Semantics, and Ontology', 1950. Reproduced in *Meaning and Necessity*, Supplement, 1956, pp. 205–221 (Phoenix edition, 1967).

empiricists' suspicion of ***abstract entities*** and their fear of falling into the trap of a Platonic ontology. He does so by conceiving a specific linguistic system with sharp boundaries which help to distinguish clearly between ***internal*** and ***external*** question:

> Are there properties, classes, numbers, propositions? In order to understand more clearly the nature of these and related problems, it is above all necessary to recognize a fundamental distinction between two kinds of questions concerning the existence or reality of entities. If someone wishes to speak in his language about a new kind of entity, he has to introduce a system of new ways of speaking, subject to new rules; we shall call this procedure the construction of a linguistic *framework* for the new entities in question. And now we must distinguish two kinds of questions of existence: first, questions of the existence of certain entities of the new kind *within the framework*; we call them *internal questions*; and second, questions concerning the existence or reality of the system of entities *as a whole,* called *external questions.* Internal questions and possible answers to them are formulated with the help of the new form of expressions. The answer may be found either by purely logical methods or by empirical methods, depending upon whether the framework is a logical or a factual one . . . (p. 205) . . . To recognize something as a real thing or event means to succeed in incorporating it into the system of things at a particular space–time position so that it fits together with the other things recognized as real, according to the rules of the framework.
>
> From these questions we must distinguish the external question of the reality of the thing world itself. In contrast to the former questions, this question is raised neither by the man in the street nor by scientists, but only by philosophers. Realists give an affirmative answer, subjective idealists a negative one, and the controversy goes on for centuries without ever being solved. And it cannot be solved because it is framed in a wrong way. To be real in the scientific sense means to be an element of the system; hence this concept cannot be meaningfully applied to the system itself. Those who raise the question of the reality of the thing world itself have perhaps in mind not a theoretical question as their formulation seems to suggest, but rather a practical question, a matter of practical decision concerning the structure of our language. We have to make a choice whether or not to accept and use the forms of expression in the framework in question . . . If someone decides to accept the thing language, there is no objection against saying that he has accepted the world of

things. But this must not be interpreted as if it meant his acceptance of a *belief* in the reality of the thing world; there is no such belief or assertion or assumption, because it is not a theoretical question. To accept the thing world means nothing more than to acquire a clear notion about the foundation on which our discipline rests.

These four instances of shifting or asserting system boundaries and their effect upon (1) goals, (2) determinacy of propositions, (3) character of variables and (4) fundamental philosophical questions, can be complemented in many other ways.

2.3 Incorporating and Externalizing Value Judgements[11a]

The design of a system usually requires value judgements about such features as the system's objective, capacity, robustness, sensitivity with regard to some aspects, efficiency and many other properties. These value judgements constitute *prescriptions* of the system-user, *via* designer, to the actual builder of the system. They ultimately *become incorporated* into the system as *relations together with parameter values*. However, *not all* value judgements need to be incorporated in this fashion. Some may be "left open" in such a way that the user may impose upon the system at any time a particular value judgement without changing the system structure.

In this section we shall use four variations of a thermostat heating system for a single dwelling as *an illustration* for the shifting of value judgements. This will demonstrate how value judgements can either be incorporated into a system proper or, alternatively, be externalized from it. It will lead in the next section to general principles underlying this illustration. The supreme goal of a thermostat system is the maintenance of the air temperature of a dwelling within certain limits. The *values which these limits* (lower bound and upper bound) shall assume, may be regarded as the more specific goals or *sub-goals*. They are determined by value judgements which in no case can be avoided, but which can either, from the very outset, be permanently incorporated into the system or be left open. In the latter case the system is more flexible but the goal setting or value judgement must be made outside the system proper. Of these four variations, three vary slightly from the thermostat systems ordinarily encountered.

[11a] The Sections 2.3–2.6 are reproduced, with minor modifications, from the author's article, 'The Incorporation and Reduction of Value Judgements in Systems', 1974a.

In System S_I we assume a heating plant constructed in such a way that the furnace is ***always automatically*** switched on at 69°F (lower bound y) and switched *off* at 71°F (upper bound x) without any possibility of outside interference by a layman (these values become, so to speak, ***parameter values,*** and any mechanical manipulation of changing them constitutes the conversion of the original system into another). This system is typically *normative* (we shall call it ***primary*** normative for reasons that will become plausible after the discussion of S_{II} and S_{III}) because the value judgements are here an integral part of the system containing the double imperative "switch on at 69°F and off at 71°F!"[12] (see Table 2-3).

TABLE 2-3

Systems with varying locations of value judgements

System type	Imperatives *incorporated* in the system	Imperatives *outside* the system	Location of value judgement
S_I	"Switch on at y = 69°F and off at x = 71°F!"	None	Two absolute value judgements x and y are incorporated. S_I is *primary normative* in respect of switching *on* and *off* temperatures.
S_{II}	"Switch on at y = (x−1)°F and off at x°F!"	"x = 70°F!" ("Let x be 70°F!")	One secondary value judgement $y = (x-1)$ is incorporated. S_{II} is *secondary normative* in respect of the switching *on* temperature.
S_{III}	"Switch on at y = $(x-1)$°F and off at z = $(x+1)$°F!"	"x = 70°F!"	Two secondary value judgements $y=(x-1)$ and $z = (x+1)$ are incorporated. S_{III} is *secondary normative* in respect of the switching *on* and *off* temperatures.
S_{IV}	"Switch on at y°F and off at x°F!"	"x = 70°F!" "y = 68°F!"	No value judgement is incorporated. S_{IV} is *positive* in respect of switching *on* and *off* temperatures.

[12] Those experts who recognize as value judgements only certain subjective sentences, might argue that values incorporated in the system should no longer be regarded as value judgements since the system has ceased to offer pertinent alternatives to individuals outside the system. But this tendency of submerging the issue, and the fallacious belief that one can get rid of value judgements by converting them into structural parameters of the system, seems to be the very reason for the confusion and controversy of the value neutrality hypothesis.

In the case of System S_{II} we shift the system boundaries slightly to create a different system structure. The value judgement determining the upper bound shall be made by a person outside S_{II} by moving an indicator on the temperature scale of the thermostat (e.g. temperature $x = 70°$F), while the lower bound is fixed relative to x and incorporated by the following imperative "switch on at $(x-1)°$F and off at $x°$F!" Obviously we still have one *incorporated* value judgement, namely the span of one Fahrenheit degree between switching on and off temperatures; and thus have a normative system. But in order to be precise we should address it as a *secondary normative system with regard to the switching on temperature* ("secondary" because not the lower bound y itself was incorporated but only the difference $x - y = 1$).

The third system S_{III} might correspond to the thermostat heating systems ordinarily encountered in our homes. We assume that it operates (e.g. $x = 70$) through the following built-in imperative: "switch on at $(x-1)°$F and off at $(x+1)°$F!" Here we might speak of a system that again is *secondary normative,* but *with regard to both switch on as well as switch* off temperatures.

Only the fourth system S_{IV} might be addressed as a *positive system* (with regard to switching on and off temperatures), since we assume that it offers the dweller the convenience of determining from outside both the upper bound (e.g. $x = 70°$F) and independently the lower bound ($y = 68°$F). Thus no *value judgements* (with regard to temperature switchings) are incorporated in the system proper, both pertinent value judgements are independent of each other, and are made by a person outside the system without changing its structure. These four structures are summarized in Table 2-3.

In studying this illustration it is important to be aware that each of these systems will be subject to a series of *other value judgements*, e.g. as to robustness, efficiency, size, etc. of the system, which have to be *incorporated*. For that reason one could argue that none of these systems, not even S_{IV} is a positive system. Precisely for this reason we have carefully specified "positive" or "normative" *in respect of which properties*.

2.4 The Method of Neutralizing Systems

On the basis of the preceding illustrations some general statements regarding value judgements and the notion of their "location" in relation to a system can now be formulated:

1. *A personal value judgement* is an individual's imperative potential and expression of his or her preference order at a specific time.

2. Every personal value judgement is ***directly manifested*** by a feeling or emotional impulse of the pertinent individual. (At present it can be observed directly only by introspection, but it can be manifested ***indirectly*** by the individual's non-deceptive behavior of making pertinent choices or statements.)

3. *A social value judgement* is the temporary, voluntary or enforced agreement of a group to accept a certain preference order and eventually to act accordingly. (It need not coincide with the personal value judgement of any member of the group, and often is the result of a compromise.)

4. A ***non-personal value judgement*** is the consequence of a preference order either ***permanently incorporated*** into a system by an appropriate choice of boundaries (i.e. by structural relations and parameter values) or ***imposed*** upon the system ***temporarily*** by the environment.

5. Every ***artificial*** system contains ***at least one incorporated***, non-personal value judgement arising out of the preference through which it and no other alternative came to be created and accepted. Every ***natural*** system possesses either personal or non-personal value judgements incorporated by the evolutionary process. Further value judgements may be incorporated into natural and artificial systems by learning processes.

6. A system is called "normative" with respect to a certain property or activity[13] if the pertinent value judgement is more or less permanently incorporated; it is called "neutral" (or "positive") with respect to this property if the exercise of some pertinent value judgement is to be imposed from the environment on a temporary basis.

7. Overall goals (as expressions of value judgements) are sometimes complex, and occasionally have to be sub-divided into sub-goals; above all, a complex goal may be constituted ***partly*** through ***incorporated*** (internal) and ***partly*** through ***external*** sub-goals.[14]

[13] This property or activity may be *limited* to a certain *range of values*. An ordinary household thermostat heating system for example may work within a temperature range between 40°F and 90°F only.

[14] Simon (1957b) may have sensed this crucial issue when he wrote the following passage:

> Another way of characterizing the given and the behavior variables is to say that the latter refer to the organism itself, the former to its environment. But if we adopt this viewpoint, we must be prepared to accept the possibility that what we call "the environment" may lie, in part, within the skin of the biological organism. (1957b, p. 243.)

This probably is one reason why in recent years he preferred to adhere to the less frequently encountered usage of calling the structure of a system its *inner environment*.

The acceptance of the above set of propositions (especially items 4 to 6) enables us *to extend the notion of value judgement beyond semantics into systems theory*. An "ordinary language" philosopher of the Oxford school may now point out that the usage of such words as "positive", "normative", etc. must be kept within the limits of common linguistic usage. Thus our terminology would be rejected by this group if it were to introduce an artificial usage violating the commonly accepted one. We do not believe that such a violation is involved in our presentation; because it is quite generally accepted to speak, for example, of "a *positive* economics" and "a *normative* economics", or of "a *neutral* scientific system". Thus not only sentences, but entire systems are addressed as positive (neutral) and normative; then obviously these systems must be able to express, on one side, incorporated descriptions and, on the other, incorporated value judgements. Thus the novelty does not lie in the usage but in a new awareness of the consequences of such usage. A typical example is the debate over the controversial issue of whether science must be free of value judgements or not, or whether only some sciences may include value judgements but not others (for surveys of this controversy see Krimerman (1969, pp. 689–758) and Brody (1970, pp. 540–570)). Yet these controversies rarely tell us when an author regards science in general, or a science in particular, as a goal-oriented *system* or merely as a body of descriptive and perhaps prescriptive sentences.

In this connection it has to be emphasized that the modern linguistic usage is constantly broadening, perhaps beyond what is convenient to some scholars and language philosophers. The fact that nowadays we are "telephoning with a computer system" which then "answers our questions, or gives its judgements and directions because they were incorporated into its program" is no less supporting our case than recent discoveries of neurophysiology and biochemistry. We now know that the utterances of the human voice are released by a complex electronic and chemical information process, furthermore we know with not much lesser certainty that our own personal value judgements are partly incorporated through our genetic code and partly through environmental learning processes. Thus an imperative shouted by a human voice is not more normative than a "Do statement" of the FORTRAN-language releasing a sequence of electrical and mechanical events. And the latter is not more normatively impregnated than an imperative transmitted by a lever- and contact-mechanism of a thermostat switching on our furnace at 69°F. In these cases, as in many others, normative "sentences" are not formed by ordinary human language but by signs of a mechanical, electrical or chemical nature.

According to the preceding investigation we may properly designate a system as normative (in regard of a specific property) if it is designed to *impose upon its environment a certain norm* which is permanently incorporated into the system (e.g. the thermostat system S_I which imposes on its environment a temperature of 70°F ± 1°F). We have also seen that a value judgement can be relocated or externalized from the system. Precisely speaking this means the creation of a new and, in at least one respect, different system, which however *fulfills a very similar function* (e.g. heating the house, except for the fact that the value judgement is no longer an integral part of the system but is imposed upon it in a flexible way by some person or element of the environment). That means the term "system" expresses, precisely speaking two different concepts. For the sake of better distinction we may in *doubtful situations* designate as "*system*$_1$" *an entity amenable to different structures, and as "system*$_2$" *a system amenable to a single structure only.* Then one is justified in speaking of eliminating a norm, and of shifting the capacity to exercise a value judgement, from the system$_1$ to the environment or super-system. Alternatively one may speak of *reducing the norm of a system*$_1$ *to the capacity of obeying an external value judgement,* and therefore of *neutralizing a system*$_1$. For lack of better terminology we may address the entire approach here developed as the "Method of Neutralizing (and De-Neutralizing) Systems", even if it is not possible to externalize simultaneously *all* value judgements of a system.

A final remark to this Section is called for. The neutralizing of a system$_1$ should be done for significant reasons only (e.g. enhancing the flexibility of the system or for the sake of analysis) but not for the sole reason of calling a system "free of values" (something some positivists seem to do with regard to science). Such a reduction for its own sake is a mere shifting away of value judgements without ability to escape their ultimate consequences.

2.5 Management Science as a System: Normative or Positive?

The question of value judgement in science in general, and in management science in particular, is fundamental to every epistemological investigation. It constitutes an unresolved and highly controversial issue, and opinions, even within the management sciences, are still divided. Many scholars persistently maintain that every science must be neutral and thus free of values. This issue became especially relevant in the social science during the past century, and Max Weber (1922, 1949) was an early and major defender of this view. In our time its chief proponent in the management and administrative sciences is Herbert A. Simon:

> In the first place, an administrative science, like any science, is concerned purely with factual statements. There is no place for ethical assertions in the body of science. (1957a, p. 253.)

> Natural science has found a way to exclude the normative and to concern itself solely with how things are. Can or should we maintain this exclusion when we move from natural to artificial phenomena . . . ? . . . In order not to keep readers in suspense, I may say that I hold to the pristine positivistic position of the irreducibility of "ought" to "is" . . . This position is entirely consistent with treating natural or artificial goal-seeking systems as phenomena, without commitment to their goals. (1969, p. 5 and footnote 2.)

It is interesting to note that in the last sentences of the above-stated quote, Simon refers to the problem of value neutrality *in connection with systems*. But to our knowledge there does not exist any literature treating in detail this problem from the systems point of view. The conditions for determining whether a sentence is prescriptive (normative) or descriptive (positive or neutral) have been much discussed and can be stated fairly clearly; but the same does not hold for examining whether *a system* is normative or whether it is neutral (with respect to a specific property).

The recent publication of the ORSA Guidelines (1971), emphasizing the need for "objectivity" in our discipline, reveal that Simon is by no means alone in pleading for a value-free Management Science. On the other side, however, there exists a growing number of experts who reject on various grounds the value neutrality of science in general, or at least of some sciences. Among these dissenters at least three groups can be distinguished. First, those like Boulding (1969), Braithwaite (1953), Churchman (1948, 1961), Rudner (1953) and others who hold that sciences are inevitably endowed with value judgements. Second, those who believe that only the natural sciences can be objective and free of values, thereby rejecting the scientific status of the social and management sciences. And, finally, those who argue that two kinds of "objectivity" must be distinguished in such a way that the natural sciences are as little objective in one sense as are social sciences in the other. In this way the proponents of the last group reclaim the designation "science" for their disciplines. To the latter group belong mainly historians, sociologists, psychiatrists, historical and social philosophers like Isaiah Berlin, Erik H. Erikson, Karl Mannheim and his followers, Norman Malcolm, Leo Strauss and others. Cf. Krimerman (1969, pp. 689–741).

The present outline rests on the belief that this controversy can be somewhat clarified if not resolved by looking at the problem of value neutrality from the viewpoint of system thinking. Whether a system (e.g. Management Science) is free of values or not, depends on the location of the value judgement in relation to the boundaries of this system, as has been demonstrated above. But since no science has sharp boundaries generally agreed upon, these boundaries can be drawn arbitrarily at least within certain limits. Indeed, the boundaries might be manipulated in such a way as to include or exclude those value judgements which causes us to regard a science as normative or positive respectively. But it must be borne in mind that every purposive system, including a scientific discipline, contains a series of *other value judgements* ("pre-scientific" ones, in Hutchison's (1964) terminology) which are generally neglected or taken for granted.[15]

As long as these pre-scientific value judgements are suppressed, the distinction between a neutral (positive) and normative system may prove useful wherever the system's boundaries are clearly defined and whenever the pertinent property is at least implied. Where this is not the case, as for example in looking at entire disciplines, the above distinction should be avoided. To know whether a system is positive or normative is less important than to have knowledge of the nature and location of the value judgements pertaining to a system. We have tried to show that this specific kind of knowledge can be revealed, and in a precise presentation ought to be revealed, by pointing out the property or activity in regard to which a system is considered to be normative or neutral.

Value judgements demand special attention in Management Science, because the latter primarily deals with hypotheses implying specific goals, or even with arguments containing imperatives. The *positing of a goal* corresponds to the expostulation of a value judgement in form of an imperative statement or *task thesis* (in Rescher's (1969, pp. 31–36, 41–45) terminology) or similar statement. The management scientist's recommendation

[15] A good illustration of pre-scientific value judgements are the rules of deductive logic. These are imperatives which the human mind feels bound to accept. For this reason many philosophers (who generally make no distinction between "pre-scientific" and "post-scientific" value judgements) regard logic as a "normative" discipline. This view is re-inforced by the insight that there exist alternative sets of norms in deductive logic:

> For some years, it was felt that there was precisely one correct system of formal logic which could be used to impose clarity and rigor on all significant verbal contexts. This is, quite simply, false. There is not precisely one correct system of logic. There are many. Which system is the appropriate one to use for a given task is, to a large extent, determined by the nature of that task. Snyder, *Modal Logic and its Applications*, 1971, p. 1.

is usually stated in form of a scientific technological rule (in Bunge's (1967, Vol. II, p. 132) terminology), also called instrumental or pragmatic hypothesis (see Mattessich (1964a, pp. 234–237; 1969 and 1974a)); out of these two kinds of premises follows a recommendation, which again is an imperative or similar statement expressing a (derived) value judgement. This sequence is best expressed by a typical argument from deontology in the broad sense hence including imperative arguments[16] (illustrated crudely in Table 2-4).

In this connection reference should be made to Herbert Simon's (1965, 1966) argument, that *deontic reasoning does not require a special deontic logic.* This assertion seems to be interpretable in at least two ways: (1) that management scientists and deontologists, etc. ought to restrict their attention to statements represented by the second premise, which are propositions (i.e. assertions or declarations) but not normative sentences, or (2) that the entire deontic arguments are acceptable, but should be handled within assertorial logic. Yet in our view the second interpretation is self-contradictory because *ultimately* assertorial logic should exclude from its arguments non-assertions (e.g. task theses) because no truth values can be assigned to them. Thus assertorial logic would require an extension; but this extension is precisely what deontic logic is all about. The first interpretation, on the other hand, would banish normative arguments, leaving merely *the instrumental hypothesis which, as a factual proposition,*[17] *neutralizes the encapsuled value judgement.* The latter is relegated to the environment, and claimed to be neither the concern of the pertinent theory nor of any scientific discipline. This of course presupposes some sweeping assumptions (that *absolute* truth is attainable; that a scientific theory can be fully understood if the underlying value judgements are eliminated from it by drawing artificial boundaries; etc.) all of which run counter to systems thinking. It is our understanding that the major recommendation of the systems approach *is to perceive a system in relation to its environment, and to avoid looking at a system in isolation.* Whoever follows this recommendation is forced to con-

[16] For a survey of deontic logic in the more narrow sense see Wright (1968). For the analogy and difference between the quantifiers of assertorial logic, and deontic as well as modal operators, see *ibid*. pp. 13–14.

[17] A proposition is a statement that has a *truth value* (i.e. it is either true or false) and an instrumental hypothesis can in principle be tested as to its truth in contrast to imperatives or other non-propositions. Bunge (1967, Vol. II, pp. 134–136) however prefers to assign to instrumental hypotheses *efficiency values* instead of truth values. To our mind an efficiency value should not substitute but supplement the truth value of an instrumental hypothesis.

TABLE 2-4

A deontic-imperative argument

1st Premise	(imperative):	Person N is to do or attain B
2nd Premise	(proposition):	Do A if B is to be attained
Therefore conclusion	(imperative):	N is to do or attain A

sider (in addition to the instrumental hypothesis) the value judgement-premise as well as the value judgement-conclusion. The latter is of course the actual recommendation the management scientist is supposed to provide.

2.6 Reduction of Value Judgements

The problem of value judgement versus value neutrality is of special importance to Management Science, and is frequently encountered in the pertinent literature (e.g. Churchman (1948, 1961, 1968a, b), Simon (1957a, 1965, 1969), Hutchison (1964), Chmielewicz (1970), Tarascio (1971), Dlugos, *et. al.* (1972)). Traditionally, the core of this problem has been summarized in the question "Can value judgements be reduced to factual statements?" Careful semantics (as used in our proposition 1 of Section 2.4) reveals that a value judgement, by definition, is an imperative, hence a non-declarative statement. But since every *factual* statement is by necessity declarative, the positivists' claim that "ought-to-sentences cannot be reduced to is-sentences" turns out to be a tautology (unless there are statements which are simultaneously imperative and declarative). Yet in spite of this obvious truth, much controversy has centered around that assertion even in circles who do not subscribe to the thesis of "ethical naturalism" – see, e.g. E. M. Adams (1960). This controversy might be due to different possibilities of interpreting the above-mentioned claim. Indeed, the *sentence expressing it, loses its tautological nature if its basis of reference is a system instead of an unbound universe.*[18] Thus the counter-argument "ought-to-sentences can be reduced to is-sentences within a system" must be carefully examined. For this purpose we again refer the reader to Table 2-4. But this time we begin with the imperative conclusion, and argue that one way of reducing this normative statement is by tracing it to its premises. Since one

[18] It seems that the following is an economic analogue to the above statement: "ex-post investment is equal to ex-post savings" is necessarily true only for an entire economy, but not for a sector of it (e.g. this identity hardly ever holds for the so-called Household Sector in the Flow of Funds Accounting).

of them is a *factual* statement (2nd premise) while the other is a more basic normative sentence (first premise), it is established that in this sense a value judgement can be reduced to a factual statement *plus* another value judgement. Although one could terminate the argument at this stage, pointing out that it presents one possible interpretation to counter the positivists' claim, a much less trivial interpretation (and possible explanation of past confusion) is attained by continuing the argument as follows: As demonstrated in the first two parts of this paper, systems can be designed such as to externalize some value judgements. Thus it would be possible to draw the system boundaries in such a way as to include within a system the factual premise of a deontic argument (i.e. its instrumental hypothesis), as well as its conclusion and perhaps consequent statements, but to exclude from the system the normative premise. In this way it would be correct to say that *from the point of view of this specific system* the ought-to-sentence (i.e. the normative conclusion) was reduced to a factual statement, because the normative premise of this argument was relegated to the environment. Of course, once the deontic mode is adopted, a complete elimination of the normative remnant is not possible, and this may never have been meant by the opponents of the behavioral positivists. On the contrary, it has been a major argument of these opponents that, in science or in any other system, *value judgements cannot be eliminated in the end* (i.e. if the environment is taken into consideration).

Another aspect must here be pointed out. In tracing value judgements to factual statements, on one side, and to more basic norms, on the other, one should not limit the analysis to a single deontic argument but ought to contemplate a larger part of the deontic hierarchy (as for example illustrated in Figure 2-1). Because frequently an instrumental hypothesis makes the fulfilment of a norm dependent on *several* less basic norms instead of a single one. Accordingly, two or more norms of lower order are *simultaneously* being reduced to a factual statement plus a norm of higher order. Figure 2-1 shows that we are dealing with a *reduction process* in the true sense of the word (working in counter-direction to the printed arrows, i.e. the derivation process). In the entire segment here depicted, seven terminal norms (all those in boxes, e.g. [Do *O*]) are ultimately reduced to a single factual statement ("If *A* is to be attained, then do *B, C,* and *D*") and a single basic value judgement "Do *A*" or alternatively "*A* is to be attained"). The situation where several norms are reduced to a single factual statement within a system, is illustrated in S_1 of Figure 2-1. The reader acquainted with the notion of "scientific explanation" as advanced by Hempel and Oppenheim (1948)

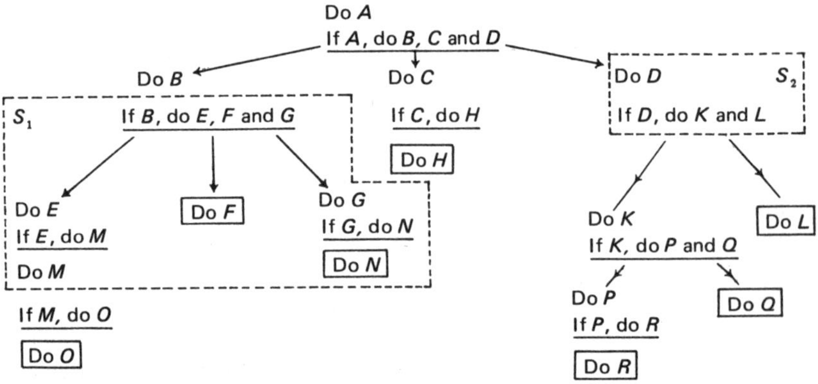

Fig. 2-1. A hierarchy of deontic-imperative arguments (reduction of value judgements in reverse order of arrows). Expressions like "If *A*, do *B*, *C* and *D*" mean "If *A* is to be done (or attained), then do (or attain) *B*, *C*, and *D*." Dashed lines indicate system boundaries. Small boxes indicate ultimate value judgements: e.g. Do *F*.

will notice an analogy between our reduction process (on the deontic level) and the process of explanation (on the assertorial level).

2.7 Institutionalized Facts as Values

However, there seems to exist a further, complementary rather than competitive possibility of reducing value judgements to factual statements. It rests on the assertion that certain sentences are not only descriptive but simultaneously prescriptive. To begin with a naive example let us look at the sentence "I am thirsty". On one hand, it expresses undoubtedly ***a value judgement***, based on my preferring, at the moment, the activity of drinking to any other. Thus it is almost synonymous with, or at least interpretable as, "give me something to drink". On the other hand, I *describe* through it an inner state, namely that I am thirsty. But as we have pointed out in Subsection 2.1 one usually does not accept such statements based on introspection (internal observation) as descriptive. Only statements based on external observation, that is on objectively verifiable behavior, are recognized as descriptive or factual sentences. But is the description of my inner state – of which I may be much surer than of any external, perhaps even deceptive, observation – less reliable than the observation performed by an intermediary? In pursuing this thought the question arises: How could sentences expressing both descriptive and prescriptive content be categorized? An attempt of such categorization was undertaken in an important paper by Searle (1964).

This author begins with the following sequence of sentences:

(1) Jones uttered the words "I hereby promise to pay you, Smith, five dollars."
(2) Jones promised to pay Smith five dollars.
(3) Jones placed himself under (undertook) an obligation to pay Smith five dollars.
(4) Jones is under an obligation to pay Smith five dollars.
(5) Jones ought to pay Smith five dollars.

Searle then demonstrates in detail (with the aid of some auxiliary but neutral premises) that we are here dealing with a sequence of deductive arguments containing apparently only descriptive premises (statements 1 to 4) but, surprisingly enough, end up with a normative conclusion (sentence 5). His analysis reveals that the critical jump from "is" to "ought" occurs as early as the first argument, i.e. in the transition from sentence (1) to sentence (2). After introducing two auxiliary hypotheses (1a) and (1b) the first argument assumes the form represented in Table 2-5.

Sentence (1) obviously is a descriptive statement but it presupposes and, together with (1a), invokes the institution of promising which prescribes an "ought". Thus the first sentence (supported by (1a) or implying it) is not merely a descriptive but simultaneously a normative statement. Only if the part in quotation marks were pronounced in jest or when play acting, would the institution of promising not be invoked, then sentence (1) would be nothing but a descriptive statement. Searle finally arrives at the conclusion that this is not simply a curiosity or an isolated example but is representative for all instances where institutions are invoked. Therefore he insists on a strict distinction between the following two kinds of descriptive sentences:

(i) Descriptive sentences expressing simple empirical paradigms (e.g. "my car goes eighty miles an hour", "Jones is six feet tall", "Smith has brown hair").

TABLE 2-5

(1)	Jones uttered the words "I hereby promise to pay you, Smith five dollars".
(1a)	Under certain conditions *C* anyone who utters the words (sentence) "I hereby promise to pay you, Smith, five dollars" promises to pay Smith five dollars.
(1b)	Conditions *C* obtain.
∴ (2)	Jones promised to pay Smith five dollars.

(ii) Descriptive sentences expressing facts that presuppose institutions (e.g. "Jones got married", "Smith made a promise", "Jackson has five dollars", and "Brown hit a home-run").

How are they different? Though both kinds of statements state matters of objective fact, the statements containing words such as "married", "promise", "Home-run", and "five dollars" state facts whose existence presupposes certain institutions: a man has five dollars, given the institution of money. Take away the institution and all he has is a rectangular bit of paper with green ink on it. A man hits a home-run only given the institution of baseball; without the institution he only hits a sphere with a stick. Similarly, a man gets married or makes a promise only within the institutions of marriage and promising. Without them, all he does is utter words or make gestures. We might characterize such facts as institutional facts, and contrast them with non-institutional, or brute, facts: that a man has a bit of paper with green ink on it is a brute fact, that he has five dollars is an institutional fact. The classical picture fails to account for the differences between statements of brute fact and statements of institutional fact.

The word "institution" sounds artificial here, so let us ask: what sorts of institutions are these? In order to answer that question I need to distinguish between two different kinds of rules or conventions. Some rules regulate antecedently existing forms of behavior. For example, the rules of polite table behavior regulate eating, but eating exists independently of these rules. Some rules, on the other hand, do not merely regulate but create or define new forms of behavior: the rules of chess, for example, do not merely regulate an antecedently existing activity called playing chess; they, as it were, create the possibility of or define that activity. The activity of playing chess is constituted by action in accordance with these rules. Chess has no existence apart from these rules. The distinction I am trying to make was foreshadowed by Kant's distinction between regulative and constitutive principles, so let us adopt his terminology and describe our distinction as a distinction between regulative and constitutive rules. Regulative rules regulate activities whose existence is independent of the rules; constitutive rules constitute (and also regulate) forms of activity whose existence is logically dependent on the rules. Searle, 'How to Derive "Ought" from "Is" ' 1964, pp. 54–55.

"One ought to pay one's debts" can be construed as saying that to recognize something as a debt is necessarily to recognize an obligation to pay it. It is easy to see how all these principles will generate counter-examples to the thesis that you cannot derive an "ought" from an "is".

My tentative conclusions, then, are as follows:

1. The classical picture fails to account for institutional facts.
2. Institutional facts exist within systems of constitutive rules.
3. Some systems of constitutive rules involve obligations, commitments, and responsibilities.
4. Within those systems we can derive "ought's" from "is's" on the model of the first derivation. (Searle, 1964, p. 57.)

We may now pose the question whether Searle's presentation cannot be fitted into the broader framework of systems analysis as previously sketched. Are not such systems constitutively subject to value judgements similar to Searle's institutions? Should such a similarity or identity hold, then a system could be described by institutional facts. But those are, according to Searle, descriptive as well as prescriptive and permit the derivation of neutral as well as normative conclusions. The next section will deal with the extension of Searle's insight to our notions of neutralizing systems.

2.8 Institutions as Systems

Assuming that institutions like those of moral (or legal) obligation, marriage, monetary regulations etc., can be treated as systems, how could the pertinent deontic arguments be represented? We begin our illustration by building upon the example presented by Searle. In such a case the entire argument (shown in Table 2-5) or at least its essential elements (see Section 2, Tables 2-5 and 2-6) should be incorporated into system S_{MO} (system of moral obligation). In addition we need the constitutive rule or *norm* (sentence (1) of Table 2-6) representative for this institution and therefore to be *incorporated* in S_{MO}. Furthermore a logical link between the general formulation of sentence (1) (Table 2-6) and the particular formulation of sentence (2) has to be introduced. This is done by the sentences (3) and (4) (Table 2-6), but in a meticulous presentation might require even more sentences. Then the conclusion (sentence (5), Table 2-6) can be drawn in the form of an imperative.

This illustration (Table 2-6) sheds further light upon Searle's analysis. Above all it indicates that an institutional fact as expressed in sentence (2) is not necessarily prescriptive, provided the usually implied value judgement is separately stated. In systems analysis the method developed by us

TABLE 2-6

A deontic argument of a system of moral obligation

System S_{MO}:

(1)	For all persons *x*, *y*, etc. bound by the moral system S_{MO} (condition *C*) and all promissory relations *P*, *Q*, *R*, etc. the following holds:
(a)	If *x* says to *y* "I promise you *p*", then *x* made the promise *P* to *y*.
(b)	*x ought to* hold his promise *P* to *y*.
(2)	Jones uttered the words "I hereby promise to pay you, Smith five dollars".
(3)	Jones and Smith are persons bound by the moral system S_{MO} (condition *C* obtains).
(4)	Jones fulfills his promise to Smith if he pays him five dollars.
∴ (5)	Jones *ought to* pay Smith five dollars.

(Mattessich, 1974a), and presented in this chapter takes care of formulating the actual value judgement in a natural way. This *institutional value judgement* as we might call it, is illustrated in sentence (1) (Table 2-6) and usually will assume the form of a *universal* imperative bounded merely by the limits of the pertinent institution. If this value judgement is made explicit and thus separated from the corresponding institutional fact (e.g. sentence (2)) then there is no need to regard the institutional fact as being imbued with a value judgement. It becomes a fact like any other, and the embarrassing duality suggested by Searle is eliminated.

This does not mean that Searle's claim, that sentences expressing institutional facts are both descriptive and prescriptive, is necessarily incorrect. On the contrary in most situations this assertion seems to be correct, simply because until recently no means were available to separate clearly and systematically the normative part from the descriptive part of an institutional sentence. We therefore suggest that *an institutional proposition ought to be regarded simultaneously as descriptive as well as prescriptive as long as it appears in isolation. But as soon as it is viewed within the context of the pertinent system, the institutional proposition loses its normative character, because a separate and universal value judgement assumes the prescriptive function.* This value judgement is incorporated in the pertinent system as its constitutive part.

CHAPTER 3

PHILOSOPHY AND EVOLUTION OF LOGIC FROM A SYSTEMS POINT OF VIEW

3.1 Some Ontological Considerations

In the preceding chapter we offered a rough outline of the system notion; we tried to make its usefulness plausible and illustrated its applications as a possible tool of analysis. But if this notion is something beyond a passing fad, it must be possible to relate it to the contemporary view about the structure of·the universe. Thus the systems approach might be enhanced by giving it an ontological grounding (i.e. by stating assumptions about the *existence* of certain entities and events) and by showing the system notion as being rooted in the foundations of science.

Reality and its mental representations are matters of high complexity, not only because of the immense variety of actual combinations but also because of an extensive hierarchy spanning the entire gamut from the energy quantum to the human being. Yet modern physics leads us to believe that the ultimate building stones and principles of design are less variegated. And one speculates that the universe (reality, nature, world, cosmos, etc.) is made up of either a single *basic substance* (event) or of a limited number of basic substances. A predominant view conceives basic as well as compound substances as possessing *properties*, and as being connected with each other by *relations*. Substances are usually called *things*; in contrast to them are *facts*, or *existing states of affairs*, which are the object of knowledge ("a thing or a property or a relation cannot be known, strictly speaking: if anything is known, it is always that the thing or property or relation in question occurs in a certain way in a state of affairs". Bocheński (1965, p. 4)). The representation of *entities* (i.e. things, properties or relations) is through (objective) *concepts* while that of facts is through (objective) propositions which possess truth values (i.e. they are either *true* or *false*, or even *probable*). The linguistic manifestation of concepts is by means of *terms*, and that of propositions by means of *sentences* (terms and sentences are both linguistic *signs*). But there is also a mental manifestation which is through mental or neurological patterns often called *subjective concepts* and *subjective propositions*. One and the same (objective) concept or proposition can be manifested by several terms or sentences respectively (e.g. in different languages). Whether all entities possess essence (stating *what* it is) as well as *existence* (stating *whether* it is) is a controversial issue. Nowadays a distinction between physical existence and mental existence is often made. Accordingly the crucial mathematical and philosophic notion of "set", for example, is regarded as having only mental but not physical existence (cf. the mind–body problem in Subsection 3.21).

Of central importance for the physical, biological and social sciences is the fact that, under appropriate conditions, substances are amenable to a process of simultaneous aggregation and integration. For lack of a better expression we shall call this process "*concrescence*" and *define it as an event through which one or several entities, possessing specific properties, are transformed into another entity with new holistic properties*. The combination of a certain number of free protons, neutrons, electrons and energy quanta into the atom of a particular chemical element, is such a process of concrescence; other examples are the combination of various DNA and RNA molecules, proteins and other chemical substances into a specific amoeba, the combination of various production factors into a particular business enterprise, or even the combination of various electronic and mechanical components into a computer. So far no general schemes for measuring the *intensity* and the *extent* of these simultaneous processes of integration and aggregation have been devised. But a systematic exploration of the pertinent measurement problems might become a serious concern of the systems approach. A major effort of every science is to describe the conditions under which certain concrescences occur. And the fact that the entities resulting from each process of concrescence can conveniently be presented as systems, gives evidence that the system notion is deeply rooted in our scientific outlook. What is less evident is the usefulness of a *cross-disciplinary abstraction* comprising all the variegated processes of concrescence. This different angle of abstraction is no less a basic idea of the systems approach than the system notion itself. It is a somewhat different and novel way of looking at the world. Whether this new outlook can survive or not, will depend on its future fertility. Yet in conformity with the spirit of scientific exploration one should give systems thinking sufficient opportunity to prove its merits instead of pre-judging it in a narrow-minded way.

Apart from systems theorists, modern philosophers have paid relatively little attention to nature's tendency of aggregating basic substances into integral entities of ever-increasing complexity. (Leibniz' monadology is the best known *traditional* theory of concretion.) Only in one area have philosophers paid attention to the hierarchy resulting from aggregation or concretion, namely in semantics where the distinction between object language and meta-language, and meta-languages of higher order, brought forth revolutionary insights. *But are the hierarchies of physical, biological and social systems of lesser philosophic significance than those of linguistic systems*?

A further ontological assumption frequently, though not generally, accepted, is that of the *interdependence of all things*. But even without it, many experts regard the basic conditions of the systems approach as fulfilled. Above all, every aggregate–integrated entity may be taken as a system, since it fits our system notion as defined in Subsection 2.22. This definition does not insist upon the mutual relations of all elements, but merely stipulates a relation between at least two elements within the system and a relation between an element within the system and one of the environment (the latter only in case of an open system).

We conclude that the ultimate justification of the systems approach has to be sought in its suitability for *a general representation of, (1) the process and result of physical, biological and social concrescence, and (2) the hierarchy and the feed-backs ensuing from these concretion processes*. If the representation of these phenomena can be executed in a more general or superior way, through the system notion, the *raison d'être* of the latter will no longer be disputed. But the ultimate proof of its usefulness or even superiority must wait for tangible results. In this connection it must be repeated that for us the systems approach is more a systematic extension of the conventional analytical framework than an entirely new paradigm (as ambitiously envisaged by Bogdanov, von Bertalanffy and others). *While the traditional analytical approach rests on a theory of aggregates (set theory), we envisage the modern extension as a theory of simultaneous aggregation and integration. A set is a loose collection of elements whereas a system is a collection of elements integrated by specific relations*. Since logic is the very basis of the analytical framework, it deserves some attention in a book of this kind.

3.2 On the Nature of Logic

In general, logic is regarded as *a formal or analytical discipline*, hence one dealing with mere forms or tautologies without empirical content. Since these tautologies need not be expressed in law-like propositions but, with increasing frequency, are presented in form of rules (prescriptive statements), the question arises whether logic should not rather be addressed as a *normative* subject matter.[1] Which in turn raises the question about the difference or relation between an analytical and a normative discipline. Some scholars even regarded logic as an empirical endeavour. But it deals with *analytical laws of reasoning, not* with *factual laws of thinking*. While the former are foundation stones of valid inference, the latter belong to psychology and should explain neuro-physiological activities, human and perhaps animal behavior, and related phenomena. Usually it is argued that those viewing logic as an empirical subject have confused the formal processes of inferring with the factual processes of thinking. In some cases this confusion may well have occurred, in others however, the reason for regarding logic as an empirical field has much deeper roots. It seems to lie in the still unanswered question: How can we know the principles of logic[2] if not through experience?

The standard reponse to this question is that the laws or norms of logic are given *a priori*. That means they are assumed to be an inescapable structural precondition of every mind and possibly even of nature in general. But this raises a host of other questions which must be dealt with in proper succession. The first refers to *the inescapability or a priori necessity of the laws of logic*: Is there only one ultimate set of such laws or are there alternatives from which one may choose? If the latter holds, then it seems that an element of arbitrariness enters the picture and neither the necessity nor the *a priori* character of logic can be maintained. Yet in spite of the fact that in recent decades alternative systems of logic begin to dominate the scene, it seems that only one or the other of those laws can be dispensed with, while the others remain unshaken. Mainly the principle of the excluded middle (*tertium non datur* – see our footnote 2) seems to be under dispute. Lukasiewicz's three-valued logic (the three truth values are: true, possible, and false) had to abandon this principle, since the latter insists that a proposition cannot assume a third value beyond the two values of true and false. This change is of special importance when inferences are based on propositions about future events. In such situations a truth value expressing the possibility or even a specific probability is of course indispensable. Thus it is not

[1] The eminent American philosopher Charles Peirce was one of the earlier proponents of this view.

[2] Typical examples of the laws or principles of logic are the following: "Either a proposition is true or it is false" (law of the excluded middle), "a proposition cannot be true and simultaneously be false" (law of contradiction), "a proposition implies itself" (law of identity). Although such laws appear to be trivial to the uninitiated, he must be warned not to underrate them; they are most powerful tools upon which the mighty structures of logic as well as mathematics rest.

surprising that areas depending on the probability calculus like quantum mechanics, modern decision theory, etc., cannot be presented, without contradiction, by means of the traditional two-valued logic. But this fact should not tempt us to pour the baby out with the bathwater; Bochenski (1965), for example, assures us that:

> Far too many thinkers have drawn premature philosophical conclusions from this state of affairs in the direction of absolute relativism and scepticism. In fact, however, there seems to be no reason for such pessimistic conclusions. On closer examination the following considerations come to light:
>
> (1) The so-called "heterodox" systems of logic are applied only in fields where signs are unlikely to acquire eidetic meaning. "Classical" logic is used in all sciences which operate with eidetically meaningful signs.
>
> (2) The metalinguistic rules used in the formalization of the system in question are thoroughly "classical". The three-valued logic of Łukasiewicz, for example, does not admit *tertium non datur*, but on the metalinguistic level it is always taken for granted that each statement has a certain truth value or does not have it, and that no third alternative is possible. For that matter there are systems in which the principle of contradiction does not hold, but these systems must themselves be constructed without contradictions, and every logician tries to provide a proof of this consistency.
>
> (3) In most cases involving apparently contradictory logical systems either one of them is without an interpretation or the signs used do not have the same meaning in both. Thus, for example, the sign of negation has completely different meanings in intuitionist logic and in the system of *Principia Mathematica*.
>
> (4) On the other hand, such systems often represent only a fraction of the whole domain of logical principles. It may be that such a partial logic is enough for the uses to which it is to be put.
>
> In this way a philosopher who was not sceptically inclined might sum up the methodological situation in this area, and this judgement is appended here because most scientists, after all, are not sceptics. Their intuitive belief in the absolute validity of the laws of logic is not in the least threatened by recent developments. (Bochenski, *The Method of Contemporary Thought*, 1965 pp. 79–80.

Further questions raised by asserting the *a priori* character of logic will be dealt within the next Subsection.

3.21 *Relation to the Mind–Body Problem*

If the laws of logic are considered to be inherent in our mind, we should ask what meaning the word "mind" has in this context. Is it identical to "brain" or is there a fundamental difference between these two expressions? This brings us back to the mind–body (or mind–brain) controversy hinted at in Chapter 2, and the interrelated problem of *consciousness*. It may appear surprising to raise this question in a chapter on logic, but there exists a close and often neglected interdependence between the views about logic and those about the mind–body problem. Since the latter is the more fundamental one, a short outline of the mind–body issue may aid in forming a consistent view about the nature of logic. A further reason for this concern lies in the bearing which the problem of consciousness has upon applied science. The phenomenon of *consciousness* (i.e. the ability to have ideas, make judgements, experience emotions, etc.) lies at the very root of *value judgements* which play a central role in any applied discipline. The emergence of preferences, the setting of goals, the prescribing of means, all these are consequences of consciousness; and it is notable that none of them are encountered in the pure, physical sciences, because to them the notion of consciousness is alien.

The classical position on the mind–body is *Descartes' duality-interaction theory*, according to which there are only two kinds of basic substances: *mind* and *matter*. While the essence of mind was deemed to be "thought", that of matter was pronounced to be "extension in space". In man both substances were supposed to *interact* and influence each other.

But if mind and matter are entirely different substances how can they possibly interact? In which way, for example, can such a mutual event as a desire in the hunter's mind lead to the aiming of the rifle and the releasing of its lock? Or, the other way round, how can the tasting of a ripe peach lead to the mental event which we consider such a delicious sensation? We may, after many intermediate steps, be in a position to trace this activity of tasting to some electro-chemical events in the brain-cortex, but on this road the transformations are all of a material nature. The last and crucial transformation, however, the one from the electro-chemical events to the sensation, is still utterly mysterious.

Leibniz too embraced the dualism of mind and matter, but avoided the embarrassing question of interaction between different basic substances by simply *denying this interaction*. According to his ingenious but startling *theory of pre-established harmony*, mind and matter are *not causally connected,* but operate independently in parallel function, they act so to say in a divinely harmonious correspondence. This phenomenon may be compared to two precisely adjusted mechanical or atomic clocks which continuously show the same time without being physically connected (the comparison would not be valid in case of *electrical* clock works *linked to the same net*).

Closer to modern views is T. H. Huxley's *epiphenomenalism* which, although being dualistic, accepts causal interaction in one direction only, namely from body to mind, and not *vice versa*. It thus recognizes a predominance of matter over mind, and regards consciousness as a secondary bodily function or by-product of some material neurological process. In many scientific quarters, at least those refusing to believe in disembodied existences, there might be little objection to the notion that mind and thought are unthinkable without material and bodily entities. But such a view does not necessarily coincide with the opinion that mental events can merely be effects but not causes of bodily events. Epiphenomenalism, however, regards the undeniable influences which the mind is capable of exercising over the body as non-causal events.

In contrast to those duality theories (of which there exist many variations) there are such *monistic theories* as *idealism*, which tries to explain material events entirely in terms of mental occurrences (e.g. Bishop Berkeley), or *materialism* which attempts to reduce mentalistic phenomena to physical events (e.g. Hobbes as well as most members of the Vienna Circle). A somewhat moderate materialistic version, taken very seriously at present, is the *mind–body identity theory* advanced by Herbert Feigl, J. J. Smart and others. It admits that mentalistic and physical expressions have different semantical *meaning*, but asserts that they ultimately *refer* to the same empirical process (cf. difference between meaning and reference in Subsections 3.25 and 3.41). This would come close to our own view that the mind is a notion pertaining to the mental *function* of being conscious (i.e. as having feelings, preferences, ideas, etc.) while the notion of the brain or, more precisely, of the entire nervous system would pertain to such functions as receiving, transferring, coordinating and transforming electro-chemical nerve impulses, etc. Thus a particular mental phenomenon would not only be dependent on a particular phenomenon in the brain, but either would be nothing but a different aspect of one and the same physical event. One objection to the identity theory is the *problem of location* (mental events might not be localized, while brain events seem to be restricted to a specific location; yet identical events must have identical locations). Another consideration refers to the fact that a person gets acquainted with his own mental events subjectively through introspection (another mental event) but *not* in the "objective" way of observation.

A final possibility of dealing with the mind–body problem is to declare it a pseudo problem (e.g. G. Ryle). This approach too relies on semantical analysis but goes beyond the identity theory by declaring the controversy of mind versus matter a "category mistake". Ryle offers an analogy designed to illustrate the possible semantic confusion here involved.

> A foreigner visiting Oxford or Cambridge for the first time is shown a number of the colleges, libraries, playing fields, museums, scientific departments and administrative offices. He then asks "But where is the University? . . . " . . . it has then to be explained to him that the University is not another collateral institution . . . The University is just the way in which all that he has already seen is organized . . . He was mistakenly allocating the University to the same category as to which the other institutions belong. (Ryle, *The Concept of the Mind*, 1949, p. 16.)

But, to return to our remark in the beginning of this Subsection, how can we establish the connection between the philosophy of mind on one side and the nature of logic on the other? Scholars who consider the conscious or subconscious awareness of the basic principles of logic, together with their validity, as a genuine *experience* (i.e. those defending the empirical nature of logic), might have to deny, for the sake of consistency, the physical as well as functional difference between mind and brain. On the other hand, those deeming the premises of logic as given *a priori* to one's mind, should be inclined to admit that mentalistic events or functions are different from physical events, since the affirmation of these principles was not attained through empirical observation but by a distinctly different mental process. Of course the connection between these two issues is more complex than this hint might suggest, but there exists an undeniable, often neglected, cross reference between them. And the decision about the nature of logic will ultimately hinge on the way in which one solves the mind–body problem and the closely related problem of consciousness.

3.22 *Analytical and Normative Aspects of Logic*

The question of logic as a normative versus an analytical discipline seems to be easier solved than the mind–body problem. Indeed the answer, in a way, was pre-empted in Chapter 2 where the conversion of neutral systems into normative ones was discussed. However, it might be of particular interest that such a conversion and shifting of system boundaries can be observed in modern logic. While the axioms of modern logic were originally formulated as propositions (i.e. as descriptive statements with truth values – apart from the rules of definition, formation, and transformation), some versions of logic (so-called *natural deduction systems*) have recently emerged in which the axioms themselves are formulated as rules of inference, hence as normative instead of descriptive statements. A. E. Blumberg (1967, p. 25) points out clearly that "as an alternative syntactical characterization of sentential logic, a natural deduction system has marked advantages. For one thing, its deductive apparatus consists of inference rules alone thus eliminating the awkward business of logical axioms (propositions instead of rules). For another, its method of testing the validity of argument forms is much closer to ordinary patterns of reasoning."

> The choice between logical axioms [propositions] and rules of inference, as Carnap noted in 1934 (*Logische Syntax der Sprache*), is a practical one rather than one of principle, in that for any logical axiom an equivalent inference rule, or rules, can be stated. Blumberg (1967), p. 25.

Of course, natural deduction systems are, strictly speaking, still axiom systems (cf. Bochenski, 1965, p. 72). And although their premises are not descriptive propositions but prescriptive rules of inference, there is no formal or material reason not to call them also "logical axioms". Yet, in the above quote, Blumberg restricts this expression to propositions in spite of the fact that the same inferences can be drawn deductively from rules.

The choice between the neutral (descriptive or "axiomatic") mode, on one side and the normative (prescriptive, or natural deductive) mode on the other, can be made on the basis of two entirely different criteria. The one criterion is *practicality*, the other *consistency* with one's fundamental beliefs about the mind–body problem. In recent years the natural deduction method is favored with the argument that it is more convenient. Those who chose this method may not even be aware that they have given preference to a normative over a neutral method. But consistency requirements might force those who believe in attaining absolute laws of logic through intuition (e.g. a phenomenological Wesensschau) to accept it as a neutral discipline. While those who doubt that the mind is capable of intuiting absolute laws of logic, and who argue that the banishment of the principle of excluded middle in modal logic might foreshadow the abandoning of other logical principles (or the acceptance of new ones) in future systems of logic, would act consistently by regarding logic as a normative discipline. But this latter view does not enforce the acceptance of logic as an empirical science. It is important to realize that *an analytical discipline may be either neutral or normative, just as an empirical science can assume both modes*.

Conditions of rationality (for details see Subsection 6.23) prescribe, among other things, that we *ought to* make our inferences in accord with the laws of logic. But obviously no one can force a person to do this. And since not all persons infer correctly all of the time, logic is prescriptive but not descriptive. However, as we have seen, the boundaries of a discipline can be shifted such as to exclude the norms; thus it is possible to present logic as a neutral discipline. But there is no reason why this shift of boundaries should affect the analytical character of logic.

In the case of an empirical science the situation is different insofar as one has no choice but to "obey" the laws of nature. (Anyone jumping out of an airplane is subject to the laws of free fall whether he wants it or not. All he can do is to change the conditions of this fall, e.g. by donning in time a parachute, such that these laws together with those of wind resistance lead to a considerably reduced falling speed.) Thus the *pure* empirical sciences and their laws describe rather than prescribe (unless nature is assumed to "prescribe" the inevitable). The applied empirical sciences, on the other side, fulfill a normative function, because they prescribe how certain actions *ought to be* performed (e.g. how an effective parachute is to be constructed). Pragmatic philosophy goes even so far as to declare all empirical sciences as applied, denying them the ability to describe and explain (at a sufficient degree of reliability) what is the case. Thus pragmatists might reject this major criterion for distinguishing pure from applied science.

3.23 *The Origin of Formal Logic*

The history of logic has two peculiarities which distinguish this field of learning from any other discipline. First, *formal logic was created by Aristotle (384–322 B.C.) virtually out of nothing*. That means, one finds hardly any trace of preceding ideas on this subject by Plato, Socrates or any other philosopher. Second, *for far over two thousand years this subject matter was believed to have been exhausted by its creator.*[3] Indeed, most of the

[3] Modern historical research has proved that fundamental advances have occurred in logic between Aristotle's time and the nineteenth century – for details see Bochenski (1956/70) and Kneale and Kneale (1962). But important manuscripts on logic were either neglected or destroyed (e.g. as those of the Stoics and Megarians who were already in possession of the sentential calculus).

eminent philosophers of past centuries, including Immanuel Kant, deemed logic as practically complete and hence as incapable of further fundamental advances. Yet, since the middle of the past century logic has experienced an explosion of ideas and achievements. Not only did the Aristotelian syllogisms turn out to cover but a minute part of the problems of logic, above all a host of exciting insights were gained that have proved to be of far-reaching significance for modern science and philosophy alike. In the following we shall indicate concisely the highlights of these achievements.

Most human communication and conversation is not by *isolated* signs (such as sounds, tokens, terms, phrases, etc.) but by sentences *related* to each other. The most important of these relations is that of *consequence* or *conclusion* which is manifested by such expressions as "because", "hence", "since", "therefore", "thus", etc. Although these words claim that one sentence follows from others, the words themselves bear no assurance that such an allegation is correct. How then can we know that a pretended conclusion is a *valid* (i.e. conclusive) consequence of the premises?

Thus the need arises for a body of general rules assuring correct reasoning. Such a theory demonstrates *what follows from what*, and offers the desired assurance for the validity of an inference. And no one should underrate the fallacies to which human inferences are prone. Besides, few minds are made to grasp at an instant inferences of even moderate complexity. Often enough we have to toil to infer the implications step by step. Logic is such a theory of inference, but it does not deal with *ultimate* arguments (*concrete* premises and conclusions), it merely *provides forms or conceptual vessels into which factual content may eventually be poured* in order to satisfy concrete situations.

This can be illustrated by reference to *Aristotelian syllogisms* (see Table 3-1). These are arguments or argument schemata comprising a limited group of deductive inferences, thus covering but a small portion of logic. The arguments to be *evaluated* by syllogisms are subject to several conditions:

(1) The propositions of a syllogistic argument must *all* be of *standard form* and thus begin with either a *universal quantifier* (e.g. "All . . . " or "No . . . ") or an *existential quantifier* (e.g. "Some . . . " or "There exists . . . "), and consist of a *subject term*, an *object term*, and a *copula* (e.g. "is" or "are") connecting the two. There exist only the following *four propositional standard forms* (to which in medieval times the vowels A, E, I, O were assigned as codes for quick identification):

"All *A* is *B*"	universal affirmative (*a*ffirmo)	A
"No *A* is *B*"	universal negative (n*e*go)	E

TABLE 3-1
Examples of syllogisms

Categorical standard forms		Illustrations (specific arguments)
(1)	All *A* is *B*	All computers are machines
	All *B* is *C*	All machines are artifacts
	∴ All *A* is *C*	∴ All computers are artifacts
(2)	All *A* is *B*	All automata are organic systems
	Some *A* is *C*	Some automata can think
	∴ Some *B* is *C*	∴ Some organic systems can think
(3)	All *A* is *B*	All teamsters are unionized
	No *B* is *C*	No one unionized is an entrepreneur
	∴ No *C* is *A*	∴ No entrepreneur is a teamster
(4)	All *A* is *B*	All norms are prescriptive
	Some *C* is *B*	Some sentences are prescriptive
	∴ Some *C* is *A*	∴ Some sentences are norms

"Some *A* is *B*"	particular affirmative (aff*i*rmo)	I
"Some *A* is not *B*"	particular negative (neg*o*)	O

(2) A syllogistic argument consists of *exactly three propositions*, of which two are premises (the major premise containing the *major term*, i.e. the term forming ultimately the *predicate* of the conclusion, and the minor premise containing the *minor term*, i.e. the term forming the *subject* of the conclusion) and the third is the conclusion.

(3) A syllogistic argument must have precisely *three terms* (e.g. *A*, *B* and *C* in Table 3-1) each of which is employed twice, and the two premises must have one of these terms in common, the so called *middle term* (e.g. *B* in the first argument of Table 3-1).

Table 3-1 shows four among many possible categorical standard forms together with some interpretations. But neither all of the 256 possible syllogistic forms nor all of the four presented in Table 3-1 are valid forms.

Which of these standard forms are *valid* syllogisms? Which of the actual premises and conclusions of the illustrations are true and which are false? Which of the actual arguments of the illustrations are sound (*soundness* of an argument requires *validity* of the inference *as well as truth* of all premises)? The correct answers to these questions may be obvious in most but not in all cases. The *standard forms* (1) to (3) (Table 3-1) are valid, but (4) is *invalid*. The premises of the *illustrations* are all true with the exception of the first (minor) premise of item 2 (the fact is that automata are *not* organic systems), the conclusions are all true propositions, but merely *incidentally true* in illustrations (2) and (4). The latter therefore are *not sound* (the argument of illustration (2) is unsound for a material reason – falsity of minor premise – and the argument of (4) is unsound for a formal reason – invalid standard form). As "truth" and "soundness" actually belong to semantics rather than logic we shall restrict ourselves to the following question: Why is standard form (4) invalid? On the basis of which evaluation procedures can we make this assertion? Which procedure did Aristotle employ to evaluate his syllogisms? Obviously the fact that all four standard forms (of Table 3-1) fulfill the conditions required for a syllogism (see above) merely guarantees the form but not its validity.

Since Aristotle dealt only with the relatively limited number of syllogistic arguments[4], it was possible for him to present a list of those syllogisms that proved to be *valid* (see Table 3-2). To facilitate the grouping he distinguished *three* "figures" (although there actually exist *four*) based on the *crucial position of the middle term*. To each figure a combination (mood) of propositional forms yielding a valid argument was assigned. In medieval times these *moods* were given Latin names, consisting of a combination of three or the four vowels A, E, I, O, thus indicating the corresponding propositional forms (see above) in the correct order (e.g. in Table 3-1 the standard form (1) could be represented by Barbara or AAA, because in both premises, as well as in the conclusion, the propositional form coded by the letter a or A occurs).

Standard form (4) of Table 3-1 obviously belongs to the "second figure" (Table 3-2) because its *middle term* is the predicate of both premises (hence appears *at the end of both premises*), but its *letter sequence* AII (characterizing the three propositions of this syllogism) is *not* to be found *among* the mnemonic names of the *second figure*. Hence it is not *a valid*

[4] Aristotle was well aware of at least some non-syllogistic arguments. Indeed the three *laws of conversion* formed, in a way, the starting point of his logic although they are inferences consisting of *only one premise* and the conclusion:

$$\frac{\text{All } A \text{ are } B}{\therefore\ \text{Some } B \text{ are } A};\qquad \frac{\text{Some } A \text{ are } B}{\therefore\ \text{Some } B \text{ are } A};\qquad \frac{\text{No } A \text{ are } B}{\therefore\ \text{No } B \text{ are } A}.$$

TABLE 3-2

List of MNEMONIC names and codes of valid syllogisms

(The letters *P* and *S* of the *figures* represent the major or minor terms of each propositional form and *M represents the crucial middle term*. The quantifiers are here omitted as being irrelevant for the purpose of this representation. In the names, only the vowels and their sequences are relevant).

First figure:	*M–P*	Barbara (AAA), Clearent (EAE),
	S–M	Darii (AII), Ferio (EIO),
	S–P	
Second figure:	*P–M*	Baroco (AOO), Camestre (AEE),
	S–M	Cesare (EAE), Festino (EIO),
	S–P	
Third figure:	*M–P*	Bocardo (OAO), Darapti (AAI),
	M–S	Datisi (AII), Disamis (IAI),
	S–P	Felapton (EAO), Perison (EIO).
Fourth figure:[4a]	*P–M*	Bramantip (AAI)*, Camenes (AEE)*
	M–S	Dimaris (IAI)*, Fesapo (EAO)*,
	S–P	Fresio (EIO)*.

syllogism.[5] But how did Aristotle find the validity of the syllogisms listed in our Table 3.2?

He accepts the moods of the first figure (all of which contain only *universal* propositions and are thus fairly obvious) as axioms, and deduces from

[4a] The moods of the fourth figure were considered by Aristotle only *indirectly*. Furthermore he did not make reference to the "sub-altern" syllogism: Barbari, Celaront, Cesaro, Camestrop and Camenop.

[5] Nowadays one rarely evaluates syllogistic arguments by checking the list of mnemonic names, but rather by means of the well known Venn Diagrams. Standard form (4) of Table 3-1 is represented in diagram (a) which clearly shows that *no* element *C* is *necessarily* contained in the set of all *A*'s. Hence the conclusion "Some *C* is *A*" is false. Diagram (b) shows a *special case* where this conclusion *may* hold (this represents incidentally the *illustration* of syllogism (4) in Table 3-1).

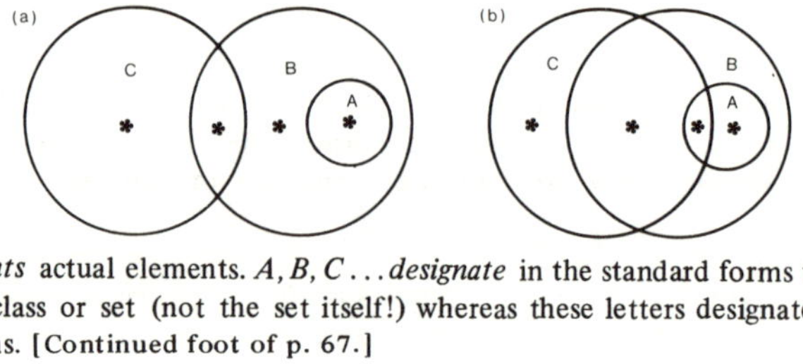

* . . . *represents* actual elements. *A, B, C . . . designate* in the standard forms the *elements* of a certain class or set (not the set itself!) whereas these letters designate *sets* in the Venn Diagrams. [Continued foot of p. 67.]

them the moods of other figures (at a later stage he even seemed to have reduced the moods known to him to those two designated in Table 3-2 with Barbara and Celarent). Thus Aristotle's logical genius is manifested in many ways: First of all, in the fundamental insight that the validity of an inference can be determined by pairing the form of the premises to the form of the conclusion; secondly, in the use of abstract forms and symbols; and thirdly, in the use of a kind of miniature axiomatic system by reducing ultimately all the *valid* syllogisms to two basic ones.

Until the middle of the nineteenth century the structure of logic outlined above dominated philosophy and science. Only then it was realized that *in addition to the syllogisms and conversions there exist many other inference forms* that have to be evaluated. These turned out to be too numerous to be presented in form of a list; they required an elaboration of the axiomatic method by which again the *validity of an argument* could be shown *by proving its form as a theorem* of the pertinent system (see Section 4.1).

Before proceeding further, an issue has to be raised which in recent years has become particularly acute. Apart from the difference between Aristotelian and modern logic, there are quite different ways by which premises can be related to their conclusions. *Deductive inference* is the most reliable way (a valid deduction holds by *necessity*) but by no means the only one; *inductive inference*, although never completely reliable, is at the very core of the empirical science, and *practical or instrumental inference* (relating means to ends), at least as reliable as induction, is the key to applied science.

The major shortcomings of traditional logic were listed by Bertrand Russell (1945, pp. 195–202), and can be summarized as follows:

Another method occasionally encountered for evaluating syllogisms, is to check whether all of the following five *rules of inference* (worked out after Aristotle) hold for a specific standard form. If so the argument is valid:

(1) The middle term must be "distributed" at least once, (a term is distributed when it refers to *all* of the members of the class (e.g. in "All *A* is *B*" *A* is distributed but not *B*, in "Some *C* is *B*" neither *C* nor *B* is distributed, because none of the two premises refers either to *all* of *B* or *all* of *C*)).

(2) If a term is not distributed in the premise, it must not be distributed in the conclusion (i.e. from two premises with existential quantifiers no conclusion with a universal quantifier can follow).

(3) No conclusion can follow from two negative premises.

(4) If one of the premises is negative the conclusion must be negative.

(5) A negative conclusion cannot follow from two affirmative premises.

The application of these rules to standard form (4) of Table 3-1 indicates that rule number (1) is violated, and this standard form is invalid.

(1) *Formal defects*: Aristotle failed to make clear the essence of the distinction between a ***universal proposition*** and an ***existential proposition.*** This essence lies in the fact that a universal proposition like "All computers are machines", never asserts the existence of anything, neither of computers, machines nor of any other entity, but merely states that something holds for all things of a certain kind, provided that these things exist. An ***existential proposition***, however, like "*Some* automata can think", or more precisely, "*There exists* at least one automaton that can think", ***does assert existence***. The failure to realize this difference proved to be a perennial source of epistemic errors, because one was prone to infer from a universal proposition the existence of something (e.g. to infer the existence of a ghost from statements like "All ghosts are ephemeral spirits").

(2) *Overrating of the syllogism*: Other kinds of deductive arguments (e.g. those used in mathematics which hardly ever state its deductions in form of syllogisms) are at least as powerful and important and should not be neglected. Russell points out that the predilection for syllogistic over other kinds of deductive arguments, misled philosophers as to the nature of mathematics. Kant who was clearly aware that mathematics is non-syllogistic, therefore believed that it used extra-logical principles.

(3) *Overrating of deduction*: Russell points out that by saying "all men are mortal", our knowledge is actually limited to something like "all men born more than one hundred and fifty years ago are mortal and so are almost all men born more than one hundred years ago" which is our reason for thinking that Mr. Smith is mortal. This, obviously is not a deductive but an ***inductive*** argument with empirical content, and hence subject merely to a ***probabilistic*** truth value. Thus non-deductive inference should also be taken into consideration. (However, Aristotle concerned himself to some extent with non-deductive inferences.)

(4) *Considering subject–predicate propositions* only: Aristotle envisaged merely *one kind* of simple propositions, those which ascribe a predicate to a subject (e.g., "Some philosophers ***are wise***"). In logic and empirical science, however, statements assigning ***qualities*** are less important than those expressing ***relations*** between ordered elements (e.g. Socrates ***is wiser than*** Aristophanes; *A is the father* of *B*; $5 < 6$; *X is preferred to Y*). But Aristotelian logic did not pay heed to the logical form of "relations", it rather subscribed to "the belief or unconscious conviction that all propositions are of the

subject–predicate form – in other words, that every fact consists of some things having some quality – has rendered most philosophers incapable of giving any account of the world of science and daily life" (Russell 1914/49, pp. 54–55). Only the advent of modern logic enabled the systematic investigation of propositions expressing ***relations and their possible properties*** (symmetry, asymmetry, non-symmetry, transitivity, intransitivity, non-transitivity, reflexivity, connectedness, closure, etc.).

To these limitations, mentioned by Russell, may be added that Aristotle concentrated on ***general*** (i.e. ***universal*** and ***particular***) propositions without taking into consideration the important category of ***singular*** propositions (e.g. "sentence *p* implies sentence *q*", "sentence *p* and *q* both hold", or "Socrates is wise" where the subjects are ***names*** and not classes). Thus his is, in a way, a ***class calculus*** (like set theory) not a ***sentential calculus*** (created after him by the Megarians). Furthermore he did not seem to have been aware of the difference between propositions and sentences; hence one does not know whether he talks about things and facts, or about words (the famous problem of ***use*** versus ***mentioning***). In spite of all these limitations Aristotle's contributions to logic were so original, fundamental, profound and versatile that he still is the undisputed top figure in the history of this discipline. His was not only the first system of logic but also the first axiomatization; he not only created assertorial or indicative logic but also modal logic (see Sections 4.2 and 4.3); he laid not only the foundation to deductive but also to inductive inference, even to "practical" inference where ***means are related to ends***.

3.24 *The Hierarchy of Semantics and Logic*

Before discussing the importance and richness of modern logic, it is advantageous to gain an overall view of the pertinent hierarchy (see Figure 3-1). This will clarify the bewildering picture of sub-areas and terms (often with a ***broad*** as well as a ***narrow*** meaning, in the following indicated by the subscripts $_B$ and $_N$ respectively) which the philosophical layman encounters in the pertinent literature. It also enables us to offer definitions of some major areas or sub-areas.

Logic is embedded in the ***theory of (linguistic) signs*** (also called semiotics or semantics$_B$ in the broad sense) of which three major sub-areas are customarily distinguished:

(1) ***Semantics***$_N$ (in the narrow sense) which deals with interpretations, that means with relations between (linguistic) signs and the things or facts to which these signs refer;

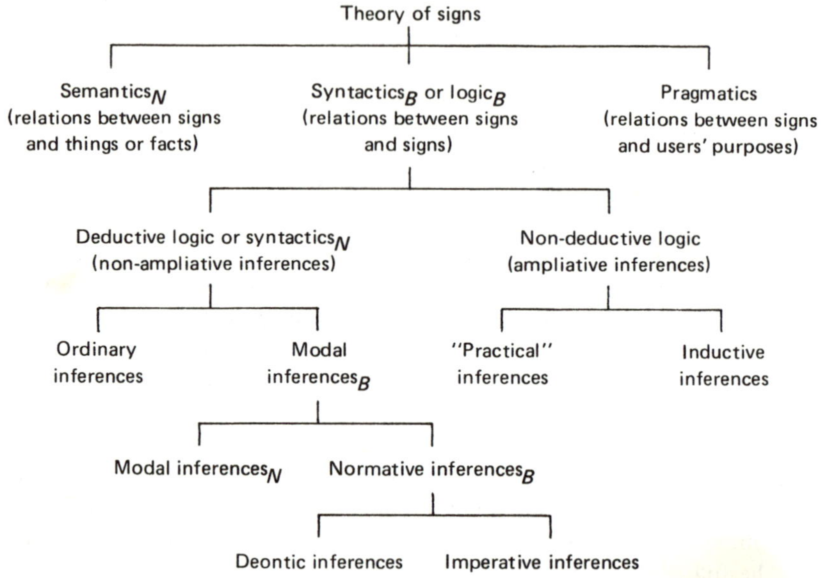

Fig. 3-1. Theory of (linguistic) signs (semiotics or semantics$_B$). The subscripts B and N stand for "in the *broad* sense" and "in the *narrow* sense" respectively. In the very *broadest* sense *logic* may even mean the theory of signs.

(2) *Syntactics$_B$ or logic$_B$* which deals with *inference relations* (e.g. deductive, inductive or other consequences) between signs and other signs (e.g. premises and conclusions). We therefore define *logic$_B$ in the broad sense as a discipline concerned with all kinds of inferences* (ampliative as well as non-ampliative[6]), analyzing the relations among linguistic signs, especially the *evidential strength* between a set of premises (evidence) and its conclusion (hypothesis);

(3) *Pragmatics* which deals with relations between linguistic signs and their *users*, especially with the *information purposes* the signs are to fulfill. This third area is the least explored, and it is expected that close ties to information economics and management science will be disclosed.

[6] *A deductive inference is non-ampliative* because its conclusion does not amplify (i.e. does not go beyond) the content of the premises, whereas inductive and other inferences are ampliative as the content of their conclusions is an amplification of the content of their premises. E.g. if one *induces* from the observation of *a thousand black* ravens (evidence or premise) the hypothesis (conclusion) that *all* ravens are *black*, the inference obviously amplifies from a small number (one thousand) of ravens to a large number (all ever in existence). Whereas in the deductive argument the conclusion is already contained in the premises.

Deductive logic (syntactics$_N$ or logic$_N$ in the narrow sense) we define as *the theory of valid (non-ampliative) inference*, stating the conditions under which a conclusion ought to be regarded as following by *a priori* necessity from its premises and providing (as far as possible) decision rules for validating such inferences. Thus it is concerned with formal questions of *validity*, but not with material questions of truth, soundness, usefulness, etc. Deductive logic deals not only with propositions (descriptive statements in the indicative mood, having a truth value) but comprises both, *ordinary inferences* (based on two truth values and operating with such quantifiers as "all", "some", "no" or "some not") as well as *modal inferences* (based on more than two truth values and, instead of quantifiers, using modal operators). The latter consist of *modal inferences$_N$* (using such ordinary modal operators as "necessary", "possible" and "impossible") and of *normative* or *deontic inferences$_B$* (using such deontic modal operators as "obligatory", "permitted" and "forbidden"). The latter can further be subdivided into *deontic inferences$_N$* (which deal only with propositions some of which *describe norms* but do not prescribe them) and *imperative inferences* (which deal with statements prescribing norms[7]).

Ampliative inferences belong to a twilight area which might be addressed as *non-deductive* logic. Many scholars reject the notion that inductive and "practical" inferences are subject matters of logic proper. Those experts (e.g. Popper and his disciples) recognize only logic in the narrow sense, insisting that logic by its very nature is limited to deductive inferences. However, during recent decades great strides have been made toward developing an *inductive logic* (see Chapter 5). Though many of its results are controversial and none of them have a fundamental status equivalent to the principles of (deductive) logic, the notion of inductive logic seems to be too deeply entrenched to ignore it or to reject it as a part of logic in the broad sense of the word.

Much less explored is the second branch of non-deductive logic. It deals with what is usually called *practical inference* (see H. von Wright, 1963). Although this concept has been traced to Aristotle, from a terminological point of view it is not a very fortunate one. First of all, other inferences are no less useful to actual practice, and second, it erroneously suggests a kind

[7] In this book we shall use the term *statements* as comprising, both, propositions (descriptive statements with truth values) as well as prescriptive statements (without truth values). The linguistic manifestation of the former are descriptive sentences, of the latter prescriptive sentences.

of "applied" logic. However what is meant by "practical" inference is *an ampliative inference in which some recommended action is inferred from a premise about a desired end together with another premise asserting the means to achieve this end.* This resembles closely those arguments listed under the headings of deontic and imperative inferences. Although the latter also result in conclusions about actions, they are non-ampliative and cannot be used in situations where the premises leave the slightest doubt about the conclusion. Since both, the *ampliative* and *non-ampliative action inferences* are of great significance for applied science we shall examine them together in Section 5.4.

3.25 *Naming and Meaning*

Modern logic and semantics cannot be understood without prior knowledge of the distinction between *extension* (*extensio, naming* or *denotation* through *classification*) and *intension* (*intensio, meaning* or *connotation* by assigning *qualities*). Every class designation like "computer", "economist", "uranium", etc. conveys *two aspects*. On the one hand it denotes an entire class of all objects of a certain kind, on the other hand it conveys meaning about each individual class element by implying some qualities, properties or attributes. The extension of white is the *class of all white things*, while its intension is the *quality of being white*. The word "computer" not only comprises all computers within a common class or set, it also implies the capability of performing certain mathematical, logical and cybernetic activities. What holds for *predicates* also seems to hold for *proper names* (the distinction between the two is important to logic). E.g. Frederic I=Barbarossa, both names designate the same person but they do not have the same meaning.

But denoting and connoting are not equal partners. The first, the assigning of a class name, is the weaker of the two notions; it *inevitably* follows from the meaning but not *vice versa* because the same class can often be named or characterized in different ways. As Frege pointed out, although the expressions "morning star" and "evening star" designate the same phenomenon (in this case a set consisting of a single element known to us as the second planet of our solar system, called "Venus"), the meaning of these two expressions is different. Not only do they *refer* to different properties ("appearing after sunset" versus "appearing before sunrise"), but the identity of these "two" phenomena could not be established by any linguistic convention but had to be discovered empirically.

The word "evening star" implies the more neutral class concept "planet

Venus", but the later not necessarily implies "evening star" because this month it might well appear as the morning star. Thus *meaning or intension is the more fundamental notion*; without it no objects could ever be grouped into a common class. But it also is an extremely complex notion and much more difficult to handle than extension (the assigning of classes). This is the very reason why the *logic of extension* (e.g. set theory) has found such an appeal among philosophers, mathematicians and above all natural and social scientists. Yet the logic of classes alone is not capable of exposing all analytical aspects, and often a translation into the logic of intension (e.g. first order predicate calculus) is required (see Section 4.2).

In recent decades philosophers have devoted much mental effort to the clarification of meaning. What then is the meaning of meaning? To the positivists it appeared that a proposition is meaningful only if there exists, at least in principle, some way of *verifying the truth* which that proposition asserts. This *referential theory* associates the meaning of a word, phrase or sentence with some kind of extra-linguistic referent like a thing or a fact. In opposition to this is John Locke's (1632–1704) *ideational theory* relating meaning to an idea of sensory image in a person's mind. In the behavioral circles the *stimulus-response* theory is in vogue; it ties meaning to the response, sometimes also to the stimulus of verbal behavior. As W. P. Alston remarks:

> Each (of these theories) is based on a real insight into the nature of language and meaning. (1) Language is used to talk about the extralinguistic world (referential), (2) it somehow expresses our thoughts and ideas (ideational), and (3) words have meaning by virtue of the ways in which they figure in human activity (stimulus–response). But all of these insights get perverted through oversimplification. Thus, (1) becomes the idea that each meaningful unit is connected with something discriminable in the extralinguistic world in the same way as any other. On the basis of (2) it is supposed that each meaningful unit has a fixed association with a particular "idea" and (3) analogously leads to a search for regular stimulus–response association in which words figure. It is important to see that things do not work out in so piecemeal a fashion. (Alston, 1967, p. 237).

The *modern analysis of meaning* is rooted in Wittgenstein's later philosophy which takes the *diversity* and *abstract nature* of language fully into account. It *seeks the meaning of an expression in its use*, and analyzes it by *explicating the usage* as well as possible. Hence meaning is not bound to a particular spatio-temporal entity but to the linguistic behavior of a specific individual and the conventions to which he or she adheres. Some theorists of this persuasion believe that a satisfactory analysis of the notion of *synonymity* would go a long way to settle the problem of meaning. By *presenting a synonymous expression* to a term or sentence we offer at least some aspect of its usage and thus its meaning. But since two synonymous expressions can hardly be substitute in every situation, a theory dealing with *degrees of synonymity* would be required.

3.3 Historical Development of Modern Logic

The view that logic was entirely stagnant between Aristotle's time and the nineteenth century is a gross oversimplification. But, apart from the fact that important logical advances of the classical age fell into oblivion, it is correct that even the high tide of medieval logic (12th to 14th century) consisted more in thoughts *about* logic than in novel contributions to logic. Even during the modern times up to the past century, one finds only very few eminent scholars whose contribution to logic is highly original: For example, Gottfried Wilhelm von Leibniz (1646–1716) who envisaged a precise symbolic language reflecting the structure of thinking, and who made concrete suggestions towards the construction of a *calculus ratiocinator* capable of representing complex thoughts through a combination of simple elements. But his writings on this subject remained unpublished for too long a time, and influenced the development of logic to a very limited extent. The same holds for others, like Bernard Bolzano (1781–1848) whose contributions to logic only recently found proper attention.

3.31 *The Advent of Boolean Algebra*

The turning of the tide did not come before the nineteenth century. Sir William R. Hamilton (1788–1856), August de Morgan (1806–71) and above all George Boole (1815–64) formed the *avant-garde*. Both de Morgan and Boole noticed structural similarities between logic and numerical algebra. But it was Boole (1847), who by an ingenious stroke invented the first workable algebra obeying the principles of logic. Boole's success is partly due to the following circumstances:

(1) He employs a *class calculus* (in contrast to the peculiar mixture of extension and intension in Aristotelian logic);

(2) he restricts the logical sum to the adjunction of classes having *no members in common* (this is initially easier, although in the modern usage of set theory, where the class *intersection* permits members common to two or more sets, is more convenient in the long-run).

(3) The statements $x \cdot x = x$ (law of tautology; in set theoretical terms $X \cap X = X$) became *the pivot of Boolean algebra*, (e.g. a set of objects in conjunction or intersection with itself always yield the same set of objects), but as algebraic formulas, they only hold for a binary number system (e.g. $1 \cdot 1 = 1, 0 \cdot 0 = 0$)[8].

(4) In adopting such a binary system and *assigning the notion "everything" (the universe class) to the number 1 and "nothing" (the null class) to the number 0*, Boole made the crucial step toward an operable algebra of logic.

Table 3-3 offers a somewhat modernized formulation of Boole's algebra – the Boole–Schroeder algebra – together with verbal approximations of the postulates (axioms).

The *universal quantifier* (x) . . . "for all x it is true that . . . " and the *existential quantifier* $\exists\, x$ . . . "there exists an x such that . . . " employed in Table 3-3, were not employed by Boole, but allow a more precise presentation. The primitive notions are here (i) the class of terms x, y, and z (which, in the abstract version of Boolean algebra, can be interpreted as *sets* as well as other entities like *areas* in a two-dimensional space, switches in electrical circuits, etc.), (ii) the *disjunction* $+$, (iii) the conjunction $\cdot$ and (iv) the *identity* $=$. The crucial formula $x \cdot x = x$ (law of tautology) is not presented in Table 3-3 as a postulate (premise) but can be deduced as a theorem (conclusion); and so can other important principles of logic as the laws of *absorption, associativity, contraposition, double negation*, etc.

3.32 *Mathematicians' Contributions to Logic*

The far-reaching significance of converting logic into an algebra became obvious to many scientists only since the advent of the computer which uses this kind of algebra to solve complex problems of deductive inference. This was facilitated by the fact that the logic of electrical circuits is nothing but an interpretation of the Boole–Schroeder algebra. Since the middle of

[8] Note that $1 + 1$ is excluded, since Boole's original class addition does not permit sets that have elements in common (see item (2)). This has later been modified in the Boole–Schroeder algebra.

TABLE 3-3

Postulates of the Boole–Schroeder algebra

Verbal approximation	Formal presentation
1. For every term there exists *a complement.*	$(x)\,(\exists -x): x + (-x) = 1$, and $x \cdot -x = 0$
2. For any two terms there exists *a sum* (in the Boolean–Schroeder algebra $x + y = z$ is equivalent to the set-theoretical expression $X \cup Y = Z$).	$(x, y)\,(\exists z): x + y = z$
3. For any two terms there exists *a product* $x \cdot y = z$ (is equivalent to the set-theoretical expression $X \cap Y = Z$).	$(x, y)\,(\exists z): x \cdot y = z$
4. For any term there exists a *universe* class (i.e. there exists at least one element 1 such that $X \cap 1 = X$).	$(\exists 1)\,(x): x \cdot 1 = x$
5. For any term there exists a *null* class.	$(\exists 0)\,(x): x + 0 = x$
6. Any two classes are *commutative* with regard to disjunction and conjunction.	$(x, y): x + y = y + x$ and $(x, y): x \cdot y = y \cdot x$.
7. Any three classes are *distributive* with regard to disjunction and conjunction.	$(x, y, z): x + (y \cdot z) = (x + y) \cdot (x + z)$ and (x, y, z): $x \cdot (y + z) = (x \cdot y) + (x \cdot z)$.

the past century the rapprochement between logic and mathematics was promoted from both sides. Not only did logicians (Boole, Jevons, Frege, Lewis, Nicod, Schroeder, Peirce, Russell, Whitehead, etc.) devise algebraic calculi for logic; mathematicians too began to scrutinize the foundations of their discipline, and in doing so put it on the basis of logic.

Paradoxes have always played a vital role in logic and philosophy. They are not mere shockers but help to delineate the boundaries of our knowledge in particular and, occasionally, of human comprehension in general. One of the most puzzling and persistent among them was the paradox posed by Zeno of Elea (born *ca.* 127–128 B.C.):

> In this capricious world, nothing is more capricious than posthumous fame. One of the most notable examples of posterity's lack of judgment is the Eleatic Zeno. This man, who may be regarded as the founder of the

> philosophy of infinity, appears in Plato's Parmenides in the privileged position of instructor to Socrates. He invented four arguments, all immeasurably subtle and profound, to prove that motion is impossible, that Achilles can never overtake the tortoise, and that an arrow in flight is really at rest. After being refuted by Aristotle, and by every subsequent philosopher from that day to our own, these arguments were reinstated, and made the basis of a mathematical renaissance, by a German professor, who probably never dreamed of any connection between himself and Zeno. Weierstrass, by strictly banishing from mathematics the use of infinitesimals, has at last shown that we live in an unchanging world, and that the arrow in its flight is truly at rest. Zeno's only error lay in inferring (if he did infer) that, because there is no such thing as a state of change, therefore the world is in the same state at any one time as at any other. This is a consequence which by no means follows; and in this respect, the German mathematician is more constructive than the ingenious Greek. Weierstrass has been able, by embodying his views in mathematics, where familiarity with truth eliminates the vulgar prejudices of common sense, to invest Zeno's paradoxes with the respectable air of platitudes; and if the result is less delightful to the lover of reason than Zeno's bold defiance, it is at any rate more calculated to appease the mass of academic mankind. (Russell, *Mysticism and Logic*, 1929, pp. 66–67.)

This paradox (see also Subsection 3.35) actually involves three problems: the *infinitesimal, infinity* and *continuity*. The first problem was solved, though negatively, by K. Weierstrass (1815–97) while the solution of the other two begun by R. Dedekind (1831–1916) and completed by Georg Cantor (1845–1918).

After considerable groundwork by Weierstrass and Dedekind, Cantor the originator of *set theory*, generalized these paradoxes and "took pairs of contradictory propositions, in which both sides of the contradiction would be usually regarded as demonstrable, and he strictly examined the supposed proofs. He found that all proofs adverse to infinity involved a certain principle, at first sight obviously true, but destructive, in its consequences, of almost all mathematics. The proofs favourable to infinity, on the other hand, involved no principle that had evil consequences. It thus appeared that common sense had allowed itself to be taken in by a specious maxim, and that, when once this maxim was rejected, all went well. (Russell, 1929, p. 81.)

But what is this maxim? To formulate it popularly we might say it consists of the proposition "The whole is larger than its parts". This, although true for finite sets, may not hold for infinite sets. The comparison between the set of *all* integers and the set of all *odd* integers shows this quite clearly.

$$\begin{array}{ccccc}\{1, & 2, & 3, & \ldots, & \infty\} \\ \updownarrow & \updownarrow & \updownarrow & & \updownarrow \\ \{1, & 3, & 5, & \ldots, & \infty\}.\end{array}$$

Since there exists a one-to-one correspondence between the elements of each set, they have the *same magnitude*, although obviously the set of the odd integers is only part of the whole, namely the set of all integers. Dedekind used this insight to formulate his renowned definition of infinity. He thus stated that

> A set S is *infinite* if it has a proper subset S_1, such that between the elements of S and of S_1 there exists a (1-1) correspondence[9].

This might not solve the problem of *empirical infinity* (if such a concept is meaningful at all), but it does solve that of *mathematical Dedekind infinity*, and Russell might be justified in asserting that "if any philosopher had been asked for a definition of infinity, he might have produced some unintelligible rigmarole, but he would certainly not have been able to give a definition that had any meaning at all" (Russell, 1929, p. 80). Dedekind's definition and Cantor's further elaborations became one of the most fundamental and far-reaching achievements of modern mathematics, disclosing many novel ideas and connections, including the existence of *different kinds or magnitudes of infinity* (e.g. the set of all integers has a smaller magnitude of infinity, or equivalently, has a smaller transfinite number, than the set of all real numbers). Thus the mind-shaking new concept of infinity offered the first flawless solution to Zeno's paradox, and Cantor's ingenious, almost mystical notion of *transfinite cardinal numbers* was the ultimate result of a quest that lasted for a quarter of a millenium or so. If the best human minds during a good deal of the recorded history of mankind perennially returned to Zeno's paradox, and ultimately found a solution, can anyone still doubt the profundity of such questions and answers?

Although all this proved ultimately to be of utmost relevance to logic, of more immediate influence may have been Giuseppe Peano's (1858–1932) *logical exposition and axiomatization of the system of natural numbers as*

[9] Cf. Wilder, *Introduction to the Foundation of Mathematics*, 1952, p. 65. Research on the problems of "infinity", the "infinitesimal", "continuity" and related topics is continuing, and Russell's presentation might have to be revised in the light of new results.

well as of geometry. The basis consists of three primitive or undefined terms ("number", "zero", "is a successor of") and the following handful of postulates:[10]

P1. 0 is a number.

P2. The successor of any number is a number.

P3. No two numbers have the same successor.

P4. 0 is not the successor of any number.

P5. If P is a property such that
(a) 0 has the property of P, and
(b) whenever a number n has the property P, then the successor of n also has the property P, then every number has the property P (*principle of mathematical induction*).

On this basis Peano was in a position to erect all of arithmetic and algebra (for geometry a separate axiomatic basis was conceived). But for him logic was merely the hand-maid of mathematics, whereas logicians like Frege and Russell regarded logic as the very foundation of mathematics. Indeed their supreme goal was to reduce all parts of mathematics to the primitive notions and postulates of logic. We shall see later in this section to what extent they succeeded in this ambitious undertaking and in which regard it proved to be a failure.

3.33 *The Logistic Thesis of Mathematics*

In the realm of logic Frege might well be regarded as ranking second after Aristotle. Or as B. Mates says:

> If there is one point upon which all recent historians of logic agree, it is the eminent place of Gottlob Frege (1848–1925) among those who have contributed to the development of the subject. Alonzo Church says flatly that Frege "is unquestionably the greatest logician of modern times"; I. M. Bochenski calls Frege "undoubtedly the most distinguished thinker in the field of mathematical logic" and says that Frege's *Begriffschrift* is comparable in importance with only one other book in the entire history of logic, namely, Aristotle's *Prior Analytics*; and William and Martha Kneale find that "the deductive system or calculus which he

[10] As reformulated (in simple language) by Hempel (1956, p. 1630).

elaborated is the greatest single achievement in the history of the subject". (Mates, *Elementary Logic*, 1965, p. 217.)

Frege was the first to propound the *logistic thesis* that all mathematical concepts are definable in terms of logic, and that all mathematical propositions are deducible from those of logic. His is also the first complete, consistent and fully axiomatic presentation of *sentence logic* (sentential calculus – see Section 4.1). Furthermore he incorporated the existential and universal quantifiers into his formal system. Under the introduction of further axioms and rules this led to *first and higher order predicate logic* (predicate calculus or logic of relations – see Section 4.2). The "rigor" of his proofs, in which "intuitive obviousness" was substituted by a step by step demonstration of the conclusions, set a shining example for future generations of logicians and mathematicians alike. Thus modern logic was born. It is "an artificial, formalized language, for which the concept of (well-formed) formula is explained by reference solely to the shapes of the expressions involved; the primitive symbols must be explicitly listed, and all others defined in terms of them; all formulas to be asserted without proof are to be listed as axioms; other asserted formulas are to be derived from these by application of formal inference rules, all of which are to be stated in advance." (Mates, 1965, p. 218).

The young Bertrand Russell conceived the logistic thesis quite independently, but in 1902 chanced upon the first volume of Frege's *Grundgesetze der Arithmetik* (1893). He discovered with surprise the similarity of thought, and sent Frege a letter inquiring whether his system dealing with classes is capable of solving the following paradox:

> Classes are groups of similar objects. Some classes are themselves members of the class they describe. For instance "the class of all phrases" is itself a phrase. On the other hand there are classes which are not themselves members of the class they describe. Thus, "the class of all cats" is not itself a cat. So one might speak of "the class of all classes that are members of themselves" and "the class of all classes that are *not* members of themselves". Is then the class of all classes that are not members of themselves a member of itself or not? If it *is* a member of itself then it is one of those classes that are *not* members of themselves. On the other hand, if it is *not* a member of itself then it must be a member of the other classes that are members of themselves.[11]

[11] This is not the original wording of Russell but is expressed in most simple and purely verbal terms, and is taken from Isaac Assimov. [Continued on p. 81.]

Frege was not in a position to resolve this contradiction satisfactorily, and admitted it faint-heartedly in the second volume (1903) of his *Grundgesetze*. Thus his aspiration to create a common basis of logic and mathematics free of contradictions, seemed to be shattered. Besides, Russell's own work of even wider scope stagnated for years due to his inability to solve the paradox he himself conceived so brilliantly.[12] It ultimately led to Russell's theory of description (1905) and his so-called "ramified" theory of types (1908). Due to its complexity and the need for the much disputed *axiom of reducibility* (explainable only in the entire context of this theory), the ramified theory has now largely been replaced by other solutions,

---

Cf. Assimov, *Biographical Encyclopedia of Science and Technology*. 1964, p. 356. See also a more detailed presentation in Wilder, *Introduction to the Foundations of Mathematics*, 1952, pp. 55–57.

The Russell paradox is a *generalization* of a series of paradoxes appearing in many forms. Russell himself seems to have popularized this contradiction by the example of the *village barber*: Assume a barber whose imperative is to shave every male of his village who does not shave himself. If the barber shaves himself he obviously violates his own imperative, but if he does not shave himself he also violates his imperative. (Here, obviously the class of all males not shaving themselves assumes the role of the class of all classes that are not members of themselves, while the class of all males shaving themselves compares to the class of all classes that are members of themselves). As with the barber, it can be proved that the class of all classes that are not members of themselves is *both* a member of itself and is not a member of itself. This contradiction can only be resolved if the barber or the class of all classes that are members of themselves, are put on a *higher level* making comparison with entities of lower levels meaningless.

Further similar paradoxes as well as those of other types are listed in Kasner and Newman's, 'Paradox Lost and Paradox Regained', 1956, and by Runes, 1960, pp. 224–225.

[12] Russell acknowledged in Vol. I of the *Autobiography of Bertrand Russell*, 1968, pp. 195, 200–201:

> This led me to consider those classes which are not members of themselves, and to ask whether the class of such classes is or is not a member of itself. I found that either answer implies its contradictory. At first I supposed that I should be able to overcome the contradiction quite easily, and that probably there was some trivial error in the reasoning. Gradually, however, it became clear that this was not the case (p. 195).
>
> I was trying hard to solve the contradictions mentioned above. Every morning I would sit down before a blank sheet of paper. Throughout the day, with a brief interval for lunch, I would stare at the blank sheet. Often when evening came it was still empty . . . the two summers of 1903 and 1904 remain in my mind as a period of complete intellectual deadlock. It was clear to me that I could not get on without solving the contradictions . . . what made it the more annoying was that the contradictions were trivial, and that my time was spent in considering matters that seemed unworthy of serious attention (pp. 200–201).

especially by a modification known as the *simplified theory of types* developed by Chwistek (1924), Ramsey (1926) and above all the further developments by Carnap (1929) and Tarski (1934)[13] such as the *theory of language levels.* The task of these attempts is to make language more consistent, introduce the notion of "meaningless" expressions, indicate the necessity for *formation rules* and above all make the fundamental distinction between object language and meta-language, hence between different language levels. "The language spoken about in some context is called the *object language*; the language in which we speak about the first is called the *meta-language*."[14] Hence, a formula which the instructor puts on the board might be in the object language, the words in which he explains the formula, however, belong to the meta-language. If one mentions the sets that are not members of themselves, one may speak in an object language; if one compares these sets with the *set of all sets* that are not members of themselves, one speaks in the meta-language and might commit the error of inappropriately equating propositions of two different language levels, the result of which is the famous Russell paradox.

3.34 *Principia Mathematica*

To most laymen the *Principia Mathematica* (1910–1913) by A. N. Whitehead and B. Russell is, at least by title, much better known than the more original and more rigorous work of Frege. Partly this is due to language and to the less convenient symbolism employed by Frege; partly it is due to the colorful personality of Bertrand Russell who gained such eminent status not only as a logician but also as a general, well-rounded philosopher. But the *Principia* (in spite of the fact that some parts on geometry, originally assigned to A. Whitehead, were never finished) is more comprehensive and, in a way, a natural extension of Frege's work. For some time it seemed indeed that the problem of proving that mathematics can be reduced to logic had been solved – that is to say until Kurt Gödel (1933) presented the proof to his *incompletability theorem*, the most famous or infamous theorem in the entire history of logic and mathematics (see next Subsection).

For the sake of comparison with Boolean algebra (an extensional logic)

[13] Although the simplified theory of types and the theory of language levels are not creations of Whitehead and Russell they rest on Russell's insights, and his Introduction to Wittgenstein's *Tractatus* gives evidence that Russell came very close to the need of distinguishing between two or more levels of language.

[14] Carnap, *Introduction to Semantics*, 1942, p. 3.

TABLE 3-4

Postulates of the calculus of elementary propositions (plus the definition of material implication)

	Verbal approximation	Formal presentation
Definition of:		
Material implication	"A proposition *implies* another one" means that either the negation of the first proposition is true or the second proposition is true.	$(p \supset q) \equiv \text{def.} (\sim p \vee q)$
Postulates of:		
1. Inference	The implication of any true proposition is true.	Must be given informally.
2. Tautology	It is asserted that a proposition implies itself.	$\vdash : (p \vee p) \supset p$
3. Addition	It is asserted that a true proposition implies that either it or another proposition (or both) are true.	$\vdash : q \supset (p \vee q)$
4. Commutativity	It is asserted: If "either a proposition or another one (or both) are true", then "either the other one or the first (or both) are true".	$\vdash : (p \vee q) \supset (q \vee p)$
5. Associativity	It is asserted: If "either proposition *p*, or the proposition '*q* or *r*' is true", then "either proposition *q* is true, or proposition '*p* or *r*' is true".	$\vdash : [p \vee (q \vee r)] \supset [q \vee (p \vee r)]$
6. Summation	It is asserted: If "proposition '*q* implies *r*' is true" then "proposition '*p* or *q*' implies proposition '*p* or *r*' ".	$\vdash : (q \supset r) \supset [(p \vee q) \supset (p \vee r)]$
7. and 8. Assumptions of Elementarity	If a proposition is an elementary proposition then its negation is an elementary proposition.	Must be given informally.
	If two propositions *p* and *q* are elementary then "either *p* or *q* (or both)" is an elementary proposition.	Must be given informally.

we present in Table 3-4 the postulates of the propositional calculus (logic of propositions or sentences – an intensional logic) of the *Principia.* This work operates with a set of undefined terms and premises different from Boolean algebra, but is translatable into it and other systems of logic. Although it begins with a propositional calculus, it soon introduces a calculus of classes and relations and ultimately expands into logic of arithmetic etc. The primitive or undefined notions[15] of the calculus of *elementary propositions* are: "*elementary proposition*" such as p, q, r, . . . , "assertion" $\vdash$, "negation" $\sim$, and "propositional disjunction" $\vee$. Before the primitive propositions can be listed, the important definition of *material implication* $\supset$ has to be given, as it is not included in the set of undefined terms. Yet every deductive inference obviously hinges on the notion of implication (of which *material* implication is the most frequently used version).

In this calculus of elementary propositions further principles like those of the *disjunctive syllogism, simplification, transposition, reductio ad absurdum, identity*, etc. follow as theorems. These fundamental propositions of logic, whether those of Boolean algebra, the propositional calculus or of any similar system may sound trivial. *Yet what counts is the fact that no deductive inference can be made without taking for granted propositions of this kind, and that all logic and mathematics rests on such so-called "trivialities".* These principles are, of course, nothing but alternative and rigorous formulations or derivations of such common sense rules as "don't contradict your statement", "if a statement is true, then it is true", "a statement cannot be both true and false", etc.; suppositions which any sane person accepts more or less subconsciously as rules for drawing his many everyday conclusions.

3.35 *Paradoxes and the Axiom of Choice*

Paradoxes or antinomies have been the testing ground of logic since its very inception. Indeed, if a philosopher before Aristotle deserves to be called a logician, one would have to choose Zeno of Elea who so brillantly posed one of the most notorious paradoxes (see Subsection 3.32). Zeno's example

[15] The assertion sign $\vdash$ is only necessary where a clear distinction between the *description* and the *assertion* of a proposition is called for. Thus $\vdash$ stands for "It is asserted that the following is true: . . . " The negation $\sim$ denies the pertinent proposition, while the disjunction $p \vee q$ stands for "*either* proposition p *or* proposition q is true *or both* are true." The *material* implication $p \supset q$ stands for "*If* p is true *then* q is true" in a purely logical sense (see Section 4.1).

To facilitate the understanding we employed in Table 3-4 *Algebraic parentheses and brackets* instead of the system of the point bracketing used by Russell and Whitehead.

bears witness that it is not merely the finding of a solution but above all the conception of a paradox that reflects the profundity of a philosopher. Zeno saw better than anyone else, that such notions as the infinitesimal small, infinity, and continuity must lead to contradictions within the framework of our conventional thinking (i.e. without abandoning for infinite sets the notion that the whole is larger than its parts). He presented three versions of this paradox of which the best known passes under the slogan of *Achilles and the Tortoise*:

> Let Achilles and the tortoise start along a road at the same time, the tortoise (as is only fair) being allowed a handicap. Let Achilles go twice as fast as the tortoise, or ten times or a hundred times as fast. Then he will never reach the tortoise. For at every moment the tortoise is somewhere and Achilles is somewhere; and neither is ever twice in the same place while the race is going on. Thus the tortoise goes just to as many places as Achilles does, because each is in one place at one moment, and in another at any other moment. But if Achilles were to catch up with the tortoise, the places where the tortoise would have been would be only part of the places where Achilles would have been. Here, we must suppose, Zeno appealed to the maxim that the whole has more terms than the part. Thus if Achilles were to overtake the tortoise, he would have been in more places than the tortoise; but we saw that he must, in any period, be in exactly as many places as the tortoise. Hence we infer that he can never catch the tortoise. (Russell, 1929, pp. 84–85.)

Whether Russell's interpretation is accepted or not, no one will deny that Zeno's argument was a most serious matter, the more so as everyone knew that the conclusion was absurd. Nevertheless it took millenia before Euclid's axiom, that the whole is greater than its parts, was rejected for infinite sets by Dedekind and Cantor. Only then could Zeno's paradox be solved because a distance between *any* two marks consists of infinitely many places or points.[16]

Another famous antinomy, one of even greater influence upon modern logic, was encountered in Subsection 3.34 under the name of Russell's para-

[16] The set of infinite points on a line, as well as the set of all real numbers, etc. are characterized by the trans-finite cardinal number $\mathfrak{c}$ (Gothic c) or $\aleph_1$ (aleph$_1$), while the infinite set of all natural numbers $\{1, 2, \ldots, \infty\}$ as well as that of odd numbers, belong to a lower level of infinity $\mathfrak{a}$ or $\aleph_0$. Cantor could show that there exist an infinite number of infinities by proving the following theorem: "For any arbitrary infinite set, there exists a set having a greater cardinal number than that of the selected set."

dox. Here was at stake no less than the notion of class or set itself. As long as this concept involved a fundamental contradiction – namely *that the class of all classes that are not members of themselves, is both a member of itself and at the same time not a member of itself* – the entire set-theory and all modern logic was highly suspect if not downright useless. In the first decade of this century one became aware that Russell's paradox actually comprises *a whole family of related antinomies*, (e.g. the Liar's paradox, the Burali-Forti paradox and the Cantor paradox) the first of which is almost as old as logic itself. It is attributed to Eubulides of the Megarian school who says: "I am lying." Is he telling the truth or not? If he does, he is lying, but if he lies he tells the truth and thus is not lying. This contradiction and those of related antinomies can be removed in the same way as that of the Russell paradox; at best by distinguishing between different language levels ("I am lying" belongs to the *metalanguage*, while the actual lie or truth he says belongs to the *object language*; and the two must not be mixed or confused with each other, because any kind of system must be distinguished from its environment).

If toward the end of the past century the opposition of many mathematicians toward set-theory was overcome, the time of almost universal acceptance lasted only about a decade. Then the new resistance from the camp of the neo-intuitionists was fueled by those emerging antinomies. At this stage another renowned mathematician, Zermelo (1871–1953), made his fundamental contributions. He formulated set theory as an axiomatic system, and by introducing the much disputed *axiom of choice* (Zermelo postulate, 1908) obviated the need for a more satisfactory definition of the set concept. Indeed a link between the theory of infinity and Russell's paradox may be found in Zermelo's postulate which eventually leads to an alternative way of solving Russell's paradox, as well as to a new vision of set-theory. The choice axiom became the basis for the modern distinction between Zermelian set-theory (which includes this axiom) and non-Zermelian set-theories which try to get along without it, thereby renunciating many important theorems. This distinction has been compared to that between Euclidean and non-Euclidean geometries, comprehensible in the face of the independent status of Zermelo's postulate. But whether it should be called a postulate or axiom at all, or whether it is a principle more absolute in nature than an axiom of logic or geometry, is still a controversial question. But what is the content and function of this postulate that was compared to a match which started a forest fire?

If we are confronted with an infinite number of sets and are asked to form new sets by *choosing* from each of the original sets the *first* member, then forming another set choosing from each original set the *second* member and so on, we shall not encounter any difficulties if we are able to discern what is a first member, a second one and so on. Often, however, such identification is not given, and has to be "arbitrarily assumed" by the *axiom of choice*: "Given a set of *N* sets, having no members in common, it is assumed there exists a set that has exactly one member in common with each of the *N* sets". If *N* is finite the assumption is fulfilled and does not need to be introduced separately, if *N* is infinite it also will be fulfilled, but only if all members of these sets are "labeled". Russell illustrated the problem underlying the axiom of choice in a popular way, here paraphrased from memory: In the Western world shoes are made in such a fashion that the right and left shoe of each pair can be distinguished from each other, but the distinction between right and left cannot be made for pairs of stockings. If we imagine an infinitely rich man possessing an infinite number of pairs of shoes and of pairs of stockings, he may select, for instance, the left shoe of each pair and form an infinite set of all left shoes, but he cannot do the same with his stockings unless he employs the axiom of choice, that is to say, unless he acts as though one stocking of each pair were labeled as the left one. Wilder (1952, p. 74) points out that it is in such *cases with insufficient information about the nature of the sets involved*, that one is forced to appeal to Zermelo's postulate. But its significance reaches even further, for it has been proved that the choice axiom is equivalent to the *well-ordering theorem* (also by Zermelo),[17] as well as to the *comparability principle*, which play an important role in the controversy about the existence of infinite sets. And if the reader might wonder why it is so important to know whether infinite sets exist or not, he might ask himself whether the systems of natural numbers, of rational numbers, of real numbers, etc. – so familiar to him from everyday use – all have cardinality. If his answer is affirmative he has accepted, in a way, the axiom of choice, the well-ordering theorem as well as the comparability principle. Although this is a simplistic way of conveying it, it shows strikingly the ultimate meaning of these principles.[18]

[17] *Well-order*: Every set *S* can be *well-ordered* (in regard of $<$ and similar relations) if every of its non-empty subsets has a first element.

Comparability: Of two well-ordered sets that are not similar, one is similar to a section of the other (i.e. either two ordinals, and also transfinite cardinals, are equal or one is less than the other).

[18] There exists another fundamental problem, the *continuum problem* also arising out of Cantor's set theory. The so-called "continuum hypothesis" is even more controversial than Zermelo's postulate but closely related to it since it *implies* the choice axiom (as shown by Sierpinski). The *continuum hypothesis* assumes that there is no

Concluding this section, Frank P. Ramsey's (1900–26) distinction between *syntactical* (logical) versus *semantical paradoxes* ought to be pointed out. While the paradoxes of Russell, Burali-Forti, and others belong to the former, because they rest on nothing but logical notions, the paradoxes of Eubulides, Berry, Richard, etc. are semantical paradoxes since they "contain some reference to thought, language, or symbolism, which are not formal but semantical and empirical terms. So they may be due not to faulty logic or mathematics but to faulty ideas concerning thought and language" (Ramsey, 1925/31, pp. 20–21).

3.36 *Consistency and Gödel's Proof*

The endeavour to create a logic free of contradictions encountered many difficulties in form of paradoxes and the need for some additional assumptions beyond the ordinary laws of logic. Already Frege saw the need for a *consistency proof* of formal systems and, as we know, his attempt to construct such a proof was wrecked by the Russell paradox. Later on, Russell's theory of types (defining numbers as classes of equivalent classes) yielded a consistency proof but only relative to set-theory. Yet a *relative proof* rests on some preceding theory, and does not constitute an ultimate solution. Therefore an *absolute* consistency proof as sketched for arithmetic by Hilbert (1904) was required. Nevertheless, by 1930 many scholars believed that the major paradoxes were mastered, and that the internal consistency (freedom from contradiction) of modern logic was no longer in question.

This confidence was shattered, not by presenting a new paradox but in a much more fundamental way – by an achievement that was called "a milestone in the history of modern logic and mathematics" – see Nagel and Newman (1958, p. 1668). A twenty-five year old Austrian mathematician, Kurt Gödel, proved in his "epoch-making" paper, "Über formal unentscheidbare Sätze der Principia Mathematica und verwandter Systeme" ("On Formally Undecidable Propositions of Principia Mathematica and Related Systems" – 1931)[19] that neither in Whitehead and Russell's nor in any

infinity between infinity $\mathfrak{a}$ (the one characterizing the set of natural numbers as well as all other infinite denumberable sets) and infinity $\mathfrak{c}$ (characterizing the set of all real numbers as well as the set of infinite points on any line, etc.). In other words, there does not exist an infinity $\mathfrak{b}$: hence $\mathfrak{a}$ is $\aleph_0$, the first transfinite number and $\mathfrak{c}$ is *indeed* the second transfinite number $\aleph_1$.

[19] This paper was not only spectacular because of its results but even because of its method. Gödel employed a novel analytical technique (associating with each elementary

other comprehensive analytical system, is it possible to prove or disprove *all* derived propositions as being validly inferred. That means, any axiomatic system of even moderate complexity will possess *undecidable* propositions, namely those of which neither their affirmation nor their contradiction can be proved within the specified system. A proof for those theorems can be attained only by incorporating the next higher system, e.g. the pertinent metasystem into the analytical framework, but then *new undecidable propositions arise*. To decide those, the framework requires further expansion and so on *ad infinitum*.

3.4 Some Highlights in the Evolution of Semantics

Gödel's theorem was not the only impetus within logic and mathematics that led to the consideration of *hierarchies of systems*; the new area of *formal semantics* created by Tarski, Carnap and others is explicitly concerned with the hierarchy of language systems. But before modern semantics can be approached, it is necessary to get aquainted with the evolution of traditional semantics (in the current section) as well as with sentential and predicate logic (in Chapter 4).

3.41 *From Ancient Times to the Twentieth Century*

Thoughts on semantics go back to ancient Greece, that is to say to records on Parmenides (born *ca*. 515), the Sophists, Democritus (*ca*. 460–370 B.C.) and above all Plato (*ca*. 428–347 B.C.). During this time concern with the relation between *a thing and the name assigned to it*, resulted in two opposing semantical theories. These arise out of the following question: Are names (i.e. *common* names such as "horse" or "philosopher" or "king" – in contrast to *proper* names like "Pegasus" or "Socrates" or "Alexander") assigned by mere convention or does some necessity in nature influence the process of naming. According to Plato his teacher Socrates (*ca*. 470–399 B.C.) seems to have defended a "naturalistic" view according to which synonymous words of different languages like the Greek word "hyppo" and the Latin word "equus" (or the English word "horse") are but different

sign as well as each formula and proof, a so-called Gödel number), the fertility of which was compared to that of Descartes' analytical geometry. He also provoked a reappraisal of traditional views of epistemology. For details see Nagel and Newman (1958) as well as J. van Heijenoort (1966).

sounds for a single *ideal name* (concept, idea, mental image). If a language had merely one common name for both horses and cattle, this name would prevent any linguistic distinction necessary for recognizing the true state of nature. Opposed to this *doctrine of ideal names* is the *conventionalism* of Democritus who maintains that names are assigned on the basis of convention and nothing else.

The search for the *meaning* of *words* as well as of *sentences* – which aroused so much interest in many twentieth century philosophers – goes back to Plato's writing. There we find already the *distinction between meaningfulness and truth* (e.g. sentence may be meaningful if the combination of its names and verbs follows a preconceived pattern that makes sense even if it does not correspond to any fact). Or as Aristotle said "falsity and truth are not in things . . . , only in thought; whereas for *simple* concepts (names and verbs) . . . falsity and truth is not even in thought . . . "[20] And the Stoics were the first to express clearly the difference and relation between the three fundamental notions of (1) the *sign* (sound, written symbol, etc.), (2) the *conceptual idea* ("lekton", meaning) communicated by sign, and (3) the actual *object* or *event* behind the concept. They furthermore seemed to have held the sound view that the *explication of meaning* must not be limited to the subject and the ideas conveyed, but must be *extended to the linguistic functions* performed by a sequence of signs (e.g. to *assert*, or to *order*, or to *ask* something, or to *express an emotion*).

The highlights of medieval semantics are found in St. Augustine's (354–430) writings. Among his many contributions, one of the most outstanding is the notion of *meaning* as related to the *effect upon the person* receiving the sign. Some medieval writings on semantics reflect "a distinction between two levels of signification" which approaches the important modern distinction between object language and meta-language. In post-renaissance times the major contributions to semantics are (1) Hobbes' (1588–1679) reflections on the question whether linguistic signs are names of things rather than names of ideas or conceptions, (2) Arnauld's (1612–1694) distinction between the *intension* (called "comprehension" by him) and the *extension* of a term, and (3) Leibniz' doctrine of propositions as extra-linguistic, even extra-mental, schemata. He also pointed out that "it is clearly not necessary that that which expresses be similar to that which is expressed as long as a certain analogy of relations is preserved".[21] This suggests that *there does not*

[20] Quoted by Kretzmann (1967, p. 363) from Aristotle's *Metaphysics* (1027b23).

[21] Quoted by Kretzmann (1967, p. 382) from Leibniz' collected works (Gerhard edition 7.263–264).

need to be a one-to-one correspondence between a language pattern and a factual pattern in order to represent the latter. If the logical atomists (e.g. Russell and the "early" Wittgenstein whose aim was to create an ideal language in which atomic propositions would correspond to atomic facts – in order to represent reality more accurately) had heeded this assertion, they would have been spared a long and cumbersome roundabout way.

Philosophers of the eighteenth century pursued the interest in signification and stressed the importance of grammar and above all *universal grammar* – concentrating on principles fundamental to *all* languages. They fully recognized that an analysis of language and an understanding of its evolution and usage are important preconditions for logic and the philosophy of science. Thus it is hardly surprising that in the early nineteenth century eminent scholars like J. S. Mill (1806–1873) and C. S. Peirce (1839–1914) envisaged logic in the broadest sense, including in it the process of naming and sign-giving (cf. our caption to Figure 3-1). But Mill opposed the attempts of creating formalized languages of logic, favoring rather a reform of natural languages. While the division (of semiotics or logic in the broadest sense) into semantics, syntax and pragmatics goes back to Peirce, who also anticipated the pragmatic idea that the *meaning of an expression lies in its use*. Frege's distinction between *sense* (Sinn) and *reference* (Bedeutung) has great similarity to Arnauld's and Hamilton's *extension*, but shows subtle differences and highly original traits:

> The reference of a proper name is the object itself which we designate by its name; the idea, which we have in that case, is wholly subjective; in between lies the sense, which is indeed no longer subjective like the idea, but is yet not the object itself . . . A proper name (word, sign, sign combination, expression) *expresses* its sense, *stands for* or designates its reference. By means of a sign we express its sense and designate its reference. (Frege, 1892, in Geach and Black, 1952, pp. 60–61).

Further contributions to semantics were made by Edmund Husserl (1859–1938), the founder of phenomenology, and his student Alexius Meinong (1853–1920). The following controversy between Russell and Meinong became especially prominent: According to Meinong's theory (Gegenstandstheorie) objects that do not exist physically are not nonsensical, they are constituted in one way or the other (e.g. mentally) and can be made the subject of a meaningful or even true sentence. Opposed to this is Russell's *theory of description*, which may be concisely illustrated through the following sentence (see also Subsection 4.23): "The round square does not exist."

Does this assert the *non-existence of* an *object* or the *existence of a non-object*? Meinong would opt for the former, Russell for the latter. If there were such an object as a "round square", Russell would argue, then it would exist and the above sentence would be false. Already Frege was confronted with this *profound problem of asserting that something does not exist.* A problem apparently restricted to common names or denoting phrases but not affecting *proper names* since they *are the objects they denote*. "Since the round square does not exist, there is *no* object to be named, and if it were taken as a proper name, 'the round square' would necessarily be meaningless. But if it were meaningless, the assertion, 'The round square does not exist' would also be meaningless. Since it is not meaningless but true, it follows that 'the round square' is not a proper name . . . According to Russell's analysis this becomes 'It is false that there is one and only one object which is both round and square'. Here the descriptive phrase 'the round square' does not appear at all." (Linsky, 1967, p. 97.) Nevertheless Meinong maintained that the sentence "The round square is round" is a true proposition about a non-existent object, it does not convey *being* (Sein) but merely *being-so* (Sosein). In other words he denied that there are only existential and non-existential sentences (e.g. universal sentences), and asserted a third category which we might call quasi-existential sentences.

3.42 *Carnap's and Tarski's Major Contributions*

For the logical positivists,[22] with their rigorous scientific approach to philosophy, the meaning of a proposition was originally given by the way in which that proposition can be verified (the *criterion of meaning* and *principle of verification*). In the attempt to banish metaphysics from epistemology they were tempted to declare any proposition which is not amenable to empirical and intersubjective verification as meaningless. Later they realized that such a view, equating knowledge with experience, was untenable. After all, science needs generalizations containing *theoretical terms* (such as energy quantum, electron, probability, utility, capital, etc.) which, unlike *observational terms*, do not correspond to anything given by immediate sense experience. Therefore, Carnap who became the leading figure among the logical positivists, concluded that a scientific hypothesis can never be completely verified. He therefore relaxed the meaning criterion and shifted his emphasis from verifiability to the broader notion of *confirmability*. He furthermore

[22] Usually identified with the "Viennese Circle" (Rudolf Carnap, Otto Neurath, Moritz Schlick, Friedrich Waismann) and their followers.

regarded analytical sentences as (non-factually) meaningful since they convey information about the structure of linguistic forms for expressing empirical statements. Carnap in his first major work *Der Logische Aufbau der Welt* (*The Logical Construction of the World*, 1928) attempted to undertake for empirical science what Whitehead and Russell did for analytical science, the *reduction* of the pertinent concepts and relations to a small number of basic notions (sense experiences and similarity relations). Although this undertaking remained a sketch, it is considered an "enormous intellectual achievement". Because "ever since the days of Locke and Hume, empiricist philosophers have repeatedly assured us that it must be possible to reduce all the concepts of the empirical sciences to that which is given directly in internal and external perception. But there the matter rested; the assurance remained an unrealized program until Carnap set out to convert this program into a reality. W. V. Quine, one of the most important contemporary American logicians, has remarked that Carnap has succeeded, in his system, in defining numerous concepts that no one ever dreamed could be defined on such a slender initial basis." (Stegmüller, *Main Currents in Contemporary German, British, and American Philosophy*, 1969a, p. 290.)

Later Carnap had to abandon the phenomenalistic basis of the early work in favour of *protocol sentences* which report in a language based on physical data rather than sense data. Carnap's research is characterized by a constant shifting and revising which is in full accord with the program and the *scientific* methodology of logical positivism. Just as scientists are obliged to abandon hypotheses in the face of a refutation, so Carnap was willing to revise his constructs as soon as he discovered improvements and new avenues. But a permanent major vocation of his was the *elimination of metaphysical expressions* through a logical language analysis, pointing out that such "pseudo-statements" come into being either (1) by taking non-empirical words for empirical ones, or (2) by organizing empirical words countersyntactically into meaningless sentences. Carnap (1934) then aimed at creating *a theory of linguistic expressions* to clarify the formulation of epistemological problems. There he adopted a conventionalistic attitude and ultimately pointed at *a major source of pseudo-problems, the use of a word for designating another word instead of an object* (e.g. "Five is not a thing but a number" which Carnap would properly formulate as "Five is not a thing-word but a number-word"). But stimulated by Tarski's work, Carnap (1942, 1943, 1947) recognized that the problems of philosophy (epistemology) cannot be solved by syntax alone, but require an extension into semantics. Thereby such concepts as "range of variables", "analytic", "contradiction", "implication", "synthetic" and others, turned out to be semantical and not syntactical in nature, although some of them have syntactical counterparts (e.g. "analytical" versus "logical", "implication" versus "derivability" – for further details see Subsection 4.32). Thus he began to formalize *sentence logic as a semantic system* and even constructed a modal functional logic (see Sections 4.3 and 4.4). The last phase of this highly creative and "constructive" philosopher was occupied with the foundation of probability, inductive logic and the measurement of confirmation, all to be hinted at in our Chapter 5.

The actual creator of the semantic method or formal semantics is Alfred Tarski (born 1902). He set out and solved one of the perennial problems of philosophy, namely "to construct – with reference to a given language – a *materially adequate and formally correct definition of the term 'true sentence'.*" Semantics had the great advantage over syntactics that it enabled the representation of relations between languages and extralinguistic objects. Of special importance was the subtle and meticulous representation of such notions as formal or *uninterpreted calculus* and the semantical *interpretation* of such a calculus by means of more specific *models*. In more general terms "the fruits of Tarski's approach are, first, a precise set-theoretical description of the semantic notions, together with a meticulous discussion of the language in which these definitions are expressible, second, the discovery of general properties of these notions which sometimes are very startling, and third, the discovery of a broad field of applications."

"The semantic notions, which before Tarski were used in solving relatively special problems concerning consistency and independence, now turned out to be powerful tools in dealing with meta-mathematical investigations. For a philosopher the most important application of the semantic method is Tarski's theory of truth." (A. Mostowski, 1967, p. 79.) Tarski accepts the medieval notion that the expression "*true*" is an adjective of a sentence, but he improves upon it by not regarding it an adjective of the object language *L* (which we are using to express something) but *an adjective of the metalanguage M* in which the sentence of *L* are *not used* but *mentioned* and discussed. Let us designate the sentence "This sentence is not true" by the symbol *c*. "By the ordinary Aristotelian criterion for the truth of sentences we may say '*c* is not a true sentence' is a true sentence if and only if *c* is not a true sentence'. But '*c* is not a true sentence' is precisely the sentence *c*, so we may equate the preceding with '*c* is a true sentence', which is self-contradictory. The contradiction is eliminated if we put 'of *L*' after 'true sentence' throughout and deny the principle ≪ '*c* is not a true sentence of

L' is a true sentence of *L* if and only if *c* is not a true sentence of *L* ≫ on the ground that *c* is not a true sentence of *L* under any conditions whatever, because it is not a sentence of the language *L* at all but of its meta-language *M*." (A. N. Prior, 1967, Vol. 2, p. 230.)

3.43 *Wittgenstein's Two Philosophies*

Wittgenstein's concern with language goes far beyond semantics in the ordinary sense; yet he never ceased to focus on *the miracle that we are capable of representing the real world by means of linguistic signs*. How is it possible that things and facts can be depicted by something so different as words and sentences? This crucial question characterizes not only the earlier but also the later inquiries of one of the most revolutionary philosophers. Both, Wittgenstein's *picture theory* as well as his later, quite opposite, *theory of language games* grew out of that query. This may seem contrary to Russell's remark that Wittgenstein in his later philosophy disregarded the connection between language and reality. Such an objection may not do full justice to this perennial searcher who finally regarded *language not as being apart from but closely integrated with human life and action* – but this seems to establish an even closer connection between language and the world than his earlier theory or any other correspondence theory could ever achieve. Indeed the *theory of language games* (or "the chess theory of language" as Stegmüller calls it in contrast to the earlier "mosaic theory") is another important example that modern philosophy is penetrated by systems thinking. For us Wittgenstein's emphasis that a language game ought to be seen in the context of social activity, is *evidence of the awareness that a system should not be looked at in isolation but must be analyzed under consideration of its environment*.

Wittgenstein's early philosophy is contained in the *Tractatus Logico-Philosophicus* (1922). There he perceived *the world* as an aggregation of *facts*, not of things ("1. The world is all that is the case." "2. What is the case, the fact, is the existence of states of affairs."[23]). Composite propositions are for him truth functions of elementary propositions, something easy to comprehend if one is reminded that Wittgenstein, independent of E. L. Post, invented the *method of truth tables* (see Section 4.1). Above all he regarded *propositions as logical pictures or models of reality* which *show* their meaning just as actual pictures show it by means of correspondences between its own

[23] For Wittgenstein every fact is a state of affairs, but for a state of affairs to be a fact *existence* is necessary since there are also *potential* or *possible* states of affairs.

elements and those of reality.[24] Thus a proposition and the corresponding portion of reality are supposed to have the same logical structure. (2.172 "A picture cannot, however, depict its pictorial form: it displays it.") But "we cannot say how language represents the world ... We understand the elements of a sentence, and we see how they are combined. But we cannot say what this combination means. Yet we *grasp* its meaning. In some sense we know what it means, because the sentence *shows* its meaning. Anything that can be said can be said clearly, but not everything that is understood can be said. In a letter to Russell, Wittgenstein remarked that his 'main contention' was this distinction between what cannot be said but can only be shown. This he said was 'the cardinal problem of philosophy'." (N. Malcolm, 1967, p. 330.) The *Tractatus* exercised much influence upon logical positivism, although the former does neither defend the verification theory of meaning nor abhor metaphysics.

After years of putting philosophical work aside, and more years of philosophical re-examination, Wittgenstein wrote the *Philosophical Investigations* (1953, published posthumously) which summarizes his later philosophy. In it he abandons the belief that a proposition presupposes the whole of language. He discovered that it merely presupposes a small portion of it, which he called a *language game*. Its rules must be mastered before the meaning can be comprehended. No longer does he accept the notion that a generalized expression reveals the *essence* of a thing or fact; he asserts that terms and sentences have no common features but merely *family resemblances*. The latter are due to many features that "overlap and criss-cross" as can best be seen from a comparison of such words as "game" and "play". They have many meanings that resemble each other – as two sisters may resemble a brother without resembling each other – but there is no essential feature which *all* of them have in common. A system theorist might say that the young Wittgenstein took all of language for a *closed* system, whereas the old one realized that it is an *open* system. But the most influential change occurred with regard to the notion of meaning. According to the *Tractatus* the meaning of a name is the object of which it is a logical picture, whereas the *Philosophical Investigations* declare that *the meaning of a word or sentence is in its use*. In the face of the many meanings which an expression often has, Wittgenstein no longer believed that "we understand the sense of a propositional sign without its having been explained to us", he rather

[24] However, on one side a single proposition may represent different facts, and on the other different propositions may represent the same fact. This insight that meaning is not definite led Wittgenstein later to abandon his ingenious picture theory.

reminds us that a knowledge of the usage, that is to say the rules of the language game, is prerequisite for grasping the meaning. He even compared a sentence to a tool, and the meaning to its application. But *meaning and use of a sentence are not identical*, the former is *revealed by* the latter, but the latter is *based on* the former. The major objection to Wittgenstein's philosophies was succinctly summarized by Gellner's (1959) following words:

> Wittgenstein's idea – though, I think, mistakenly – was based on the immensely powerful insight that we cannot say how language fits the world, nor improve its *fit*, because to do so would involve our looking at things as they are prior to being described or specified in language. Once this insight is abandoned, once it is conceded that we *can* look at things and decide whether language fits or does not, the whole position crumbles. Its sole persuasive prop has collapsed. Of course, it is still possible to argue in favour of the validity of usage from its age . . . Yes, it *has* survived. But this, by itself, is neither new nor persuasive nor interesting.[25]

3.44 *Recent Developments*

During the last two decades semantics and linguistic philosophy have experienced a most significant revolutionary impetus through Noam Chomsky (e.g. 1957, 1965, 1968) who is generally regarded the most eminent contemporary linguistic theoretician (cf. Stegmüller, 1975a, p. 1). He emerged out of the camp of the older structuralistic school but must be regarded as a neostructuralist as well as a neo-rationalist who vehemently opposes positivistic behaviorism and who denies the empiristic assertion that all our knowledge is gained by experience alone. For him the learning of language, one of the most important ways to acquire knowledge, is based on two endowments inborn in the brain of human beings: *the basic structure of human grammar* and *an evaluation mechanism* for selecting the appropriate grammatical rules in specific situations. The "linguistic competence" would thus be rooted in certain structural components and programs of the nervous system. The resulting *linguistic universalia* are shared by all humans, but are possibly shared by them only. Intelligent beings, if existing on other planets, according to Chomsky, are likely to be "programmed" in quite different linguistic patterns. Therefore the communication with such a trans-terrestrial intelligentsia might be a much more difficult undertaking than is generally sup-

[25] Ernest Gellner, *Words and Things*, 1959; quoted from the Pelican edition, 1968, pp. 283–284.

posed – yet not for technical but genetic reasons. However, Chomsky's theory of language acquisition should not be confused with his much better substantiated semantic theory.

Traditional linguistics has been dominated by the collection of factual material and its classification, together with the formation of a conceptual hierarchy which comprises *phonemes* (basic sounds), *morphemes* (basic combinations of such units), various kinds of *phrases, sentences* and *types of sentences*. Thus the goal of the *traditional approach* has to be sought in *the collection of a systematic linguistic corpus of actually encountered characteristics*. In contrast to this stands *Chomsky's* different and more ambitious goal, *the construction of a theory with testable hypotheses about rules regulating the formation of all meaningful expressions ever possible*. Such a theory deviates radically from that of the older school which hardly paid attention to the modern philosophic notions of *usage* and *meaning*. Before Chomsky, linguists were in no position to explain the logic behind the phenomena manifested, for example, by multiple meanings of a single sentence (e.g. "I like her cooking") or by different sentences with apparently identical, but actually different grammatical structures (e.g. the two sentences "She expected her lover to murder her husband" and "She persuaded her lover to murder her husband" possess, according to the superficial, traditional grammar, the same structure – nowadays therefore called *surface* structure. Actually, however, they have different structures – deep structures – as revealed by the following transformation: "She expected her husband to be murdered by her lover" versus "She persuaded her husband to be murdered by her lover" only the latter but not the former statement is close to absurdity).

Chomsky not only exposed the traditional grammar as a mere *surface grammar*, but showed how a *depth grammar* (supplementing the surface grammar and revealing the deep structural differences between various meanings of a single sentence, or between various sentences possessing a common meaning, or between sentences of different meaning or depth structure but identical surface structure) could be created. His *generative grammar* produces, by means of a *phrase marker* (nowadays usually presented in form of a schematic tree), simple sentences, and reveals their deep structure. For the analysis of complex sentences he developed a *transformation marker*, in which the variables of the structural tree are themselves derivation trees, to attain a reduction to simple forms and a derivation of the deep structure.

For Chomsky, language is a much more complex phenomenon than was previously believed, which explains why his theory is a theory *in nuce* only. He and his disciples have been working on further elaborations but, apart from many external controversies, tensions in his own camp have arisen. Above all, it turned out that Chomsky's generative transformation grammar was not in a position to clarify many pertinent, *semantical* issues, because the core of his grammar is formed by syntax rather than semantics – hence the occasionally encountered reproach that Chomsky neglects semantics at the cost of logic (cf. Stegmüller, 1975a, p. 32).

A very different, perhaps even more promising way was chosen by Richard Montague (e.g. 1969, 1970a, 1970b, 1970c) who by an untimely, murderous death perished before further elaborating his ground-breaking work. Montague's general or universal grammar is no less revolutionary than Chomsky's generative transformation grammar. The gist of Montague's variegated but highly formalistic contributions lies in the creation of a *link between natural and artificial languages: it also lies in a simultaneous and balanced development between syntax and semantics*. The neglecting of this link by traditional scholars led to the most unfortunate separate development of logic, on one hand, and semantics, on the other. The logicians aimed at the construction of efficient and precise artificial languages while the linguists tried to classify structural elements of natural languages and, at best, to comprehend their functioning. Montague's general or *universal grammar* has been the first successful attempt to reconcile these two estranged areas. He starts from the idea that, at bottom, *there does not exist any fundamental theoretical difference between artificial languages of logic and natural languages of every day usage*. This idea is less surprising if one considers the rare fact that in Montague himself the tension between the logician and the linguist was kept in perfect, even harmonious, balance. In spite of the great difference between Montague and Chomsky, it is being asserted by Stegmüller that Montague virtually created the semantics required for the syntax of Chomsky's generative and transformational grammar (cf. Stegmüller, 1975a, p. 60). But for the layman the most interesting among the many significant results brought forth by Montague's investigations is *his first successful attempt to supply proofs for the validity of deductive arguments in a natural language – in contrast to a formal language*. Of course, everyone believed that traditional logicians fulfilled this task a long time ago, but the latter did so only with regard to artificial languages. The step from these to the proofs of arguments of natural languages, was erroneously deemed to be selfevident or trivial, and thus was never really undertaken. (Many of the so-called "deductive" arguments encountered in the non-formalistic sections of scientific literature might not stand up to logical proofs, and thus might have to be regarded as inductive rather than deductive arguments.)

A prerequisite to Montague's success was *the conception* of *a standardized natural language* which combines the precision and other advantages of a formal language with the variety and flexibility of everyday languages. To achieve this, Montague developed a set of syntactic as well as semantic principles. In the following these principles shall be hinted at on the basis of a concise adaption from Stegmüller's (1975a, pp. 35–64) elaborate and more precise presentation:

(1) The analysis of natural languages must exploit the achievements of modern logic.

(2) The semantics of natural languages and its implication notion must be based on the *notion of a true sentence* (as developed by Tarski – see Subsection 3.42).

(3) The formalization of the sentences of natural languages must be based on a precise algorithm.

(4) The analysis must treat the elements as *atoms within a standardized framework*.

(5) The standardization must preserve the syntax of the natural language.

(6) There exists a unique correspondence between an entity and the set of its attributes (e.g. the name "IBM-Computer 370" designates the set of all qualities possessed by such a computer).

(7) A semantics always interprets by ascribing to a well formed formula (wff) a definite meaning or denotation respectively.

(8) Meaning as well as denotation of a wff of complex structure is a unique function of the meaning or denotation respectively of the well formed components of the complex wff.

(9) A linguistic expression possesses an *extension* (reference to an object) as well as an *intension* (a meaning).

(10) Intensions are taken to be functions determining the extensions on possible words (Carnap Intension).

(11) The semantics has to be constructed *within a context*, (i.e. its extensions and intensions must take into consideration all relevant factors such as *speaker, addressee, place, time, object,*

and *preceding context* and its interpretations must indicate a fixed point of reference).

(12) The sentences of a natural language are to be translated into a standardized task language reducible to predicate logic of first degree.

(13) Grammars are linguistic systems relating symbols to aspects of possible worlds.

These principles merely convey the basis on which Montague's ingenious system rests. If it is here not possible to discuss this system in any detail, at least two further features should be pointed out. In contrast to traditional logic, Montague formulated adjectives (e.g. "versatile") *as syntactic operators* to be applied to simple names or designations (like "machine") producing complex names (like "versatile machine"). This avoids incorrect conclusions that might occur in traditional grammar (e.g. the latter does little to declare, for example, the following deduction as invalid: "Desdemona is a presumed adulteress" therefore "Desdemona is an adulteress"). Furthermore it is important to note that Montague is one of the first to apply an intensional logic of second degree which, however, is ultimately reduced to a predicate logic of *first* degree.

As a third important breakthrough one might regard J. L. Austin's (1962) *theory of speech acts* which reveals the obvious yet previously not applied insight that different kinds of actions can be performed by linguistic expressions. He therefore made the distinction between *locutionary* acts which express something and the *illocutionary acts* which perform something beyond that particular expressions, namely that which is conveyed or achieved but which remains unspoken (a third category, or subcategory, the *perlocutionary* acts, contains only those illocutionary acts that were successful in achieving the intended goal). This distinction is significant because even where there is only one semantic interpretation there may exist several interpretations regarding speech acts involved (one and the same sentence may be taken either as a description, a hidden order, a thread, a warning etc.). Searle's analysis (see our Sections 2.7 and 2.8) is an application and extension of Austin's theory to a particular area, namely to the institution of obligation.

Another recent significant and most provoking contribution begins in language philosophy but overcomes it by reaching far beyond its boundaries, it is Saul Kripke's work on "Naming and Necessity" (1972, pp. 253–255 and 763–769). The essence and achievement of this famous article shall be outlined in a few strokes. Kripke revitalizes and revises the language theory of John St. Mill. Above all, *Kripke regards names as fixed designators, designating the same object in all possible worlds*[26] (in contrast to Frege's and Russell's theories in which names are symbols assigning bundles of qualities, and thus being valid only in one world or in *some* possible worlds). Out of Kripke's theory of names arises his distinction between *necessary qualities* (holding in *all* possible worlds) and *contingent qualities* (holding in one world or *some* possible worlds only). All this leads him to question the unjustified Kantian *identification* of the *epistemic* notion of *a priori truth* (knowledge gained prior to experience) with the *metaphysical* notion of *necessary truth.* The result is Kripke's startling conclusion that *there also exist analytical a posteriori truths, as well as contingent a priori truths* (beside the uncontended notions of analytical *a priori* and contingent *a posteriori* truths). This can best be comprehended by comparing such sentences as the following four with each other:

(1) A bachelor is an unmarried man (contingent *a priori*).

(2) Napoleon lost the battle of Waterloo (contingent *a posteriori*).

(3) "Barbarossa" is identical to "Frederic I" (necessary *a posteriori*).

(4) A proposition is either identical in all respects with another proposition or it is different from it (necessary *a priori*).

In contrast to traditional philosophy *Kripke would not accept the first sentence as a necessary a priori truth*, he would argue that the word "bachelor", being not a name but a designation, does not hold in all possible universes. Indeed we all know that it does not hold in the universe of academia where "bachelor" refers to the first academic degree in countries of English language. The nature of the second sentence is obvious and undisputed. The third sentence would, in contrast to the traditional view, be a necessary *a posteriori* sentence because of a special reason: as we have seen in his theory of names, Kripke regards a name as a fixed designation which holds in all possible worlds. Thus the sentence must be a necessary one, since it involves two identical *names*. On the other hand, this identity had to be determined by empirical research, therefore the sentence must be an *a posteriori* one

[26] Apart from the important theoretical function which the *modal* notion "possible world" plays in Kripke's theory, the notion also assumes increasing practical significance through the method of computer simulation.

(determined *after* the experience of historical fact finding). The nature of the fourth sentence again is undisputed, it is obviously *a priori* (based on laws of deductive logic) and no possible world is imaginable where it would not hold, thus it is true by necessity.

But Kripke carried his investigations much further, even into the mind–body problem where he reveals by means of this method the immense *complexity* of this particular issue. It seems to be necessary to distinguish not merely between two events (the physical and the psychic event) but between three, (cf. Stegmüller, 1975a, pp. 250–251), first the *physical micro-phenomenon* (e.g. the molecular movement called heat), second, the *physical macro-phenomenon* (e.g. the every-day behavioral symptoms of feeling heat), and finally the actual, at present unexplainable, psychic or *mental experience.* But this threefold differentiation may not be possible in the case of analyzing the causal nexus of pain, because the *actual situation* of *being in pain* is no longer distinguishable from the *epistemic situation* of *feeling pain* (cf. Stegmüller, 1975a, p. 250). However, we would suggest to say that the feeling of extreme warmth or heat undoubtedly becomes a certain kind of pain. In this case the feeling of heat and that of pain merge, and the distinction between the two seems to vanish.

CHAPTER 4

MODERN DEDUCTIVE LOGIC

4.1 Sentence Logic or the Theory of Truth-Functions

In Subsection 3.23 the reader got somewhat acquainted with syllogisms which constitute the oldest but not the most basic form of logic. The latter deals neither with classes nor with quantifiers, but with simple, unanalyzed sentences (or propositions, designated in the following by $p, q, r, s, t, \ldots$, etc.), their combinations by means of *sentence connectives* (also called logical or propositional connectives) to compound sentences (e.g. $p \vee q$, $p \cdot q$, $p \equiv q$), and above all with the pertinent inferences. Thus this *sentence (or sentential) logic* is not a logic of extension but a *logic of intension*, in which the sentences p, q, etc. do not constitute classes but may be regarded as elements of such classes as P, Q, etc. (e.g. $p \in P$, $q \in Q, \ldots$; $\in$ stands for "is an element of", see Table 4-1).

4.11 *Sentence Connectives*

Of crucial importance are the sentence connectives, the meanings of which correspond closely to the everyday usage of such words as "or", "and", "not", etc. (see Table 4-1). But since this everyday usage is occasionally ambiguous (e.g. "or" may be used in the exclusive sense as in "either *p* or *q* but *not* both", or in the inclusive sense as in "either *p* or *q* *or* both"), a precise definition of each connective must be given in a formal logic that cannot tolerate any ambiguity. By means of those sentence connectives, simple or *atomic sentences* are combined into *molecular sentences* such that the latter are regarded as *truth functions* of the former.

In Table 4-2 we offer semantical definitions of the six most common connectives. Such an assignment of truth values is actually an interpretation and thus belongs, precisely speaking, to the realm of semantics and not syntactics (cf. Figure 3-1). But it must be pointed out that it would be sufficient to give a semantic definition of only one or the other connective (e.g. of "$\vee$" and "$\sim$") and define the remaining ones not semantically (i.e. by means of truth tables) but syntactically by means of such nominal defini-

TABLE 4-1
Sentence connectives

Verbal approximation	Whitehead and Russell notation	Designation	Hilbert's notation	Polish notation
"or"	$p \vee q$	Disjunction	$p \vee q$	*Apq*
"and"	$p \cdot q$	Conjunction	$p \& q$	*Kpq*
"not"	$\sim p$	Negation	$\bar{p}$	*Np*
"if . . . then"	$p \supset q$	Material implication	$p \rightarrow q$	*Cpq*
"if and only if"	$p \equiv q$	Biconditional or identity	$p \sim q$	*Epq*

The symbols *p* and *q* stand for sentences with truth values. In the following Whitehead and Russell's notation of the *Principia Mathematica* shall be used, but since others are occasionally encountered in the literature we presented two further important notations.

TABLE 4-2
Semantical (truth-table) definition of sentence connectives

p	q	$p \vee q$	$p \cdot q$	$\sim p$	$\sim q$	$p \supset q$	$p \equiv q$
T	T	T	T	F	F	T	T
T	F	T	F	F	T	F	F
F	T	T	F	T	F	T	F
F	F	F	F	T	T	T	T

tions[1] as "$p \cdot q = \sim(\sim p \vee \sim q)$", and "$p \supset q = \sim p \vee q$", etc. This obviously means that not all of the six connectives listed and defined in Table 4-2 need to be considered as primitive notions (indeed apart from "assertion" *Principia Mathematica* regards only negation and disjunction, as primitive notions – see Subsection 3.34).[2] As just shown, the notion of conjunction and material implication can be derived from (i.e. defined in terms of) the notion of disjunction.

In Table 4-2 the letters *p* and *q* represent simple sentences (e.g. *p* . . . "The motor is in order"; *q* . . . "Gasoline is in the tank"). The first two columns give all possible combinations of truth values for these two propositions *p*

[1] A *nominal definition* does not give meaning to a term but merely substitutes a novel (usually simpler) expression for an already introduced (and usually more complex) expression.

[2] Sheffer (1913) demonstrated that sentence logic can be built on the basis of *a single binary connective* – e.g. the so-called *stroke connective* $p \mid q$ or "alternate denial" equivalent to $\sim(p \cdot q)$ from which all other connectives can be derived.

and q (two truth values n sentences = 2^n combinations). Since we are here working with a *two-valued* logic, the truth value of a sentence is either "true" (T) or "false" (F) but cannot be both. In the case of a compound sentence (e.g. "The motor is in order *and* gasoline is in the tank" = "$p \cdot q$"; see fourth column of Table 4-2), the sequence of truth values will be *a function* of the truth value combinations of the components p and q. For example, according to this definition the sentential conjunction (fourth column) will be true only if both components are true. From the third column, defining the sentential disjunction, $p \vee q$, – which is false only in the case that both components are false – we recognize that modern logic interprets the expression "or" *in the inclusive sense* (in contrast to the *original* Boolean algebra which employed "or" in the exclusive sense). The definitions of the remaining connectives will be fairly obvious to the reader with the possible exception of the *material implication* (seventh column of Table 4-2). In reading the truth table of $p \supset q$ the uninitiated reader will probably accept the truth values in the two top rows, but may wonder about those in the last two lines. Why should a false sentence p validly *imply* a true sentence q (line before last of Table 4-2) or a false sentence q (last line of Table 4-2)? This is a peculiarity of material implication; the latter facilitates the precise definition of the consequence relationship so important for deductive inference. Thus it should be borne in mind that the notion of material implication is a purely logical notion which need not correspond to all our everyday usages of the word "imply" or the expression "if . . . then". (Occasionally the notion of "ordinary implication" is mentioned in the literature and defined in such a way that the last two controversial truth values are assumed to be undecided, occasionally one encounters other implication notions).

4.12 *Conditional Form versus Argument Form*

At this stage we may introduce the ***argument form*** (already encountered in Subsection 3.23) to sentence logic, and compare it to the *conditional form* based on the notion of material implication. In Table 4-3 we present (i) specific arguments together with their (ii) corresponding argument forms and (iii) corresponding conditional forms, expressing each deductive argument in a single compound sentence which consists in each case of the implication $p \supset q$.

Indeed every deductive argument is ultimately such a conditional form and therefore can be presented by means of a material implication $p \supset q$ which in turn reveals the importance of this notion. But here the implica-

TABLE 4-3

	(i) Specific argument	(ii) Argument form	(iii) Conditional form
(1)	If $1 < 2$ then $2 < 3$	$r \supset q$	$\underbrace{\overbrace{((r \supset q) \cdot r)}^{p} \supset q}_{s}$
	$1 < 2$	r	
	$\therefore\ 2 < 3$	$\therefore\ q$	
(2)	Either $3 < 4$ or $3 \geqslant 4$	$r \vee q$	$\underbrace{\overbrace{((r \vee q) \cdot \sim r)}^{p} \supset q}_{s}$
	$3 \geqslant 4$ is not true	$\sim r$	
	$\therefore\ 3 < 4$	$\therefore\ q$	

tion sign $\supset$ is not merely a substitute for the conclusion sign "therefore" ($\therefore$) connecting p and q, because it also occurs *within* the sentence p, since the latter stands for the conjunction of both premises: $(r \supset q) \cdot r$. These two occurrences of the material implication sign are somewhat different in nature and ought to be kept strictly apart. In the case $r \supset q$, the implication sign refers to the *object language of* sentence p, whereas in the case $p \supset q$ the implication sign refers to the *meta-language about* sentence p (where it represents the implication *of p* but not an implication contained in p). Since the conditional form does not reveal this distinction at a first glance, some authors recommend the use of different signs for these two different instances of material implication. D. S. Clarke (1973, p. 35) for example suggests the use of the symbol $\Rightarrow$ as a substitute for $\supset$ wherever the material implication no longer serves as a mere sentence connective but becomes an *entailment relation* of an argument (i.e. between its antecedent and its consequent – for further discussion of "entailment" see Subsection 4.32).

In the following are the most important principles of logic (some of which were previously encountered in connection with the discussion of Boolean algebra and the *Principia Mathematica*) presented in form of compound (or molecular) sentences (most of them are conditionals or biconditionals):

Rules of Inference

Modus ponens:	$((p \supset q) \cdot p) \supset q$
Modus tollens:	$((p \supset q) \cdot \sim q) \supset \sim p$
Hypothetical syllogism:	$((p \supset q) \cdot (q \supset r)) \supset (p \supset r)$
Disjunctive syllogism:	$((p \vee q) \cdot \sim p) \supset q$
Constructive Dilemma:	$(((p \supset q) \cdot (r \supset s)) \cdot (p \vee r)) \supset (q \vee s)$
Absorption:	$(p \supset q) \supset (p \supset (p \cdot q))$

Simplification: $(p \cdot q) \supset p$

Conjunction: $(p \cdot q) \supset (p \cdot q)$

Addition: $p \supset (p \vee q)$

Logical Equivalences

De Morgan's Theorems: $\sim(p \cdot q) \equiv (\sim p \vee \sim q)$
$\sim(p \vee q) \equiv (\sim p \cdot \sim q)$

Commutation: $(p \vee q) \equiv (q \vee p)$
$(p \cdot q) \equiv (q \cdot p)$

Association: $(p \vee (q \vee r)) \equiv ((p \vee q) \vee r)$
$(p \cdot (q \cdot r)) \equiv ((p \cdot q) \cdot r)$

Distribution $(p \cdot (q \vee r)) \equiv ((p \cdot q) \vee (p \cdot r))$
$(p \vee (q \cdot r)) \equiv ((p \vee q) \cdot (p \vee r))$

Double Negation: $p \equiv \sim(\sim p)$

Transposition: $(p \supset q) \equiv (\sim q \supset \sim p)$

Material Implication: $(p \supset q) \equiv (\sim p \vee q)$
$(p \supset q) \equiv \sim(p \cdot \sim q)$

Material Equivalence: $(p \equiv q) \equiv ((p \supset q) \cdot (q \supset p))$
$(p \equiv q) \equiv ((p \cdot q) \vee (\sim p \cdot \sim q))$

Exportation: $((p \cdot q) \supset r) \equiv (p \supset (q \supset r))$

Tautology or Idempotency: $p \equiv (p \vee p)$
$p \equiv (p \cdot p)$

Other Principles

Excluded Middle: $p \vee \sim p$

Non-Contradiction: $\sim(p \cdot \sim p)$

With regard to the *Logical Equivalences* one may again distinguish between the employment of the material equivalence as a sentence connective, on one side, and as an equivalence relation between two sentences (for which Clarke suggests the symbol $\Leftrightarrow$ to distinguish it from the connective $\equiv$) on the other.

4.13 *Decidability and Formalization*

In the previous Chapter we learned that the major function of logic is to determine whether an argument is valid or not. But this is not always an easy matter, and in Subsection 3.23 we noticed that in the case of Aristotelian logic the task to decide on the validity of a syllogism became fairly awkward. *In sentence logic however, the conditional form and the notion of tautology offer excellent means for deciding whether an argument is deductively valid or not*. Indeed, as Blumberg (1968, p. 17) states "the entire theory of sentential inference may be formulated in one rule: *a sentential logic argument form is valid if and only if its corresponding conditional* – consisting of the conjunction of its premises as antecedent and its conclusion as consequent – *is a tautology*." In Table 4-3, for example, the conditional forms (i.e. the sentences *s* of each argument) are valid provided they are tautologies. In Table 4-4 we derive the truth values of the two conditional forms first presented in Table 4-3. They are indeed tautologies since all possible combinations yield nothing but *true* truth values. Thus both argument forms are valid – indeed both are well known logical principles – the first is the *modus ponens*, and the second the *disjunctive syllogism*.

If the reader takes time to examine (by means of truth tables) such other argument forms as for example the following six:

(i) $p \supset q$	(ii) $p \supset q$	(iii) $p \equiv p$	(iv) $p \supset q$	(v) $p \supset q$	(vi) $p \vee q$
$q \supset r$	$\sim q$		p	q	q
$\therefore p \supset r$	$\therefore \sim p$	$\therefore p$	$\therefore \sim q$	$\therefore p$	$\therefore \sim p$

he will notice that argument forms (i) to (iii) yield nothing but *true* truth values, therefore are *tautologies* supplying valid arguments; argument forms

TABLE 4-4

Determination of two tautologies

(1)	r	q	$r \supset q$	p: $(r \supset q) \cdot r$	s: $((r \supset q) \cdot r) \supset q$
	T	T	T	T	T
	T	F	F	F	T
	F	T	T	F	T
	F	F	T	F	T

(2) r	q	$r \vee q$	$\sim r$	p: $(r \vee q) \cdot \sim r$	s: $((r \vee q) \cdot \sim r) \supset q$
T	T	T	F	F	T
T	F	T	F	F	T
F	T	T	T	T	T
F	F	F	T	F	T

(iv) to (vi) yield *mixed* truth values, therefore are invalid (their conditional forms are thus *contingent*). Furthermore, there are molecular propositions like "$p \equiv \sim p$" or "$\sim (p \supset q) \equiv (\sim q \supset \sim p)$" which yield nothing but *false* truth values and thus are called *contradictions*.

Therefore the truth tables serve not merely the semantical definition of sentence connectives and the determination of the truth values of molecular sentences (on the basis of the truth values of atomic sentences), but provide *an algorithm or decision procedure for evaluating the validity of deductive arguments*. This is commonly expressed by saying that *sentence logic is decidable*. Unfortunately, sentence logic seems to be the only complete branch of logic which has such an algorithm and which therefore is decidable. Other branches like the various echelons of predicate logic (see Section 4.2) are not decidable in this sense, and require axiomatic or similar treatment. This does not provide algorithms but enables the evaluation of the pertinent arguments by more wearisome deductions and proofs. However, even sentence logic will require some formalization wherever a large number of atomic sentences makes the method of truth tables too cumbersome a procedure. Yet some *parts* of predicate logic are decidable.

4.14 *Formalization of Sentence Logic: Sentence Calculi*

This book is not a text on logic and its task is not to present a comprehensive survey of the sentential calculi developed hitherto. In this Subsection we merely offer a few hints to clarify the picture and to guide the reader, interested in further details, to the pertinent literature.

A sentence calculus is formulated for a well specified *object language L* and consists of the following four or five parts:

(1) A *vocabulary* in form of a *list of primitive signs* of *L*. Some of these symbols will refer to *logical constants* (the sentence connectives), others to *variables* (for the atomic sentences *p, q*, etc. as well as punctuation signs).

(2) The *formation rules* stating, in the meta-language *M*, which expressions of *L* (e.g. atomic and molecular sentences) are acceptable and thus considered as *well-formed formulas* (in short: wffs). These rules would, for example, accept such an expression as "$p \vee q$" as a wff, but would not permit an expression like "$\vee p \sim q \supset$".

(3) The *axioms* are statements in *L* expressing those principles of sentence logic assumed to be basic or primitive (e.g. the axioms of Boolean algebra or those of the *Principia Mathematica* – see Subsection 3.31 and 3.34). Since many principles of sentence logic can be derived as theorems, care must be

taken that, on one side, a sufficient number of them are chosen as axioms in order to ensure *completeness*, i.e. to cover the entire field of sentence logic, on the other hand, not too many are incorporated as axioms to avoid redundancy (no single axiom must be derivable from the remaining axioms). However, in comparing different calculi it is likely that all or some principles which are axioms in one system will be theorems in the other system and vice versa.

(4) The *rules of transformation* or *inference* express, in the meta-language M of L, the conditions for permissible inferences. They assume the following general form: "From well-formed formulas of the form $A_1, A_2, \ldots, A_n$, it is permissible to infer a well-formed formula of the form B". (B. A. Brody, 1967, p. 74.) In some axiomatic systems the transformation rules are not explicitly stated but implied or hidden in the set of axioms.

(5) The *rules of interpretation* may or may not be an integral part of the actual calculus. If the latter is an uninterpreted calculus the rules will not be incorporated, if it is an interpreted calculus they will be part of it.

The above stated first four parts form the *syntax* of the formalized system S (the *uninterpreted calculus*) and offer all ingredients of the deductive apparatus. The *semantics* for the object language L in which S is embedded, offers one or several *interpretations* by giving meaning(s) to the signs and expressions of L (e.g. assigning the words "or", "and", "not" to the symbols "$\vee$", "$\cdot$", "$\sim$" . . . or, even better, stating their truth tables).

This five-part structure is by no means restricted to the sentence calculus, but holds for all axiomatic systems, even those of empirical areas. But, as pointed out in Subsection 3.22, in most branches of deductive logic one has the choice between *formal axiomatization* and *natural deduction*. The latter substitutes all axioms by, in a way normative, *rules of inference*.

The best known axiom system of the sentence calculus is that of *Principia Mathematica* (see Subsection 3.34), while natural deduction systems of the sentence logic have recently come into higher vogue. The latter use some of the rules of inference listed at the end of Subsection 4.12. For a general survey we refer the reader to Blumberg (1967), and for an examination of a complete system we refer him to Clarke (1973), who offers a natural deduction system not only for sentence logic but also for predicate logic and various branches of modal logic including imperative and deontic modalities (see our Sections 4.3 to 4.5).

4.2 Predicate Logic

Sentence logic is neither in a position to analyze the internal structure of simple sentences nor to handle universal or existential quantifiers. For this reason sentence logic cannot evaluate most arguments encountered in the pure or applied sciences or in everyday life. The previously encountered argument for example:

all computers are machines	p
all machines are artifacts	q
∴ all computers are artifacts	∴ r

if translated into sentence logic, has the following structure $(p \cdot q) \supset r$. This neither shows the tautology, nor can it be evaluated on the basis of sentence logic alone, because the sentence variables p, q and r do not reveal any relationships between premises and conclusion. The disclosure of such internal relationships requires a kind of logic that permits the formal treatment of predicates and relations. Then it is no longer necessary to rely on the mere recurrence of complete sentences of the premises in the conclusion, but it becomes possible to utilize the recurrence of subjectives, predicates and relations (in the above example the subjective of the first premise and the predicate of the second one recur both in the conclusion). Thus *predicate logic evaluates deductive inferences the validity of which depends on the recurrence of constitutive terms in premises and conclusion.* But these constitutive terms are not limited to predicates (apart from subjectives), as the misnomer "predicate logic" might suggest, but extend to all kinds of relations. Therefore the less frequently encountered term "logic of relations" would seem to be more appropriate – the more so since predicates may no less be regarded as one-place relations than true relations may be regarded as many-place predicates. The symbolic representation of the following sentences shall illustrate this (lower case letters are used for *individual constants* representing objects, and capital letters are used for *predicate constants* representing predicates or relations):

The bridge *is wide*	bW	or	Wb
The computer *is large*	cL	or	Lc
Socrates *is the teacher* of Plato	sTp	or	Tsp
Machines (m) *will be shipped* (S) *from Boston* (b) to Los Angeles (l)	$Smbl$	or	$S(m, b, l)$.

All these are *singular* sentences which either state that a certain property pertains to an individual object or that a certain relation holds between two or more individual objects. (The preferred symbolism in predicate logic is to *list first the predicate constant followed by the individual constants* without the use of parentheses.) Sentence connectives can here be used in the same way as before, e.g.:

The bridge is wide *or* the computer is large $Wb \vee Lc$.

4.21 *Quantification*

Non-singular sentences require quantifiers (Table 4-5) which enable us to formulate either universal or existential generalizations (cf. Subsection 3.34).

We shall use in the following the most common variation of the Whitehead and Russell notation: $(x)\,(Fx)$ and $(\exists x)\,(Fx)$.

The symbolism of the following predicative argument deviates somewhat from the symbolism described and thus has to be explained:

All automata (A) are systems (S)	$(x)\,(Ax \supset Sx)$
Some automata (A) can think (T)	$\exists x\,(Ax \cdot Tx)$
∴ Some systems (S) can think (T)	∴ $\exists x\,(Sx \cdot Tx)$

First of all, it should be noted that the *universal quantifier* (x) stands for "For all (things or individuals) x it is true that . . .", while the *existential quantifier* $\exists x$ stands for "There is (at least) one x such that . . . ". Furthermore the reader will have noticed that both object (subject) and predicate are designated by capital letters while the lower case letter was reserved for the impersonal variable x. One reason for this lies in the fact that certain terms change their role in the course of the argument (e.g. the predicate of the first premise "are systems", itself consists of an object, and ultimately becomes the subject of the conclusion). From this we may conclude that A and S actually do not designate such objects as automata and systems but

TABLE 4-5
Various notations of logical quantifiers

Whitehead and Russell notation	Verbal approximation	Hilbert notation	Polish notation	Other notations
$(x)\,\Phi x$	All x are Φ (or F) or Every x is Φ (or F)	$(x)F(x)$	$\Pi x \Phi x$	$\forall x\,F(x)$ or $\wedge xFx$
$(\exists x)\,\Phi x$	Some x is Φ (or F) or There is (at least) one x which is Φ (or F)	$(Ex)\,F(x)$	$\Sigma x \Phi x$	$\exists x\,F(x)$ or $\vee xFx$

TABLE 4-6

Formulas of predicate logic

1.	*Ba*	*Andrew* (*a*) *is building* (*B*) something.
2.	*Bab*	Andrew is building a *bridge* (*b*).
3.	*Bx*	*x* is building.
4.	$(x)(Bx)$	Everyone is building (= For all *x* it is true that *x* is building).
5.	$(\exists x)(Bx)$	Someone is building (= There is an *x* such that *x* is building).
6.	$(x)(\sim Bx)$	No one is building (= Everyone is not building).
7.	$(\exists x)(\sim Bx)$	Not everyone is building (= Someone is not building).
8.	$\sim(x)(\sim Bx)$	Not everyone is not building (= Someone is building).
9.	$\sim(\exists x)(\sim Bx)$	No one is not building (= Everyone is building).
10.	$(x)(Bx \supset Cx)$	Whoever builds *is creative* (*C*) (= Everyone who builds is creative).
11.	$(\exists x)(Bx \cdot Cx)$	Some (of those) who build are creative.
12.	$(\exists x)(Bx) \cdot (\exists x)(Cx)$	Some (persons) are building and some are creative.
13.	$(x)(Fx) \supset Fa$	If everyone *is fallible* (*F*) then Andrew is fallible.

a, *b*, . . .	*terms* naming or describing individual objects.
A, *B*, *C*, *F*, . . .	*predicate constants* representing predicates or relations.
x, *y*, . . .	*individual variables* serving as placeholders for terms.
(x), $(\exists x)$ . . .	*quantifiers* (universal and existential respectively).
Bx	*propositional* or sentential *form* (open formula).

stand for such relations as "things called automata" and "things called systems". Table 4-6 offers some important formulations and illustrations of predicate logic.

Some peculiarities of this formulation are of special interest. All formulas of Table 4-6 represent propositions with exception of item 3 which is a propositional form. More importantly, it should be noted that the negation of item 4 is 7 and not, as might be thought, 6, and the negation of item 5 is 6 and not 7; this is best shown by the negations of items 6 and 7 which yield items 8 and 9 (which in turn are logically equivalent to items 5 and 4 respectively!). A comparison of items 10 and 11 shows that *universal sentences involve material implication*, while *existential sentences involve conjunction* – thus it would be incorrect to write: $(x)\ (Bx \cdot Cx)$ or $(\exists x)\ (Bx \supset Cx)$, something worth pondering about by means of Venn diagrams (cf. Subsection 3.23). A comparison of items 11 and 12 is no less interesting: it shows that in item 12 the existential quantifier *cannot* be bracketed out to obtain item 11 – the two sentences have different meanings. Item 13 is *the only complete argument contained in Table 4-6*, because it is the only so-called *valid formula* (for details see below); it also reveals (like a comparison of items 1 and 3) the difference between the free variable x, bound merely by the quantifier, and the term or constant a.

4.22 *Valid Formulas*

Most "first-order logic" admits only individual variables and their quantification; all other sorts (for example, predicate variables) are reserved for predicate logic of second and higher orders.

> However, the class of first-order formulas or sentence forms is still a rather wide one. It includes the following:
>
> (1) all formulas consisting of single n-place predicate constants and their n-individual constants (these formulas interpreted, are singular sentences);
>
> (2) all universal and existential generalizations of open formulas – that is, those that contain one or more n-place predicate constants and at least one individual variable (these generalized formulas, when interpreted, become general sentences);
>
> (3) all truth-functional compounds of (1) or (2) or both.
>
> Such first-order formulas (sentences) serve as components for a correspondingly wide class of first-order argument forms (arguments) whose validity or invalidity it is the business of elementary logic to determine.
>
> The key to inference in first-order logic is the notion of *valid formula*. This, in turn, rests on the notion of interpretation of formula F relative to a domain of individuals D if S is obtained from F by (a) replacing the predicate constants of F with predicates defined for the individuals of D and (b) replacing the individual constants of F with proper names of individuals of D. Then a formula F in predicate logic is said to be *valid* (or universally valid) if it becomes a *true* sentence under *every* interpretation in *any* (non-empty) domain of individuals. (Blumberg, 'Logic, Modern', 1967, pp. 20–21.)

Such a *valid formula* for example is shown in item 13 of Table 4-6. There the expression "everyone" indicates that x ranges over the *domain* (D) of *all* human beings and the predicate constant F stands for "is fallible", and "a" stands for "Andrew", a human being. Then the sentence "If everyone is fallible then Andrew is fallible" is *true under all possible interpretations*, while for example the formula presented in item 1 of Table 4-6 is not a valid formula because it does not hold in all possible circumstances (e.g. Andrew actually may or may not be building). In sentence logic the validity of an argument was demonstrated by showing it to be a tautology; similarly *in predicate logic the validity of an argument requires the demonstration that its corresponding conditional is a "valid formula"*. (Table 4-7 summarizes some important *valid* formulas.) But it is much more difficult to show which formulas are valid ones than to demonstrate the tautological character of a valid argument in sentence logic. Although all tautologies are valid formulas, the reverse is not true (e.g. item 13 of Table 4-5 does not *seem* to be a tautology).[3] In contrast to sentence logic which can use truth tables as a decision procedure for testing the validity of its arguments, *predicate logic*

TABLE 4-7

Important valid formulas of predicate logic[3a]

1.	$[(x)(Fx) \cdot (x)(Gx)] \supset [(x)(Fx \vee Gx)]$
2.	$[(\exists x)(Fx \cdot Gx)] \supset [(\exists x)(Fx) \cdot (\exists x)(Gx)]$
3.	$[(x)(Fx \supset Gx)] \supset [(\exists x)(Fx) \supset (\exists x)(Gx)]$
4.	$[(x)(p \vee Fx)] \equiv [p \vee (x) Fx]$
5.	$(y)[(x)(Fx) \supset Fy]$
6.	$(y)[Fy \supset (\exists x) Fx]$
7.	$(x)(Fx) \equiv \sim(\exists x)(\sim Fx)$
8.	$(x)(Fx \cdot Gx) \equiv (x)(Fx) \cdot (x)(Gx)$
9.	$(x)(p \cdot Fx) \equiv [p \cdot (x)(Fx)]$
10.	$(\exists x)(Fx \vee Gx) \equiv [(\exists x)(Fx) \vee (\exists x)(Gx)]$
11.	$(\exists x)(p \cdot Fx) \equiv [p \cdot (\exists x)(Fx)]$
12.	$(\exists x)(p \vee Fx) \equiv [p \vee (\exists x)(Fx)]$
13.	$(x)(Fx) \supset Fy$
14.	$Fy \supset (\exists x)(Fx)$
15.	$[(\exists x)(Fx) \supset p] \equiv (x)(Fx \supset p)$

[3] Let p and q express the following two sentences "Everyone is fallible" and "Andrew is fallible" respectively, then item 13 of Table 4-6 becomes $p \supset q$ which here, however, is a tautology because the term "everyone" implies a human like Andrew.

[3a] Adapted from Stegmüller (1969b, pp. 52–54).

has no such decision procedure and thus is said to be "*undecidable*". The major way to determine the validity of an argument of predicate logic is deductively through either an axiomatic system or a natural deduction system.

Especially the last of these valid formulas (item 15 of Table 4-7) may at first be puzzling, since it seems to identify an existential sentence with a universal sentence; but that is not the case, it merely identifies an implication (containing but not asserting an existential sentence) with a universal sentence. The following interpretation of item 15 will facilitate the understanding of this valid formula: Let F stand for the predicate " . . . is a philosopher" and p stand for the sentence "he (or x) is a person", then item 15 (Table 4-7) says:

> "If there is a philosopher then he is a person" is logically identical to "all philosophers are persons".

4.23 *Russell's Theory of Description and Recent Reactions*

A major problem behind all this awkward symbolic representation of fairly simple sentences manifests itself in the question: How can words and sentences *describe* reality? One answer to this question is Bertrand Russell's well known theory of description. To illustrate it concisely let us take the following sentence:

> "The man first on the moon is an American".

This not only seems to be a meaningful but even a true sentence. However, how should one have reacted to such a sentence before the first manned moon landing in 1969? Disregarding the problem of perfect foresight and predestination (cf. Section 4.3) one could then have argued that this is a meaningless description without any possibility of truth value. On one side the sentence asserts a certain person to be an American, on the other, that person, or better said that particular aspect of this person (who later turned out to be Neil Armstrong) did not then exist. Russell asserted that sentences of this kind are grammatical deceptions because they appear to be of the subject–predicate form, yet from a logical point of view are conjunctions of three different sentences (complex symbols). Thus by carefully analyzing such conjunctions he interpreted them as consisting of three components. In our example these would be the following sentences 1 to 3:

1. There is *at least one* man (stepping) first on the moon.
2. *At most one* man is (or stepped) first on the moon.
3. Whoever that man first on the moon is, he is an American (*identification*).

According to Russell such incomplete descriptions, as contained in our complex sentence, are meaningless unless three conditions hold. The conditions are generalizations of the above sentences 1 to 3 and are roughly indicated by those numbers in the concise symbolic representation which Russell offered for such sentences[4]:

$$\exists x\,[(y)Fy \equiv (y=x)\cdot Ax]$$

1

2

3

Let x and y stand for man (or men) and F and A for the predicates "being first on the moon" and "being American" respectively, then this symbolic representation of our complex sentence reads:

> "There exists at least one man x, such that all men y, first on the moon, are identical to one man x who is an American".

Of course the true description "first man on the moon" may be replaced, under certain circumstances, by e.g. the proper name "Neil Armstrong" (or *vice versa*) which itself is not a description, and ought to be distinguished from it.[5] At the same time Russell provided a vehicle for *distinguishing*

[4] This may also be expressed by writing $A\,℩\,[(x)Fx]$ which is the *definiendum* to the above stated *definiens*. In everyday language such a *definite description* begins with the definite article "the" followed by a predicate. The description symbol (a reversed lower case iota) may be regarded as a kind of singular quantifier such that (℩x) means "there is one and only one x . . . ". But as Russell showed us (℩x) can be dispensed with through the above stated formulation. Quine (1957), however, uses such expressions as "(℩x) Fx" or "(℩x) Gx" as the "F-er" or "G-er" for replacing names by definite descriptions. He would then read "Socrates" as "the socratizer", possessing the set of properties to single out this particular person or object. As Smart (1968, p. 31) says: " 'The socratizer' sounds artificial, but it is no different in principle from replacing 'Moon' by 'the natural satellite of the Earth'."

[5] In Russell's own words: "What we call proper names – e.g. 'Socrates' (or in the above case 'Neil Armstrong') – can, if I am right, be defined in terms of qualities and spatio-temporal relations, and this definition is an actual analysis . . . . Subject–predicate

clearly between the *non-existence of an object* and the *existence of a non-object*: Assuming the above statements were made before 1969, then "the first man on the moon" would not describe Neil Armstrong but, according to Russell, a non-object or non-person; yet the fact that at a later date the description referred to an existent object, proves that the latter is different from such a genuine non-object as a "round-square". Indeed, Russell disregarded, even rejected Frege's previously mentioned distinction between *sense* (i.e. meaning or descriptive content) and *reference* (i.e. the object to which description refers); and it is at this point on which recent critics turn away from the theory of description (e.g. Searle, 1971).

In contrast to Russell, Frege would not have regarded a sentence like "The man first on the moon is an American" as meaningless before 1969. Because in Frege's view a sentence may have sense (i.e. could be meaningful) even though the expression has no existing object or reference. "Frege asks: how do proper names and definite descriptions refer to things? His answer is: in virtue of their sense. Russell rejects the question. He argues, in effect, that neither definite descriptions nor ordinary proper names . . . refer at all. Rather, he says they have no meaning 'in isolation' . . . but sentences containing them are to be analyzed . . . " (Searle, 1971, p. 4). Searle then asks how Russell thinks that "words hook on to the world" if neither descriptions nor proper words do refer. The answer is that for Russell as well as for the early Wittgenstein they stand for entities of unanalyzable simplicity without any further meaning: "The name means an object. The object is its meaning" (Wittgenstein, *Tractatus* item 3.203). The meaning of the sentence is then derived from the specific arrangement of these names, descriptions etc., in a *word picture* of a *state of affairs*. Different arrangements would yield different pictures. The truth of the sentence depends on the existence or non-existences of the state of affairs depicted. If the latter exists it is called a *fact*. Thus Searle (1971) says:

> Notice that all these theories which I have sketched – Frege, the Tractatus, logical positivism – have certain characteristics in common. They all assume that the only, at any rate the primary, aim of language is to represent and communicate factual information, that the part of the

---

propositions, such as "Socrates is snub-nosed", assert that a certain quality, named by the predicate, is one of a bundle of qualities named by the subject – this bundle being a unity in virtue of compresence and causal relations. Proper names in the ordinary sense, if this is right, are misleading, and embody a false metaphysic." (Russell, 1948, pp.98–99.

language that really counts is the "cognitive" part. The aim of language, in short, is to communicate what can be true or false. Secondly, they treat the elements of language – words, sentences, propositions – as things that represent or things that are true or false, etc., apart from any actions or intentions of speakers and hearers. The elements of the language, not the actions and intentions of the speakers are what count. In the late thirties and especially after the Second World War these assumptions came to be vigorously challenged, especially by Wittgenstein. Wittgenstein argued that stating facts is only one of the countless jobs we do with language and that the meaning of elements lies not in any relationship they have in the abstract, but in the use we make of them. "Language", says Wittgenstein, "is an instrument"; and "for a large class of cases, . . . the meaning of a word is its use in the language." (*Philosophical Investigations*, para. 569 and 43.)

Austin, in a similar vein, called attention to a class of utterances that do not even set out to be true or false. For example, a man who says, "I promise I will come", is not stating a fact about himself to the effect that he promises, but rather he is *making* a promise. Austin called such utterances "performatives", contrasting them with "constatives".

There was a good deal of carelessness in the way philosophers in this period talked about the *use* of expressions and – with the notable exception of Austin – they did not always distinguish among the different sorts of "use" to which expressions could be put. But this approach has certain real advantages which have survived to the present day . . . Most importantly it recasts the discussion of many problems in the philosophy of language into the larger context of the discussion of human action and behaviour generally. Questions of meaning and reference can be seen in the context of speakers meaning something by something and referring to something in the utterance of an expression. Instead of seeing the relations between words and the world as something existing *in vacuo*, one now sees them as involving intentional actions by speakers, employing conventional devices (words, sentences) in accordance with extremely abstract sets of rules for the use of those devices. For example, the real strength of Frege's theory of sense and reference as opposed to Russell's theory of definite descriptions emerges in Strawson's conception of reference as a speech act (Strawson, 1950). Once one sees referring as an action that is performed in the utterance of an expression with a particular sense provided by the rules for the use of the expression, then it is easier to see that it is subject to the sorts of error that plague actions generally (one can fail to refer to a king of France for the same reason that one can fail to hit a king of France: there is no such person), and on this account there is much less motivation for trying to identify referring (one kind of speech act), with asserting an existential proposition (quite another kind of speech act), as Russell in effect does.[6]

4.3 Multivalued and Modal Logic

4.31 *Lukasiewicz' Many Valued Logic*

So far we have dealt with a logic capable of handling only propositions to which one of two truth values ("true" or "false") could be assigned. But neither everyday nor scientific discourse seems to be restricted to such sentences. Frequently we encounter situations in which a third possibility ought to be contemplated. Should one therefore *add a third truth value*, like "possible" to "true" and "false", *or* should one even *provide an infinite number of truth values expressing all probability values* between and including truth and falsehood? Some logicians would reject both alternatives by arguing that the *law of bivalence* (one version of the law of the excluded middle – see Subsection 4.12) asserts that a proposition can be either true or false but nothing else. While there is less doubt about this with regard to propositions concerning past and present events, the situation is different for future-tense propositions conveying contingent subject matters. Aristotle already raised this issue which may have led to the controversy between the ancient Epicureans who rejected the law of bivalence and the Stoics who could not afford to do so, since their doctrine of determinism (predestination) would have been put in jeopardy by any kind of multivalued logic. This issue was revived in medieval times when the problem of "God's foreknowledge" assumed special importance. A certain Peter de Rivo was then the main proponent for a neutral third truth value. But when all events are assumed to be preordained, then they must occur by necessity, and a proposition asserting an event, whether past, present or future, must either be true or false even if it may appear to a mortal human as merely possible. Thus the controversy of "two-valued versus many-valued logic" became an epistemological as well as metaphysical battleground.

[6] Reprinted from Searle's Introduction to *The Philosophy of Language*, 1971. Frege's semantic relations between name–meaning–object possess on a much more general, *phenomenological* level an analogy in Husserl's distinctions between act–noema–object. See Stegmüller (1975a, pp. 86–103).

Jan Lukasiewicz (1878–1956) developed in the early 1920s a multi-valued logic based on three-valued truth tables offering semantical definitions of various sentence connectives. In this system the number 1, 2 and 3 represent the truth-values "true", "possible" and "false" respectively. Furthermore the sentence connectives "if . . . then", "not", "or" "and" etc. have to be newly defined. Table 4-8 shows those definitions but they are not the only possible ones of three-valued logic, and others have been offered as alternatives.

It is noteworthy that in this three-valued logic the implication ($p \supset q$) has only one instance of falsity (see line (iii) of Table 4-8) just like the material implication of the two-valued or classical logic, but in contrast to the latter it has *two neutral values* (see lines (ii) and (vi) of Table 4-8) of which the second case, as well as the case expressed in lines (viii) of Table 4-8, may surprise the uninitiated. But these are hardly stronger cases than those familiar from two-valued logic which we again encounter in lines (vii) and (ix) of Table 4-8.

Of special interest is Lukasiewicz' introduction of a *possibility operator*, which we shall designate with M, and the resulting *functor Mp* (meaning "possibly p"). It can be defined in terms of p as shown in the truth table of Table 4-9. The left hand side of this table shows the truth values of proposition p within the three-valued logic, while the right hand side shows the truth values of the functor or proposition Mp based on the traditional two-valued logic extended by the possibility operator M and thus moving in direction of modal logic (see next Subsection). This Table 4-9 reveals, in a way, the transition from multi-valued logic (left) to modal logic (right) among which M is an especially significant operator. Thus multi-valued logic and modal logic might be interpreted as either two facets of the same coin, or as

TABLE 4-8

Semantical definition of sentence connectives in a three-valued logic

	p	q	$p \supset q$	$\sim p$	$p \vee q$	$p \cdot q$
(i)	1	1	1	3	1	1
(ii)	1	2	2	3	1	2
(iii)	1	3	3	3	1	3
(iv)	2	1	1	2	1	2
(v)	2	2	1	2	2	2
(vi)	2	3	2	2	2	3
(vii)	3	1	1	1	1	3
(viii)	3	2	1	1	2	3
(ix)	3	3	1	1	3	3

TABLE 4-9

Comparison of truth functions: multi-valued versus dual-valued logic*

Multi-valued truth values of *p*	Dual-valued truth values of *Mp*
1	T
2	T
3	F

* This is a mere juxtaposition and does not imply that the value of *Mp* is a truth function of *p*.

two alternatives of handling the problem of indeterminism in logic. Both deal with the notion of *possibility* (as well as the notions of *necessity* and *impossibility*), but the former tries to solve the problem of contingent propositions by introducing a multitude of truth values, while the latter adheres to the traditional two truth values of "true" and "false", solving the problem of contingency through the introduction of modal operators. Although many versions of multi-valued logic (some with an infinite number of truth values) have subsequently been developed, and although some interesting applications (in designing signalling systems, quantum mechanics etc.) were found, it seems that modal logic proved to be a more promising development.

Nevertheless there are recent indications that multivalued logic may become useful in dealing with *the problem of vagueness* so prominent in the social and applied sciences (the notion of vagueness must not be confused either with that of uncertainty nor that of inexactness)[6a]. Indeed Menges and Skala (1974) believe that the most natural way to handle vague concepts by means of a formal language is to start with a multi-valued logic. In particular they refer to the notion of a *fuzzy set* (and an *L*-fuzzy set) developed by Zadeh (1965) and Goguen (1967), and arising out of the attempt to apply logic to probabilistic concepts and to reduce or even formalize vagueness. Perhaps a way can thus be found to harness systematically the dialectical nature and polarity of many concepts that have been playing havoc with the social sciences (see also our Section 7.4).

[6a] Whereas *vagueness* is meant to be a conceptual problem arising out of the discrepancy between the logical form of a concept and its empirical manifestation, *uncertainty* refers to the absence of insufficiency of a certain kind of knowledge, and *inexactness* to the deficiency of a description or measurement.

4.32 *Modal Logic*

As we have seen, multivalued logic and modal logic are two alternative solutions arising out of the same problem.[7] But for the applied sciences modal logic is of special significance for two reasons. First of all, it may be regarded as the logical foundation of probability theory which became so pre-eminent during recent decades. And second, modal logic in the broad sense comprises such sub-divisions as the deontic and imperative modalities. The latter deal with "ought-sentences" and normative statements and enable us to incorporate value judgements and goals into the formal framework. Indeed these two modalities form the backbone of instrumental reasoning and thus are presented separately in Section 4.4. Modal logic (in the narrow sense) explores the formal characteristics of *necessity, possibility,* and *impossibility*. This logical trichotomy we find repeated, on one side, in predicate logic (Section 4.2) as well as in deontic logic (Subsection 4.42). These similarities are best exposed by juxtaposing the quantifiers of predicate logic to the modal operators as well as deontic operators (see Table 4-10).

Applying the modal *possibility operator M* (or $\diamond$ called "diamond") to the sentence p (e.g. "a missile will be launched tomorrow"), the *operand Mp* means:

> "The statement 'a missile will be launched tomorrow' is possible" or simply "It is possible that 'a missile will be launched tomorrow' ".

Both of these versions reveal the important fact that *the entire statement belongs to the meta-language* with regard to sentence p which itself belongs to the object language. Similarly, if q stands for "$3 > 5$", then $\sim Mq$ expresses the fact that

> " '$3 > 5$' is impossible".

Furthermore, if r stands for "the sum of all angles of a triangle is 180°", then the *necessity operator N* must be applied, and the operand Nr (or $\Box r$) says:

> " 'The sum of all angles of a triangle is 180°' is necessary (or is true by necessity)".

[7] "In fact the entire problem of relating modal and many-valued logics can be brought into sharper focus. It becomes clear that there are two distinct ways of effecting such a relationship. One way is to keep the logic-values of many-valued calculi neutral, and another way is to identify the logic-values with modalities or modal-values". Turquette (1963, pp. 266–267).

TABLE 4-10

A comparison of basic concepts from predicate logic, modal logic and deontic logic

Quantifiers:	$(\exists p)(Bp)$	equivalent to	$\sim(p)(\sim Bp)$	Some p are B
	$\sim(\exists p)(Bp)$	equivalent to	$(p)(\sim Bp)$	No p are B
	$\sim(\exists p)(\sim Bp)$	equivalent to	$(p)(Bp)$	All p are B
Modal operators:	Mp	equivalent to	$\sim N\sim p$	p is impossible
	$\sim Mp$	equivalent to	$N\sim p$	p is impossible
	$\sim M\sim p$	equivalent to	Np	p is necessary
Deontic operators:	Pp	equivalent to	$\sim O\sim p$	p is permitted
	$\sim Pp$	equivalent to	$O\sim p$	p is forbidden
	$\sim P\sim p$	equivalent to	Op	p is obligatory

But unlike p, the operands Mp, $\sim Mq$ and Nr are not truth functions of p, q or r respectively. Thus "r is true" does not imply Nr ("r is necessary").

But these three modalities of *necessity* Np, *contingency* $Np \vee N\sim p$, and *impossibility* $\sim Mp$ can be interpreted in three different senses. If they represent *sentences*, as was the case above, we speak of the *alethic sense,* but if they represent instead *beliefs* or *events* we speak of the *epistemic* or *physical sense* respectively. In the following (Table 4-11) we state some important definitions and propositions of modal logic.

Of special significance are the definitions of entailment $\Rightarrow$ and compatibility $\circ$, offered in items 6 and 7 of Table 4-11. Item 6 defines the *entailment relation* $\Rightarrow$ between p and q in two equivalent ways. On one side, as *the necessity of p materially implying q*, on the other side, as the *impossibility of a conjunction between p and* $\sim q$ – which corresponds to the definition of $p \supset q = \sim(p \cdot \sim q)$ as an alternative to $p \supset q = \sim p \vee q$ – see Subsection 3.34, Table 3-4. Item 7 defines the *compatibility relation* $\circ$, on one side, as the *possibility of p in conjunction with q*, on the other, as *the negation of p* entailing non-*q* (in all these cases the symbols p and q stand for *names* of sentences, not for sentences themselves).

A further important subdivision of analytical sentences, is that between *material analytical* and *logical* (or formal analytical) sentences. All logical sentences represent necessary propositions, like:

"Event x has either occurred or not occurred"

or

"A proposition is logically identical to its double negation".

Whereas material analytical propositions are necessarily true only if a further

TABLE 4-11

1.	$Mp = \sim N \sim p$
2.	$\sim Mp = \sim(\sim N)\sim p$
3.	$\sim M \sim p = Np = \sim(\sim N)p$
4.	$\sim Mp \Rightarrow N(p \supset q)$
5.	$Nq \Rightarrow N(p \supset q)$
6.	$p \Rightarrow q = \text{def.}\, N(p \supset q) = \text{def.}\, \sim M(p \cdot \sim q)$
7.	$p \circ q = \text{def.}\, M(p \cdot q) = \text{def.}\, \sim(p \Rightarrow \sim q)$
8.	$N(p \cdot q) = Np \cdot Nq$
9.	$N(p \supset q) \Rightarrow (Np \supset Nq)$
10.	$(Np \vee Nq) \Rightarrow N(p \vee q)$
11.	$M(p \vee q) \equiv Mp \vee Mq$
12.	$M(p \cdot q) \Rightarrow Mp \cdot Mq$

sentence specifying the meaning of a pertinent word, is explicitly or implicitly given.

"All spinsters are unmarried females".

or

"5 is a number".

Obviously the last two sentences are necessary merely by virtue of certain linguistic conventions conveyed by such words as "spinster" or "number" respectively. Each of which presupposes a meaning-specifying sentence. Although many modal arguments are deductive (the following one designated by (1) and (2)), others are not (see (3) and (4)).

(1) " 'There will be mass starvation and a World War III' is possible".

∴ " 'There will be mass starvation' is possible".

or symbolically $M(p \cdot q) \Rightarrow Mp$,

(2) " 'There will be mass starvation' is possible".

∴ " 'There will be either mass starvation or a World War III or both' is possible".

or symbolically $Mp \Rightarrow M(p \vee q)$.

Inferences of the type represented by arguments (1) and (2) can be proved as deductively valid within modal logic.[8] But this is definitely not the case for inferences of the type represented by (3) and (4).

(3) " 'If there will be continuing droughts there will be mass starvation' is possible".

" 'There will be continuing droughts' is possible".

∴ " 'There will be mass starvation' is possible".

(4) " 'If there will be mass starvation there will be a revolution' is possible".

" 'There will be no revolution' is possible".

∴ " 'There will be no mass starvation' is possible".

Although the arguments (3) and (4) seem to be modal applications of the *modus ponens* $((p \supset q) \cdot p \Rightarrow q)$ and *modus tollens* $((p \supset q) \cdot \sim q \Rightarrow \sim p)$ respectively, the conclusions do not follow by necessity from their premises. Hence such modal or any other *weak* form of the *modus ponens, modus tollens* etc. are not deductive but inductive inferences[9] which will be discussed in Chapter 5.

Concluding this extremely sketchy Subsection, we should point out that there exists a vast and growing literature on this subject with a variety of alternative systems of modal logic.[10] Indeed the fact that the axiomatic bases of those alternatives vary considerably, sheds light on the many meanings, or shades of meaning, attributed to the words "possible" and "necessary".

[8] Proof of the form of argument (2) above is offered for example in Hughes and Cresswell (1968, p. 231) for Lewis' system S_2, while argument (1) is an interpretation of one of the axioms of system S_2 (see also footnote 10).

[9] Cf. Bunge (1967, Vol. 2, p. 293).

[10] The first comprehensive treatment of modal logic was contained in Lewis and Langford (1932). There "possibility" constitutes the primitive operator (from which "necessity" and "impossibility" are derived) and axiomatic systems, usually addressed as S_1 and S_2, were developed, and further systems S_3 to S_5 were outlined in an appendix. Other systems of modal logic were developed by authors like G. H. von Wright, A. N. Prior, etc.

Interesting comments on the essence and evolution (with literature references) of modal and multi-valued logics, deontic logic as well as such new branches as epistemic logic, temporal logic, nominalistic logic, decision logic and the quantum logic are found by Stegmüller (1975a, pp. 147–208).

4.4 Imperative Arguments and Deontic Modalities

In recent years authors of applied fields, especially of the administrative and management sciences, began to concern themselves more intensively with arguments in which at least one premise (as well as the conclusion) consists of a value judgement. But most of those social or administrative scientists seem to be quite unaware of the problems and additional assumptions involved in making normative and especially imperative inferences. Many applied scientists seem to believe that such inferences are permissible within the framework of the traditional, deductive logic of assertions (i.e. assertoric or declarative logic). Since this is not the case, the major purpose of this Section is to make the reader aware of the pitfalls and further requirements of arguments based on value judgements. Thus this Section offers nothing but a glimpse of the present efforts to create a logic of imperative and deontic arguments, and concentrates mainly on aspects immediately relevant to instrumental reasoning.

The dilemma of imperative inference has been summarized succinctly with the following words:

> "According to the usually accepted definition of a logical inference, an imperative is precluded from being a constituent part of such inference. Nevertheless instances may be given of inferences the logical evidence of which seems obvious in spite of the fact that imperatives form part of them. And, further, those instances must be considered typical of the way in which reasoning actually takes place in practical life and in the sciences operating with normative expressions, especially the science of law. Wherever an ordinary norm is applied to a concrete case – such as, for instance, where a judge imposes a punishment on a criminal in accordance with the general norm of the penal code – it is a case of a practical inference . . ."[11] Furthermore, Rescher in dealing with commands, the most important sub-group of imperatives, points out that the "giving of a command is a performance. From this angle, a 'logic of commands' is difficult to envisage. Performances cannot stand in logical relations to one another, and specifically, one performance cannot entail or imply another, nor can the *description* of one performance entail that of another . . . We shall abstract from this performative aspect of command-giving just as the logic of assertion abstracts from the performative aspect of statement-making."[12]

[11] Ross, 'Imperatives and Logic', 1944, pp. 32–33. (Ross understands by practical inference an inference with at least one imperative as constituent part.)

[12] Rescher, *The Logic of Commands*, 1966, pp. 8–9.

Such reflections raise questions about *the nature of practical inference*. Is it possible that we are dealing here with a process of reasoning which is neither deductive nor inductive? This question appears less absurd in view of Aristotle's explicit distinction of practical reasoning.[13] Nevertheless there seems to be some doubt of the meaning which Aristotle assigned to this expression. Modern interpretations of the term "practical inference" vary, and Clarke recommends that it "should not be applied to all inferences bearing on conduct, but only to those whose premises describe or express a desire and belief. In particular, it should not be applied to the imperative and deontic inferences. (D. S. Clarke, 1973, p. 11.) This interpretation is in opposition to that of Ross (1944) who seems to regard imperative arguments as either identical with or at least belonging to practical inference. For these reasons we shall here not use the term "practical reasoning" but instead the related one of "*instrumental reasoning*". To this we shall give the following definition:

Instrumental reasoning is *any* process of *deductive or non-deductive* inferences dealing with arguments *containing premises that relate means to ends leading to conclusions about pertinent actions.*[14]

We shall also distinguish between *instrumental reasoning* and *cognitive reasoning.*[15] The latter comprises all those assertoric inferences (deductive or non-deductive) which do not deal with premises relating means to ends (instrumental hypotheses). Hence instrumental reasoning is not regarded as

[13] *Nicomachean Ethics*, Chapter 3, Book 7. See also Clarke (1973, p. 2) who clearly distinguishes between *three* different categories of inference under the headings: "Practical Inference", "Inductive Inference" and "Deductive Inference".

In recent years there exists growing interest in practical reasoning as the following quotation from Rescher attests:

> An active revival of interest on the part of philosophers in practical reasoning is currently in progress . . . This interest relates both to the history of the problem and to the substantive issues. (Rescher, 1969, p. 29.)

But in text books on logic, practical inference is still being grossly neglected as Clarke indicates:

> That a form of reasoning central to everyday life and the formulation and application of the law has been largely ignored thus far is nothing short of a scandal, and it is high time we begin to set the matters right. (Clarke, 1973, pp. i–ii.)

[14] This definition may resemble that of von Wright's (1963, p. 160), definition of *practical inference* which, however, seems to exclude all non-deductive inferences while we recognize that instrumental inferences may be of deductive as well as of inductive form.

[15] This distinction again bears some resemblance to von Wright's (1963, p. 177) distinction between *practical* and *theoretical* inference on the purely deductive level.

TABLE 4-12
A two-dimensional classification of inference

	Deductive inference	Inductive inference
Cognitive inference	Non-ampliative arguments excluding instrumental premises	Ampliative arguments excluding instrumental premises
Instrumental Inference	Non-ampliative arguments relating means to ends	Ampliative arguments relating means to ends

constituting a third category of inference beyond deduction and induction, but leads to a double two-dimensional classification of inference processes as represented in Table 4-12.

According to this classification scheme instrumental reasoning comprises not only imperative but also deontic arguments. The conclusions of the latter are "ought-sentences" instead of imperatives. Out of this further differences arise which will be discussed in Subsections 4.41 to 4.43.

4.41 *Imperative Inferences*

The dilemma mentioned by Ross (1944) that imperatives, as having no truth values, cannot be recognized as premises in traditional (assertoric) logic has been circumvented by the imperative modality in different ways, none of which seems to be perfectly satisfactory. A favored approach of extending traditional logic to imperative arguments is the systematic distinction between two essentially different aspects of a sentence: (1) the *sentence radical* (which reflects the subject–predicate structure of the sentence and thus is independent of the mood) and (2) the *mood-determiner* of the sentence. This may be illustrated by the following examples:

(i) "Charge the battery". (Imperative sentence).

(ii) "The battery is charged". (Assertoric or indicative sentence).

(iii) "The battery, to charge". (Sentence radical).

The three sentences (i) to (iii) all possess the same subject and predicate, but in (i) the predicate expresses an activity while in (ii) it expresses an attribute, whereas (iii) is called the *sentence radical* because the sentence presents the same subject–predicate structure in a *moodless* or neutral form. By means of such sentence radicals it is possible to analyze an imperative argument in the following way:

(iv) *Purely Imperative Argument* (no sentence has truth value).

Charge the battery or destroy it.	$p! \vee q!$
Do not destroy the battery.	$\sim q!$
∴ Charge the battery.	$\therefore p!$

(v) *Assertoric Argument* (corresponding to iv – each sentence has a truth value).

The battery is charged or it is destroyed.	$p\dagger \vee q!$
The battery is not destroyed.	$\sim q\dagger$
∴ The battery is charged.	$\therefore p\dagger$

(vi) *Argument of Sentence Radicals* (corresponding to iv and v).

The battery, to charge or to destroy.	$p \vee q$
The battery, not to destroy.	$\sim q$
∴ The battery, to charge.	$\therefore p$

The symbolic representation (see right-hand side of the arguments) here used, corresponds to sentence logic and requires the adoption of our conventional symbolism (as used in our Chapter 3 and the preceding Sections of Chapter 4) for the sentence radicals, and the introduction of the mood-symbols (or mood-determiners) ! and † for the imperative and assertoric moods respectively. The argument of *the sentence radical* is then considered to be the basic logical form on which the imperative as well as the assertoric forms are based, and from which they are derived. The dilemma of the truth values is solved by attributing corresponding *performance values* (e.g. *O* . . . for obeying and *D* . . . for disobeying the imperative) to the sentences. The *performance tables* for the sentence connectives "or", "and", and "not" are identical to the corresponding truth tables (merely T, would be substituted by *O*, and F by *D*); but difficulties arise with regard to material implication and equivalence. For the sake of illustration the performance table for the joint premises of argument (i) is represented in Table 4-13.

Since the entire argument (including the conclusion) is not an imperative, it would be incorrect to assign performance values to $(p! \vee q!) \cdot \sim q! \supset p!$ in correspondence with our previous assignment of truth to the conditional forms of Table 4-3 of Subsection 4.12.

TABLE 4-13

Performance values of simple and compound imperatives

$p!$	$q!$	$p! \vee q!$	$\sim q!$	$(p! \vee q!) \cdot \sim q!$
O	O	O	D	D
O	D	O	O	O
D	O	O	D	D
D	D	D	O	D

In contrast to the above-stated practice – which follows Clarke's (1973) presentation – Rescher (1966) in his logic of commands developed a different symbolism as well as a different technique explicitly stating the person at whom the command is directed. This author bases his system on the imperative for $[X!A/P]$ which is to be interpreted as "You X, realize A whenever P is the case." A great many different variations (action–performance versus state-realization commands, do-it-always versus do-it-now commands, one-shot conditional versus conditional standing order commands etc.) as regards time and other circumstances are derived and discussed by Rescher (1966a). He also deals with the representation of commands by "programs" (i.e. computer and similar programs) and like Clarke (1973) discusses mixed inferences which are of greater interest from our point of instrumental reasoning.

4.42 *Arguments with Mixed Premises*

We have repeatedly emphasized that instrumental reasoning rests on arguments consisting of a normative statement (e.g. an imperative) together with an instrumental hypothesis relating means to ends. While the first premise, if an imperative, is non-assertoric, the second, the instrumental hypothesis, was considered by us as a proposition with truth values derived from experience, hence assertoric. Thus it seems that such an instrumental argument is a mixed inference. But here again the opinions are divided. To explain this let us compare the following two arguments (vii) and (viii):

(vii)	Maximize function f.	$M!f$
	To maximize f, apply the differential calculus.	$M\dagger f \supset A!d$
	∴ Apply the differential calculus.	$\therefore\ A!d$
(viii)	There is a storm.	$p\dagger$
	If there is a storm, don't fly.	$p\dagger \supset q!$
	∴ Don't fly.	$\therefore\ q!$

Apart from the fact that the symbolic representation in (vii) follows from first order predicate calculus (*M* stands for "maximize", *f* for "function *f*" and *d* for "differential calculus") while that in (viii) follows the sentential calculus (*p*† stands for the sentence "there is a storm" and "*q*!" for "don't fly"), the major difference between these two arguments lies in the first premise. In argument (vii) the first premise is *imperative*, while in argument (viii) it is *assertoric* – in both cases the second premises consist of conditional hypotheses, and the conclusions of imperatives. Which of these two arguments is a mixed inference?

The answer hinges on the question whether the second premise is considered to be an assertoric or an imperative statement. Clarke would in both cases (vii and viii) regard the second premise as an imperative, and consequently could accept only (viii) as a mixed inference. In case (vii) we can hardly object since the second premise, although a conditional, is certainly not an instrumental hypothesis in our sense (the "storm" is not an end to be achieved by "flying") – apart from the fact that the first premise is assertoric. But the situation is much less straight forward in argument (vii) where the second premise seems to be precisely what we call an instrumental hypothesis. Are the following formulations not all synonymous expressions?

(α) To maximize *f*, apply the differential calculus.

(β) If *f* is to be maximized, then the differential calculus ought to be applied.

(γ) Unless the differential calculus is applied, *f* cannot be maximized.

The expressions (α) to (γ) may appear to be synonymous but, from a logical viewpoint, cannot be considered equivalent to each other. The first one (α) must be regarded as an imperative, while the second (β) is an ought-sentence (deontic sentence) which many logicians consider an indicative statement. While the third (γ) is undoubtedly assertoric. This last formulation is also a much stronger one, leaving no doubt that the application of the differential calculus is the only way to determine the maximum of function *f*, whereas (β) left open the possibility that there might be other ways to determine this maximum. Thus the relation between means and ends can be presented in different ways, and it will require further analysis to determine which of them are best suited for instrumental reasoning. This can best be done in the subsequent Subsection 4.43 which deals with deontic modalities.

Here we shall merely spell out some difficulties encountered with mixed inferences. Deductive arguments of the type of (vii) would be permissible as straight imperative arguments provided the second premise too is regarded as an imperative instead of an assertoric sentence. But (viii) is a genuine mixed argument and the question of its validity is inevitable. Difficulties arise out of the peculiar form of the conditional imperative (second premise) which assumes the general form of: $p\dagger \supset q!$. According to this an antecedent indicative sentence is supposed to imply an imperative consequent. If this is acceptable, the following truth and performance table (Table 4-14) would define the implication of a mixed conditional.

But, as Clarke (1973, pp. 198–199) points out, this precarious semantic definition would not permit nominal definitions analogous to $(p \supset q)$ = def. $\sim(p \cdot \sim q)$ or to $(p \supset q)$ = def. $\sim p \vee q$, because a conjunction $(p\dagger \cdot q!)$ or disjunction $(p\dagger \vee q!)$ of an indicative *and* an imperative sentence is difficult to envisage. Furthermore, one would have to obtain from defining the mixed material equivalence as an analogue of $(p \equiv q)$ = def. $(p \supset q) \cdot (q \supset p)$, since the second implication of the definiens would contain an imperative antecedent $(q! \supset p\dagger)$, which according to Clarke (1973, p. 198) is never permissible, since no imperative can be an antecedent of an indicative consequent (only the reverse is possible). One would have to define the mixed material equivalence as follows: $(p\dagger \equiv q!)$ = def. $\sim(p \cdot \sim q!)$.

In spite of such weaknesses one does operate with mixed inferences on the basis of the principle of radicals and the definition offered in Table 4-14, and even applies quantifiers to such inferences, provided the important *principle of mood constancy* ("The constituent elements of an inference must be in the same mood for every occurrence") is obeyed.

TABLE 4-14

Truth and performance values defining the material implication of a mixed conditional

$p\dagger$	$q!$	$p\dagger \supset q!$
T	*O*	*O*
T	*D*	*D*
F	*O*	*O*
F	*D*	*O*

4.43 *Deontic Inferences*

The normative premise of an instrumental argument can be formulated either as an imperative or as a deontic sentence, (i.e. in form of an ought-sentence). The instrumental hypothesis too will then assume a deontic form and so will the conclusion (see Table 4-15).

To the non-logician these two forms seem to be equivalent, and from a grammatical point of view the sentence "you ought to . . . " often enough is regarded as an imperative. But from a logical point of view this is hardly acceptable. Indeed the major school of thought (represented by von Wright, Rescher and others) *regards ought-sentences not at all as expressing prescriptions but as being in the indicative mood* representing a proposition with truth values. The argument in favor of such a treatment is based on the view that a deontic sentence is true if the addressee is indeed under obligation (moral, legal, etc.) to obey this sentence, otherwise it is false. Thus the institutional setting, justifying this obligation, and Searle's (1964) distinction between ordinary and institutional facts (mentioned in Section 2.7) may again become relevant in this connection. But the fact that ought-sentences are now regarded as indicative or descriptive and not, or not only, as prescriptive does not all-together erase the distinction between "is-sentences" and "ought-sentences". The deontic mode still requires an expanded basis, and the question arises as to the supplementary axioms necessary for expanding traditional logic into deontic logic. However, before we concern ourselves with this problem, we should investigate why there should exist a fundamental difference between an imperative and its corresponding deontic sentence.

A comparison of the following imperative and deontic sentences (see Table 4-16) illustrates the surprising fact, first revealed by Ross (1944), that *the imperative has only one negation* while *the deontic sentence has two possible negations* each conveying a very different meaning.

Sentence 1 (of Table 4-16) states the imperative and its negation 1a, sentence 2 states the deontic sentence (with a meaning similar to

TABLE 4-15

The two modalities of an instrumental argument

Imperative modality	Deontic modality
Fire the missile. To fire the missile push the red button.	You ought to fire the missile. To fire the missile you ought to push to red button.
∴ Push the red button.	∴ You ought to push to red button.

TABLE 4-16

Sentence	Negation
1. Fire the missile.	1a. Do not fire the missile.
2. You ought to fire the missile.	2a. "You ought to fire the missile" is not valid.
	2b. You ought not to fire the missile.
3. It is your duty to fire the missile	3a. It is *not your duty* to fire the missile.
	3b. It is your duty *not to fire* the missile.

sentence 1) and its negation 2a, the meaning of which is very different from sentence 1a, while the negation 2b again comes close to sentence 1a. In order to recognize better the difference between 2a and 2b, we have listed the sentences 3, 3a and 3b which constitute nothing but a more explicit expression of the sentences 2, 2a and 2b. Obviously the sentences 1, 2b and 3b express the desideratum that "you should *not fire* the missile" *while the sentences* 2a and 3a express the fact that "the firing of the missile does not fall under your obligation". But if two similar sentences have different negations they must possess a fundamental difference. Since scholars are inclined to interpret deontic sentences as disguised sentences of a meta-language, (similar to modal sentences – see Subsection 4.32), it is understandable that sentence 2a is taken to be the more correct or official negation of 2.

Such a meta-linguistic interpretation of deontic logic permits the introduction of the *deontic operators O* (for "it is obligatory . . . ") and *P* (for "it is permissible . . . ") already encountered in Table 4-10, and corresponding to the alethic modal operators *M* ("it is possible . . . ") and *N* ("it is necessary . . . "). In the system presented by Clarke (1973) a sentence like "You ought to fire the missile" is taken as equivalent to " 'Fire the missile' is obligatory" or symbolically $Op!$ rather than $Op\dagger$ (since one does not say " 'The missile is fired' is obligatory"). Based on such linguistic usages one would have to accept the following deontic definitions and formulas:

1. $O(p\dagger \supset q!) = \text{def.}\, p\dagger \supset Oq!$
2. $P(p\dagger \supset q!) = \text{def.}\, p\dagger \supset Pq!$
3. $O(p\dagger \equiv q!) \Leftrightarrow p\dagger \equiv Oq!$
4. $P(p\dagger \equiv q!) \Leftrightarrow p\dagger \equiv Pq!$
5. $O(p!q!) \Leftrightarrow Op! \cdot Oq!$

6. $P(p! \cdot q!) \Leftrightarrow Pp! \cdot Pq!$

7. $(Op! \vee Oq!) \Leftrightarrow O(p! \cdot q!)$.

Von Wright (1968) begins with a different deontic system in which the deontic operators *O* and *P* are applied to indicative sentences representing states of affairs only (and not at all to imperatives) (Table 4-17). Thus *Op* stands for "It is obligatory that (it is the case that) *p*". But as this system does not sufficiently integrate the "states of affairs" with the contents of norms to be dealt with, he develops an expanded *deontic logic of actions* (with the *T–I*-calculus). The axioms of this systems consist of those of the traditional predicate calculus and the following axioms using two newly introduced binary connectives *T* (for "and is next") and *I* (for "and was before"). Thus *pTq* says: "the state of affairs is now *p* and *is next q*." Analogously *qIp* says: "the state of affairs is now *q* and *was before p*."

A third system, probably best suited for instrumental reasoning, was presented by Rescher (1969) and operates with the important notion of *task thesis*[16] $T(X: p)$ to be read as: "One thing for *X* to do is to make it true that *p*."

Rescher (1969) admits that "the familiar criterion on validity of assertoric logic – that an argument is valid when it is the case that *if* its premises are true, then its conclusions must (given these premises) also necessarily be true – is not directly applicable to arguments containing task theses, since

TABLE 4-17

Von Wright's (1968) *T–I*-calculus for a deontic logic of action (axioms and definition supplementary to those of the predicate calculus)

$A_T1.$	$(p \vee qTr \vee s) \equiv (pTr) \vee (pTs) \vee (qTr) \vee (qTs)$.
$A_T2.$	$(pTq) \cdot (pTr) \supset (pTq \cdot r)$.
$A_T3.$	$p \equiv (pTq \vee \sim q)$.
$A_T4.$	$\sim (pTq \cdot \sim q)$.
$A_I1.$	$(p \vee qIr \vee s) \equiv (pIr) \vee (pIs) \vee (qIr) \vee (qIs)$.
$A_I2.$	$(pIq) \cdot (pIr) \supset (pIq \cdot r)$.
$A_I3.$	$p \equiv (pIq \vee \sim q)$.
$A_I4.$	$\sim (pIq \cdot \sim q)$.
$A_D1.$	$P(p \vee q) \equiv Pp \vee Pq$.
$A_D2.$	$Pp \vee P \sim p$.
$D_m.$	$Op = \text{def.} \sim P \sim p$.

[16] Rescher's operator *T* must not be confused with von Wright's binary connective *T*, possessing an entirely different meaning. See Rescher (1969, p. 30 ff).

task theses cannot be characterized as "true" or "false" in any direct and unproblematic way" (pp. 38–39). Since *task theses*[17] *are deontic sentences*, and not imperatives, the preceding quote by Rescher seems to stand in opposition to the presentations by von Wright, Clarke and others who have little hesitation to assign truth values to deontic sentences. On the other hand Rescher (1969) asserts that "no sharp line of separation can be drawn between statements of value and statements of facts: value theses are always shot through with factual considerations. Value theses are not matters of taste, but are either well founded or ill founded, either right or wrong" (p. 10). Thus we may conclude that due to Rescher's factual interpretation of value judgements he may ultimately, though hesitatingly, be prepared to assign truth values to task theses. Nevertheless he recognizes the difficulties that arise in arguments that mix traditional assertoric premises with task theses (Table 4.18).

While Rescher has no hesitation to accept the inference patterns presented in arguments 1 and 2 (of our Table 4-18), he points out that the principles under which the inferences in arguments 3 to 5 (of Table 4-18) are made "are not unqualifiedly valid." Only if "$p \supset q$" is interpreted in an *action–performing* sense to mean "to make true that p also requires making it true that q" might the inference patterns represented by 3 to 5 (of Table 4-18) be acceptable. But the following example demonstrates that even then pitfalls can arise from an inappropriate application of such a deontic inference. Since the existence of Japanese is an established fact, and certainly is beyond the control of a single person, the following inference cannot be accepted as valid:

X is to make it true that this book is translated into Japanese.	$T(X{:}p)$
If X makes it true that this book is translated into Japanese, then by necessity the Japanese language exists.	$p \supset q$
∴ X is to make it true that the Japanese language exists.	$\therefore\ T(X{:}q)$

From the above outline on imperative and deontic arguments one may recognize that the pertinent logical situation is much more complex than it appears to be at a first glance. A closely related problem concerns the

[17] Rescher's (1969) deontic logic operating with tasks theses must not be confused with Rescher's (1966) imperative logic of commands.

TABLE 4-18

(1)	*X* is to buy merchandise. If *X* is to buy merchandise, then *X* has to procure the funds.	$T(X{:}p)$ $T(X{:}p) \supset T(X{:}q)$
	∴ *X* has to procure the funds	∴ $T(X{:}q)$
(2)	*X* is to buy merchandise. If *X* has not to procure the funds, then *X* is not to buy merchandise.	$T(X{:}p)$ $\sim T(X{:}q) \supset \sim T(X{:}p)$
	∴ *X* has to procure the funds.	∴ $T(X{:}q)$
(3)	*X* is to buy merchandise. If merchandise is bought then the funds are procured.	$T(X{:}p)$ $p \supset q$
	∴ *X* has to procure the funds.	∴ $T(X{:}q)$
(4)	*X* is to buy merchandise. If the funds are not procured then merchandise is not bought.	$T(X{:}p)$ $\sim q \supset \sim p$
	∴ *X* has to procure the funds.	∴ $T(X{:}q)$
(5)	*X* is not to buy merchandise. If the merchandise is bought then the funds are procured.	$T(X{:}\sim p)$ $p \supset q$
	∴ *X* has not to procure the funds.	∴ $T(X{:}\sim q)$

supposed derivation of prescriptive sentences from descriptive-causal sentences. Several German text books of business administration, for example, assert that *means–ends relations* can be attained through simple *tautological transformations* from *cause-and-effect relations.* That this assertion is incorrect was demonstrated by D. J. G. Schneider (1976, 1977). He showed that – due to the possible non-fulfilment of the norm – such a transformation is neither possible

(1) *as a definitional translation within one language system,* nor

(2) *as a translation from one language system into another language system* (both in the object language), nor

(3) *as a translation from an object language into its metalanguage*, and not even

(4) through the *additional introduction of a normative statement* (non tautological transformation).

If Schneider's results hold, then the chances of deriving "ought" from "is" on the linguistic level are slim indeed. Exceptions might be the cases of the so-called *institutional facts* (see Section 2.7); but there one deals already with institutions hence with structural systems and no longer with mere sentential configurations. We may therefore presume that if there is any hope at all for connecting normative with positive aspects, the realm of systems might be more amenable to such a task than any linguistic realm.

CHAPTER 5

THE CONTROVERSY AROUND INDUCTIVE LOGIC

> These two propositions are far from being the same *"I have found that such an object has always been attended with such an effect"* and *"I forsee, that other objects, which are, in appearance, similar, will be attended with similar effects,"* I shall allow, if you please, that the one proposition may justly be inferred from the other. But if you insist that the inference is made by a chain of reasoning, I desire you to produce that reasoning. The connection between these propositions is not intuitive. There is required a medium, which may enable the mind to draw such an inference, if indeed it be drawn by reasoning and argument. What the medium is, I must confess, passes my comprehension; and it is incumbent on those to produce it, who assert that it really exists, and is the origin of all our conclusions concerning matter of fact.[1]

The above-stated quote from Hume might well be considered the most important and crucial passage in the literature of science of knowledge. Whether it reflects the most enlightened vision or a misunderstanding, is still a matter of dispute, but it summarizes succinctly a major aspect of the problem of induction thus far unsolved. A firm grasp of this passage is prerequisite for understanding the endeavors of inductive logic: its failures, its achievements, its promises and its limits. Since ultimately "logic is concerned with the real world just as truly as zoology, though with its more abstract and general features",[2] no empirical discipline can escape either this profound dilemma or the various attempts to overcome it. None of the numerous endeavors to find "a medium . . . which may enable the mind to draw such an inference", has led to an ultimate and generally accepted *justification* of inductive reasoning. Whether the inductive medium can be found in an "independent logical principle, incapable of being inferred either from experience or from other logical principles", as Russell believed,[3] or by concentrating on the process of

[1] David Hume, *An Enquiry Concerning Human Understanding*, 1748, Section IV.

[2] Russell, *Introduction to Mathematical Philosophy*, 1920, p. 169.

[3] "Hume's scepticism rests entirely upon his rejection of the principle of induction. The principle of induction, as applied to causation, says that, if A has been found very often accompanied or followed by B, and no instance is known of A not being accompanied or

refutation proposed by Popper, or through a systematic and purely *logical* development of induction, as Carnap suggested, or by relying on subjective judgements as Ramsey, Savage and many management scientists believe, or by any other means, is still unresolved. In contrast to the well founded deductive logic, each solution proposed for inductive logic is accompanied by strong arguments on both sides, arguments favoring as well as opposing it. Thus, to choose one or the other solution, the reader will have to rely on his own judgement. But his decision should be made hesitatingly, on a provisional basis only, and not before having carefully examined other positions.

This controversy generated a host of exciting ideas and still exercises great stimulus upon the applied sciences no less than on any others. The empirical scientist who fails to acquaint himself with these ideas, who bypasses major insights gained in this weary search, resembles a sleepwalker unaware of the precipice crossing his path. The benefits to be gained from studying the puzzle of induction may go beyond sharpening one's mind, they will help in recognizing the boundaries set to the scientific approach, perhaps narrowing the apparent gap between pure and applied sciences.

Inductive logic is essentially the logic of uncertainty – that same uncertainty that lately has indelibly impressed itself upon the social and management sciences, leading to the center of decision theory. This created a growing realization that only by probing at the logical and epistemological roots of their

---

followed by *B*, then it is probable that on the next occasion on which *A* is observed it will be accompanied or followed by *B*. If the principle is to be adequate, a sufficient number of instances must make the probability not far short of certainty. If this principle, or any other from which it can be deduced, is true, then the causal inferences which Hume rejects are valid, not indeed as giving certainty, but as giving a sufficient probability for practical purposes. If this principle is not true, every attempt to arrive at general scientific laws from particular observations is fallacious, and Hume's scepticism is inescapable for an empiricist. The principle itself cannot, of course, without circularity, be inferred from observed uniformities, since it is required to justify any such inference. It must therefore be, or be deduced from, an independent principle not based upon experience. To this extent, Hume has proved that pure empiricism is not a sufficient basis for science. But if this one principle is admitted, everything else can proceed in accordance with the theory that all our knowledge is based on experience. It must be granted that this is a serious departure from pure empiricism, and that those who are not empiricists may ask why, if one departure is allowed, others are to be forbidden. These, however, are questions not directly raised by Hume's arguments. What these arguments prove – and I do not think the proof can be controverted – is that induction is an independent logical principle, incapable of being inferred either from experience or from other logical principles, and that without this principle science is impossible." Russell, *A History of Western Philosophy*, 1945, pp. 673–674. Copyright © 1945, 1972 by Bertrand Russell.

disciplines, can administrative scientists bring order, stability, and coherence to their work. Yet inductive logic is still in turmoil and beset by conflict. Whether or not it will be able to answer the call may depend no less on the new generation of administrative and management scientists than on professional logicians.

5.1 Essence and Early Evolution of Induction

At the beginning of the preceding chapter a *deductive argument* was shown as consisting of a series of propositions, called premises, from which one or more further propositions *follow by logical necessity* as conclusions. An *inductive argument* too consists of a series of propositions (sometimes a great many of them), regarded as premises, and one or more further proposition(s), regarded as conclusions, but the former do *not necessitate*, but merely *support* the latter.[4] The following inductive arguments will illustrate this:

All top administrators are vigorous personalities. All top administrators have a good memory. All top administrators can handle people well. Mr. *A*, 30 years old, a vigorous personality with good memory, is not a top administrator, and can handle people well.	} Evidence or premises
Mr. *A* will become a top administrator.[5]	} Hypothesis or conclusion

Provided the premises (*evidence*) are correct, what *confidence* do we have in this argument and its conclusion (*hypothesis*)? Even if the premises are correct, there may still be considerable doubt whether Mr. *A* will become a top administrator, but we can hardly deny that the previous argument seems to be *stronger* than the following one:

[4] *Induction* is a non-demonstrative inference leading to a conclusion referring to some or all members of a class, based on some evidence of these members. This kind of *logical* (or incomplete) induction must by no means be confused with mathematical (or complete) induction nor with *electric* induction, neither of which is the subject of this chapter.

[5] This example may disprove the erroneous belief that inductive inference *must* proceed from the particular to the general, (just as it is false to think a deductive argument *must* proceed from the general to the particular). The reader will notice that the first three premises above are indeed universal propositions and the conclusion is a particular one.

All top administrators are vigorous personalities.

All top administrators have a good memory.

All top administrators can handle people well.

Mr. *A*, 30 years old, having a vigorous personality and a good memory, can handle people well and is not a top administrator.

Mr. *A* is a successful artist who dislikes administrative responsibilities.

Mr. *A* will become a top administrator.

Although the second argument contains all the premises of the first, and has merely been enriched by one further premise (Mr. *A* is a successful artist who dislikes administrative responsibilities), and although the conclusion is precisely the same, the strength of the argument and confidence in the hypothesis is weaker. From this we may draw several lessons:

(1) A change in the premises (evidence) creates a different argument.

(2) One and the same hypothesis may rest on different evidences.

(3) The *confidence* we have in a hypothesis is *dependent on the evidence* with which it is associated, hence it cannot be asserted independently from the strength of the entire inductive argument (evidence plus hypothesis). By adding certain statements it is even possible to convert the inductive argument into a deductive one (see footnote 7).

(4) We do not yet know whether the strength of the argument is an objective and logical relationship (degree of *confirmation*) or whether it is merely psychological and a subjective matter (degree of *confidence*, personal or actual belief etc.).[6]

(5) If the strength of an inductive argument is a relationship of logic then, like the deductive argument, the inductive one is a conditional statement (*If* all administrators . . . , *then* Mr. *A* . . .) and its strength does not depend on the truth of the premises (but the *actual* belief of a specific person in this hypothesis would depend on the truth of the premises). Even if the "strength" is a logical relationship, we do not know whether it will be possible to measure it generally on a ratio-scale, that is whether it can be expressed in terms of measurable objective probabilities.

[6] We should like to adhere throughout the book to this *inductive agnosticism* which seems to be justified in the face of the unresolved controversy between logical positivists and subjectivists (see Subsection 5.24, 5.32 and 5.33).

To the above examples of *non-statistical* inference let us add one of *statistical* inference:

Assume an urn containing an unknown number of balls some of which are red. Assume further that after a series of draws from the urn it is noticed that, thus far, each red ball consists of metal. Does this observation entitle us to conclude that the *unobserved* red balls still contained in the urn *all* consist of metal? Are we justified in saying that every additional draw of a red metal ball from this urn strengthens our belief, thus yielding a *stronger* argument and conclusion? Can we *measure* the strength of these various beliefs and arguments at various stages of draws? Would the measure be influenced by the knowledge of the number of red balls in the urn, would it be different for a finite than an infinite set of balls? Is this belief a purely personal matter or is there something like an objective or *rational* belief independent of subjective judgements? Although this example depicts a highly simplified situation compared with the induction of scientific *laws*, it does illustrate the essence of the general problem of induction and raises many, though not all, of its fundamental questions.

The method of *enumerative* induction[7] is the most primitive inductive approach; it goes back at least 350 years and probably much farther.[8] By

[7] Induction by *simple enumeration* would "enumerate" the individual evidences as follows:

1. The first red ball is of metal
2. The second red ball is of metal
....
n. The *n*th red ball is of metal

Hypotheses: All red balls are of metal.

It is interesting to note that any *inductive* argument can be converted into a *deductive* argument by appropriate additional premises, e.g. in the above instance by adding the statement: "Balls of the same color are of the same material."

[8] G. H. von Wright asserts that it was Aristotle who made the first attempt of a systematic treatment of induction, and summarizes Aristotle's contributions as follows:

(i) Aristotle was the first to point out the non-demonstrative character of the type of inference which we treat under the name of induction, and to contrast it with conclusive reasoning. The contrast, however, was obscured by his own terminology which has become established in traditional logic.

(ii) Aristotle was aware of the double aspect of inductive method as a process of inference and as a process of definition (formation of concepts). *A Treatise on Induction and Probability*, 1951, pp. 151–152.

Yet Aristotle in his *Topics* describes induction as "a passage from particulars to universals" which, as our first examples illustrate, need not be the case.

subjecting it to criticism, by pioneering in the logical systematization of the inductive procedure and by introducing the somewhat superior method of *induction by elimination*, Francis Bacon[9] became the founder of modern inductive logic. Within a few decades another event occurred that, in the long-run, proved of decisive influence for the analysis of the inductive process: the emergence of a *mathematical theory of probability*. Pascal and Fermat, incited by gambling problems posed to them by Chevalier de Mere, demonstrated that by means of the theory of permutations and combinations the *probability* of winning a game of chance *can be calculated*. But the calculus of probability (further developed by Christian Huygens, Jacob and Daniel Bernoulli, Montmort, De Moivre, Thomas Bayes and above all Pierre S. de Laplace) for the time being, went its own independent path. David Hume's scepticism, so aptly expostulated in the first volume (Part IV) of his "still-born" *Treatise of Human Nature* (1738) and his *Enquiry Concerning Human Understanding* (1748), more popular among his contemporaries, became another major milestone in the history of induction. Next, one might think of Immanuel Kant's *Kritik der reinen Vernunft* (1781) which was considered by many scholars of the nineteenth century to be the major refutation of Hume's sceptical attitude toward induction and causation. But meanwhile Kant's major weapon, the belief in the existence of *a priori synthetic* propositions (*factual* statements about space, causation etc., which are not derived from experience but given *prior* to *all* experience), has been so strongly undermined that many twentieth-century scholars lost faith in this kind of refutation. Then John Stuart Mill's *System of Logic* (1843) became a further milestone in the history of this philosophic area. Mill held that the assumption "the course of nature is uniform" is the warrant for all

[9] In his *Novum Organum* (1620) he points out that "the induction which is to be available for the discovery and demonstration of sciences and arts, must analyze nature by proper *rejection and exclusions*; and then after a sufficient number of negatives, come to a conclusion on the affirmative instances" (our italics). Depending on which aspects of F. Bacon's work one concentrates, it may be praised or criticised. Russell asserts (1) that F. Bacon "missed most of what was being done in science in his day . . . (and) . . . rejected the Copernican theory" and (2) that his "inductive method is faulty through insufficient emphasis on hypothesis . . . [hoping] . . . that mere orderly arrangement of data would make the right hypothesis obvious", *History of Western Philosophy* (p. 544), whereas G. H. von Wright emphasizes that "it is the immortal merit of Bacon to have fully appreciated the importance of . . . asymmetry in the logical structure of laws" (*op. cit.*, p. 152), namely that these laws are *not verifiable* but merely *falsifiable*, thus anticipating the core of Popper's dogma by more than three centuries. Although Popper discusses Bacon's work on induction at many places, we are not certain whether he would agree to such a strong assertion.

inductive inferences and the major axiom of the logic of induction. But this is neither a self-evident assumption nor can it be proved by anything but induction. Yet if induction is justified by induction, then some circular reasoning seems to be involved which at best leads to an infinite regress. But Mill's canons or methods of inductive inference proved to be of some practical consequence and their modern versions will be discussed in Subsection 5.23.

5.2 Modern Views on Induction

In the twentieth century the interest in inductive logic was reborn with *A Treatise on Probability* (1921) by John Maynard Keynes. A highly productive period of intense concern for and dispute about the probability concept and its implications on induction ensued.[10] But during the years of the second World War this concern ebbed away, and as late as 1951 G. H. von Wright could assert that "considering the importance of the subject, the number of books which deal with induction is extraordinarily small."[11] Meanwhile this situation has changed drastically. The last decades brought forth an abundance of profound and subtle studies in this area. The recent work on *Probability and Inductive Logic* by Henry E. Kyburg (1970) lists a bibliography of almost *twelve hundred* publications. It is remarkable that most of them appeared during the Fifties and Sixties, and that Kyburg admittedly included only publications that seemed to him "of greatest philosophic interest," excluding the many technical or purely mathematical papers. The vastness of this literature allows nothing more than outlining in broad strokes the major views and issues involved.

5.21 *Hume and the Sceptics*

Hume deemed it impossible to justify the process of induction on grounds of logic. He showed (1) that *demonstrative* (e.g. deductive) arguments cannot justify induction, since demonstrative reasoning is not ampliative (does not

[10] To mention the most important names and publications we draw attention to: Ramsey, 'Truth and Probability', 1926 and 'Further Considerations', 1928, both contained in his collection *The Foundations of Mathematics*, Kegan Paul, Trench, Trubner & Co., London, 1931, pp. 156–211. Richard von Mises, *Probability, Statistics and Truth*, in German 1928; English translation, 1957. Reichenbach, *The Theory of Probability*, in German 1934; English translation, 1949 Jeffreys, *Theory of Probability*, 1939.

[11] *A Treatise on Induction and Probability*, 1951, p. 11.

extend beyond what is already known) whereas induction is ampliative (claims to create *new* knowledge), and (2) that justifying induction by non-demonstrative arguments (e.g. by induction itself) constitutes ***circular*** reasoning. Several recent attempts to justify induction inductively,[12] failed to convince the profession in general. Hume asserts rather that out of sheer "force of habit" we are associating certain pairs of events with each other, thus conceding merely a psychological explanation of inductive behavior.[13] If he could have anticipated Ivan Pavlov's famous experiments with conditioned reflexes,[14] he would most likely have admitted that the inductive behavior of Pavlov's dog, just as that of any other animal and man, can be traced to associations based on inborn as well as learned reflexes. A great number of scholars adhere to this view, including Wittgenstein who said "this process, however, has no logical justification but only a psychological one."[15]

Nevertheless, many of Hume's epigones attempted to explain the phenomenon of induction on purely logical grounds; a search that still goes on. Almost as many, however, believe that this problem is misconceived. By asserting that, in contrast to deduction, inductive arguments cannot lead to "valid" inferences and true conclusions, Hume tried to press induction into the Procrustean bed of deduction, something that obviously would not work. Thus, it is claimed, Hume created nothing but a linguistic confusion, a pseudo-problem, asserting nothing beyond the triviality that induction is not deduction. Hence, the occasionally encountered call for dissolution, instead of solution, of this problem. Nevertheless, many would disagree with this view. Barker's words, and his hint toward an applied science, are characteristic for rejecting the negation of Hume's problem:

> No doubt it is a psychological fact that we in our culture do happen to pay more attention to scientists than to gypsies; but that is not all there is to it. There is a further important fact: we are ***right*** to do so, for scientific

[12] E. g. see Black, *Problems of Analysis*, 1954, Chapter 11, and Braithwaite, *Scientific Explanation*, 1953.

[13] Karl Popper, although agreeing with Hume's rejection of logical justification, disagrees with Hume's formulation of the "psychological justification." See Popper's *Conjectures and Refutations*, 1962, pp. 42–46.

[14] *Unconditioned* reflex: the salivation of a hungry dog when shown food. *Conditioned* reflex: the salivation of a dog when a bell is rung after the dog has been conditioned by previously ringing a bell every time when food was presented to him.

[15] Ludwig von Wittgenstein, *Tractatus Logico-Philosophicus*, 1961, first ed., 1922, item 6.3631, p. 142.

> methods somehow are more logical, more rational, than are gypsy methods (crystal gazing). Only someone who was thoroughly disingenuous (or perhaps thoroughly confused) would actually go about advocating the hiring of engineers rather than of gypsies yet at the same time maintaining that no method of appraising hypotheses is any more reasonable than any other. To advocate a thorough skepticism here, to maintain that all methods of appraising hypotheses are equally irrational, would be to embrace a stultifying philosophy.[16]

With this argument the problem of induction is gently led in a new direction. No longer is it crucial whether extrapolation into the future is justifiable; ultimately the following methodological question might turn out to be a more meaningful one: "Which among several inductive approaches is the one to be justified?" If this question can ever be answered, then familiarity with various suggestions and approaches will be a prerequisite. Most recently philosophers and scientists, especially K. Lorenz (1973, p. 135), pointed out that the *principles of causality and induction* as well as those of *deductive logic*, equally, exist prior to any experience within the genetic and mental apparatus of individual creatures, yet not by *a priori*, i.e. analytical necessity, merely through the evolutionary process of phylogenesis. Because creatures obeying those principles in a relatively consistent fashion seem to have in the long-run a better chance of survival and propagation than creatures who possess a less developed urge to follow those norms. This, of course, raises two questions: Why do just those principles have a survival value? And is the fact that they do, perhaps an indication of a kind of inevitability tantamount to *a priori* necessity?

5.22 *The Hypothetico-Deductive Approach and Popper's Falsificationism*

The dilemma of induction has led to several attempts of justifying the choice or the confirmation of a certain hypothesis by somehow reducing induction (non-demonstrative reasoning) to deduction (demonstrative reasoning). This way of justification spans a fairly wide spectrum of variations and is usually known as the hypothetico-deductive model or approach. As Brody says:

> This model for the confirmation of scientific hypothesis is clearly preferable to the simpler model of *induction by enumeration*. According to this latter model, hypotheses of the form "All *A*'s are *B*'s" are accep-

[16] Barker, *Induction and Hypothesis*, 1957, pp. 12–13.

table when one has examined a sufficient number of *A*'s and seen that they are all *B*'s. The trouble with this simpler model is that it is only applicable to hypotheses of a particular form which are such that one can determine by observation whether or not objects have properties *A* and *B*. The hypothetico-deductive model, on the other hand, seems applicable to all hypotheses. For this reason, most contemporary philosophers of science have adopted some version of the hypothetico-deductive model of confirmation, and recent work in the theory of confirmation has been devoted to an elaboration and formalization of this intuitive model.[17]

It proceeds by inverting the premise with its hypothesis and thus converting an inductive into a deductive argument.

	Inductive	*Deductive*
Premise:	(*e*) All balls *drawn from* this urn are red.	(*h*) All balls *in* this urn are red.
Conclusion:	∴ (*h*) All balls *in* this urn are red.	∴ (*e*) All balls *drawn from* this urn are red.

In an ordinary inductive argument the premise consists of the empirical evidence (*e*), while the conclusion consists of the conjectured hypothesis (*h*). But if the hypothesis is used as the premise and the evidence as the conclusion, then the argument becomes deductive (as seen in the above illustration), because if "all balls *in* this urn are red" then by necessity "all the balls *drawn from* this urn are red". The idea behind this magic is very similar to the conversion of an inductive argument into a deductive one by adding a further premise – as demonstrated in footnote 7 of this Section. Whereas inductive inference is concerned with the creation of the hypothesis *h* and therefore has to concentrate on the *ex-ante* relationship between *e* and *h*, the *hypothetico-deductive method* disparages the importance of inductive inference and tries to avoid it. by concentrating on the *ex-post* relationship between *h* and *e*. In this case one merely *deduces* from *h* an observable consequence *e* of the hypothesis. After running the appropriate experiment, either *h* has withstood the test or not. If it has, one might regard *e* as confirming the hypothesis *h* or, at least, a failure to refute it, and will provisionally accept *h* until a refutation occurs.

But the hypothetico-deductive method reaches from John Dewey, whom Kyburg regards as one of its earliest defenders, through Cohen and Nagel,

[17] Brody, *Readings in the Philosophy of Science*, 1970, 'Introduction to Part 3', p. 376.

Barker, Wisdom, von Wright, (some even include Carnap and Kemeny) above all to Popper. Thus, this general method overlaps with many divergent views and is not well suited for the purpose of juxtaposing those views. Therefore we shall discuss in this subsection mainly the most extreme proponent of this version of the hypothetico-deductive approach: Karl Popper and his *falsificationism*.

According to Popper it is not the *confirmation* but the *falsification* of a hypothesis which is crucial for a sound application of the scientific method. He correctly claims that no hypothesis, law or theory can ever be verified or confirmed, hence their acceptance cannot depend on confirmation but merely on the failure to refute them. Thus he suggests to test a hypothesis (1) by applying to it deductive logic in order to infer singular observation statements open to refutation, and (2) by subjecting those observation statements to attempts of refutation. For him it makes little difference how a hypothesis comes into being, the important thing is that, at least in principle, it is refutable. Only then would he admit it as an empirical statement. He definitely prefers *bold conjectures* to self-evident and commonplace hypotheses, because the former are more *risqué* and hence, if unrefuted, have greater empirical content than a hypothesis that is so obvious that it has little chance to be refuted. Einstein's relativity theory when first announced was startling, its conclusion incredible. It thus constitutes an example *par excellence* of Popper's bold conjectures, whereas a statement like "the sun will rise tomorrow", although an empirical hypothesis, is far too much a matter of course to be scientifically significant. Or the statement "The Earth orbit is an ellipse" is less falsifiable (i.e. has a lesser degree of corroboration) than the statement: "The orbits of all solar planets are ellipses". The less likely a statement, the higher its degree of corroboration and the more significant its factual import, provided it remains unrefuted in spite of all possible tests (i.e. attempts of falsification).

Popper arrived at these ideas and the logical *asymmetry* of testing hypotheses (by refutation versus verification) in the winter of 1919–20[18] and summarizes his conclusions as follows:

(1) It is easy to obtain confirmations, or verifications, for nearly every theory – if we look for confirmations.

[18] Since this time Popper has vastly elaborated upon his system, but his *magnum opus* remains his *Logik der Forschung*, 1934, and its English version *The Logic of Scientific Discovery*, 1959.

(2) Confirmations should count only if they are the result of *risky predictions*; that is to say, if, unenlightened by the theory in question, we should have expected an event which was incompatible with the theory – an event which would have refuted the theory.

(3) Every "good" scientific theory is a prohibition: it forbids certain things to happen. The more a theory forbids, the better it is.

(4) A theory which is not refutable by any conceivable event is non-scientific. Irrefutability is not a virtue of a theory (as people often think) but a vice.

(5) Every genuine *test* of a theory is an attempt to falsify it, or to refute it. Testability is falsifiability; but there are degrees of testability: some theories are more testable, more exposed to refutation than others; they take, as it were, greater risks.

(6) Confirming evidence should not count *except when it is the result of a genuine test of the theory*; and this means that it can be presented as a serious but unsuccessful attempt to falsify the theory. (I now speak in such cases of "corroborating evidence".)

(7) Some genuinely testable theories, when found to be false, are still upheld by their admirers – for example by introducing *ad hoc* some auxiliary assumptions, or by re-interpreting the theory *ad hoc* in such a way that it escapes refutation. Such a procedure is always possible, but it rescues the theory from refutation only at the price of destroying, or at least lowering, its scientific status.[19]

Thus Popper exploits the feature of boldness or riskiness, in choosing between two or more competing hypotheses. Provided all of them are unrefuted he would choose the hypothesis with the greatest risk of possible refutation, or in his formal terminology, the hypothesis with the highest *degree of corroboration*. This concept he confronts with Carnap's *degree of confirmation* and emphasizes that in contrast to Carnap (or Carnap's precursors, Keynes and Jeffreys) he would not recommend the hypothesis best confirmed or *most* probable, but the one least confirmed or *least* probable.

[19] Popper, *Conjectures and Refutations*, 1962; quotations from Basic Books edition, 1962, pp. 36–37. Originally presented under 'Philosophy of Science: a Personal Report', in *British Philosophy in the Mid-Century*, ed. C. A. Mace, 1957.

But apart from the fact that in this connection a distinction between *a priori* and *a posteriori* probability might have to be made,[20] Kyburg points out that: "Indeed the most interesting thing about this entire conflict is that neither Barker, Popper, Jeffreys, nor any other inductive logician or analyst of scientific procedure would have any difficulty at all in deciding what hypothesis to accept in an ordinary experimental situation. This suggests that the very hypothesis 'most probable' for Jeffreys is precisely that which is 'least probable' for Popper."[21]

Kyburg even demonstrates, through tabular juxtaposition,[22] that the probability measures for ranking hypotheses as applied by Carnap, Rescher, Popper, Finch, Kemeny–Oppenheim, and Levi, in spite of the polemics carried out between these authors, are similar and based on the "same criteria" for "acceptance" (or serious consideration) of a scientific hypothesis.

Further objections to Popper's approach are:

(1) The degrees of corroboration of competing hypotheses are difficult to determine, occasionally defective in ranking hypotheses and frequently not comparable at all. (But similar arguments could be made against Carnap's degree of confirmation.)

(2) Popper's criterion of acceptance seems to allow the acceptance of non-empirical hypotheses. To this Barker offers the following illustration:

> More concretely: If "All swans are white" is a falsifiable statement, then "All swans are white, and the World Spirit informs all activity" must be just as falsifiable a statement, since any observational statement which contradicts the former must contradict the latter also; hence whatever the evidence may be, the latter statement can be no less well confirmed than the former.[23]

(3) Popper's theory is concerned neither with the process nor with the logic of scientific discovery. It deals rather with a later phase, namely with the testing, refutation and perhaps revising of theories. Therefore it is difficult to accept the claim that it proves induction to be superfluous. Parabolically, Popper is so much concerned with tasting the cake, that he forgets the baking. It is usually a combination of observation and decision processes, against a background of existing theories and rules, which trigger the creating

[20] Cf. Harsanyi, 'Popper's Improbability Criterion for the Choice of Scientific Hypotheses', 1960–61, pp. 41–56.

[21] Kyburg, *Probability and Inductive Logic*, 1970, p. 157.

[22] *ibid*. p. 161.

[23] Barker, *idem*., p. 159.

of new hypotheses. Ignoring these processes may constitute the cardinal sin of the Popperian approach.

(4) Wellmer[24] regards Popper's theory as merely a *dogma* for setting a demarcation line between scientific and non-scientific hypotheses and theories. But since this dogma rests on the assumption that "to fail empirically, means to fail experimentally" Wellmer points out that it is not acceptable for social and other sciences which cannot rely as much on experimentation as the physical sciences.

On the other hand it has to be admitted that Popper greatly contributed to the clarification of the insight that *an empirical theory can never be verified* in the rigorous sense of the word, as well as to understanding the relation between theory and experimental control. Even in the economic sciences his influence is felt, and Paul Samuelson obviously thought of Popper's falsificationism when he wrote in his renowned *Foundations of Economic Analysis*:[25] "By a *meaningful theorem* I mean simply a hypothesis about empirical data which could conceivably be refuted, if only under ideal conditions."

(5) Salmon, finally asserts that "Popper has not succeeded in purging the logic of science of all inductive elements . . . Popper furnishes a method for selecting hypotheses whose content exceeds that of the relevant available basic statements. Demonstrative inference cannot accomplish this task alone, for valid deductions are non-ampliative and their conclusions cannot exceed their premises in content . . . Popper has claimed that scientific inference is exclusively deductive. We have seen, however, that demonstrative inference is not sufficient to the task of providing a reconstruction of the logic of the acceptance – albeit tentative and provisional – of hypotheses . . . I do claim that Popper is engaged in the same task as many inductivists – namely, the task of providing some sort of justification for a mode of non-demonstrative inference. This enterprise, if successful, *is* a justification of induction."[26]

(6) "Furthermore, his critics claim, there is apparently an *inductive* inference embedded in Popper's doctrine – the inference from the fact that a theory has thus far escaped refutation to the conclusion that it will continue to do so."[27]

(7) " . . . Popper has failed completely to provide any kind of rationale

[24] Wellmer, *Methodologie als Erkenntnisproblem – Zur Wissenschaftslehre Karl R. Poppers*, 1967.
[25] 1947, p. 4.
[26] Salmon, *The Foundations of Scientific Inference*, 1966, pp. 26–27.
[27] Quinton, 'Popper, Karl Raimund', 1967, p. 399.

for the methodological rules he advocates. That is, he has failed to provide us with any reason for holding that Popperian rules give us a better hope of realizing the aims of scientific enquiry than any other set of rules. Nor is it easy to see how this failure can be made good with a general Popperian framework. Consequently, Popper has failed to solve his fundamental problem – the problem of demarcation. He has also failed to exhibit science as a rational enterprise. For in order to do this, it is not enough simply to specify an aim for science and a set of methodological rules: we need in addition some reason for holding that the rules give us a better hope of realizing the aim than any other set of rules."[28]

(8) The decisive and perhaps most devastating criticism was launched by Thomas Kuhn (1962), the renowned historian of science, who pointed out that no single scientific process disclosed by historical studies has the least similarity with the pattern of Popper's falsificationism. Actual research just does not proceed the way that Popper describes, because according to T. Kuhn, *it is not possible to falsify a theory.* This view has recently been reinforced and clarified by the work of Sneed (1971) and Stegmüller (1973a, 1976) who have shown why *empirical theories should not be regarded as collections of statements but rather as mathematical structures or systems. Obviously, an instrumental structure, unlike a proposition, is neither true nor false and thus there is no truth to be refuted.*[28a] Stegmüller (1975a, pp. 520–521) even speaks of *a three-fold immunity of theories against falsification*: (i) because the stability of the *theory core* (i.e. the first structural component of a theory – for details see Subsection 7.32) is combined with possible variations through "core-extensions" which cannot be anticipated. Thus even if a theory were a statement, a potential falsification could

[28] Maxwell 'A critique of Popper's Views on Scientific Method', 1972, p. 137.

[28a] The situation is different for hypotheses, which according to Stegmüller (1975a, p. 510) are not structures, like theories, but provisionally accepted sentences, and thus are open to refutation. The notion of a mathematical structure can be defined by an axiomatic representation in which the predicate "is an *S*" is introduced to represent a structure that belongs to the category of the *S*-structures (suppose *S* stands for "planetary system" then various phenomena can be described as planetary structures in the following way: e.g. "The *atom* is a planetary structure", "the *lunar* system is a planetary structure", "the *solar system* is a planetary structure"; or suppose *S* stands for "double-classification accounting structure", then we can say "*Leontief's input–output system* is an accounting structure" or "*The U.S.-National Income and Product Statistic* is an accounting structure", etc. In both cases a *fundamental mathematical structure* is being attributed to structurally similar phenomena). Such structures refer to the core of a theory while hypotheses may refer to constraints, to extensions of a core, etc. (cf. Subsection 7.32.)

possibly be refuted by a still unknown core-extension; (ii) the collection of *intended applications* (the second component in the structural interpretation of theories) is an *open set*; thus a persistent failure to apply the theory to a special area might lead not to a falsification of the theory but to an exclusion of this particular area from the set of intended applications; (iii) the Ramsey criterion for determining what constitutes a theoretical concept (elaborated and improved upon by Sneed) is the basis for a third kind of theory immunity, the explanation of which is complex enough to refer the reader to Stegmüller (1973a, pp. 12–17, 69–75).

(9) "Refutations of the view that falsifiability proves a criterion of empirical significance, or at least of scientific status, have left an important legacy. Now it is thought that scientific hypotheses, whatever the correct analysis of their significance or scientific character, have been discovered to be unfalsifiable. The claim, popularly identified as the Duhemian Thesis (D-Thesis), is that no possible piece of evidence conclusively falsifies any scientific hypothesis."[29] Indeed the D-Thesis is of special interest to us, because it ultimately rests on the systems point of view that "in every test it is not only the theory under investigation which is involved, but also the whole system of our theories and assumptions; so we can never be certain which of all these assumptions is refuted in a falsifying experiment."[30]

But all this criticism hardly means that one can afford to by-pass Popper's contribution to epistemology, it rather means that one must try to transgress beyond him. He played a most important role in the Philosophy of our century – mainly as "the guilty conscience" of the Viennese School. Although he had contact with this circle and shared many interests with this group, he was neither a member of it, nor must he be regarded as a positivist. He calls himself a "critical rationalist", and rightly so, because (1) he believes that errors can be disclosed mainly through criticism, (2) for him the formulation of a hypothesis seems to be more a mental than an empirical or, more precisely, experiential act, (3) he rejects the very basis of positivism, namely the truth criterion of verifiability (substituting for it the criterion of falsifiability), and (4) he also rejects the notion of logical positivism that theories should be analyzed by means of an artificially created calculus. For him the growth of scientific knowledge cannot be reduced to a study of symbolic logic and semantics. His sceptical creed that in science we are never certain but can only guess, has found general acceptance. It is nowhere more aptly expressed than in the following passage, overleaf:

[29] Leplin, 'Contextual Falsification and Scientific Methodology', 1972, p. 476.
[30] Suppe (ed.), *The Structure of Scientific Theory*, 1974, 'Introduction', p. 168.

> The more we learn about the world, and the deeper our learning, the more conscious, specific, and articulate will be our knowledge of what we do not know, our knowledge of our ignorance. For this, indeed, is the main source of our ignorance – the fact that our knowledge can be only finite, while our ignorance must necessarily be infinite . . . This state of learned ignorance might be a help in many of our troubles. It might be well for all of us to remember that, while differing widely in the various little bits we know, in our infinite ignorance we are all equal.[31]

5.23 *Von Wright and Mill's Methods of Induction*

George Henrik von Wright in his *Treatise on Induction and Probability* (1951), following, in a way, the footprints of J. S. Mill, presented an interesting and thorough analysis of the inferential mechanism of induction by restricting himself mainly to the ***truly deductive aspects*** of the inductive process,[32] thereby deliberately neglecting the other two major aspects of induction, namely the problem of *scientific discovery* and the problem of *justifying* induction (von Wright treated the latter in a separate book[33]). His aim was to *reconstruct* various arguments encountered in the inductive process by means of the rigorous tools of deductive logic at a degree of precision thus far unknown in this area. He thereby succeeded in greatly clarifying, among other aspects, J. S. Mill's five canons or methods of induction which, in the following, will be discussed in their new and disentangled version.

To do so, we shall start with the following definitions of three crucial concepts:

1. A property n is a *necessary condition* for a property x, means: if x is present, then n is present; or equivalently, if n is absent then x *is* absent ($x \supset n$, or $\sim n \supset \sim x$; for *material* implication see Subsection 3.34 and Table 3-4). For example: An undergraduate degree is a *necessary* condition for admission into this MBA-program.

2. A property s is a *sufficient condition* for a property x, means: if s is present, then x is present; or equivalently, if x is absent then s is absent ($s \supset x$, or $\sim x \supset \sim s$). For example: An undergraduate degree with an average of 75% is a *sufficient* condition for admission to this MBA-program.

[31] Popper, *Conjectures and Refutations*, 1962, pp. 28–29.

[32] Kyburg therefore speaks in this connection of "demonstrative induction".

[33] *The Logical Problem of Induction*, 1945; 2nd rev. ed., 1957.

3. A property *ns* is a *necessary-and-sufficient condition*, means: *if and only if ns* is present, then *x* is present (symbolically this may be written $ns \equiv x$, and is equivalent to: $sn \supset x$ *in conjunction with* $x \supset sn$). For example: An undergraduate degree with an average of at least 72% is a *necessary and sufficient* condition for admission to this MBA-program.

The concept of *causality*[34] has haunted induction since Hume's time or longer, and a clear distinction between the above three concepts is all the more important since the expression "*cause*" is often interpreted as "being a necessary condition," often as "being a sufficient condition", while in the purest form it ought to be used in the sense of "being a necessary and sufficient condition"; only then is it possible to attribute a *unique* cause to an effect and *vice versa.*

The Method of Agreement: Assuming that among several circumstances (e.g. the presence of properties: *m, n, o, p*),[35] one of them is *suspected* of being a necessary condition for a specific phenomenon or property *d* (for instance declining profit figures during the current period in four occurrences or branches of a firm). Then the attempt is made to eliminate (by observation etc.) those circumstances which were unjustly suspected as being a necessary condition for the phenomenon.

According to Table 5-1, the only circumstance which all four branches have *in common*, is the conditioning property *n*, all others were *eliminated*. Thus by the *method of agreement* one would infer that no other circumstance but *n* could be a *necessary* condition for the occurrence of phenomenon *d* (hence $d \supset n$ or $\sim n \supset \sim d$). The more complex case, where two or more properties *in disjunction* (e.g. $n = v \vee w$; see Section 3.3) to each other constitute a possible and necessary condition, can be solved in analogous fashion (e.g. $d \supset v \vee w$). In all these cases one may speak of the *direct* method of agreement.

Where properties are suspected of being *sufficient* conditions, the *indirect* version of this method is employed. There, one searches for a circumstance or property *s* which is absent *in the absence* of the phenomenon or property *d* (e.g. $\sim d \supset \sim s$ or $s \supset d$). In this case the circumstance may consist of two or

[34] See also Simon, *Models of Man*, 1957, Chapters 1–3.

[35] Such a "cause" need not be the presence of a property, but could be its absence, which then may be listed as the presence of a separate property.

TABLE 5-1

Occurrences	Suspected circumstances				Phenomenon
1	*m*	*n*	–	*p*	*d*
2	–	*n*	*o*	*p*	*d*
3	*m*	*n*	*o*	–	*d*
4	*m*	*n*	*o*	*p*	*d*

more properties *in conjunction* (e.g. $s = v \cdot w$; see Section 3.3) with each other.[36]

The Method of Difference: If an instance (1) in which the phenomenon (*d*) occurs and other instances (2 to 4) in which it does not occur, have suspected circumstances in common (*r, t, u*), except one (*s*) occurring only in the former, then *s* is the ***sufficient*** condition of the phenomenon in the ***particular*** instance (1).

Assuming one does not intend to investigate the necessary or the sufficient condition for declining profits in general (as in our previous example, see Table 5-1), but only the sufficient condition for a declining profit of a particular case, say in branch 1, then the method of difference is to be applied (see Table 5-2). Excluding joint occurrences as causes, property *s* is inferred to be the sufficient condition of the phenomenon *d* in instance 1 (both *s* and *d* occur only in 1). This method may be expanded to allow complex properties and conjunctions, similar to the inverse method of agreement.

The Joint Method: This method serves the inference of the ***necessary and sufficient*** condition of a phenomenon, and consists of either a combination of the direct and the inverse version of the method of agreement (*double method of agreement*) or a combination of the direct method of agreement with the method of difference (*joint method of agreement and difference*). Since the individual components of these methods have been hinted at, no further illustration is offered here.

J. S. Mill distinguished two further methods, the method of *residues* and

[36] In this case the disjunction does not need to be emphasized, because a disjunction $v \vee w$ is a sufficient condition for *d*, *if and only if* *v* is a sufficient condition for *d* and *w* is a sufficient condition for *d*. Therefore in discovering all the sufficient conditions that are not disjunctions one necessarily attains all the sufficient conditions that are disjunctions. For an analogous reason we did not emphasize *conjunctions* in connection with the *direct* method above.

TABLE 5-2

Occurrences	Suspected circumstances				Phenomenon
1	*r*	*s*	*t*	*u*	*d*
2	*r*	–	–	*u*	–
3	–	–	*t*	*u*	–
4	*r*	–	*t*	–	–

the *method of concomitant variations*.[37] but von Wright has shown that both of them are basically contained in the above stated three methods. Mill's methods, anticipated by Herschel,[38] constitute the fulfilment of Francis Bacon's not altogether successful attempt at constructing an inductive system of elimination. Although they hardly solve Hume's problem, they have significance for the practice of science and constitute valuable guidelines.

It is appropriate to close this Subsection with the following remarks made by Kyburg:

> If all the possible combinations of conditioning properties are allowed, von Wright shows, it is still possible for inductive elimination to lead to certainty: when all the possible sufficient conditions but one are eliminated, the one that remains will be the conjunction of all the possible conditioning properties; and when all the possible necessary conditions but one are eliminated, the one that remains will be the disjunction of all conditioning properties (p. 114).
>
> In principle at any rate there is nothing problematic about the logic of elimination at work here: the law is a general statement, and the observation report can be a singular statement that contradicts the law . . . Where does a useful set of possible laws come from? On what kinds of grounds do we accept the empirical hypothesis that one of these laws will be found to hold? Do such sets of hypotheses exhibit an internal structure? They clearly do not exhibit the complex and exhaustive structure Mill and von Wright suppose they do. But so far as I know, very little has been done to answer these questions, least of all by those whose maxim is: Examine usage and discover concepts (p. 120).[39]

[37] Often implicitly used in correlation analysis. Cf. Goode and Hatt, *Methods in Social Research*, 1952, pp. 86–87.

[38] Cf. Herschel, *A Preliminary Discourse on the Study of Natural Philosophy*, 1830. Another contemporary of Mill concerned with inductive logic and scientific discovery was William Whewell. See his *History of Inductive Science*, Vols. I–III, 1837 and *Philosophy of the Inductive Sciences*, 1840.

[39] Kyburg, *Probability and Inductive Logic*, 1970, pp. 114, 120.

5.24 *Carnap and Theories of Confirmation*

Rudolph Carnap's theory of confirmation, as the name implies, seems to be the very antithesis of Popper's falsificationism. Although Carnap's is the most impressive and massive theoretical structure of confirmationism, he is neither its first nor its only exponent. Again, several or at least two main branches of this camp ought to be distinguished, one, basing its system on the concept of *logical* probability (see Subsection 5.32) and the other operating with *subjective* probability (see Subsection 5.33). The difference between the two branches, as far as inductive behavior is concerned, seems to us less drastic than occasionally supposed. First of all, both approaches pivot around the well-known *Bayesian theorem*, and secondly, to practice confirmationism, some kind of personal judgement is required, either as regards the more or less arbitrary evaluation of certain constants (e.g. Carnap's λ and η, or Hintikka's α and λ) or directly as regards the assumption of subjective probabilities.

A series of impressive names may be found in this camp: John Maynard Keynes, Nicod, Ramsey, Jeffreys, Carnap, Savage, Kemeny and many others. They all would agree that there exists a ***relationship of strength between the evidence (premises) and the hypothesis (conclusion) of an inductive argument; a relationship that might increase with accumulation of appropriate evidence, and which ought to be measured.***

The proponents of the *logical theory of confirmation* (Keynes, Jeffreys, Carnap, Kemeny, Hintikka and Hilpinen, Levi, Kyburg, etc.) believe:

(1) that the relationship *c*, between the hypothesis *h* and the evidence *e*, to which a numeral *q* (a probability $0 \leqslant q \leqslant 1$) might be assigned,

$$c(h, e) = q,$$

expresses a degree of *rational* belief, independent of personal moods and judgements, and thus constitutes a purely *logical* relationship (called by Carnap, the degree of confirmation resulting from the confirmation function *c*);

(2) that the *degree of confirmation* can be measured within precise and well structured *language systems* (Carnap bases his system on a *semantic* theory, operating with *sentences* instead of propositions, and describes the pertinent language systems rigorously).

Thus the logical inductivists are not so naive as to assert that the degree of confirmation can be determined by merely adding up the number of evidences: If you saw in your life altogether not more than 150 black ravens, and if I should be in the more fortunate position of having observed 450 black ravens (and if we both never saw ravens of any other color), you as well as I might conclude: "All ravens are black". But the difference in the number of our evidences does not necessarily mean that the degree of confirmation of my argument is larger, or three times as large, as that of yours. Surprisingly enough in Carnap's system the *degree of confirmation in both cases could be zero*, namely if it is assumed that the number of objects (e.g. ravens, past, present and future) is *infinite* or approaches infinity.

But the logical theory of induction cannot be fully grasped without studying various artificial language systems devised for this purpose, usually operating with such concepts as atomic sentence, formation rule, state description, structure description, measure function, etc. So far only highly simplified language systems, adequate for nothing but the most simple situations of induction, could be constructed. But even in these cases, a subjective element in the form of more or less arbitrarily assumed constants has crept into the theory. A fairly lucid explanation of one of Carnap's artificial language systems can be found in Salmon (1966, pp. 68–83);[40] for a full grasp, we recommend Rudolf Carnap's *Logical Foundations of Probability*.[41] Carnap, until his recent death, seems to have continued to elaborate his work along these lines,[42] and other authors too have tried to improve upon his vast pioneering effort.

The confirmation theories developed by Hintikka and Hilpinen, Levi as well as Kyburg,[43] belong to such efforts of continuation. These three theories pay particular heed to the construction of simple and natural rules of *accepting* hypotheses[44] (Kyburg therefore speaks of *Acceptance Theories*), thus

[40] Another, more sophisticated, introduction to Carnap's theory and original language system may be found in Tintner, 'Foundations of Probability and Statistical Inference', 1949.

[41] 2nd rev. edition, 1962; first ed. 1950.

[42] A forthcoming *posthumous* publication by Rudolf Carnap, *Basic Systems of Inductive Logic*, is announced in the bibliography of Kyburg's recent (1971) book.

[43] See, e.g. Hintikka, 'A Two-Dimensional Continuum of Inductive Methods', 1966, pp. 113–132. *Ibid.*, pp. 1–20, 'Knowledge, Acceptance, and Inductive Logic', by Hintikka and Hilpinen. Levi, *Gambling with Truth: An Essay on Induction and The Aims of Science*, 1967. Kyburg, *Probability and Inductive Logic*, 1970, pp. 77–93, 180–198.

[44] This is a deviation from Carnap's viewpoint. He deemed it rather to be a mistake to "regard the result of inductive reasoning as the acceptance of a new position" whereas the objective of inductive logic ought to be above all, the assignment of a degree of confirmation to this new position. Indeed, a serious argument against theories of acceptance, is the fact that people, whose behavior cannot be declared as "irrational", do buy lottery tickets although realizing that their chance is so small (even where they deal with a *fair* lottery system), that no acceptance theory could ever recommend such a purchase.

avoiding some problems arising in Carnap's system. The acceptance theories too operate with artificial language systems. But the disadvantage of assigning only *small* or even *zero* probabilities to universal generalization (characteristic for Carnap's theory) could be avoided, and respectable probability figures could then be assigned to universal hypotheses. Whereas Hintikka's theory constitutes a *global* approach to justification, and Levi's theory a *local* and therefore more flexible approach, Kyburg in his system tries to combine the virtues of both. Two major tenets of these theories of acceptance are: (1) One frequently *accepts* a probable statement as an indication of a *true* statement, (2) Carnap, in order to start from a firm basis, must regard *protocol sentences*[45] (those reporting sense experience) as certain, while the acceptance theorists can afford to be more realistic, declaring it highly probable and therefore only "practically certain".

The superabundance of competing hypotheses often puts the hypothetico-deductive approach into the embarrassing situation of undecided choice, from which there is no escape other than to state some criteria of confirmation and acceptance. At this point Bayes' Theorem becomes relevant to induction. To understand the connection we must distinguish between the *a priori* probability of the evidence $c(e)$, the *a posteriori* conditional probability of the hypothesis, given the evidence, $c(h, e)$ and the joint probability of hypothesis *and* evidence together $c(h \cdot e)$; then the relation between this theory and Bayes' Theorem might be expressed as follows:

$$c(h, e) = \frac{c(h \cdot e)}{c(e)}.$$

A more precise presentation of the application of Bayes' Theorem to the logical theory of induction is offered by Carnap in the following form:

$$c(h, e \cdot i) = \frac{c(i \cdot h, e)}{\sum_{p=1}^{n} c(i \cdot h_p, e)}.$$

This $c(h, e \cdot i)$ expresses the *degree of confirmation* of hypothesis h after a predicted information i (in addition to evidence e) is confirmed.[46] Thus $c(i \cdot h, e)$ represents the likelihood of i, and $c(i \cdot h_p, e)$ is the likelihood of one hypothesis h_p, being one of the n competing hypotheses among

[45] Popper and other philosophers not subscribing to positivism would deny that there are incorrigible protocol sentences forming the ultimate empirical basis of all science.

[46] In contrast to this posterior confirmation $c(h, e \cdot i)$, the expression $c(h, e)$ would then be regarded as the prior confirmation of h. Cf. Carnap (1962, pp. 326 ff).

which one and only one (h) is true. Thus the question arises: "By how much is the confirmation of h increased when the observation predicted by i actually occurs?" But Bayes' Theorem does not allow computation of the degree of confirmation for any pair of sentences, it merely indicates how some confirmation values are connected with others.

The following example should help to grasp the idea of *determining the degree of confirmation of a hypothesis* on the basis of some empirical evidence and by means of Bayes' Theorem. Let us assume our universe of discourse consists of an urn or set U with ten balls of equal size of which two balls are black in color and made of metal, four other balls are also black but of vinyl, three balls are white and of metal, and one further ball is white but of vinyl. We then can form the following four sets (see Figure 5-1):

B the set of all black balls (6 members)

M the set of all metal balls (5 members)

V the set of all vinyl balls (5 members)

W the set of all white balls (4 members).

Now suppose one draws randomly a ball from urn U, and upon inspection the ball turns out to be black (evidence e). One may then ask what is the degree of confirmation c measured by a number $0 \leqslant q \leqslant 1$ – i.e. the conditional probability $P(M|B)$ – that this ball is of metal (hypothesis h)? In

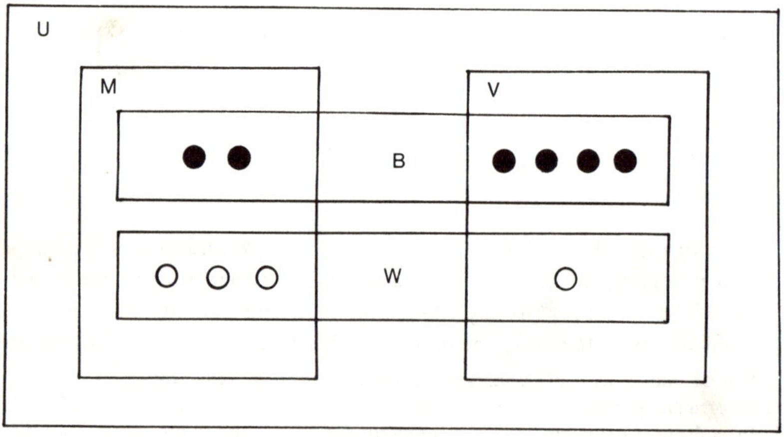

Fig. 5-1. An urn with ten balls of different colors and different materials.

such a case the determination of the degree of confirmation is a straightforward mathematical problem with a precise solution given in Bayes' well known theorem:

Specific Set-Theoretical-Probabilistic Symbolism:[47]

$$(1) \qquad P(M|B) = \frac{P(M \cdot B)}{P(B)} = \frac{P(B|M) \cdot P(M)}{P(B|M) \cdot P(M) + P(B|V) \cdot P(V)}$$

Carnap's General Symbolism:[48]

$$c(h, e) = \frac{m(h \cdot e)}{m(e)} = q = \frac{m(e, h) \cdot m(h)}{\sum_{p=1}^{n} m(e, h_p) \cdot m(e)}.$$

To find the specific solution one has to determine the various *a priori*, joint, and conditional probabilities required. In our case we obtain the following values directly from Figure 5-1 (count number of dots of a sub-set and divide it by the total dots of a specific main set – *replacement* of ball drawn is always assumed):

$P(M) = \frac{5}{10} = 0.5$ probability that a metal ball is drawn;

$P(B) = \frac{6}{10} = 0.6$ probability that a black ball is drawn;

[47] Bayes' Theorem is a version or immediate consequence of the definition of "conditional probability":

$$P(A_i|B) = P(A_i \cdot B)/P(B) = P(A_i \cdot B)/\sum_{i=1}^{n} (A_i \cdot B) = P(B|A_i) \cdot P(A_i)/$$

$\sum_{i=1}^{n} P(B|A_i) \cdot P(A_i)$ because by definition and inversion $P(A_i \cdot B) = P(B|A_i) \cdot P(A_i)$.

[48] The *c*-functions often become in Carnap's system measure-functions *m*.

$$P(V) = \frac{5}{10} = 0.5$$ probability that a vinyl ball is drawn;

$$P(M \cdot B) = \frac{2}{10} = 0.2$$ joint probability that a black metal ball is drawn;

$$P(B|M) = \frac{2}{5} = 0.4$$ conditional probability that the drawn ball is black provided it is of metal;

$$P(B|V) = \frac{4}{5} = 0.8$$ conditional probability that the drawn ball is black provided it is of vinyl;

hence

$$P(M|B) = \frac{0.2}{0.6} \quad \text{or} \quad \frac{0.4 \cdot 0.5}{0.4 \cdot 0.5 + 0.8 \cdot 0.5} = \frac{1}{3},$$

thus the degree of confirmation in hypothesis h (that the ball is of metal), provided the evidence e shows that it is black, is $c(h, e) = q = 33.33\%$. In this way we succeeded in measuring the degree to which a certain evidence confirms a specific hypothesis. In a similar way one may determine the degree of confirmation of the competing hypothesis "The black ball drawn is of vinyl", or one may reverse the case and assume a blind-folded person (not seeing the colors of the balls but feeling the material) draws and asks: "what is the degree of confirmation that a ball is black if it is of metal?" or alternatively "what if it is of vinyl?" or "what is the degree of confirmation that a ball is white if it is of metal?" or alternatively "what if it is of vinyl? Table 5-3 shows the pertinent probabilities (*a priori*, joint, conditional etc.). The reader may check these values against his own conclusions based on Figure 5-1 and may assign the proper values of degree of confirmation to the pertinent hypotheses mentioned above.

The difficulty with *this approach* is that it *cannot take cognizance of any learning process based on the collection of evidence*. This has to be explained in some detail: Assume that an *experimentor draws three balls in succession* from our urn. Let us designate the first ball by a, the second by b and the third by c. Then we write Ba for "the first ball is black", or Wb for "the second is white" etc. The probabilities pertaining to the eight possible combinations (two colors and three balls $2^3 = 8$) is shown on the left-hand side of Table 5-4 under the designation "state descriptions", while the right hand side shows the assignment of probabilities or weights on the more arbitrary

TABLE 5-3

Various probability values derived from figure 5-1

$P(M)$	= 0.5	$P(M \mid B)$	= 0.333
$P(V)$	= 0.5	$P(M \mid W)$	= 0.75
$P(B)$	= 0.6	$P(V \mid B)$	= 0.666
$P(W)$	= 0.4	$P(V \mid W)$	= 0.25
$P(M \cdot B)$	= 0.2	$P(B \mid M)$	= 0.4
$P(M \cdot W)$	= 0.3	$P(B \mid V)$	= 0.8
$P(V \cdot B)$	= 0.4	$P(W \mid M)$	= 0.6
$P(V \cdot W)$	= 0.1	$P(W \mid V)$	= 0.2

basis of some different classification scheme under the heading of "structure descriptions" (recommended by Carnap to achieve some feedback by evidences).

Here we disregard the different materials and concentrate exclusively on the color difference of the balls. Let us then measure the degree of confirmation or relationship between the hypothesis that "the third ball drawn is black" Bc, and some evidence e, as for example "the first and second ball is black" $Ba \cdot Bb$. The *a priori* probability of h (i.e. the probability of h prior to any evidence) obviously is $P(Bc) = 0.6$ since 60% of all balls are black. The degree of confirmation of h or *ex post* probability of h (i.e. after evidence has been obtained) is determined as previously indicated by Bayes' Theorem $c(h, e) = m(h \cdot e)/m(e) = P(Ba \cdot Bb \cdot Bc)/P(Ba \cdot Bb \cdot Bc) + P(Ba \cdot Bb \cdot Wc)$ = $0.216/(0.216 + 0.144) = 0.6$. Hence the *ex post* probability is equal to the *a priori* probability which means that no change in belief and hence no learning has taken place in spite of the additional evidence of obtaining black balls at the first as well as second draw.

"To circumvent the difficulty about learning from experience, Carnap proposed a different system for assigning weights to state descriptions which he designated 'm^*'. He argued for its plausibility along the following lines. The only thing that significantly distinguishes individuals from one another is some qualitative difference, not a mere difference of name or identity. Hence the fundamental possibilities to which we assign equal weights should not discriminate on the basis of individuals" W. Salmon (1966, p. 72). In consequence Carnap would summarize the state descriptions into *structure descriptions* according to new classificational criteria, e.g. those given under I, II, III and IV of the right hand side of Table 5-4. Then he would assign equal weights to each of these new classes or structures, something that

TABLE 5-4

State and structure descriptions of events (3 balls *a, b, c* of black or white color drawn in succession, but after immediate *replacement* of ball drawn)

State descriptions	Probabilities	Structure descriptions	Weights	
1. $Ba \cdot Bb \cdot Bc$	$= 0.6 \cdot 0.6 \cdot 0.6 = 0.216$	I. All balls drawn are black	1/4	
2. $Wa \cdot Bb \cdot Bc$	$= 0.4 \cdot 0.6 \cdot 0.6 = 0.144$	II. Two balls drawn are black and one is white	1/12	1/4
3. $Ba \cdot Wb \cdot Bc$	$= 0.6 \cdot 0.4 \cdot 0.6 = 0.144$		1/12	
4. $Ba \cdot Bb \cdot Wc$	$= 0.6 \cdot 0.6 \cdot 0.4 = 0.144$		1/12	
5. $Wa \cdot Wb \cdot Bc$	$= 0.4 \cdot 0.4 \cdot 0.6 = 0.096$	III. One ball drawn is black and two are white	1/12	1/4
6. $Wa \cdot Bb \cdot Wc$	$= 0.4 \cdot 0.6 \cdot 0.4 = 0.096$		1/12	
7. $Ba \cdot Wb \cdot Wc$	$= 0.6 \cdot 0.4 \cdot 0.4 = 0.096$		1/12	
8. $Wa \cdot Wb \cdot Wc$	$= 0.4 \cdot 0.4 \cdot 0.4 = 0.064$	IV. All balls drawn are white	1/4	

results not only in a weight distribution to individual events or their state descriptions different from the original events, but that reflects the change in probabilities due to new evidence. Suppose again, the first two draws yield black balls, then the degree of confirmation is

$$c^*(h, e) = \frac{m^*(h \cdot e)}{m^*(e)} = \frac{1/4}{1/4 + 1/12} = \frac{1/4}{4/12} = 0.75.$$

Since the *a priori* probability $c(h) = 0.6 < 0.75 = c^*(h, e)$, the evidence[49] $Ba \cdot Bb$ has strengthened the belief that "the third ball will be black" Bc, which means that learning from experience has occurred. Of course, the assignment of the structural weights was fairly arbitrary, and Carnap cannot claim to have provided us with an absolute measure of the degree of confirmation. But for comparative purposes the assignment of weights to structure descriptions might be acceptable and has definitely the advantage of reflecting learning through evidence. But the fact that such state- and structure descriptions are available only for comparatively simple language systems and the infinite number of possibilities of assigning measures within

[49] The probability as well as the measure m^* of e are based on lines 1 and 4 (of Table 5-4) which reflect the only state descriptions in which $Ba \cdot Bb$ occur, while the probability as well as measure m^* of $(h \cdot e)$ are based on line 1 only because no other state description reflects the event $Ba \cdot Bb \cdot Bc$.

such language systems as well as other difficulties have impeded practical application of Carnap's system.

In latter years Carnap tended toward "inductive intuition", as Salmon calls it, enunciating a series of intuitively justifiable axioms, and thus moving somewhat in the direction of the postulational approach[50] (see also next Subsection 5.26). However, the major hurdle of the *logical* approach to confirmation remains: the fact that we are not in (and might never get into) possession of an artificial language system sophisticated enough to satisfy the complex requirements for measuring the degree of confirmation when inducing universal scientific hypotheses. The *subjective* approach to confirmation is not fraught with this difficulty, but suffers under the arbitrariness of evaluating various competing hypotheses by a system which, in spite of such restrictions as coherence, consistency etc., rests on *personal* judgements – see Subsection 5.33 and Ramsey's (1931) posthumous pioneering work. The subjectivists reject the notion of a *logical* concept of *rational* belief, but are willing to describe a person's degree of *actual* belief in the form of an *a priori* probability distribution. The latter ought to be derived empirically from the person's *betting* or *action behavior*. As Raiffa says:

> The split between the necessarists [logical confirmationists] and the subjectivists gains operational significance when we discuss whether there is a "scientifically objective" prior distribution that appropriately captures the state of "no prior information". The necessarists think there is a logically appropriate prior distribution and their posteriors build up in a formal manner on this prior. The subjectivists disagree. They feel the necessarists' suggestions for "informationless" prior distribution are *ad hoc* and do not stand up to careful scrutiny; they feel the necessarists are seeking a scientifically objective basis for inference which will forever remain elusive.[51]

The subjectivists, are still in the minority among inductive philosophers and statisticians, but in recent decades have gained majority among administrative and management scientists as well as among economists,[52] and seem

[50] See Carnap and Jeffrey (eds.), *Studies in Inductive Logic and Probability*, Vol. 1, 1971.

[51] Raiffa, *Decision Analysis*, 1968, pp. 284–285.

[52] Cf. Fellner, *Probability and Profit*, 1965, p. 37: "I share the belief that the subjectivists' view will continue to gain ground over the frequentist (objective) view, and I expect distinct benefits from this change." A more recent and most impressive defence of the personalistic approach has been advanced by a leading epistemologist: Stegmüller (1973b and c).

to be on the way of conquering the applied sciences in general. Their forbear is James Bernoulli who in his *Ars Conjectandi* (1713) suggested interpreting "probability" alternatively as a "degree of confidence" that an individual attaches to an uncertain event, and that this degree depends on his knowledge and can vary from individual to individual.[53] The Reverend Thomas Bayes, in spite of the significance of his theorem, leading to the combination of *a priori* with *a posteriori* probabilities, surprisingly enough, might not be counted among the subjectivists (or Bayesians, as they are frequently, but perhaps erroneously, called). It was Ramsey's genius which led him – in addition to other profound philosophical and mathematical ideas, bursting forth during a short lifetime of hardly twenty-seven years – to the first formulation of inductive and probabilistic subjectivism. Ramsey conceived as early as 1926 what Raiffa calls, "an operational theory of action based on the dual intertwining notions of judgemental probability and utility." But this aspect of Ramsey's work remained hardly noticed for many years until the elements of the subjective approach of probability were rediscovered step-wise by De Finetti, Borel, von Neumann and Morgenstern, Wald, and Savage. The latter merged ideas of De Finetti with von Neumann and Morgenstern's modern utility theory and thus laid the corner stone on which modern subjectivism rests.[54] For a discussion of "subjective probability" and competing interpretations we refer the reader to Section 5.3.

5.25 *Von Mises, Reichenbach and others: the Frequentists' Approach to Induction*

In the previous section we discussed inductive methods based on either the logical or the subjective concept of probability. However, confirmationism may also be based on the *statistic-empirical* concept or *relative frequency* (see Subsection 5.31). This method, on one side is as *objective* as the logical approach, on the other side it has an *empirical* aspect like the subjective one, with a statistical rather than personal slant. The frequentist camp, no less than the others, reflects different shades. Within the area of philosophy of probability and inductive logic, Richard von Mises, Hans Reichenbach

[53] Cf. *idem*., p. 274 (degree of confidence should not be confused with degree of confirmation).

[54] See Savage, *The Foundations of Statistics*, 1954. He confesses that at the time this work was created, although interested in personal probabilities, he was not yet a subjectivist, or "personalistic Bayesian", as he prefers to say.

and, more recently, Wesley Salmon[55] are the most notable representatives of frequentism of philosophy, while in the area of frequency statistics names like Denis Poisson, Leslie Ellis, John Venn, Ronald A. Fisher, E. S. Pearson, Jerzy Neyman and many others have a brilliant ring.

Whereas von Mises[56] builds his theory on the restrictive definition of a random sequence ("irregular collectives" such as 11000101 . . .), Reichenbach also accepts regular sequences (e.g. 10100100010000 . . .) and intermediate types, and launches a *pragmatic* justification of induction.[57] Kyburg calls the frequentists' attempts to provide a general *probabilistic* justification of induction "one of the most clear-cut failures of philosophy," but Reichenbach did not claim to have any probabilistic justification. He would merely assert that wherever nature is uniform (e.g. *all* red balls in this urn are *in fact* of metal), the standard inductive method *must* be successful, while any competing method (e.g. crystal gazing) *might*, but need not be so. Where nature is not uniform, no method, neither, induction nor any other would succeed. This would still prove induction superior to other approaches, and constitutes the core of its pragmatic justification. Whereas most statisticians seem to prefer the more rigorous method presented by von Mises, some pragmatic philosophers like Feigl and Salmon defend the pragmatic justification or *vindication* of induction and attempt to extend this approach.[58]

At this juncture it might be appropriate to discuss the statisticians' approach to inductive behavior, and to relate it to scientific induction. This relation cannot be understood properly without making a clear distinction between *the probability that a given hypothesis is true* (something with which we were concerned so far) and *the probability of the occurrence of an event* or of kinds of events. The importance of this distinction as well as of the fact that *statistical hypotheses*[59] play a decisive role in modern science is well expressed by Braithwaite:

[55] Richard von Mises, *Probability, Statistics and Truth* (original German ed., 1928; 2nd rev. English ed., 1957). Reichenbach, *The Theory of Probability* (original German ed., 1935; English ed., 1949). *idem., Experience and Prediction*, 1938. Salmon, *The Foundations of Scientific Inference*, 1966.

[56] Richard von Mises, *op. cit.*, p. 103.

[57] A recent innovative defence of the frequentist point of view can be found in several articles by G. Menges (ed.), *Information, Inference and Decision*, (1974).

[58] Herbert Feigl introduced the seemingly important distinction between "justification" and "vindication" of induction. See his frequently quoted article 'De Principiis non Disputandum . . . ', 1950, pp. 113–147.

[59] A statistical hypothesis may be defined as "an assumption about the frequency function of a random variable." Cf. Hoel, *Introduction to Mathematical Statistics*, 1954, p. 30.

> It will be safer for the philosopher to take statistical hypotheses as being the normalcy, and to regard universal (i.e. non-statistical) hypotheses as being extreme cases of statistical hypotheses when the proportions in question are 100 or 0% (p. 116).
>
> Besides speaking of the hypothesis that the probability of a radium atom disintegrating within a period of 1700 years is 1/2, we also speak of Einstein's theory of gravitation being probable, or of being more probable than Newton's theory, where it is a whole scientific theory that is asserted to be probable. The importance of this distinction between probability of kinds of events and probability of hypotheses has been emphasized by many recent logicians (Footnote omitted). It is the first sense of probability which we use in translating statistical laws; it is probability as used within the system of a science, probability which enters into the hypotheses themselves. That the probability of a radium atom disintegrating within 1700 years is 1/2 is a hypothesis within the body of physics; since it is reasonable to believe this hypothesis at the present time, the hypothesis itself may be said to be probable in the second sense of probability (p. 119).[60]

Within the area of statistical induction one ought to distinguish between two related activities of inductive behavior: (1) *the estimation of parameters* (i.e. the mean, the standard deviation, or similar characteristics) of the hypothesized frequency distribution and (2) *the testing* of this hypothesized frequency distribution (i.e. its shape and/or parameter, hence deciding whether to accept or reject it). The first activity in a way corresponds to hypothesis construction, the second to the hypothesis confirmation or refutation, but bearing in mind that the statistical hypothesis is usually only *part* of the scientific or over-all hypothesis. The *theory of testing statistical hypotheses*, in which tests may be derived as solutions of optimization problems, was developed by Neyman and Pearson.[61] These solutions were limited to *two-valued* statistical decision functions; that is to say, the approach was ultimately based on a two-valued logic in which only one of the two truth values ("true = 1" or "false = 0") could be assigned to a statistical hypothesis. Statistical hypothesis testing begins by accepting normatively a certain *level of significance* ($\alpha = 0.10$ or 0.05 or 0.01 etc., expressing the type I error

60 Braithwaite, *Scientific Explanation*, 1960, pp. 116, 119.

61 Neyman and Pearson, 'On the Use and Interpretation of Certain Test Criteria for Purposes of Statistical Inference', 1928; and *idem*, 'On the problem of the most efficient tests of statistical hypotheses', 1933.

probability – the acceptable probability rejecting a true hypothesis, thus corresponding to a *confidence level* of 0.90, 0.95 or 0.99 etc. respectively) for the hypothesis to be tested. On the basis of an *experimental test* (e.g. observation, sample) the decision will be made whether the hypothesis is to be accepted or rejected. If the hypothesized value of the parameter tested lies outside the critical region (corresponding to the significance level chosen), the hypothesis is accepted; if it lies inside the critical region, the hypothesis is rejected.

Since this decision is also based on a value judgement, as well as on other incidental occurrences (e.g. the confidence level chosen, the sample size available, the kind of parameter and hypothesis to be tested, the critical region to be constructed) there is the danger of either rejecting a true hypothesis as false (*type I error*), or accepting a false hypothesis as true (*type II error*).[62] Therefore the scientist must examine the *error characteristics* of each of his strategies for each of the possible states of reality.

To illustrate the essence of the testing of statistical hypotheses in a few strokes we refer to Figure 5-2 where the characteristics for the type I and type II errors (α and β values respectively) of a highly simplified case are represented. Assume the hypothesis h_0 (null-hypothesis) says "population parameter $\mu = 1$", while the counter hypothesis h_c says "population parameter $\mu = 2$". The evidence upon which h_0 is to be accepted or rejected is here assumed to be a single sample test. If the sample parameter $\hat{\mu}$ lies within the confidence interval, that means if it lies *outside the area of significance* (the double shaded α-area), the null-hypothesis is accepted, but if it lies within the α-area the null-hypothesis is rejected and the counter hypothesis h_c is accepted. Before the test can be made, the *significance level* α has to be arbitrarily chosen. In Figure 5-2(a) an α-value of 0.10 was chosen, which implies one is satisfied that the probability of making a wrong decision (rejecting a true null-hypothesis) is 10 per cent; while in Figure 5-2(b) a more rigorous α-level of $\alpha = 0.05$ was chosen (probability of rejecting a true null-hypothesis is only 5 per cent). But it is important to realize that this greater reliability or, better said, lower type I error is traded against a higher type II error: while in the case (a) the value of $\beta = 0.30$ (30% probability that a false counter hypothesis h_c is accepted as true) in case (b) $\beta = 0.40$ (40% probability that a false h_c is accepted). The only way to improve both the α and β

[62] The type I error (α) expresses the probability that a sample point will fall in the critical region when the *hypothesis to be tested* is actually true. The type II error (β) expresses the probability that a sample point will fall in the non-critical region when the *alternative* hypothesis is actually true.

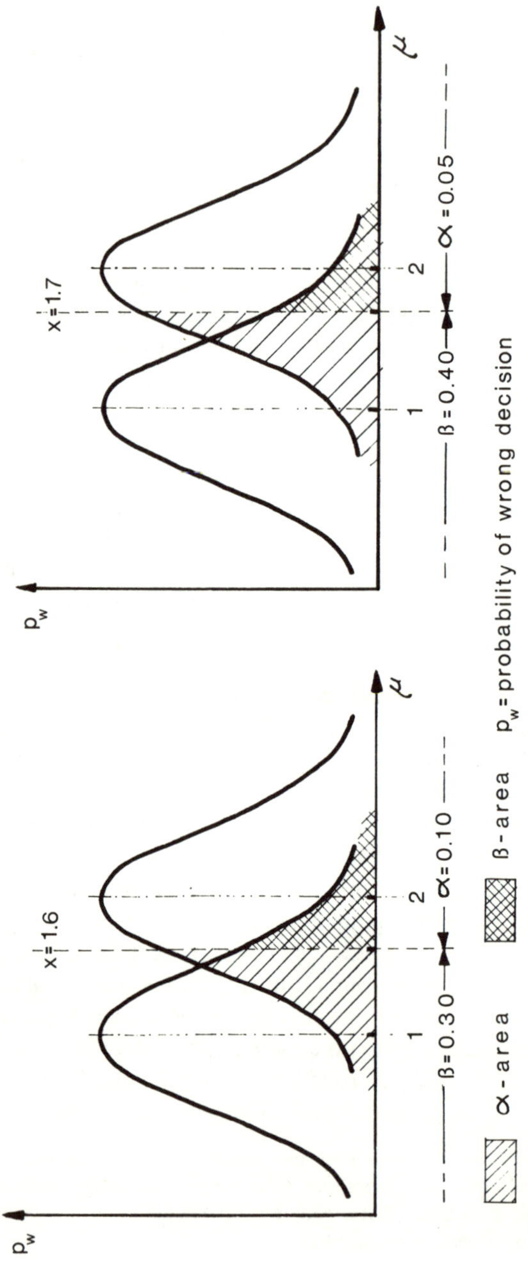

Fig. 5-2 Error characteristics in hypothesis testing.

values simultaneously is to increase the sample size (the larger the sample, the more reliable is the test with regard to both type I as well as type II errors – a larger sample would mean steeper probability functions, a smaller sample means flatter ones). Usually a relatively small type I error is chosen (since it seems often more important to avoid rejection of a true null-hypothesis than to avoid the rejection of a true counter hypothesis). In our particular case the demarcation lines are situated at 1.6 for (a) and 1.7 for (b), that means if the sample parameter $\hat{\mu} \leqslant 1.6$, the null hypothesis is accepted under $\alpha = 0.10$ and $\beta = 0.30$, while it is rejected if $\hat{\mu} > 1.6$; on the other hand, if the more reliable $\alpha = 0.05$ together with the less reliable $\beta = 0.40$ are chosen, then $\hat{\mu} \leqslant 1.7$ would still yield our acceptable h_0.

The other statistical theory of inductive behavior, that of *statistical estimation*, is based on multi-valued statistical decision functions and is usually applied to estimating parameters of frequency distributions. Two approaches have to be distinguished: *point estimation*[63] and *interval estimation* (method of confidence intervals).[64] A point estimate (namely the hypothesis) states a number derived from observed values of the pertinent random variable. This number serves as an approximation to the unknown population parameter (e.g. as in the methods of least squares and maximum likelihood estimation[65]). The interval estimate, however, has the advantage of yielding, in addition to a point estimate, an interval indicating the range of accuracy of the estimated parameter. The *normative* aspect rests on the arbitrarily assumed *confidence level or confidence coefficient* (e.g. $1-\alpha = 0.95$), from this the *confidence interval* (e.g. 95% of the area of the frequency distribution) follows on the basis of the sample information. If one were to compute on the same basis confidence intervals for all future samples, then, in the *long run*, these intervals would contain the unknown population parameter in approximately 95 per cent of the cases. Obviously there is a close relation between statistical estimation and hypothesis testing, between level of confidence and level of

[63] Pioneering work in this area was done by Markoff, *Calculus of Probability* (in Russian; 1913); Fisher, 'On Mathematical Foundations of Theoretical Statistics', 1921; Hotelling 'The Consistency and Ultimate Distribution of Optimum Statistics', 1930; Dobb, 'Probability and Statistics' 1934.

[64] Developed by Neyman, 'Outline of a Theory of Statistical Estimation Based on the Classical Theory of Probability', 1937.

[65] "A maximum likelihood estimator $\hat{\theta}$ of the parameter θ in the frequency function $f(x;\theta)$ is an estimator that maximizes the likelihood function $L(x_1, \ldots, x_n; \theta)$ as a function of θ". Hoel, *Introduction to Mathematical Statistics*, 1954, p. 40. As Kyburg (1970, p. 133) remarks, the *estimators* or estimation functions of the statisticians correspond to the *inductive rules* of the philosophers.

significance. The error of rejecting a true hypothesis, indeed, corresponds to the error of excluding the correct value of a population parameter from the confidence interval. But where the hypothesis does not refer to a population parameter but to some other characteristic parameter, (e.g. *the shape of the frequency distribution*), then these methods diverge from each other. By no means, however, must the *confidence level* be confused or equated with Carnap's *degree of confirmation*. The former is an empirical concept based on statistical frequency procedures, the latter is an *a priori* concept based on procedures of logic. Yet there are authors (e.g. James Bernoulli) who have used the similarly sounding expression "degree of confidence" for probability in the subjective sense and later we shall return to such a usage. In this connection let us point out that the decision rules originally developed for inductive behavior on a frequency basis, as outlined above, can be and have been combined by means of Bayes' Theorem with *a priori* probabilities. Thus these statistical tools based on relative frequency, without major modification, are also used in the camp of subjectivism.

A major criticism of the statistical approach points to the necessity of prescribing certain properties an *estimator* ought to have (consistency, unbiasedness etc. – the assertion of these desiderata seems to push in the direction of a postulational approach, see 5.26), and to the fact that these desiderata usually cannot be fulfilled simultaneously, i.e. all at a high degree, but often have to be traded against each other. Yet no absolute or hard and fast rule for this trading procedure exists. Further criticism levelled against the frequentists' approach in general is closely related to the relative frequency interpretation of probability. Therefore these objections will be discussed in Subsection 5.31.

5.26 *Russell and the Postulational Approach*

Instead of attempting to *justify* inductive inference, one may approach the problem of induction by asking: What has to be *assumed* before scientific induction can operate as a rational procedure? This line of attack, which does not meet Hume's problem head-on, but rather circumvents it, was chosen explicitly by Bertrand Russell, John Wisdom, Arthur Burks[66] and, perhaps implicitly by other authors, as pointed out previously. To ask for the postulates of induction is like grappling for the basic *confessions of a creed*.

[66] See Russell, *Human Knowledge, Its Scope and Limits*, 1948. Wisdom, *Foundations of Inference in Natural Science*, 1952. Burks, 'The Presupposition Theory of Induction,' 1953. *idem*., 'On the Presuppositions of Induction', 1954/55.

Indeed, Salmon (1966, p. 48) complains that this approach "is tantamount to making scientific method a matter of faith." For this reason probably, the explicit postulational approach has not been adopted widely. For those, however, who argue that science is nothing but a special kind of faith – hopefully a more reliable creed than the others, but still a creed – this approach should have particular appeal. We do not regard such a point of view as scientific heresy. On the contrary, it seems to be proven by everything so far discussed about induction. If one agrees (1) that the truth of no universal scientific hypothesis is known with certainty and (2) that some inferences (e.g. inductive inferences) are better than others (e.g. crystal gazing), then it is difficult to deny that all our knowledge consists of nothing but beliefs, though some more reliable than others. This does not deny the existence of absolute truth, it denies only the certainty of knowing this truth which induction enables us to approximate more or less, but not necessarily to reach.

The following five postulates suggested by Russell* are not claimed to be definite or optimal formulations; but as a first attempt in this direction, and coming from such an eminent philosopher, they have path-breaking significance and may ultimately lead to a more satisfactory solution.

A. *THE POSTULATE OF QUASI-PERMANENCE. "Given any event A, it happens very frequently that, at any neighboring time, there is at some neighboring place an event very similar to A."*

As an illustration of this postulate, Russell mentions the *gradual* development of a three months' embryo (event *A*) into an adult human being. The difference between both stages is enormous, yet both represent the same "person" or "thing" which is to be considered as a series of such events. John Wisdom's "second postulate of spatio-temporal proximity" corresponds to Russell's first postulate.

B. *THE POSTULATE OF SEPARABLE CAUSAL LINES: "It is frequently possible to form a series of events such that from one or two members of the series something can be inferred as to all the other members."*

Motion, i.e. a thing changing its position but maintaining certain characteristics, is listed as the most obvious example for such an event or, equivalently, a series of events.

**Human Knowledge: Its Scope and Limits.*

C. *THE POSTULATE OF SPATIO-TEMPORAL CONTINUITY. "This postulate is concerned to deny 'action at a distance' and to assert that when there is a causal connection between two events that are not contiguous, there must be intermediate links in the causal chain such that each is contiguous to the next, or (alternatively) such that there is a process which is continuous in the mathematical sense."*

A number of people listening to a speaker, is given as an illustration for the causal spatio-temporal connection between what the various listeners hear and what the speaker says. Various movie and television pictures exploiting the confusion often created by identical twins, are illustrations of what happens when this postulate is not observed (taking one twin for the other without tracing in time and space who is who).

D. *THE STRUCTURAL POSTULATE. "When a number of structurally similar complex events are ranged about a center in regions not widely separated, it is usually the case that all belong to causal lines having their origin in an event of the same structure at the center."*

Russell's illustration refers to a given object photographed by several cameras simultaneously, but from different angles and positions. Then obviously there are causal relationships between each picture and the central object and therefore between the pictures as well.

E. *THE POSTULATE OF ANALOGY. "Given two classes of events A and B, and given that, whenever both A and B can be observed, there is reason to believe that A causes B, then if, in a given case, A is observed, but there is no way of observing whether B occurs or not, it is probable that B occurs; and similarly if B is observed, but the presence or absence of A cannot be observed."*

Russell points at the distinction between, for example "observing that it is *not* raining" and "*not* observing that it is raining." This fifth postulate refers to the second kind of non-observation and the reason for supposing why an unobserved fact, if happening, remains unobserved.

The reader will have noticed that each of the preceding postulates is couched in terms of frequencies, i.e. it is supposed that something happens frequently (but not necessarily all the time) in cases of a certain sort (objective aspect) and leading to expectations of a greater or lesser degree of "rational credibility" (subjective aspect). But Salmon (1966) criticizes (1) that in Russell's induction postulates there is a "certain amount of vacillation between the search for necessary conditions and for sufficient conditions, (2) that it is not always clear to which kind of ampliative inference these conditions refer and hence which of the many alternative methods is the appropriate one to choose, and (3) that Russell assumes the soundness of present-day scientific knowledge; this is an assumption even stronger than assuming that knowledge is possible at all. Barker's (1957) objections concentrate rather (1) on the fact that there might exist various competing sets of equivalently valid postulates underlying the scientific approach and (2) on the doubt that any of these sets of postulates are "true". An objection to which Kyburg (1970) adds that all these kinds of presuppositions are nothing more than "a pious wish". Most of these considerations may well be correct, but are perhaps irrelevant, because those who accept postulates of this kind do not, or at least should not, expect them to be more than *the basis of the creed of science.*

5.27 *Uniformity of the Universe and Goodman's Paradox*

The postulational approach leads to the question whether or not a strict distinction between scientific or *cognitive* inductive inference[67], on one side and *pragmatic* inductive inference, on the other, should be made (both together might be called *general inductive inference*). The definition and examples offered in the beginning of this chapter refer to induction in general, i.e. to non-demonstrative inferences on the basis of some evidence which is expected to prove more useful in the long run than any other non-demonstrative inference (e.g. necromancy), but the result of which cannot necessarily be assumed to yield a truth in the scientific-cognitive sense. The following simple comparison will illuminate our distinction.

Imagine three urns, U_1 containing 1000 red balls, U_2 with 999 red balls plus *one* white ball, and U_3 with 990 red balls plus 10 white balls. Let us assume that from each urn a sample of 50 balls is taken, and that each sample consists of red balls only. If the experimenter possesses no other than the sample information, he may infer inductively on the basis of his evidence that in each of the three urns "the next draw will yield a red ball". However, let us assume (1) he is shown that U_1 contains nothing but red balls, (2) he has received reliable evidence that the balls of U_2 are all made of a material

[67] In the sense of leading to the *cognition* of lawlike statements or hypotheses based on the uniformity of the universe of discourse.

created by a certain kind of coral of which marine zoologists believe it can produce only red calcium compounds and (3) he is shown that U_3, in addition to red balls, also contains balls of a different color. Then each of his three inferences acquires a character basically distinct from that of the other two – in spite of the fact that they share the common conclusion or hypothesis: "the next draw will yield a red ball". In the case of U_1 the inference becomes a *deductive* one, because the conclusion follows by logical necessity. In the case of U_2 we may speak of a *cognitive inductive inference* because the experimenter possesses the scientific expectation (though not certainty) that his universe of discourse is uniform (i.e. with regard to color the balls in U_2 are the same). While in the case of U_3 he is certain that his universe of discourse is not uniform. This prevents him from accepting the hypothesis as a cognitive-scientific truth, but it might not impede him from assigning perhaps a relatively high probability to the hypothesis, and may thus lead him to expect a red ball at the next draw from U_3 (for such pragmatic purposes as, for example, betting).

But what happens when the experimenter continues with his draws from U_2 and finally encounters the one white ball in this urn? If he can assure himself that the white ball is made of the same coral material as the other balls, being neither bleached nor dyed, then he may revise the scientific law on which his cognitive hypothesis was based; namely that this kind of coral can also produce white calcium compounds (perhaps at a young or early stage). Such revisions again and again occur in science, the most famous of which is the exception to the second law of motion (Newton: "The change of motion is proportional to the motive force impressed; and is made in the direction of the right line in which that force is impressed" translate from Latin). All experience confirmed this law until A. A. Michelson with the assistance of Edward W. Morley drew in 1887 the "rare white ball". They performed the most celebrated negative experiment in the history of science by showing that in at least one category (in the case of light) motion is not proportional, i.e. speeds of various bodies cannot be superimposed upon each other in an additive way, and thus supplying the empirical cornerstone to the independently developed theory of relativity. If the second law of motion continues to be used, it is in a revised form, namely by an absolute upper limit to any kind of speed. Thus many scientific lawlike statements can be maintained in a slightly modified way by drawing some boundary which limits their universality. *From a system's point of view this means that certain, perhaps all, lawlike statements are acceptable within the confines of a specific system but not beyond them.*

From all this we recognize that the assumption of the uniformity of nature or more precisely, the uniformity of the universe of discourse (which is bound to be a more or less limited system) plays a decisive role in scientific methodology. Among the many versions which this assumption of regularity assumes, we encounter Hume's principle that the future resembles the past, Mill's principle of spatio-temporal homogeneity, J. M. Keynes' principle of limited variety (ensuring that the attributes of individuals cluster together in a finite number of groups), Russell's postulate of natural kinds, etc. As Russell (1948) points out: "... the postulate is adequate logically as a basis for induction, ... it can be stated in a form in which science to some degree confirms it ... It therefore satisfies two of the three requisites of a postulate. But it does not, in my opinion, satisfy the third, namely that of being discoverable, by analysis, as implicit in arguments which we all accept." (p. 456). In consequence of this deficiency Russell developed the postulates discussed in the preceding Subsection.

In more recent times *Goodman's Paradox*, frequently encountered in the modern literature, has shed further light, from the linguistic point of view, upon this assumption of regularity. In general we may say that induction *projects* an observed regularity into the future by assigning a probability to the pertinent argument. But Nelson Goodman not only demonstrated that *projectibility* is a matter of degree (that is to say some regularities are highly projectible, others less so and some hardly at all), but that *the degree of projectibility may depend on the language system used to describe the pertinent regularity*. This startling result can be illustrated best by Goodman's famous "grue-bleen" paradox. He begins his illustration by introducing two new color words. For him an object is said to be "grue" if (and only if) it is *green before 2000 A.D. and blue after this time.* On the other hand, an object is said to be "bleen" if (and only if) it is *blue before 2000 A.D. and green after this time.* A live chameleon, for example, sitting on a green cloth before the year 2000 and afterwards being transferred to a blue one, would be regarded first as "green" and later as "blue" in terms of traditional English, but would be called "grue" in both cases from the viewpoint of Goodman's linguistic convention. Alternatively, this convention would force us to call the color of a sapphire "bleen" before 2000 A.D. and "grue" afterwards. If now two experts (one using the traditional color words, the other using the new ones) observe all newly extracted sapphires, they both would agree on the existence of a regularity provided the observations are before 2000 A.D. If the observations are continued after this date only the expert using the traditional language would have to admit a continuing regularity; the other expert would have to abandon, after 2000 A.D., his belief in the regularity that all sapphires are bleen.

The purpose of this almost absurd example, is to show (1) that some regularities (e.g. to call a sapphire blue in traditional English) are projectible, while others (e.g. to call a sapphire "bleen" in the Goodman language) are not projectible, and (2) that the degree of projectibility depends on the linguistic apparatus employed in describing the objects under observation. With this emerges another, even more surprising, result: "For any prediction whatsoever, we can find a regularity whose projection licenses that prediction. Of course most of these regularities will be unprojectible. The point is that we need rules to eliminate those predictions based on unprojectible regularities."[68] (In general the Goodman-Paradox is taken to represent a serious objection against Carnap's inductive logic.)

The illustration offered by Skyrms for example (see Figure 5-3) shows that, given only the data plotted for the years 0, 10 and 20 on the abscissa, at least three different but equally possible population projections of a

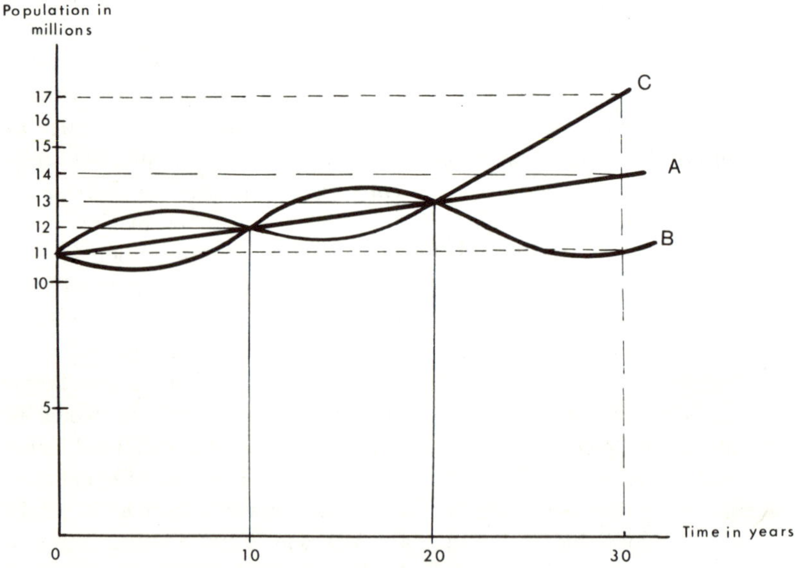

Fig. 5-3[69]

[68] Skyrms, *Choice & Chance: An Introduction to Inductive Logic*, 1966.
[69] Reprinted from Skyrms (1966).

fictitious country can be made for the year 30, depending whether the curve *A* or *B* or *C* is fitted upon the original data.

5.3 Probability and Its Interpretation

Probability is a fascinating and still fairly controversial concept. It is amenable to a variety of interpretations, and also constitutes the crucial link between the logic of induction and probability theory, on one side, and between statistics or decision theory on the other. This section contains a concise sketch of the various interpretations of the probability concept (as far as these aspects have not yet been illuminated in Section 5.2) and points out interrelations resulting from it.

One way to look at this concept, envisaging even a *hierarchy* of probabilities, is offered by Bertrand Russell:

> We have . . . a hierarchy of probabilities. The primary level is: Probably it will rain. The secondary level is: Probably the symptoms I noticed are a sign of probable rain. The tertiary level is: Probably certain kinds of events make certain future events probable. Of these three levels, the first is that of common sense, the second that of science, and the third that of philosophy.
>
> In the first stage, we have observed that, hitherto, *A* has been followed nine times out of ten, by *B*; in the past, therefore *A* has made *B* probable in the sense of finite frequency. We suppose without reflection, at this stage, that we may expect the same thing in the future. In the second stage, without questioning the general possibility of inferring the future from the past, we realize that such inferences should be submitted to certain safeguards, such, for example, as those of Mill's four methods. We realize also that inductions, even when conducted according to the best rules, are not always verified. But I think our procedure can still be brought within the scope of the finite frequency theory. We have made in the past a number of inductions, some more careful, some less so. Of those made by a certain procedure, a proposition *p* has, so far, been verified; therefore this procedure, hitherto, has conferred a probability *p* upon the induction that it sanctioned. Scientific method consists largely of rules by means of which *p* (as tested by the past results of past inductions) can be made to approach nearer to 1. All this is still within the finite frequency theory, but it is now inductions that are the single terms in our estimate of frequency. That is to say, we have two classes *A* and *B*, of which *A*

> consists of inductions that have been performed in accordance with certain rules, and *B* consists of inductions which experience hitherto has confirmed. If *n* is the number of members of *A*, and *m* is the number of members common to *A* and *B*, then *m/n* is the chance that an induction conducted according to the above rules will have, up to the present, led to results which, when they could be tested, were found to be true.[70]

But Russell's hierarchy, as illuminating as it may be, does not touch the major controversy about probability. This controversy pivots on the question whether probability is an objective empirical concept (like *relative frequency*), or an objective logical concept (like the *rational degree of belief*) or a subjective empirical concept (like *actual degree of belief*), etc. Part of the dispute is settled by the fact that there exists a general and purely mathematical theory of probability,[71] the axioms of which are assumed to be valid for various *interpretations* of the probability concept. Thus the point of gravity of this controversy has shifted and now focuses on two main questions. (1) Does each of the three interpretations mentioned, *actually* obey the axioms of the probability calculus, thus deserve the name "probability"? And (2) under which circumstances is which interpretation applicable?

The oldest or *classical view* on probability, as for instance stated by Laplace, is difficult to categorize, since both, frequentists as well as subjectivists lay claim to the classical ancestry. It might be best to regard this notion

[70] Russell, *Human Knowledge, Its Scope and Limits*, 1949, p. 377. Copyright © 1948 by Bertrand Russell; © 1975 by the estate of Bertrand Russell.

[71] One of the earliest and most renowned set theoretical axiomatizations of a general probability calculus is that by A. N. Kolmogorov, presented first in *Grundbegriffe der Wahrscheinlichkeit* (Berlin, 1933) and translated as *Foundations of the Theory of Probability* (1950). Kolmogorov's axiomatic basis in its simplest version is familiar to everyone acquainted with the rudiments of probability theory. Although the latter is a highly complex body of theorems, definitions etc., it rests ultimately on nothing but the following two primitive notions and three axioms:

Primitives:

U	the universe of discourse as the set of all possible elements or events, etc.
$P(A) = p$	the probability of A (or B or C, etc. as subsets of U) taking a real value p (the probability value or measure).

For various interpretations of U and $P(A)$ see Table 5-5.

Axioms

1. Any probability value is larger or equal to zero: $P(A) = p \geqslant 0$.
2. The probability value of the entire universe of discourse is 100 per cent: $P(U) = 1$.
3. The probability value of a joint set $A \cup B$ (the component sets of which do not intersect, hence are mutually exclusive: $A \cap B = 0$), is the sum of the probability values of each component set:
   $P(A \cup B) = P(A) + P(B)$ if and only if $A \cap B = 0$.

as an insufficiently articulated precursor of both interpretations. Its major characteristic is the crass assumption that all events of the same kind are *equally possible*. If this is taken to mean "equally probable" the definition of probability may become circular, unless an additional principle, e.g. the much disputed *principle of insufficient reason or indifference*,[72] is adopted. If, however, "equally possible" means *realizable to the same degree*, there is the danger that for some events that are actually not equally probable (like the throwing of a loaded die) one may erroneously assume equal realizability. Indeed, in the earlier stages of probability theory many errors of this kind did occur.

Since the *principle of indifference*, as the very core of the classical interpretation, leads to contradictions[73] and other difficulties, the classical view is mainly of historical significance and is here not treated as a separate interpretation.

5.31 *Relative Frequency*

The majority of statisticians still seem to adhere to the *empirical objective* interpretation of probability. Most of the various shades of interpretation encountered in this camp can be traced to Richard von Mises' fundamental epistemological work on *Probability, Statistics and Truth* (1928). There probability is viewed as *the limit of the relative frequency* of an *infinite* sequence of occurrences. But if the set of all events (e.g. the flipping of a coin) is infinite, then its subset (e.g. flipping of heads) will also be infinite (as we may conclude from our discussion of infinite sets, see Subsection 3.32). In this situation, therefore, the relative frequency cannot be determined as a ratio of the number of favorable occurrences to all occurrences[74]

[72] Kyburg (1970, p. 31) for example points out that "defining probability as a ratio of equiprobable alternatives" *need not be circular* "as long as there is some way, not involving reference to probability, for identifying the equiprobable alternatives. That is, . . . if we can define equiprobability in general terms of equiprobable alternatives, and then define equiprobability of alternatives in terms of something that does not involve reference to probability." The *principle of indifference* fulfills this requirement of individuating the alternatives to be counted. This principle assumed *equal probabilities for events which do not indicate any reason to believe otherwise*.

[73] For illustrations of such contradictions see Kyburg (1970, pp. 34–38), and Salmon (1966, pp. 67–69).

[74] If both the number of favorable occurrences and that of all occurrences is infinite, the ratio would be ∞/∞ which is not meaningful at all. To attain a meaningful solution, the mathematical notion of "limit" has to be employed: The sequence $f_1, f_2, f_3 \ldots f_n$ has the limit f as n tends to infinity if, corresponding to any positive number ϵ (no matter how small), there exists an integer N such that $|f - f_n| < \epsilon$ for all $n > N$.

as is possible under the classical and finite notion; it rather has to be interpreted as the *limit* of the sequence of ratios. This may be illustrated below where H stands for "heads" and T for "tails" of a coin:

Number of flips n:	1	2	3	4	5	6	7	8	...
Sequence of outcomes:	T	H	H	T	H	H	T	T	...
Sequence of ratios f_n:	0/1	1/2	2/3	2/4	3/5	4/6	4/7	4/8	...
(head flips/total flips)									

It is *assumed* that the limit of this relative frequency exists and that, in case of an unbiased coin, the sequence of ratios f_n converges to 1/2.

This infinity assumption obviously is an unrealistic idealization, but von Mises, in conformity with his intellectual precursors A. A. Cournot, John Venn and George Helm, considers:

> Theory of probability as a science of the same order as geometry or theoretical mechanics . . . just as the subject matter of geometry is the study of space phenomena so probability theory deals with mass phenomena and repetitive events. By means of the methods of abstraction and idealization . . . a system of basic concepts is created upon which a logical structure can then be erected. Owing to the original relation between the basic concepts and the observed primary phenomena, this theoretical structure permits to draw conclusions concerning the world of reality.[75]

A further objection was raised against von Mises' insistence that the set of events must be a *random* sequence (irregular sequence, see Subsection 5.2). This assumption was abandoned in Reichenbach's system which also contains a metalinguistic probability interpretation leading to "truth frequencies", without, however, trespassing into the area of logical interpretation (see 5.32). In this connection Russell refers to Reichenbach's theory as one "which substitutes 'probability' for 'truth' ".[76]

Further branches of this camp are the "finite frequency interpretation"[77]

[75] Richard von Mises, *Probability, Statistics and Truth*, 1957, p. vii.

[76] Russell, *An Inquiry into Meaning and Truth*, 1940; quoted from the Pelican edition, 1962, p. 272.

[77] Cf. Russell, *Human Knowledge*, p. 69 ff.

which is based on *finite* sequences only, the "conceptual-counterpart view" which does not necessarily identify probability statements with statements about observable frequencies,[78] but regards the theory as an abstract counterpart of empirical events with much looser ties to actual, repeated observations. Finally there is Hacking's "chance-set up view" related to Popper's "propensity interpretation" both of which will here be mentioned without any further discussion.[79]

The major objection to the frequency interpretation is its inapplicability to events not based on mass phenomena, hence its disregard to many legitimate usages of the word probability in everyday language:

> Even the frequentist must admit that the phenomena which they accept as having a probabilistic character make up a spectrum ranging from *strong* cases, such as Mises' drawing from a bag, to *much weaker* cases, such as those illustrated by some of the less conventional insurance problems. Where one draws the line is clearly a matter of subjective judgement. This in itself greatly weakens the methodological foundations of the frequentist objectivist position. Secondly, it has become obvious by now that a considerable number of highly intelligent people – including the prominent representatives of purely probabilistic decision theory – consider it compelling to apply the rules of probability to sets of events *in general* that is, also to events which no one would consider more or less analogous to the idealized processes generating convergent frequency ratios. The frequentist-objectivist position is inadequate.[80]

5.32 *Degree of Confirmation*

Degree of confirmation nowadays identified with the logical or entailment interpretation of probability (by Carnap also called probability$_1$, in contrast to relative frequency which he calls probability$_2$)[81] is ultimately connected with inductive logic. This concept is claimed to be an objective but purely *logical* one, expressing the degree of belief in an hypothesis by a purely *rational* being on the basis of some given evidence. It arises out of the *partial* entailment of an evidence by its hypothesis (in contrast to the *complete*

[78] Cf. Braithwaite, *Scientific Explanation*, 1953; reference to 1960, p. 191.

[79] For further details see Hacking, *Logic of Statistical Inference*, 1965, and Popper, 'The Propensity Interpretation of Probability', 1960. See also Stegmüller (1973c).

[80] Fellner, *Probability and Profit*, 1965, p. 46.

[81] Thus Carnap recognizes both kinds of probability and occasionally recommends probability$_2$ as an estimate of probability$_1$ or vice versa.

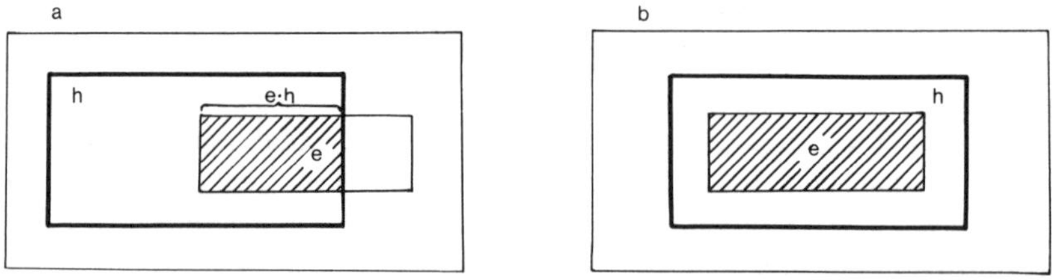

Inductive logic

$c(h, e) = 2/3$ means that the sentence e is implied to 2/3 only by the hypothesis h (i.e. only 2/3 of the range of e is contained in h).

Deductive logic

The sentence e (evidence, or premise) implies the sentence h (hypothesis or conclusion).

Fig. 5-4[82]

entailment of the evidence by its hypothesis in a deductive argument) as Figure 5-4(a) illustrates.

The concept of logical probability was first systematically developed, though not defined, by John Maynard Keynes in his *Treatise on Probability* (1921).[83] But to explain induction, Keynes had to introduce his "postulate of limited variety" (explained popularly in Part 6, Chapter III of Russell's *Human Knowledge*); he also emphasized that not all probabilities are measurable in terms of real numbers (i.e. on a ratio scale). In spite of thorough further developments by Nicod, Carnap and others, it was not possible to make it a generally measurable concept. The complex, artificial language systems developed by Carnap (for some explanatory readings on this subject see Salmon (1966, pp. 68–83)) enable the measurement of the degree of confirmation merely in highly simplified situations. But even there, *unique* measures do *not* seem to be attainable.[84] Much interesting theoretical work has been added by Kemeny (e.g. relaxing the rather stringent language restrictions imposed by Carnap), by Hintikka and Hilpinen (attainment of reason-

[82] Adapted from Carnap (1960, p. 297); cf. Salmon (1966, p. 69). These rectangles represent *sentences* and not sets, thus the figures are *not* Venn-diagrams. In Figure 5.2 (a), therefore $e \supset h$ (if e and h were sets, one would have to write $e \subset h$).

[83] Although Jeffreys, whose *Theory of Probability* did not appear before 1939, raises some claim of priority, referring to two articles which he published in co-authorship with Dorothy Winch. Cf. *Essays in Biography*, 1933. Cf. Raiffa (1968, p. 275).

[84] This is manifested in Carnap's *The Continuum of the Inductive Methods*, 1952, where the availability of a continuum of infinitely many inductive methods and possibilities to measure the degree of confirmation is revealed.

ably high probability measures in cases of universal generalizations etc. see Subsection 5.24), by Kyburg, who presented a probability interpretation especially oriented toward epistemology (epistemological probability[85]), and others.

However, in spite of all efforts and the high desirability of an objective measure, the degree of confirmation, there are no signs that the problems of "objectivity" and "measurability" have been mastered to make this probability notion applicable to empirical sciences and decision making processes.[86]

5.33 *Subjective Probability*

The concept of subjective probability (also called personal, or judgemental, or Bayesian probability) abandons the confirmationists' trust in the existence of an objective and rational degree of belief, and merely expresses a person's *actual* degree of belief as manifested in his betting and action behavior. The foundations to a systematic development were laid by Ramsey and further expanded by De Finetti. But the concept found wide attention and application only after the appearance of the fundamental work by Savage (see also Subsection 5.24). The intertwining notions of subjective probability and utility originally discovered by Ramsey, but independently rediscovered by von Neumann and Morgenstern, are vital for a complete understanding of this probability interpretation. A person confronted with such a combined probability–utility situation may, so to speak, *trade probability against utility* or vice versa (i.e. to trade a higher amount of uncertain utility against a smaller amount of a more certain utility, or the other way round). It is this betting and action behavior which makes subjective probability much more easily accessible to measurement than logical probability. Thus it is hardly surprising if this concept found wide acclaim and practical application during the last two decades, especially in the administrative sciences.

The major weaknesses of subjective probability obviously lie in the *personal bias* to which this concept or its measurement are subject, and in the *instability* with which some of these probabilities are anchored in a person's mind. Individual beliefs vary from person to person and are occa-

[85] Kyburg, *Probability and the Logic of Rational Belief*, 1961.

[86] Some authors regard the "degree of confirmation" problem a dead issue, as the following colorful titles of recent publications indicate, e.g. Settle, 'Confirmation as a Probability: Dead, but it Won't Lie Down', 1970, p. 200; and Schlesinger, 'On Irrelevant Criteria of Confirmation', *ibid*., p. 282.

sionally neither coherent nor consistent and thus may lead to contradictions. For this reason Savage recommended the concept of subjective probability not so much as a direct guide to action but foremost as *a check on the consistency of one's actions*:

> According to the personalistic view, the role of the mathematical theory of probability is to enable the person using it to detect inconsistencies in his own real or envisaged behavior. It is also understood that, having detected an inconsistency, he will remove it. An inconsistency is typically removed in many different ways, among which the theory gives no guidance for choosing. Silence on this point does not seem altogether appropriate, so there may be room to improve the theory here.[87]

But the subsequent development of decision theory, growing out of subjective probability, concentrates less on this indirect guide to action, than on the direct one, requiring decision makers to express explicitly their specific probabilities and preferences. These behavioral data are fed into a decision model which in due process supplies the recommended action. Whether this *decision round-about-way* is preferable to an immediate evaluation of the various action alternatives, is still a controversial matter and cannot be answered generally. Just as the choice of a specific production round-about-way should be based on an investment analysis, a decision round-about-way might need a preliminary investigation as to its desirability. Yet whatever the outcome of such a specific investigation or the general argument is, it will not affect the usefulness of *subjective* evaluations of probabilities and preferences. Whether such evaluations are far removed from the ultimate decisions, through a long chain of analytical processes, or very close to the actual decisions, in both cases *subjective* estimations are often inescapable. Only where mass phenomena are within reasonable reach, will it be possible to combine the subjective and frequency approaches.

In concluding this Section we should like to point out two things:

(1) That none of the three interpretations mentioned is quite independent of the others, and depending on the specific objectives to be attained, each interpretation has its area where it can be justified and other areas for which it is unsuitable. There is no room for the general and exclusive adoption of one interpretation at the cost of the others. To ostracize subjective probabilities would be as unreasonable as to do away with relative frequencies. Even the degree of confidence definitely has its place, if in no other way, than as an idealization of the subjective approach.

[87] Savage, *The Foundations of Statistics*, 1954, p. 57.

TABLE 5-5

Six interpretations of mathematical probability (after Mario Bunge[88])

Designation of interpretation	Interpretation of the set U, the universe of reference	Interpretation of the probability $P(A)$
1. Semantic	Set of all the propositions of a given kind.	Likelihood that the proposition(s) A be true.
2. Statistical	Set of empirical data of a given kind.	Relative frequency of the data (or datum) A in U.
3. Physical 1	Set of random events of a given kind.	Probability of the event(s) A.
4. Physical 2	Set of events of a given kind.	Propensity or disposition of the event(s) A to occur.
5. Psychological	Set of judgements of a given kind (about, e.g. the possible outcomes of an action).	Credibility (or degree of confidence, or certainty) of the judgement(s) A.
6. Ontological interpretation	Set of possibilities (possible facts) of a kind.	Weight of the possibility of A.

(2) More interpretations than the three can be derived. Indeed Bunge does list six interpretations which we have summarized in Table 5-5. Thus the concept of "probability" falls into the same category as such concepts as value, income, capital etc. In all these cases an unambiguous answer can only be given if one refers to the *uninterpreted concept*. Then one can point to a system of conditions (e.g. the axioms of the probability calculus) that must be fulfilled before a concept can be designed as "probability", or "value" or "income" etc. If one deals with an *interpreted* concept, it is recommendable to add the adjectives or nouns indicating the specific interpretation, thus speaking of *subjective* probability, or of *market* value, or of national income at *factor cost* etc.

5.4 Conclusion

Whether one accepts Carnap's analogy between deduction and induction or whether one opts for weaker similarities, one cannot deny that both, deduction and induction are methods of inference. A more precarious question is

[88] See Bunge, *Scientific Research, I – The Search for System*, 1967, p. 428. Interpretations 1 and 2 yield conceptual models, while the other interpretations yield factual models.

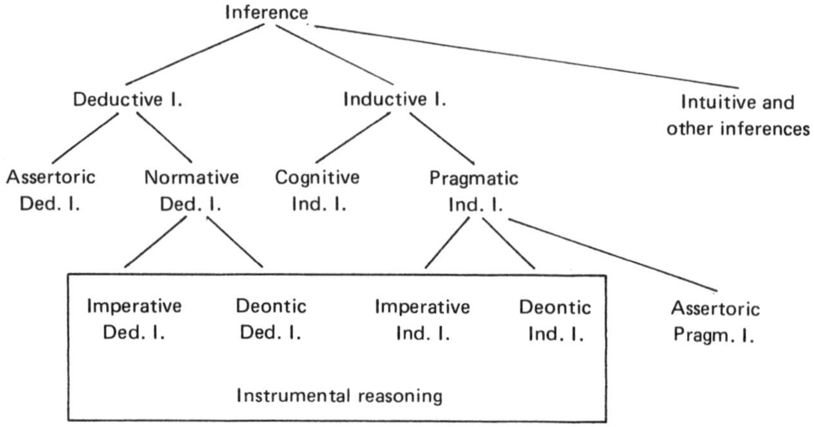

Fig. 5-5. Different forms of inference.

whether beyond these two, there exist other kinds of inference. If inference is the derivation of one set of sentences or propositions[89] from another, then one might also speak of intuitive and heuristic inferences, extra sensory perception etc. Whether "unconscious inference" is non-inferential or even non-propositional knowledge (in the Kantian sense) is a controversial issue: cf. R. Rorty (1967, pp. 207–210). Figure 5-5 presents a tentative classification of the concept of inference. This figure reconfirms our previously discussed notion of "instrumental reasoning", but also reveals some gaps in our discussion. We may be pardoned for not covering at all "Intuitive and Other Inferences" since those are presently still too remote from the kinds of inferences employed in cognitive or instrumental sciences – although the valid point could be made that heuristic inference, as recently applied in computer science and artificial intelligence, would deserve special recognition. We suspect, however, that heuristic methods, if being inferences at all, come closer to inductive than to intuitive inference.

As to the various types of induction we may distinguish the categories sketched in Figure 5-6 and outlined overleaf.[90]

[89] It is not necessary that a proposition must manifest itself in a sentence (in the narrow linguistic) sense; that it can also manifest itself in an *action-configuration* of mechanical, electrical and chemical events, has been discussed by this author elsewhere: see Mattessich, 'Epistemological Consequences of Artificial Intelligence and Systems Research', *Methodology and Philosophy of Science*, London, Ont., 1975b, pp. V-85 to V-86.

[90] This outline is based on the discussion by Bunge, 1967, Vol. 2, pp. 291–294.

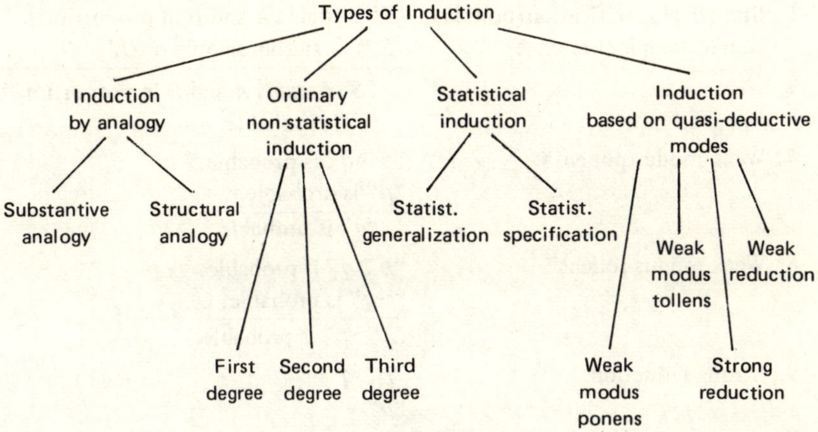

Fig. 5-6

Name of subcategory	*Illustration*
1. Induction by substantive analogy	"$A_1, A_2 \ldots A_n$ are automobiles." "A_1 to A_{n-1} all have four wheels." ∴ "A_n has four wheels" is probable.
2. Induction by structural analogy	"Y is a common physiological trait of animals A_1 to A_n." "X-rays cause cancer in A_1 to A_{n-1}." ∴ "X-rays cause cancer in A_n" is probable.
3. First degree induction (from instance to low level generalization)	"A_1 to A_n are B." ∴ "All A are B" is probable.
4. Second degree induction (from low level to a higher level of generalization)	"Law L holds for A_1 to A_n." ∴ "Law L holds for all A" is probable.
5. Statistical generalization (sample to population inference)	"S is a random sample of U." "S contains A and B in proportion p." ∴ "U contains A and B in proportion p" is probable.

6. Statistical specification (population to sample inference)	"*U* contains *A* and *B* in proportion *p*." "*S* is a random sample of *U*." ――――――――――― ∴ "*S contains A* and *B* in proportion *p*." is probable.
7. Weak modus ponens*	"$p \supset q$" is probable. "p" is probable. ――――――――――― ∴ "q" is probable.
8. Weak modus tollens*	"$p \supset q$" is probable. "$\sim q$" is probable. ――――――――――― ∴ "$\sim p$" is probable.
9. Strong reduction	"$p \supset q$" "p" ――――――――――― ∴ "q" is probable.
10. Weak reduction*	"$p \supset q$" is probable. "q" is probable. ――――――――――― ∴ "p" is probable.

* In items 7, 8 and 10 any one of the two premises (but not both) may be certain instead of probable, and yet the argument form would not change (however the probability attached to argument and conclusion, if measurable, might then change).

Another gap in our discussion is the lack of attention paid to induction with regard to imperative and deontic arguments. Obviously *not* all of these normative arguments are deductive in nature, as the illustrations of Table 5-6 show.

In spite of the existence and probable importance of inductive normative arguments, the literature of logic has to our knowledge, so far ignored them.[91] Several reasons can be advanced for this omission. Above all, the major problems of induction – its explanation, its justification, and its rules – are not yet solved and it seems appropriate to attack first the primary issues before

[91] Under "inductive normative arguments" we understand arguments as illustrated in Table 5-6, something that must not be confused with what Stegmüller (1973b, pp. 389–543), calls "Normative Theorie des induktiven Räsonierens" (normative theory of inductive reasoning). By this somewhat unfortunate expression Stegmüller does not refer to inductive arguments in which a premise and the conclusion are imperatives or ought-sentences, but refers to a reconstruction of Carnap's inductive logic (which of course is based on some *norms* or value judgements *in the meta-language*). Thus there does exist literature (even extensive one) in the area of inductive reasoning with norms in the meta-language but hardly in the area of inductive reasoning where the norms refer to the object language, that is to say to the premises and the conclusion.

TABLE 5-6

Imperative inductive argument	Deontic inductive argument
"*P* attain goal *G*". "*G* can be attained by doing *A*" is probable.	"*P* ought to attain *G*". "To attain *G*, *A* ought to be done" is probable.
∴ "*P* do *A*" is *probably* the true command for *P* to attain *G*.	∴ "*P* ought to do *A*" is *probably* the true advice for *P* to attain *G*.

turning to secondary ones. Furthermore, once the major problems of induction are resolved, the inductive normative arguments seem to fall into one and the same pattern with other inductive arguments. They do by no means appear to create difficulties of the same magnitude as normative arguments in deductive logic. Because, as we know by now, induction *per se* is a much less rigorous kind of inference than deduction, and one does not need to worry whether a consequence follows by necessity from the premises. In inductive logic the relation between evidence (premises) and hypothesis (conclusion) is much looser, and all that could be affected by switching from an assertoric inductive argument to a normative inductive one, might be the probability attached to it. But as the measurement of this probability is still unsolved, if solvable at all, it does not or not yet constitute a problem for this future area of inductive imperative and deontic arguments. Therefore it may suffice at this stage to have vented that problem and point at some of its aspects.

Another aspect so far unmentioned refers to the relation of introspection to induction. The problem of induction could never have attained such crucial importance without the advent of science and its empiricist philosophy. Thus the question arises whether the abandoning of an *uncritical* empiricism that rejects introspection as a mode of knowledge acquisition would basically affect the problem of induction. We do not think so, provided introspection is regarded as a kind of inductive inference. This idea is less absurd than it sounds since introspection is the inference of some electro-chemical pattern or action-configuration from other electro-chemical patterns (derived genetically or from lower level memory storage) within the nervous system of an animal or similar entity. We believe that such introspective inference must not necessarily be deductive, often enough it seems to correspond to inductive inference. Perhaps the category of "Intuitive and Other Inferences" in Figure 5-5 is primarily inductive inference based solely on information *internal* to the pertinent system (i.e. congenital information or information drawn from the sub-conscious).

Since the time of F. Bacon many aspects of the problem of induction have been illuminated but none of the three core-problems has been solved satisfactorily. These are:

(1) *The explanation of induction.* Is induction an epistemological or a psychological problem, or is it a pseudo-problem; and what are the criteria for regarding some inductive inferences as rationally acceptable and others not?

(2) *The justification of induction.* Why should we accept hypotheses attained by inductive inference as true or probable, and why should rules of induction be accepted for attaining such true or probable hypotheses?

(3) *The comparative and measurement problem of induction.* Why should the inductive strength of an argument be greater than that of another one, and how can one measure this inductive strength?

From a systems point of view it seems to us that Max Black's institutional approach (which he regards as a specific version of the "linguistic approach") has much to commend it. He conceives human beings as involved in a complex process of learning from experience, and calls this process *the inductive institution.*

> The philosophical problem of justifying induction can arise only for somebody who is a member of the inductive institution and is therefore already bound by its constitutive rules . . . The constitutive rules of the inductive institution (whose precise delineation remains a still unfinished task for philosophers of induction) are highly abstract, schematic and limited in their practical usefulness. Indeed, the general principles of inductive inference are about as relevant to practice as the abstract principles of justice are to decisions or concrete legal issues. In particular situations concerning the soundness of empirical hypotheses the reasoner is compelled to fall back upon his specific knowledge of relevant facts and theories. In this way the conduct of concrete inductive inference resembles the exercise of a craft or skill more than it does the automatic application of a decision procedure. Yet the constitutive rules provide important general constraints that cannot be violated without generating nonsense . . . To be in command of inductive language, whether as a master of advanced techniques of statistical inference or as a layman constantly and more or less skillfully anticipating future experience, is necessarily to be subject to the implicit norms of belief and conduct imposed by the institution.[92]

This view not only accords with ours (that induction too is a normative area and implies some basic value judgements) but recalls our presentation at the end of Chapter 2 where the relationship between systems or institutions, and the norms incorporated in them was discussed.

[92] Black, M. *Induction*, 1967, pp. 178–179.

CHAPTER 6

DECISION THEORY AND THE ECONOMISTS' METHODOLOGICAL ENDEAVORS

6.1 An Appraisal of Carnap's Inductive Logic

Modern decision theory is intricately connected, on one side with inductive logic and probability theory, and on the other with economics and utility theory. Thus the train of thought developed in the preceding chapter will here continue and will lead quite naturally to economic considerations. We first summarize a critique of Carnap's inductive logic and show that the latter has recently led to two decision-theoretical reinterpretations, a subjective one (Stegmüller 1973b and c) and an objective one (Menges, 1967, 1974).

Carnap's system has been criticized by Stegmüller (1973b, pp. 91–95), on the ground that the idea of developing induction as a logic of *partial* implication (as a weak analogue to deduction, the logic of complete implication; see our Figure 5-4) encounters several difficulties (see items 1 to 4) on technical as well as on other grounds (see items 5 and 10):

(1) Partial implication is no logical implication at all, since the notion of the latter excludes any kind of non-implication (this is our interpretation of Stegmüller's lengthy and more complex formulation).

(2) If one regards partial implication as neither logical implication nor as complete logical independence, then its only explication is the so-called Wittgenstein-Function (which assigns the same value to all states or descriptions); this, however, would not permit any learning by experience, so prominent in Carnap's system. This in turn makes the latter *intuitively*, though not logically, *inconsistent*.

(3) Carnap's system is also intuitively *circular* since, on one side, partial implication serves to explain inductive probability, on the other side, the latter is used to explain the notion of partial implication.

(4) This method seems to conflict with Hume's assertion that conclusions about the future cannot analytically be inferred from past experience.

(5) Carnap's inductive logic is in no position to recommend a specific confirmation-function but merely an infinite continuum of such functions. This neither provides an adequate definition of the "degree of confirmation" nor does it constitute a solution to the confirmation problem.

(6) A theory, like Carnap's, which assigns only zero-degrees of confirmation to natural laws cannot be used for evaluating universal scientific-conclusions based on experience.

(7) Carnap did not provide any rules of hypothesis acceptance or rejection without which scientific practice cannot operate.

(8) The logical status of Carnap's axioms of inductive logic is not clear. On one side the axioms are supposed to be neither deductively nor inductively justifiable; on the other side, they are assumed to be neither empirical nor *a priori* synthetical principles.

(9) The fact that Carnap even *refused* to provide rules of acceptance (or rejection), indicates that his system may not but *must be interpreted decision theoretically* (i.e. instrumentally and not cognitively).

(10) A further objection lies in the strong restrictions imposed by the highly simplified, artificial language systems which led Carnap himself, in his last phase, to shift from a linguistic to a model-theoretical or axiomatic approach.

(11) Another objection lies in the arbitrariness implicit in Carnap's structure descriptions (λ-principle), as well as in the strong restrictions imposed by the highly simplified artificial language systems. For this very reason Carnap, in the last phase, shifted from linguistic considerations of inductive logic to a model-theoretic or axiomatic methodology which approaches that of modern decision theory. Thus Carnap's original *theoretical* goal to solve the Humean problem of induction by means of a probabilistic theory of hypothesis confirmation, cannot be regarded as fulfilled, but there are strong indications that his work presents a basis for fortifying and elaborating the *practical* decision-theoretic approach.

All this strengthens the suspicion that Carnap's original theoretical vision of finding a solution to Hume's problem of induction by means of a probabilistic theory of hypothesis confirmation cannot be attained. However, it also offers a hint that a decision-theoretic reinterpretation may not only salvage Carnap's gigantic effort but may enrich the present body of statistical decision theory.

6.2 Formal Decision Theory and Its Evolution

6.21 *Early Beginnings and the Probabilistic Utility Notion*

Modern decision theory is a mighty river with many diverse contributaries. It mixes not only the waters of philosophy, pure mathematics and statistics, but also those of the economic, behavioral, as well as administrative and other applied sciences. It is undoubtedly one of the most fundamental achievements of the "humanistic" sciences of our century, and, in spite of its emphasis of the utility notion, it must not be identified with a hedonistic philosophy. Its philosophic as well as behavioral basis rests on the insight that *the most fundamental of human judgements* are those concerning *belief* (knowledge, expectation, probability, etc.) and *usefulness* (preference, utility, etc.). To this must be added the further revelation that these two kinds of judgements, although different in some respects, have certain analogies, and above all are more closely tied to each other than one might expect. Finally, the longstanding controversy around *the problem of rationality* may find at least a partial answer in decision theory. Because the task of the latter is not merely to provide a method for improving our administrative, economic, scientific, technical, political as well as every-day decisions, but also to search for criteria of rational behavior. Such criteria comprise not only the basic *deduction principles* but also some kind of *induction principles* as well as *preference or choice principles*. For none of these principles there exists an ideal consensus, but, as we may conclude from the preceding chapters, the agreement on the principles of deductive inference is greater than on those of inductive inference. As far as the theoretical formulation of utility or preference principles are concerned, they have undergone the greatest metamorphosis and provide us with a fascinating history.

One may begin with Jeremy Bentham's (1748–1832) hedonistic ethics which recommends maximizing utility by securing *the greatest happiness for the greatest number of people*. But to measure happiness proved to be a most exacting if not impossible task. To substitute the notion of utility for happiness did not help very much, in spite of the fact that scholars like W. S. Jevons (1835–1882) were convinced that sooner or later, a way will be found to measure utility as a *cardinal* entity. Vilfredo Pareto (1848–1923) was less convinced of this, and took the next crucial step by demonstrating that the economists' marginal utility theory does not require cardinal utilities but can easily be reformulated in terms of the much weaker notion or *ordinal* utility (a mere *comparative* preference measure). But even then the measurement problem could be overcome in none but the simplest cases. All of this rests on the assumption that the decision maker has *no uncertainty* about the consequences of the alternatives involved. Nevertheless such concepts as indifference curves, preference functions, etc. became indispensable standard economic tools, and the notion of ordinal utility dominated the scene for half a century or so. Modern economics, one might say, begins not so much with Keynes' *General Theory*, as with the formulation of the probabilistic theory of utility and its paraphernalia as presented in John von Neumann and Oskar Morgenstern's highly significant and widely influential *Theory of Games and Economic Behavior* (2nd ed. 1947). The N–M utility concept (see also our Subsection 6.23), anticipated by Ramsey (1926), is a peculiar kind of cardinal concept applicable to risk situations. It enables one to predict which among several risk alternatives (e.g. lottery tickets) a person will prefer. Given a person's ranking of the alternative prices he is willing to pay for gaining different amounts at different risks (ranging from lower gains at lower risk to higher gains at higher risk) one can derive his utility function by interpolation. This probabilistic utility notion demonstrates the interdependence of utility and probability in risk situations[1] and thus establishes the *theory of expected utility* (to be illustrated concisely by the following example).

Assume a risk situation (e.g. a gamble) in which n states $s_j (j = 1, \ldots, n)$ can occur, and x_j is the corresponding net gain (or loss) and p_j is the corresponding probability $(\sum_j p_j = 1)$ that s_j will occur; then the expected value of the entire gamble is $\sum_j x_j p_j$. But if there are m such gambles $a_i (i = 1, \ldots, m)$ with different outcomes, then the one with the maximal expected value should be chosen: $\max_i \sum_j x_{ij} p_j$.

[1] "The essence of the notion underlying the N–M utility (Neumann–Morgenstern utility) is that its measurement (on an interval scale) can be derived from preferences or lack of preferences among options involving two variables: commodities and probabilities. We first assume that, if a person shows no clear preference for either of a pair of options, the two options have the same utility for him . . . We get to an interval scale of N–M utility by assuming that within equivalent options we can, so to speak, trade probability for utility. How this is done can be illustrated as follows:

> Suppose the subject in our experiment says he is indifferent between the prospect of receiving \$10 for certain and a fifty-fifty chance of gaining either \$25 or \$1. Since we are concerned with an interval scale and can, therefore, assign two values arbitrarily, let us say that the utility of \$1 is 1 utile and the utility of \$25 is 25 utiles. The utility of \$10 is then assumed to be determined by an equating of the *expected* utilities of the two options.
>
> $$\begin{aligned} 1.0 \times U(\$10) &= 0.5 \times U(\$25) + 0.5 \times U(\$1) \\ &= 0.5 \times 25 \text{ utiles} + 0.5 \times 1 \text{ utile} \\ &= 13 \text{ utiles.} \end{aligned}$$
>
> In this example, then the utility of \$10 is 13 utiles. By starting from these known utility values, and by devising additional options that combine other probabilities and other sums of money, we could proceed to determine, on an interval scale, the utility of other numbers of dollars." (Stevens, 1959, p. 48.)

Assume a risk situation (e.g. a bet, gamble, business or war-like venture) in which n states (or events $j = 1, \ldots, n$) can occur; then we designate the corresponding *utility of* s_j (gain or loss in monetary or other terms) with $u(s_j)$ and the corresponding *probability that event* s_j *occurs* with $p(s_j)$ whereby $\sum_{j=1}^{n} p(s_j) = 1$. Then the utility or value of each event is $u(s_j) \cdot p(s_j)$ and the expected value of the entire risk situation (the worth or highest amount a bettor is willing to pay for participating in this bet) is $E(s_j) = \sum_{j=1}^{n} u(s_j) \cdot p(s_j)$. But if the decision maker (bettor) has different actions $a_i (i = 1, \ldots, m)$ at his disposal (e.g. in a roulette game he can choose between the highest risk situation of betting on a specific number or the lowest risk situation of betting on color, or on many intermediate risk situation, we have to take into consideration this action-dimension by some formula for the expected value of action a_i provided event s_j occurs):

$$(1) \qquad E(a_i) = \sum_{j=1}^{n} u(a_i \mid s_j) \cdot p(s_j)$$

hereby $u(a_i \mid s_j)$ stands for the utility measure of an action a_i, given an event s_j (similar to the *conditional* probabilities encountered in the preceding chapter but with the difference that the *condition* is here *imposed on an action* and not on a hypothesis). If we choose the *simple criterion of maximizing the expected value*, we have to determine the latter for each of the m actions and choose from this range, thus using the decision rule of Bayes–Bernoulli, here called BB, we state:

$$(2) \qquad \text{BB} = \underset{\text{over } i}{\text{maximize}}\ E(a_i).$$

Equation (1) clearly reveals the two decisive factors of such risk situations, the utility and the probability component, as well as their interdependence (in the sense that an increase in one could be traded against a corresponding decrease of the other by maintaining the same expected value).

Let us illustrate the basic decision model by means of the following examples overleaf.

Here the events (or states of nature) s_1, s_2, and s_3 might stand for economic depression, recession, and prosperity respectively, while the actions (or strategies) a_1, a_2, and a_3 might stand for capital intensive, balanced, and

		s_1	s_2	s_3
Probability space:		$p_1 = 0.4$	$p_2 = 0.1$	$p_3 = 0.5$
Event space:		s_1	s_2	s_3
Action space:	a_1	–8000	4000	5000
	a_2	–6000	1000	40000
	a_3	–3000	1500	5000

Consequence matrix $u(a_i \mid s_j)$

$$E(a_1) = \sum_j u(a_1 \mid s_j) \cdot p(s_j) = -3200 + 400 + 2500 = -300$$

$$E(a_2) = \sum_j u(a_2 \mid s_j) \cdot p(s_j) = -2400 + 100 + 20\,000 = 17\,700$$

$$E(a_3) = \sum_j u(a_3 \mid s_j) \cdot p(s_j) = -1200 + 150 + 2500 = 1450.$$

labor intensive operations (of an enterprise) respectively. The consequence space (in our case directly expressed as a "utility matrix" in $ measures) expresses the net gains or losses anticipated. Which action should be chosen? Under the Bayes–Bernoulli rationality criterion, suggested previously, the following decision rule is applied:

$$\text{BB} = \max_i E(a_i) = E(a_2) = \$17\,700.$$

But obviously this is not the only possible decision rule, because such a rule depends also on the temperament of the decision maker. If he is a *risk avoider* or pessimist, he might prefer the *maximin criterion* MI (of Wald, or Neumann and Morgenstern who call it *minimax* criterion), according to which the maximum among the minimal gains (or minimum among the maximal losses) of each action is chosen:

$$\text{MI} = \max_i \, [\min_j u(a_i \mid s_j)]$$

$$= \max_i \, [-8000, -6000, -3000] = u(a_3 \mid s_1) = -3000.$$

In our case the decision maker would have some assurance or hope that he cannot lose more than $3000.

However if he is a *risk seeker* or optimist he might choose the *maximax criterion* MA according to which that action is chosen which gives a chance (as slight as it may be) of the *highest* gain:

$$\begin{aligned} MA &= \max_i \,[\max_j u(a_i \mid s_j)] \\ &= \max_i \,[5000, 40\,000, 5000] \\ &= u\,(a_2 \mid s_3) = 40\,000. \end{aligned}$$

There exist other decision criteria among which the *criterion of minimum regret* (of Savage) is best known. It is based on the idea that the decision maker might want to minimize his regret (i.e. the difference between his actual gain and the possible maximal gain, had he known which event would occur). Also mixed criteria (combinations of some of those mentioned as well as others) are occasionally encountered (e.g. the Hodges–Lehmann criterion – see our discussion of Menges' contribution at the end of Subsection 6.22, as well as Subsection 6.23 dealing with the "sure thing" principle).

The mystique of modern decision theory however does not lie in these simple formulas but in the great variety of ways in which this model can be modified and extended. Its event or consequence space can be greatly enriched, or its probability space, or both; ordinal or cardinal, monetary or non-monetary utility measures can be chosen, so can be objective or subjective probabilities; the axiomatic frame may be on a behavioristic or an introspective basis, it may assume probability measures as given and utility measure to be determined, or the reverse may be assumed, and so on and on. As we shall see in Subsection 6.24 even the entire modern theory of information economics may be derived from our decision model by emphasizing the information dimension hidden in it. We shall also demonstrate the close connection which this model has with inductive logic as well as with the statistical theory of hypothesis testing.

6.22 *The Statisticians' Contributions*

In our historical survey we also have to pay some attention to the contributions made by statisticians to decision theory. As we have noticed, philosophy (among other things) examines the foundations of inductive behavior, and searches for the extra-logical premises on which it rests. Probability theory, though closely related to it, is concerned rather with formulating the purely logical–mathematical foundations (axioms of the probability calculus) underlying the various probability concepts required for induction; furthermore, probability theory is concerned with the theorems following from these axioms, the various interpretations and possible circumstances (possible kinds of probability distributions, etc.) of such a theory.[2] In contrast to this formal concern we find statistics, with its strongly empirical overtone, forging practical tools (e.g. sampling and decision rules) of inductive behavior for situations where large enough sequences of observations are available or, recently, also where *a priori* probabilities are conceivable. Modern statistics, in the eyes of many, is inseparably connected with decision making processes and thus with concepts of risk, value, utility, cost–benefit ratios and certain value judgements. It is this insight which in recent decades welded statistics so tightly to the economic and administrative sciences. And it is this connection which enforces a methodological examination of the economic and administrative sciences that may have repercussions upon pure and applied sciences alike.

The decision-oriented branch of statistics[3] begins, in a way, with a most eminent statistician, Sir Ronald A. Fisher (1890–1962), who developed the first, or one of the first, theories of testing statistical hypotheses, as well as experimental designs, and thereby created a host of important tools – among them the *likelihood principle* and the *fiducial argument* of confirmation which recently have regained prominence in philosophic circles, see Hacking (1965), Stegmüller (1973c), etc. Although Fisher was no less inference-oriented, he also had a strong practical bent and did indeed lay the groundwork for statistical decision making. But his analysis did *not* explicitly take into consideration either losses due to possible errors or *a priori* probabilities. "It is primarily concerned with the probability of rejecting a null hypothesis . . . if the null hypothesis happens to be true" Raiffa (1968, p. 281).

The next major step in this development was taken by Neyman and Pearson (see our Subsection 5.25) who regarded from the very outset the rejection or acceptance of a hypothesis as a decision or action problem. As we have seen in the preceding chapter, the Neyman–Pearson approach

[2] 'Just as geometry started its existence from such questions as "how large is the area of this piece of land," the theory of probability was born of the question "how frequently" will this or that event occur in the course of a long series of trials . . . In recent times, the ideas on the purpose and the scope of the theory of probability became diversified, with various claims being made relating to "inductive reasoning" and "intensity of belief".' Neyman, *First Course in Probability and Statistics*, 1950, p. 3.

[3] The other two branches of statistics are the induction-oriented branch and the descriptive branch. The latter reports (without making inferences), by analyzing, categorizing and "massaging" statistical data, while the former covers the areas of hypothesis construction (estimation) and testing without heed to practical actions. Cf. Raiffa (1968, pp. 278–280).

operates with error characteristics to be evaluated for each strategy by the decision maker (see Figure 5-2); but this approach although already cognizant of various risks (and hence risk losses) in choosing between alternatives does not yet incorporate explicitly losses or benefits. To illustrate the extension of this important and widely used method, and to show the connection to decision theory, we present an example of optimizing the experimental design for hypothesis testing summarized in Table 6-1. There we assume that the decision maker, in selecting his experimental design, can choose between four different sample sizes, on one side, and two different confidence levels, on the other. If costs could be neglected, the largest sample would be chosen, but it still would be difficult to make a choice between the two confidence levels (0.95 versus 0.99). Yet if costs and benefits of various experimental designs are known or can reasonably be conjectured, then an optimal choice in testing the statistical hypothesis can be made. Table 6-1 reveals that the net benefit (gross benefits of a design with a certain accuracy, minus sample cost) of sample size 500 together with a confidence level of 0.95 is *optimal* with $400.00 (all other net benefits are smaller). Of course, in reality it is difficult to determine the sample costs, and almost impossible to measure the gross benefits associated with designs of various degrees of accuracy. But this is here beside the point; the purpose of this example is to illustrate that the decision-theoretical conception of the Neyman–Pearson

TABLE 6-1[4]

A fictitious illustration of 8 alternative experimental designs for optimizing sample-design

	n: Sample size	100	200	500	1000
	C: Cost of sample	$1000	$1600	$3100	$5000
Confidence level $1-\alpha_1 = 0.95$	Significance level α_1	0.05	0.05	0.05	0.05
	Significance level β_1	0.35	0.30	0.20	0.10
	B_1: Gross benefit	$800	$1700	$3500	$4700
	B_1-C: Net benefit	$-200	$100	**$400**	$-300
Confidence level $1-\alpha_2 = 0.99$	Significance level α_2	0.01	0.01	0.01	0.01
	Significance level β_2	0.42	0.36	0.27	0.16
	B_2: Gross benefit	$600	$1800	$3400	$5000
	B_2-C: Net benefit	$-400	$200	$300	$0

α_1 and α_2 . . .type I errors β_1, β_2 . . .type II errors

[4] For an explanation of such terms as "confidence level" and "significance level" refer to Subsection 5.25.

approach of hypothesis testing, if extended toward testing the sample-design, can lead to a kind of optimization calculus.

The next step in elaborating the Neyman–Pearson approach, by introducing a loss concept, is found in the fundamental work by Abraham Wald[5] who also created a "general theory of statistical decision functions *embracing both* the theory of testing statistical hypotheses and the theory of estimation"[6] (cf. our Subsection 5.25).[7]

Then Leonard J. Savage elaborated upon Wald's endeavors in the following two major ways:

(i) formal introduction of utilities (instead of the loss concept),

(ii) assignment of *personal* (*a priori*) probabilities to the various states of nature (or of the world, as he calls it).[8]

Thus the decisive switch from Wald's frequentist point of view to the subjectivist standpoint of Ramsey and De Finetti was made, and was greatly fortified, not only within the area of gambling and scientific induction, but within practically all areas of decision making. This approach was further elaborated, applied, promulgated and occasionally modified by Fishburn, Markowitz, Koopman, Pfanzagl, Raiffa, Schlaifer and many others.[9]

More recently another statistician, Günter Menges, reacted to the subjec-

[5] See 'Contributions to the Theory of Statistical Estimation and Testing Hypotheses', 1939, and his *Statistical Decision Functions*, 1950.

[6] Neyman (1950, p. 12).

[7] The essence of his approach, employing mainly *linear* value functions, pivots on the determination of a *family* of *admissible* strategies (not an optimal strategy!) for statistical experimentation or action. Thus $w(\sigma \mid S)$, the *expected* loss or *worth* of strategy σ given the state of nature S, can be calculated (without assigning probabilities to states of nature) and σ tested as to its admissibility or efficiency. Then the choice of the best strategy among the admissible ones remains a matter of value judgement. Attempts to overcome this flaw by finding principles leading to a more objective determination of an optimal strategy were not successful, but led to the reversal of the problem by specifying "compelling desiderata that any 'reasonable' principle ought to fulfill" and investigating implications and compatibility of these desiderata. Cf. Raiffa (1968, pp. 277–278).

[8] See Savage (1954).

[9] See, e.g. Luce and Raiffa, *Games and Decisions*, 1957; Schlaifer, *Probability and Statistics for Business Decisions*, 1959. Markowitz, *Portfolio Selection: Efficient Diversification of Investment*, 1959. Raiffa and Schlaifer, *Applied Statistical Decision Theory*, 1961. Fellner, *Probability and Profit*, 1965. Fishburn, *Decision and Value Theory*, 1964, *idem., Utility Theory for Decision Making*, 1970. Menges, *Grundmodelle wirtschaftlicher Entscheidungen*, 1969. *idem.* (ed.), *Information, Inference and Decision*, 1974; Pfanzagl, *Theory of Measurement*, 1968. Koopman, 'The Bases of Probability', 1940.

tive approach by further developing decision theory along objective lines. He "presented an epistemological justification of R. A. Fisher's philosophy of scientific inference in terms of a modification of the etiality principle proposed by Hartwig in 1956" – Leiner (1974, p. 65). The *etiality principle* is the stochastic analog to the deterministic causality principle. Just as the latter relates to a certain cause a unique effect, so does, in cases where there is no unique consequence, the etiality principle relate all the possible consequences, weighted by their probabilities, to the probable cause. Leiner claims that it was the consistent application of this principle that led Menges to a counter-position against probabilistic subjectivism. His philosophy on that score was summarized by Menges (1970) in the following words:

(1) Axiomatization of subjective probability is non-sensical and useless.

(2) Axiomatization of (e.g. Kolmogorov) probability is sufficient for probability calculus and for the stochastic parts of decision theory.

(3) Beside the axiomatization of probability, that of utility (let us say, in the sense of von Neumann–Morgenstern) is legitimate. It plays a part in judging of decision making behavior.

(4) Subjective probability, together with the principle of insufficient reason, expresses the relationship of logical possibility (Meinong: Vermutungswahrscheinlichkeit).

(5) The three classical "positions" (objective *a priori*, objective *a posteriori*, subjective) characterize different methods of numerical specification of probabilities.

(6) Subjective probability as "degree of dispositional belief" is a surrogate for numerical *a priori* or *posteriori* specification of probability.

(7) Probability as component of a statement on matters of fact is the expression of the relationship of ontological possibility.

(8) Relationships of ontological possibility are founded upon the etiality principle which connects complexes of causes with 'laws of distribution', or, mathematically speaking, distribution functions.

For decision theory, . . . the following consequences ensue: The process of decision making, as a rule, relies upon a measure of utility, on the one hand, and a statement on probability, on the other. For the acquisition and utilization of probability statements we need that calculus of probabilities which, for its part, rests on (e.g. Kolmogorov's) axioms. Moreover, probability must be numerically specified – a problem of statistics. Such measurement can be *a priori, a posteriori*, or (at last need) subjective. The (objective) real validity of the probability statement is warranted by the etiality principle. For the acquisition and utilization of the utility measure we need utility theory which, for its part, rests on (von Neumann–Morgenstern's) axioms. The utility measure must be numerically specified (i.e. measured in reality). This measurement can also be *a priori, a posteriori*, or subjective; it is again a statistical problem.[10]

Further fundamental problems dealt with by Menges were: (1) the stability problem considering the time-dependence of decision criteria, (2) the accommodation principle separating every decision-theoretical model into an objective and subjective part and (3) separating sharply the inference problem from the decision problem proper.

6.23 *Principles of Rational Choice*

One of the basic problems of instrumental reasoning is to be found in the question: "What are the prerequisites for rational behavior?" This question finds a partial answer in the "axioms" which von Neumann and Morgenstern (1947) advanced in their probabilistic utility theory. Although several of these axioms later turned out to be theorems, we shall offer in the following – for historical as well as pedagogic reasons – a *version* of the original formulation in which the "objects or events of preference" u, v, w, etc. (originally called "entities") have the same designation as their "numerical utilities" – while properly these utilities should be designated differently, e.g.: $U(u)$, $U(v)$, $U(w)$, etc. This distinction would be all the more important as the pertinent probabilities p, $1-p$, q, r, etc.(expressing the degrees of expecting those objects or events) can be *multiplied* with the utilities but *not* with the objects or events.[11] Therefore an expression like $u \cdot p + v \cdot (1-p)$ should, first of all, be interpreted as a risk situation (e.g. a lottery ticket) with an outcome of either u (at a probability of p) or v (at a probability of $1-p$). Later on, when we present a numerical example, *multiplication* is justified only under the assumption that $(u \succ v) \Leftrightarrow [U(u) > U(v)]$ such that the *expected value* of $u \cdot p + v \cdot (1-p)$ expresses the utility of this risk situation.

1. *Complete Ordering*. Among two alternatives (choices of actions, goods, prizes, etc.) u and v, one is either preferred to the other, or they are equally desirable:

[10] Quoted from Menges, 'On Subjective Probability and Related Problems', in *Theory and Decision*, **1**, 1970, p. 55–56.

[11] Furthermore the symbols $>$, $=$, $<$, are *here* used for designating non-numerical preferences (nowadays designated by $\succ$, $\sim$, $\prec$) *as well as* order relations of utilities.

Either $u > v$ or $u < v$ or $u = v$.

2. *Transitivity of Preference Relation*. If u is preferred to v, and v to w, then u is preferable to w:

$((u > v) \cdot (v > w)) \supset (u > w)$.

3. *Willingness to Accept Risk*. If v is preferred to u, then a risk situation in which u and v are attained at likelihoods of p and $1-p$ respectively is preferable over u (attained with certainty):

$(u < v) \supset (u < (u \cdot p + v \cdot (1-p)))$.

4. *Preference of Certainty to Risk*. If u is preferred to v, then u is preferable over a risk situation in which u and v are attained at likelihoods of p and $1-p$ respectively:

$(u > v) \supset (u > (u \cdot p + v \cdot (1-p)))$.

5. *Continuity I*: If v is preferred to w, and w to u, then there exists some risk situation (in which u and v are attained at likelihoods of p and $1-p$ respectively), which is less preferable than the certain attainment of w:

$\exists (p, u, v, w)$: $(u < w < v) \supset ((u \cdot p + v \cdot (1-p)) < w)$.

6. *Continuity II*: If u is preferred to w, and w to v, then there exists some risk situation (in which u and v are attained at likelihoods of p and $1-p$ respectively) which is preferable to the certain attainment of w:

$\exists (p, u, v, w)$: $(u > w > v) \supset (w < (u \cdot p + v \cdot (1-p)))$.

7. *Irrelevance of Order Arrangement*. The order in which alternatives of a risk situation are arranged is irrelevant:

$(u \cdot p + v \cdot (1-p)) = (v \cdot (1-p) + u \cdot p)$.

8. *Decomposability*: Complex risk situations are decomposable (according to the probability calculus) into simple risk situations (without affecting the desirability of each of them):

$(u \cdot q + v \cdot (1-q)) \cdot p + v \cdot (1-p) = u \cdot r + v \cdot (1-r)$ where $r = p \cdot q$.

These axioms are the basis of the probabilistic utility notion, and are best comprehended in the light of this notion. Since the N–M-utility function is calibrated by confronting the decision agent with betting situations (e.g.

lottery tickets, as Ramsey discovered already in the twenties) one cannot escape the spelling out of the basic assumptions on which this calibration and that kind of rationality rest. The axioms 3 to 6 are of course crucial. Of special interest is the fact that 3 and 4 are in a way *universal* propositions since they are valid for all probability values ($0 \leqslant p \leqslant 1$) whereas 5 and 6 are *existential* propositions valid only for at least one probability value p. The axioms 3 and 4 can be made plausible in the following way: Assume the following values:

$$u_1 = 13 \qquad p = 0.9$$

$$v_1 = 15 \qquad 1-p = 0.1$$

then

$$(u_1 < v_1) \supset (u_1 < (u_1 \cdot p_1 + v_1 \cdot (1-p_1)))$$

$$(13 < 15) \supset (13 < (13 \cdot 0.9 + 15.0.1))$$

$$(13 < 15) \supset (13 < 13.2)$$

which illustrates axiom 3 while the next example illustrates axiom 4:

$$u_2 = 15 \qquad p = 0.9$$

$$v_2 = 13 \qquad p = 0.1$$

$$(u_2 > v_2) = (u_2 > (u_2 \cdot p + v_2\ (1-p)))$$

$$(15 > 13) = (15 > (15 \cdot 0.9 + 13 \cdot 0.1))$$

$$(15 > 13) = (15 > 14.8).$$

This should make it obvious that the values attributed to the *risk* situations (with p and $1-p$ – in the above case 13.2 and 14.8 respectively) must lie between the values of the situations with *certainty* (between the values 13 and 15).

The axioms 5 and 6 can be made plausible as follows. Assume:

$$u_1 = 12 \qquad p = 0.9$$

$$w_1 = 13$$

$$v_1 = 15 \qquad 1-p = 0.1$$

then

$$(u_1 < w_1 < v_1) \supset ((u_1 \cdot p + v_1 \cdot (1-p)) < w_1)$$

$$(12 < 13 < 15) \supset ((12 \cdot 0.9 + 15 \cdot 0.1) < 13)$$

$$(12 < 13 < 15) \supset (12.3 < 13)$$

which illustrates axiom 5 while the next example illustrates axiom 6:

$$u_2 = 15 \qquad p = 0.9$$
$$w_2 = 13$$
$$v_2 = 12 \qquad 1-p = 0.1$$

then

$$(u_2 > w_2 > v_2) \supset (w_2 < (u_2 \cdot p + v_2\,(1-p)))$$

$$(15 > 13 > 12) \supset (13 < (15 \cdot 0.9 + 12 \cdot 0.1))$$

$$(15 > 13 > 12) \supset (13 < 14.7).$$

However if

$$u_3 = 12 \qquad p = 0.9$$
$$w_3 = 13$$
$$v_3 = 100 \qquad 1-p = 0.1$$

then

$$(u_3 < w_3 < v_3) \supset (u_3 \cdot p + v_3(1-p) < w_3)$$

$$(12 < 13 < 100) \supset ((12 \cdot 0.9 + 100 \cdot 0.1) < 13)$$

$$(12 < 13 < 100) \supset (20.8 < 13)$$

which obviously is *incorrect*. This demonstrates that the above stated formula does not hold for all values of *p, u, v, w*, but *only for some*, as axiom 5 states. Something analogous can be shown for axiom 6.

The construction of a utility or desirability scale may be illustrated in the following way (see Figure 6-1): Assume the utility of \$0 as zero *utiles* and of \$20 as 20, then we may determine the utility value of, e.g. \$1 by interpolation, provided the decision maker can give us his subjective (betting) probabilities (e.g. for a wager of \$1 he expects to win \$20 with a 15% chance) in the following indifference situations:

$$U(w) = u \cdot p + v\,(1-p)$$
$$U(\$1) = 0 \cdot 0.85 + 20 \cdot 0.15 = 3 \text{ utiles}$$
$$U(\$2) = 0 \cdot 0.775 + 20 \cdot 0.225 = 4.5 \text{ utiles}$$

$$U(\$3) = 0 \cdot 0.70 + 20 \cdot 0.30 = 6 \text{ utiles}$$

$$U(\$14) = 0 \cdot 0.15 + 20 \cdot 0.85 = 17 \text{ utiles}$$

$$U(\$18) = 0 \cdot 0.05 + 20 \cdot 0.95 = 19 \text{ utiles.}$$

It is claimed that Ramsey (1926/31) showed us a way to construct such a utility scale even "without" an indication of subjective probabilities, provided the "certain" value to be measured (e.g. w) corresponds to a risk situation in which there exists an indifference – ethical neutrality[11a] – in expecting the extreme points (e.g. u or v respectively). But the indication of this kind of indifference is nothing but an expression of the two subjective probabilities which now are both 0.5. Ramsey's method however may be easier to apply and thus constitutes a genuine improvement. This is illustrated (in Figure 6-1) by finding the following points on our utility scale.

$$U(\$6) = 0 \cdot 0.5 + 20 \cdot 0.5 = 10 \text{ utiles}$$

$$U(\$12) = 10 \cdot 0.5 + 20 \cdot 0.5 = 15 \text{ utiles}$$

$$U(\$9) = 10 \cdot 0.5 + 15 \cdot 0.5 = 12.5 \text{ utiles.}$$

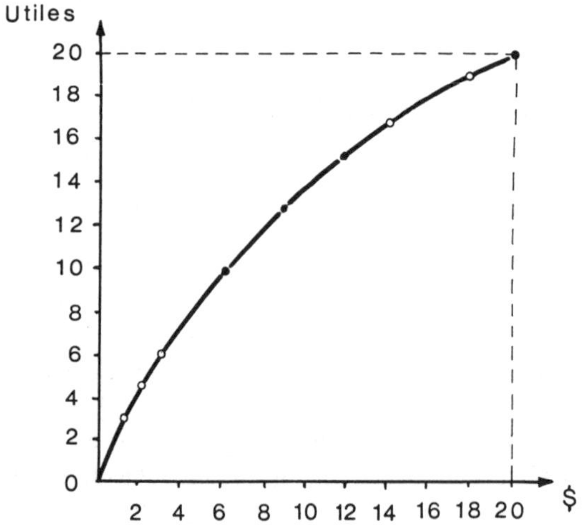

Fig. 6-1. Construction of a utility scale.

[11a] A condition is *ethically neutral* for a decision maker if his preference order is independent of his belief as to the occurrence or non-occurrence of this condition. The bettor now indicates the amount (e.g. $6) he is willing to wager (e.g. for winning either $20 or nothing at a 50–50 chance).

In this example it has to be noted, first, that the scale is an interval scale, in the sense that its extreme points, as well as its intervals, are chosen arbitrarily, and, second, that the abscissa need not necessarily show monetary values but could be expressed in commodity units, etc. Third, in the case of Ramsey's technique a double indifference is involved, on the one side, an indifference between an event at certainty and a risk situation (with two alternative events with complementary probabilities of occurrence) has to be specified; on the other side, an indifference must hold between these two uncertain events such that the probability assigned to each is 1/2. Fourth, the problem can be inverted such that the utilities are given but the pertinent probabilities are to be determined. In this case the same set of equations are utilized. Fifth, it should be pointed out that Jeffrey (1965), apart from substituting the notion of "desirability" for that of "utility", succeeded in bringing to *a common propositional basis* the three kinds of entities involved in statistical decision theory: possible actions, possible states of nature and possible effects or consequences. Finally, it has to be taken into consideration that *in our view a normative theory is valid only for those decision makers whose value judgements conform to the pertinent norms*. This means in the above case, that the axioms or postulates of choice or similar ones (together with other rules, e.g. the Bayes–Bernoulli rule) constitute the basic norms of rationality as expressed in this kind of statistical decision theory. Now we recognize another reason why the formulation and exposition of axioms is so important, they often *reveal the norms* contained in the theory.

Those axioms proved immensely fertile in stimulating many scholars and in inciting a vast amount of literature. But the underlying assumptions have been criticized on various grounds and the axioms have been restated, improved upon, extended, and some of them have been refuted by behavioral experiments. Does a decision maker believe in the probabilities he assigns to future events? Do these subjective probabilities correspond to the true chances? Is a one-dimensional utility approach sufficient? Is it correct to assume that every utility is expressible as a linear combination of every other? Is a deviation from these axioms and the Bayes–Bernoulli decision criterion really "irrational"?

A major step towards improving these axioms is found in Savage's (1954) reformulation and extension. Thereby the frequently mentioned *sure-thing-principle* plays an important role. If a subject is, for whatever reason, not in a position to assign probabilities to future events, then he is forced to rely on some weaker decision criterion than that of maximizing expected utility. Some of these criteria were mentioned in Subsection 6.22, but not the one bearing the unesthetic name of "sure-thing-principle" (preferably called *dominance principle*). Yet notwithstanding its designation, it seems to be the simplest and least controversial among various alternatives. "This principle asserts that if two decisions are such that for each possible state of nature the consequences of choosing the first decision are at least as desirable as those of choosing the second, then the first one should be weakly preferred to the second. The obvious central weakness of the sure-thing principle is that it can rarely be applied. In general, neither of two given decisions is better than the other in the sense of the sure-thing principle."[12]

An especially interesting and philosophically consequential analysis of rational behavior was made by John Milnor (1954). He not only proposed the following nine axioms for any fully acceptable principle of action, but also demonstrated that there cannot exist a precisely formulated set of coherent principles that would correspond to the conventional ideas of rationality. Milnor's results, similar to those of Russell's paradox for the foundations of set theory, yield an impossibility theorem. "Briefly, Milnor proposes the following nine axioms for any fully acceptable principle of choice. First, the principle must order the alternative courses of action. Second, this ordering must be independent of the arbitrary ordering of the rows and columns of the matrix. Third, the principle must be compatible with the sure-thing principle mentioned earlier; that is, if one row dominates another row in every column, that first row must be preferred. Fourth, the principle must satisfy an obvious condition of continuity. Fifth, the preference ordering of the courses of action must be unaffected by a linear change in all entries in the matrix. (This principle reflects the general result that the utility of consequences is measured only on an interval scale.) Sixth, the principle of choice must satisfy the condition of independence from irrelevant alternatives, namely that the ordering between old rows must not be changed by the addition to the game of a new row. The seventh axiom asserts that the principle must be invariant under a linear change of any column; in other words, the ordering among courses of action must not change if a constant is added to some column. Eighth, the ordering generated by the principle of choice must be indifferent to a column duplication; that is, the ordering must not change if a new column identical with some old column is added to the game. The ninth axiom asserts the requirement of convexity, which means simply that, if a row is equal to the average of two other rows judged equivalent in the preference ordering, then the first row must not be judged worse than the

[12] Suppes, 'Decision Theory', 1967, p. 312.

two equivalent rows of which it is an average. This axiom is sometimes described as asserting that the decision maker should not be prejudiced against randomization . . . None of the familiar criteria of rationality for the decision maker is compatible with all nine of these axioms. Milnor shows, for example, that the Laplacean [Bayes'] criterion is characterized by axioms 1, 2, 3, 6, and 7 and the Wald minimax criterion by axioms 1, 2, 3, 4, 6, 8, and 9. The undesirable negative result is that no criterion satisfies all nine together . . . Closely related paradoxical results in confirmation theory suggest that the naive theory of rationality, like the naive theory of sets, cannot easily be systematically reconstructed in any simple and consistent fashion."[13]

One of the most surprising results of the decision theoretic analysis within Neumann and Morgenstern's game theory, is the fact that in certain non-zero sum game strategies, the most rational decision is the one based on flipping an unbiased coin or using some other randomization device. As Suppes (1967, p. 312), says, "it is a result at variance with naive intuition, which urges us to deliberate and to use all possible information available in making a decision."

6.24 *Further Contributions by Philosophers and Economists*

One of the most recent and substantial contributions in the border area of induction, probability and decision theory have been made by the Austrian philosopher Wolfgang Stegmüller (1973b and c) of the University of Munich. He rejects the problem of induction in its traditional Humean version and firmly negates the question: "Do truth-preserving ampliative inferences exist?" Instead, he pleads for replacing this issue by the following two separate classes of so called *Nachfolgerprobleme* or successor problems: (1) The practice-oriented problem of decision theory which poses two main questions: "What are the norms of rational behavior?" and "How can these norms be justified?", and (2) the theory-oriented problem of statistical inference posing two further questions "What is the definition of confirmation (support, corroboration) of a hypothesis?" and "How can the adequacy of such a definition be justified?" As mentioned previously (see Subsection 6.23), Stegmüller interprets Carnap's approach in a purely decision-theoretical fashion, but Popper's approach in an inference-theoretical way. Indeed, he points out that such a viewpoint would explain many misunderstandings between Carnapians and Popperians. A confusion which may well have arisen out of Carnap's inference-theoretical interpretation of his own approach to be overcome by viewing Carnap's theory as a part of the

[13] Suppes, 'The Philosophical Relevance of Decision Theory', 1961, pp. 608–609.

metatheory of practical or instrumental reasoning, and Popper's theory as a part of the metatheory of theory-formation and cognitive reasoning.

An approach very different from that of Carnap or Stegmüller is to analyse the problems of choice, decision and action from the viewpoint of the *mind–body issue*. Then the controversy centers around the question "Which of these activities are mental acts and which are purely physical?" Different views have been advanced but a consensus can hardly be expected at this stage. Some philosophers regard choosing as a mental act that anticipates or even causes physical action, while the philosophical behaviorists oppose this view and insist that choosing is an overt action. They try to demonstrate that choosing and deciding can be explained in terms of objectively observable events and their tendencies. A third group enters a somewhat biased compromise by envisaging choosing as a mental act when identical with deciding, but as an overt physical act when separated from deciding. We cannot afford to enter into the details of this controversy and have to refer the reader to Oldenquist's (1967) survey article and its bibliography.

So far we have mainly dealt with the level of *individual decisions*; but there also exist important contributions on the level of *group and social decisions* that should here at least be mentioned. The game theory of von Neumann and Morgenstern (1944 and 1947) assumes a somewhat intermediate position, on the one side it deals with individual decisions supplying important tools to their analysis, as already emphasized. On the other side it also deals with situations in which collusion might occur – something that might be considered a group decision. But the main effort towards an analysis of the latter was made in a series of articles that culminated in the *Economic Theory of Teams* by J. Marschak and R. Radner (1972), which heavily draws on (these authors') contribution to information economics (see our Section 6.3). This theory aims at optimizing the allocation of various tasks among individual members of a management team. Thus not only the question "who should know what?" is to be answered by such a theory, but also the question "which organizational structure (information and allocation network) should be employed under consideration of cost and other constraints?" These authors summarize the major differences between the decision problem confronting a single person and that confronting several persons as follows:

1. Individual members of the organization may differ with respect to possibilities of action, with respect to their information, and with respect to their preferences. Within the expected utility framework, we may

distinguish, with regard to preferences, differences in beliefs about events from differences in preferences among (sure) consequences.

2. The multi-person character introduces the possibility of uncertainty about other members' actions as well as about the state of nature.

3. Differences among individuals with respect to preferences lead to a new problem of definition of optimality, both for the organization as a whole and for members of the organization.[14]

Another significant development points to welfare economics, i.e. to the relationship between the latter and decision theory. As Suppes claims: "From the standpoint of decision theory perhaps the most important element is the widening of the concept of welfare economics to include the more general concepts of social decision appropriate to political theory. The classical central problem of welfare economics has been the Benthamite one of devising and analyzing schemes for the distribution of economic goods .... As in the case of the normative theory of individual decisions, the results of perhaps the greatest philosophical significance are negative results that call into question the naive concept of rationality as applied to the decision making procedure of a group. The best-known impossibility theorem in this connection is that of Kenneth J. Arrow, which is concerned with the existence of a just or equitable method of social decision."[15] Arrow in his monograph on *Social Choice and Individual Values* (1951) assumes a set of five conditions that a social preference function ought to fulfill. In the following we present a somewhat simplified reformulation of these conditions:

1. *Collective Rationality*: A social preference order can be determined from any set of individual preference orders.

2. *Unrestricted Domain or Citizen's Sovereignty*: There exists a set of individual preference orders for any alternatives u and v such that society prefers u to v.

3. *Independence of Irrelevant Alternatives*: If all individual decision makers prefer in a specific situation u to v, if and only if they also prefer u to v in another situation, then the social preference orders for both situations are the same, hence they are independent of irrelevant alternatives.

Comment: A favorite example to illustrate this condition is the unchanged *relative* preference order for political candidates independent of whether one of the candidates stays in the race or drops out.

[14] Marschak and Radner, *Economic Theory of Teams*, 1972, p. 327.

[15] Suppes, 'Decision Theory', 1967, p. 312.

4. *Pareto Principle*: The social welfare function is not to be imposed (i.e., it is not permitted that some preferences of *society* are taboo in spite of different *individual* preferences).

5. *Nondictatorship*: The social welfare function is not to be dictatorial (the social preference order must not be determined by the preference order of a single individual regardless of other individual preference orders).

Arrow's achievement lies in proving that these fairly plausible conditions or axioms are mutually incompatible (i.e. cannot be satisfied simultaneously by any social decision method) provided the individuals have different preferences – something to be expected among humans. Only if narrow constraints are imposed upon the variety of individual preferences, can this incompatibility be removed, as shown by D. Black (1958). This issue forces us to have a closer look at the perennial problem of rationality in the next Subsection. But there exists another way to avoid this incompatibility (the *Arrow barrier* as it is called), namely by abandoning one or the other of the above-stated conditions. For this purpose condition 3 (Independence of Irrelevant Alternatives) is frequently mentioned as a favored candidate for elimination. The following example illustrates this dilemma to which the non-elimination of condition 3 may lead:

"This condition is extremely powerful. For example, suppose that we treat the individuals of a two-person society symmetrically in the sense that, if one prefers y to z and the other z to y, society shall be indifferent between y and z. Let us try to arrive at the social ordering for the profile:

1	2
x	z
y	x
z	y.

Since both individuals prefer x to y, it is plausible that society should prefer x to y. On the other hand, for x and z, y is irrelevant by condition 3, so the symmetry assumption requires that society be indifferent between x and z; similarly, x is irrelevant when comparing z and y, so symmetry leads to social indifference between z and y. But indifference is a transitive relation, so society is indifferent between x and y, contrary to our conclusion above that society prefers x to y."[16]

[16] Luce and Raiffa, *Games and Decisions*, 1957, p. 338.

6.3 Information Economics as an Extension of Decision Theory

The decision-theoretic approach presented in Subsection 6.22 implicitly contains already an information component which can be made explicit by further enriching the model. To illustrate this process as concisely as possible and to emphasize the salient features we juxtapose in Table 6-2 a primitive decision model with a highly simplified information model.

During the last two decades or so economists like Jacob Marschak (e.g. 1974, 3 vols. selected essays), Roy Radner (e.g. 1972 with Marschak) and many others have devoted a good deal of thought to interpreting information as a commodity. This commodity, although having a value and obeying the laws of economics, has certain peculiarities of its own. The most striking of these lies in the fact that the power and benefit of information is the ability to change the belief of a person, or more precisely, to change the degree of belief in a specific expectation which a certain person may harbour. But what is the use of such a change in belief? Can actually a value be attributed to it? Scholars more than any other group of people realize that knowledge or information *per se* can be immensely gratifying and generate utility in a person. But economists are not concerned with information as a purpose in itself, rather with information as a means to an end. Thus it is not so much the economic theory of consumption than that of production which is applied in information economics. Of course to conclude that the value of a bit of information arises out of the added benefit which one obtains by acting on the basis of this information instead of acting without it, is too simplistic an inference – ultimately this value is rooted in the belief about some expected utility. Again economists focus their interest on these probabilistic events and the overall expected value of such information. Thus information economics evolves out of economic decision theory almost as naturally as a butterfly grows out of the pupa's cocoon.[17]

A comparison reveals that through the following changes a simple decision model can be converted into a simple information model: (1) the probability of event s must be conditioned upon receipt of a specific information y; (2) the decision value therefore also refers to this information y; (3) above all the value V of the entire information system I has to be determined, and if necessary compared with that of another information system or situation in order to choose the optimal among alternative systems, e.g. $\max_I V_I^N$

[17] This paragraph is adapted from Mattessich, "Information Economics and the Notion of Management Information System', 1975a, pp. 343–344.

TABLE 6-2

Comparison of decision and information model

Primitive decision model		Primitive information model	
$E(a)$	$= \sum_s u(a \mid s) \cdot p(s)$	$E(a \mid y)$	$= \sum_s u(a \mid s) \cdot p(s \mid y)$
V_{a^*}	$= \max_a E(a)$	$V(y)$	$= \max_a E(a \mid y)$
$u(a \mid s)$	Utility of action a provided event s occurs (valid also for information model).	$V_{Ia^{**}}$	$= \sum_y V(y) \cdot p(y)$
		V_I^G	$= V_{Ia^{**}} - V_{a^*}$ and $V_I^N = V_I^G - C_I$
		V_{I^*}	$= \max_I V_I^N$
$p(s)$	Prior probability that event s will occur.	$p(s \mid y)$	Conditional probability that event s occurs, provided information y is received in information system I.
$E(a)$	Expected utility of action a.	$E(a \mid y)$	Expected utility of action a, provided information y is received in I.
V_{a^*}	Expected utility of optimal action a^* (used here in both models).	$V(y)$	Expected utility of new optimal action a^{**} upon receiving information y.
$\max_a$	Maximize over the range of all actions.	$V_{Ia^{**}}$	Expected utility of optimal action a^{**} based on information system I *before* receipt of information y.
		$p(y)$	Prior probability that information y is received in I.
		V_I^G	Expected gross value (utility) of information system I (i.e. before deduction of cost C_I).
		C_I	Cost (disutility) of operating information system I.
		V_{I^*}	Expected net value (utility) of optimal information system I^*.

(see end of Section 6.3). The following example will elucidate the operation of such an information model.

Example. Let us assume an agricultural cooperative confronted with planting one among three alternative crops a_i $(i = 1, \ldots, 3)$ whereby three possible states of nature s_j ($j = 1, \ldots, 3$, e.g. good, medium and poor weather conditions) are taken into consideration. The frequency with which each of these weather conditions occurs is given by the probability $p(s_j)$ ($j = 1, \ldots, 3$) or $p(s_1) = 0.2$, $p(s_2) = 0.3$ and $p(s_3) = 0.5$ (see also last column of Table 6-4).

$$E(a_1) = \sum_j u(a_1 \mid s_j) \cdot p(s_j) = 0 + 50 \cdot 0.3 + 10 \cdot 0.5 = 20$$

$$E(a_2) = \sum_j u(a_2 \mid s_j) \cdot p(s_j) = 30 \cdot 0.2 + 10 \cdot 0.3 + 30 \cdot 0.5 = 24$$

$$E(a_3) = \sum_j u(a_3 \mid s_j) \cdot p(s_j) = 50 \cdot 0.2 + 10 \cdot 0.3 + 0 = 11$$

$$Va^* = \max_i E(a_i) = E(a_2) = 24$$

$$E(a_1 \mid y_1) = \sum_j u(a_1 \mid s_j) \cdot p(s_j \mid y_1) = 0 + 50 \cdot 0.25 + 10 \cdot 0.25 = 15$$

$$E(a_1 \mid y_2) = \sum_j u(a_1 \mid s_j) \cdot p(s_j \mid y_2) = 0 + 50 \cdot 0.5 + 10 \cdot 0.375 = 28.75$$

$$E(a_1 \mid y_3) = \sum_j u(a_1 \mid s_j) \cdot p(s_j \mid y_3) = 0 + 50 \cdot 0.125 + 10 \cdot 0.75 = 13.75$$

$$E(a_2 \mid y_1) = \sum_j u(a_2 \mid s_j) \cdot p(s_j \mid y_1) = 30 \cdot 0.5 + 10 \cdot 0.25 + 30 \cdot 0.25 = 25$$

$$E(a_2 \mid y_2) = \sum_j u(a_2 \mid s_j) \cdot p(s_j \mid y_2) = 30 \cdot 0.125 + 10 \cdot 0.5 + 30 \cdot 0.375 = 20$$

$$E(a_2 \mid y_3) = \sum_j u(a_2 \mid s_j) \cdot p(s_j \mid y_3) = 30 \cdot 0.125 + 10 \cdot 0.125 + 30 \cdot 0.75 = 27.5$$

$$E(a_3 \mid y_1) = \sum_j u(a_3 \mid s_j) \cdot p(s_j \mid y_1) = 50 \cdot 0.5 + 10 \cdot 0.25 + 0 = 27.50$$

$$E(a_3 \mid y_2) = \sum_j u(a_3 \mid s_j) \cdot p(s_j \mid y_2) = 50 \cdot 0.125 + 10 \cdot 0.5 + 0 = 11.25$$

$$E(a_3 \mid y_3) = \sum_j u(a_3 \mid s_j) \cdot p(s_j \mid y_3) = 50 \cdot 0.125 + 10 \cdot 0.125 + 0 = 7.50$$

$$V(y_1) = \max_i E(a_i \mid y_1) = E(a_3 \mid y_1) = 27.50$$

$$V(y_2) = \max_i E(a_i \mid y_2) = E(a_1 \mid y_2) = 28.75$$

$$V(y_3) = \max_i E(a_i \mid y_3) = E(a_2 \mid y_3) = 27.5$$

$$V_{Ia^{**}} = \sum_k V(y_k) \cdot p(y_k) = 27.5 \cdot (0.2) + 28.75 \cdot (0.4) + 25.0 \cdot (0.4) = 28.0$$

$$V_I^G = V_{Ia^{**}} - V_{a^*} = 28 - 24 = 4.0$$

The utility of each action under each weather condition is given in the consequence or utility matrix of Table 6-3. While the joint probability $p(s_j, y_k)$ of Table 6-4 would reflect the management's belief in the information y provided by the long range weather forecasting system I. The relations between the actual weather condition s_j and the forecast y_k can be used to derive, by way of the Bayesian theorem, the conditional (or preposterior) probability $p(s_j \mid y_k)$ of Table 6-5. This conditional probability matrix conveys the probability of each state s_j ($j = 1, \ldots, 3$) provided some information y_k ($k = 1, \ldots, 3$) has been received. To avoid confusion it must be pointed out on one hand, that the joint probability $p(s_j, y_k)$ is a sentential

TABLE 6-3

Consequence matrix $u(a_i \mid s_j)$

	s_1	s_2	s_3
a_1	0	50	10
a_2	30	10	30
a_3	50	10	0

TABLE 6-4

Joint probability matrix $p(s_j, y_k)$

	y_1	y_2	y_3	$p(s_j)$
s_1	0.10	0.05	0.05	0.2
s_2	0.05	0.20	0.05	0.3
s_3	0.05	0.15	0.30	0.5
$p(y_k)$	0.2	0.4	0.4	1

TABLE 6-5

Conditional probability matrix $p(s_j \mid y_k)$

	y_1	y_2	y_3
s_1	0.5	0.125	0.125
s_2	0.25	0.5	0.125
s_3	0.25	0.375	0.75
$\sum_j p(s_j \mid y_k) =$	1	1	1

$$p(s_j \mid y_k) = \frac{p(s_j, y_k)}{p(y_k)}$$

conjunction and thus could also be written as $p(s_j \cdot y_k)$; on the other it is important to distinguish clearly between joint and conditional expressions if dealing with probabilities. But in case of utilities this difference vanishes in such a way that the following identity becomes acceptable $u(a_i \mid s_j) \equiv u(a_i, s_j)$ which can also be written $u(a_i \cdot s_j)$. Finally it must be noted that values of this example are expressed in some kind of utility measure (e.g. in utiles, or even in 000' of \$——— but the latter only if a linear approximation of some section of a realistic utility function is acceptable; otherwise *a separate pay-off function* transforming the utilities into monetary values is required).

If the cooperative, in planting a certain crop, does not rely on any information system (e.g. a long range international weather and harvest forecasting system), then the "rational" Bayes–Bernoulli decision rule Va^* would recommend action a_2 with an expected value of 24. If, however, the cooperative relies on an information system, it will receive one of three signals which might influence the crop decision in a different way from rule Va^*. Indeed by using the information economic approach (which constitutes a continuation of the maximization of expectations but through using additional information), different results emerge. If information signal y_1 is received, action a_3 should be chosen which then and only then has an expectation of 27.5, whereas if signals y_2 or y_3 are received, action a_1 or a_2 should be chosen respectively which then have an expected value of 28.75 or 27.5 respectively. Consequently the expected *value of the new optimal action*, resulting from information system I, is then $V_{Ia^{**}} = 28.0$, and the *gross value of the information system* alone, V_I^G, is the difference between the expected value of the decision under the influence of information $V_{Ia^{**}}$ minus the expected value V_{a^*}, i.e. without benefit of this information system, $V_I^G = V_{Ia^{**}} - V_{a^*} = 28.0 - 24 = 4.0$.

In case the information system is not free (e.g. not freely provided by government agencies etc.), but costs the cooperative $C_I = 2$, to operate, then the expected *net value* V_I^N of the information system is

$$V_I^N = V_I^G - C_I = 4 - 2 = 2.$$

This not only shows why utilization of an information system may lead to superior decisions, above all it illustrates the essence of the information economic approach. Of course, the *close connection between this approach and inductive inference* will not have escaped the attentive reader. The central notion $p(s_j \mid y_k)$, for example, expresses the probability of a hypothesized state s_j, provided some information or evidence y_k is given; this is *nothing else than Carnap's formula* $c(h, e)$ – see Subsection 5.24. But in information economics this probability is assumed to be known (e.g. subjectively) while the task of Carnap's system is to determine it. The primary functions of information economics, on the other hand, lies (1) in determining the value of a specific information system and (2) in *searching for an optimal information system* (and its expected net value V_{I^*}). For this reason the analysis illustrated above *must be extended to all feasible information systems* which then have to be compared with one another. The selection of the optimal system can then be expressed by: $V_{I^*} = \max_I V_I^N$.

6.4 Epistemo-Economics[18]

If one were to depict the chronological growth of knowledge, a progressively rising curve would appear. Or more expertly: The volume of scientific knowledge, however one might measure it, is not a linear but an exponential function of time.[19] J. Z. Young and T. Margerison (1968/69), for example, state that presently scientific information is increasing a hundred times faster than at the turn of the twentieth century, and that the volume of all research activity doubles every decade. The economic effects of such an explosive phenomenon are manyfold and are in no way limited to the material aspects of the standard of living whose growth is not assured by this development alone.

Special attention has been paid to the economic aspect of the increase of scientific knowledge by a new discipline, usually addressed as the *economics of education*. M. Blaug (1970), in an annotated bibliography, describes no less than 1,350 publications generated in this new field. Bearing in mind that most of these publications originated in the sixties of this century, there can be little doubt about the resources which the research activity of this new branch of economics is presently absorbing. But the economics of education is only a more practice-oriented part of the acquisition (production and distribution) of knowledge. A more theory-oriented part is what we might call *epistemo-economics*. It has hardly been explored and offers fascinating problems of basic research, above all it promises to reveal a close

[18] This Section is a translation from Mattessich, 'Informations – und Erkenntnisökonomik: Treffpunkt von Philosophie und Wirtschaftswissenschaft', 1974b, pp. 777–784.
[19] See for example: Michajlov, Cernyi, and Giljarevskij, *Osnowy informatiki*, 1968. German translation: *Grundlagen der wissenschaftlichen Dokumentation und Information*, 1970, Vol. I, pp. 5–19.

relationship between epistemology and economics on a completely new plane. Indeed, universities in Austria and Germany offer nowadays not only sporadic lectures in the area of economics of education but have established chairs in Bildungs-oder Erkenntnisökonomie (epistemo-economics).

6.41 *On the Attitude of the Epistemologists*

The traditional theory of knowledge hardly concerned itself with the economic problem of knowledge acquisition, and references regarding this subject only recently emerged in the pertinent literature. Ernst Mach's comment that the *efficiency* of science can only be achieved through abstraction, and that theoretical concepts are only preliminary *economic tools* of prediction, does not yet provide a basis for solving our problem. Knowledge is closely connected with the concept of truth, and theorists of knowledge found it traditionally beyond their dignity to subject such an esoteric endeavor as the search for truth, to the economic principle. The exception is perhaps pragmatic philosophy; it might have illuminated this problem, had it not overshot the mark by declaring utility the sole criterion of truth. *The naive view that something is true because it is useful should not be confused with the presumption that truth, in a global sense, proves useful*. The former is a premise of pragmatism, the latter a premise of epistemo-economics. Whoever accepts the latter without succumbing to the temptation of the former is in little danger of becoming a pragmatist.

Recently, even in non-pragmatic circles, one has come to realize that epistemology cannot ignore the relationship between knowledge and utility (e.g. see Carnap (1962, p. 269)). Above all, the introduction of the concept of "epistemic utility" into philosophy by the well-known German–American epistemologist C. G. Hempel may be regarded as an encouraging sign:

> Now, Carnap's decision principle (and analogously also such policies as the minimax principle developed in the theory of games and statistical decisions) requires, as a basis for a rational decision, a specification both of the total evidence and of the utilities attached to the various possible outcomes of the contemplated actions. In our case, the possible outcomes may be described as: enlarging e by h_1 is true; enlarging e by h_1 is false; . . . , enlarging e by h_n where h_n is true; enlarging e by h_n where h_n is false, leaving e unchanged. What utilities are we to assign to these outcomes? This much is clear: the utilities should reflect the value or disvalue which the different outcomes have from the point of view of pure scien-

> tific research rather than the practical advantages or disadvantages that might result from the application of an accepted hypothesis, according as the latter is true or false. Let me refer to the kind of utilities thus vaguely characterized as *purely scientific*, or *epistemic utilities.* [20]

Hempel further elaborates on how the relative content of epistemic utility can be measured, and provides a hypothesis-acceptance-rule based on this measure of utility. Hempel, however, realizes the limitations, one might even say inadequacy, of this solution, and explicitly emphasizes the necessity of further comprehensive research.

6.42 *On the Attitude of Economists*

Since the eighteenth century economists have been concerned with critical questions regarding knowledge, Publications, beginning with R. Cantillon (1755) through R. Malthus (1820), R. Jones (1831), J. Neville Keynes (1930) to T. W. Hutchison (1964), R. E. Emmer (1967) and others give an eloquent testimony to this interest. However, all these publications at best are concerned with the cognitive process of economics, but not with the economics of cognition. In recent times, however, we find encouraging signs also among economists. The pioneering work of F. Machlup regarding the production and distribution of knowledge in the U.S. not only provides the conceptual frame for an economics of education, but also offers a very extensive analysis of the "industries of knowledge". This analysis is based on empirical studies and estimates the share of the production of knowledge to be almost 29% of the GNP (of the U.S. in 1958). Since then this share undoubtedly will have increased considerably.

Further contributions of economics to this field of research originate in two very different areas. The one is *economics of education*, the other *research and development*. Both areas have generated a vast amount of technical literature during the past two decades. In reference to economics of education we have already mentioned Blaug's anthology; regarding research and development, we would like to refer to the anthologies of A. H. Rubenstein and E. M. Sullivan (1968), as well as to A. H. Rubenstein and R. Barth (1971). However, it is worth noting that neither Machlup's global book (1962), nor other publications in the area of economics of education, and of research and development, created a connection with epistemology. Whereas most philosophers assume that the problem of know-

[20] Hempel, *Aspects of Scientific Explanations and Other Essays*, 1965, pp. 75–76.

ledge can be solved independently from its economic aspects, most economists seem to believe that the problem of knowledge (e.g. hypothesis selection) has already been solved, and that it is sufficient to apply economic insights to the process of knowledge creation.

However, there is one branch of economics which emphasizes the interdependence of knowledge and utility. As indicated above (see the quote from Hempel), the game theory of J. von Neumann and O. Morgenstern, and the closely related decision theory by A. Wald (1950) and L. Savage (1954) revealed pertinent relations which were discovered by Ramsey (1926) a considerable time before, but then without attracting particular attention. The close relationship between the concept of probability (as a measure of belief and knowledge) and the concept of utility (as an economic criterion) has recently been expanded by the *economics of information*. One now has to decide whether the latter field is identical with the economics of knowledge or whether it stands only in close relationship to it. The micro-economic orientation of this set of problems suggests that business administration and management science come closer to the economics of epistemology than does macro-economics. These and similar relationships will be discussed briefly in the following paragraphs.

6.43 *What is the Essence of Epistemo-Economics?*

Information and knowledge systems are costly and often require long-term investments. Under what circumstances are such cost and investment expenditures justified? In other words: What are the costs, what is the expected total utility, what is the value of any given knowledge system and, finally, which one is the best among those alternative systems? These questions are nowadays dealt with within the framework of information economics, and a rigorous mathematical literature is providing partial results and, in certain cases, answers to the above-mentioned questions – see e.g. J. Marschak and Miyasawa (1968), Feltham (1972) and Mattessich (1975a). The models of information economics grow out of statistical decision theory and lead to an enriched development of the basic statistical decision model, yet are closely related to modern accounting.

However, not all information systems serve the generating of knowledge; nevertheless few experts dispute the fact that science and research are the most important activities of modern mankind in acquiring information. But the question arises whether information economics and epistemo-economics are a single sub-division of economics, or whether a distinction between two areas is justified. This problem will be discussed in Subsection 6.45. Of course, it is more difficult to subject the production of knowledge to economic controls than to subject the production of goods and services in the traditional sense. The second half of the twentieth century, however, has created conditions under which the economic aspect of information and knowledge acquisition can no longer be neglected. One might deplore the fact that such a sacred thing as *knowledge*, today, is prosaically regarded as nothing but a commodity, but the institutionalization of research activity and the related research subsidies which occasionally assume gigantic dimensions, enforce an economic control of at least part of the process of knowledge creation. Of increasing importance, is the expansion of knowledge by means of electronic data processing. The computer expands the mental capacities of man no less than the machine multiplies bodily strength. And the high costs of computer operation attract our attention to the *cost sensitivity of acquiring knowledge* much more than the unpaid overtime of scholars who pursue their projects until dawn under personal and financial sacrifices. This case can be illustrated *par excellence* through national income accounting. When a government pays computer rentals for research, the GNP figures are shown to be higher than in the case in which a scientist works unpaid overtime for the very same job.

6.44 *Epistemo-Economics as an Extension of the Philosophy of Science*

To summarize the basic problem of epistemology in a single question, one might ask: "When does a statement convey true information or knowledge?" The traditional philosophy of science tries to answer this question with the help of more or less arbitrary criteria such as degree of confirmation, degree of confidence, degree of corroboration, or even degree of coherence. In a similar way one could roughly characterize the economic extension of epistemology through the following question: Is an information worth acquiring if its opportunity cost is higher than its benefit? On the basis of modern information economics, one would have to negate this question. On the basis of epistemology, however, the answer is more difficult to give, especially for one who rejects the premises of pragmatic philosophy. Obviously the search for truth should not depend on a narrow utilitarian outlook; in other words scientific knowledge should be acquired no matter what the cost–utility relationship is. However, this assertion will remain a pious wish and cannot lead to consequent action. For, first of all, everybody would have to devote himself to the acquisition of knowledge, and to that alone, and secondly, this statement would not provide criteria for priorities among various research projects allowing a reasonable choice between them. In addition, it does not at all reflect reality. Scientific research by no means proceeds so irrationally as to completely disregard the cost–benefit relationship of a project. Intuitively and unconsciously the economic aspect of knowledge acquisition is being taken into account – however vague the basis may be. Yet only rarely is a systematic economic analysis available for such purpose, and it is only a matter of time when science itself will undertake thorough economic soul-searching. But the necessity of such an analysis only proves that an economic problem does here exist. That it is also an epistemological one is somewhat more difficult to prove.

Yet statistical decision theory, information economics, and game theory operate with the Neumann–Morgenstern utility which permits the trading of different risk situations (higher utility at higher risk against lower utility at lower risk). Applied to a simple betting situation, this means that (1) a very uncertain bet for a large amount of money may have the same *expected value* as a much less uncertain bet for a smaller amount, and (2) that between these two extremes there might exist a continuum of different alternative solutions (all with the same expected value). Then the critical question is whether this relationship is sufficient to deduce a *utility–probability continuum*, possibly similar to the space–time continuum of relativity theory. If this is feasible then utility and probability were no less separable from each other than space and time. Just as time became the fourth dimension of the space–time continuum, probability would become the complementary dimension of the utility–probability continuum. But probability is always a measure of expectancy or, more precisely, of one's strength of belief (not necessarily in a religious sense). And *empirical* scientific knowledge is such a kind of belief, because it always implies probability which rarely if ever achieves the degree of total certainty. Because even if one were to attain an *absolute* empirical truth one would never know this fact with certainty. This system of "scientific belief" has many advantages over other belief systems (with which it does not necessarily compete). Above all we deal here only with a *provisional* belief which can be adjusted in the face of better evidence, which even must be corrected accordingly. The scientist therefore has to evaluate which hypothesis is verified best, i.e. which one has the best degree of corroboration (Popper), or the highest degree of confirmation (Carnap), or the highest degree of confidence (subjectivists), etc. and which he therefore can accept as provisional truth. This acceptance or rejection, however, is a function of the total risk that is attached to each competing hypothesis. But this "total risk" is based on the product of the degree of probability and the amount of utility (including disutility) attached to it. Whether, for example, a certain vaccine will be used or not does not merely depend upon statistical tests, α and β values, sample size, confidence interval, etc. but also depends on financial or human risks. The degree of confidence of a vaccine must be high enough to use it in the prevention of illnesses. Since its application in human beings entails a considerably higher risk than in animals, it might be released only for use in veterinary medicine. This example faintly indicates something that modern decision theory, which has grown out of the theory of testing statistical hypotheses, has formulated in a very subtle way, namely the fact that the testing of hypotheses, (one of the main objectives of the acquisition of knowledge) is a *process of decision making* at which the dimension of belief should not be separated from the dimension of utility. Deliberate or unconscious suppression of the dimension of utility, of course, is possible. One even does encounter it in *traditional* statistical testing, but this notion may be conceptually as incorrect as the notion of time without the consideration of its accompanying space.

However, we do not intend to assert the existence of a utility–probability continuum; at this juncture we want to consider it as a mere possibility. Even if this conception proves to be unrealistic, it would be desirable to see the economics of knowledge being practiced by economists who are knowledgeable in the area of epistemology.

6.45 *Information as Raw Material of Knowledge*

Is information economics identical with knowledge economics (epistemo-economics)? This question we encountered before and we now should take a closer look at it. The starting point will be a comparison of the two basic concepts "information" and "knowledge". For us *information is identical with evidence (data) by which the expectation (or probability distribution) of a person, or group of persons, is changed with regard to a specific statement (hypothesis).* This definition uses the insights of J. M. Keynes (1921) and R. Carnap (1950) and refers to the relationship between evidence and hypothesis. According to this, a hypothesis is merely *supported* by evidence, it is not identical with it but reaches beyond the evidence. *Scientific knowledge, then consists of law-like statements sufficiently supported by appropriate evidence acceptable as (provisional) truth by a certain branch of science.* Thus knowledge evidently differs from information. To equate one with the other resembles the mistake of confusing the ruler with the people who bestow the power upon him. Only through relevant information does knowledge receive the elevated status traditionally assigned to scientific knowledge – but information is not its only constituent. Yet the better our information, the more dependable will our knowledge be. Admittedly, knowledge depends on information, but it contains a creative element which information lacks. Let us illustrate this point with the simple example of a cost function.

A handful of data of operating costs with varying production volume (see circles in Figure 6-2 Part (a)) offers us nothing but information (data); only after the daring and creative act of fitting a curve to these information bits (see Part (b)) do we get a *cost hypothesis*. This hypothesis can be expressed according to a formula or, even better, in form of a sentence, and becomes scientific knowledge as soon as the experts agree that, firstly, enough data have been collected and, secondly, that our cost curve is the best among all feasible alternatives (see Mattessich (1964 a, pp. 235–236)).

Nevertheless it may happen that a piece of information itself may be of hypothetical nature and may thus assume characteristics of knowledge – similar to the vassal who plays ruler in his own home. This remark points at the fact that it depends on the context whether a statement should be regarded as information or as knowledge.

All this indicates that, on one hand, information and knowledge are related concepts, on the other, that important differences exist between them, and that for this reason epistemo-economics must not be equated with infor-

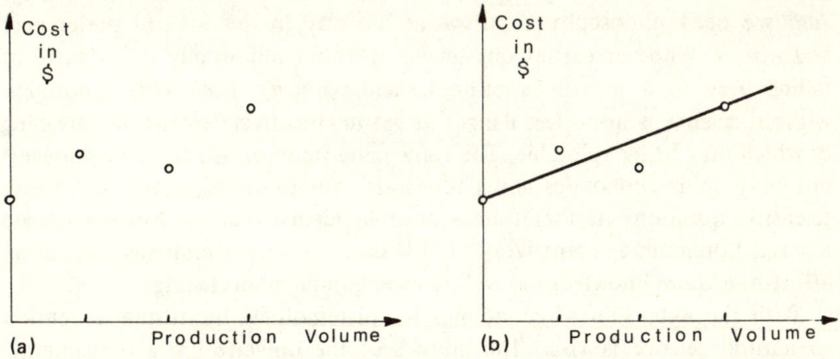

Fig. 6-2. (a) Information in form of cost data (evidence). (b) Knowledge in form of a cost hypothesis (with supporting evidence).

mation economics. The purpose of the latter lies mainly in determining the values of different information systems and in finding the optimal or quasi-optimal system for a specific purpose. Therefore, if the raw material for a certain objective can be gained in different ways (e.g. highly differentiated information at high cost versus less differentiated information at lower cost) then we expect information economics to show us the most efficient way of data processing. *Epistemo-economics on the other hand, does not so much compare competing information systems than competing areas of knowledge. Thus its task lies in determining the priorities of research goals and research projects in a systematic way by deducing them from basic value judgements.* This presupposes the assumption that scientific research can be conducted only if certain value judgements exist which enable the preference of one research project over another. An important prerequisite of epistemo-economics therefore is the general exploration of hierarchies of value judgements as well as the reduction of more specific value judgements to more basic ones (see Sections 2.4 to 2.8). Epistemo-economics also has to solve a typical economic problem. But this is so closely related to the knowledge generation that philosophy here becomes indispensable. Whereas science demonstrates what we know, philosophy makes us realize what we do not know and where the limits of our comprehension are. It is for this reason that philosophy is so eager to find paradoxes and contradictions. The latter are not only a substitute for experimentation, they also indicate the demarcation of our knowledge apparatus. From time to time we succeed in pushing this demarcation a step further into no-man's land. But if, as previously indicated, basic value judgements are prerequisites for scientific activities, then this fact represents an important demarcation of our knowledge capacity. And we need philosophy to show us the way in this area of preferences and norms. Whoever carries out science without philosophy is in danger of falling prey to a superficial outlook; and whoever deals with philosophy without science is in no less danger of getting lost in statements the meaning of which may be inexplorable. The converging trend of this circle of problems not only joins economics and philosophy, but inevitably leads to broader scientific questions. It therefore is no coincidence that the Nobel Laureate Konrad Lorenz in a recent work (1973) describes life, simultaneously, as an effort to acquire knowledge as well as an economic undertaking.

With the extension of economics to epistemology, the further extension to natural science is vital. The physics of the universe has a fundamental economic aspect which finds its expression in the *notion and law of entropy* (cf. Georgescu-Roegen (1971)). Since the universe not only contains *free* or *available energy* but also *bound energy* (unavailable or wasted), and since the percentage of available energy in the entire universe is constantly *diminishing* (increasing entropy under thermodynamic irreversibility), but especially since some parts (e.g. living beings) are able to form relatively low entropy states (higher forms of *order*) *at the cost of* other parts, it becomes obvious that the increasing scarcity of available energy is not only a problem of mankind but an issue intrinsic in the universe as a whole. Yet physics is not merely confronted with *this universal economic issue*, in its wake follow *qualitative changes* (due to the unequal distribution of free energy) that are irreducible to quantitative changes which alone can be mastered by mechanistic laws. Thus it is the advent of thermodynamics and not that of biology or the social sciences that spelled the "Götterdämmerung" of the mechanistic world view. And as Georgescu-Roegen (1971, p. 15) says "the strongest limitation to our power to predict comes from the entropic indeterminateness (i.e. the many possibilities and the different rates at which entropy may progress) and, especially, from the emergence of novelty by combination (holistic properties)." Georgescu-Roegen (1971, p. 18) furthermore expresses the conviction that an understanding of the entropy law will *not* help us to manage an economic entity in a better way, but "it may teach to anyone willing to listen what aims are better for the economy of mankind."

6.5 Other Methodological Explorations by Economists

Sir William Petty (1623–1687), Richard Cantillon (1680–1734) and above all Francois Quesnay (1694–1774) and Sir James Steuart (1712–1780) may have to be addressed as the first methodologists of economics. But there can be no doubt that the crucial methodological steps in this area were taken by Adam Smith (1723–1790) and David Ricardo (1772–1823). For purposes of analytical convenience they began to introduce assumptions valid at best for borderline cases only, but unrealistic for the ordinary range of usage. This approach has previously proved immensely successful, especially in classical physics, but it has created novel and complicating implications in the economic and management sciences. In physics the elimination of "disturbing" forces, like the *air resistance* in an object's free fall, enables a clearer cognition of fundamental relationships, whereas in the social sciences the distinction between "disturbing or secondary" forces and "major or primary" forces is by far more difficult to make and often altogether impossible. This approach puts predominant stress on the deductive process and introduces complexities which thus far have not been mastered; it restricts a good deal of our knowledge to the twilight area of reasoning by analogy. It seems to have been the ultimate reason why men like Robert Malthus (1766–1834)[21] and others (e.g. Richard Jones[22]) criticised Ricardo and pleaded for a greater emphasis on the inductive method and for a more realistic analysis of facts.[23] Since that time the hiatus between the daring "theorist" and the more earthbound "fact-finder" formed an ebbing but relentless tension, which in recent decades spread to the administrative, management and systems sciences in general. Most of these methodological contentions, whether it is that between John Stuart Mill, Nassau Senior (1790–1864) and J. E. Cairnes, or the embittered controversy exploding into the extended and weary *Methodenstreit* (the battle of methods between the Austrian "theoretical school" of Menger (1840–1921), Böhm-Bawerk (1851–1914) etc. and the German "historical school" of Schmoller and his disciples), or the skirmishes fought by the American institutionalists, and even the "modern methodological dispute" (see Subsection 6.52), are not so much a matter of principle but one of degree. They all have similar roots, and rest primarily in the difficulty of reconciling theory and facts by means of models that rarely can give justice to the complexity of economic reality; secondarily they are rooted in the fundamental behavioral differences between academic temperaments and are thus frequently a matter of taste and value judgement.

6.51 *Positive versus Normative Economics*

Another group of methodological controversies center around the general question of value neutrality of this field. Indeed, a good deal of the fairly comprehensive methodological literature of economics[24] deals with this or other closely related issues.

[21] *The Principles of Political Economy*, 1820.

[22] *Essay on the Distribution of Wealth and on the Sources of Taxation*, 1831.

[23] Cf. Stravenhagen, *Geschichte der Wirtschaftstheorie*, 1969.

[24] Some of the best known recent books in this area are listed below; but the number of pertinent journal articles is too large, thus we refer the reader to Sections 1.0 and 1.1 of the *Index of Economic Journals,* Vols. I to VII of the American Economic Association, R. D. Irwin, Inc., Homewood, Ill., 1961–1967: Myrdal, *The Political Element in the Development of Economic Theory*, origin, 1930; 1954; Hood and Koopmans (eds.), *Studies in Econometric Method*, 1953; Friedman, *Essays in Positive Economics*, 1953; Knight, *On the History and Method of Economics,* 1956; Koopmans, *Three Essays on the State of Economic Science*, 1957; Papandreou, *Economics as a Science*, 1958; Hutchison, *The Significance and Basic Postulates of Economic Theory*, 1960; *idem.*, *"Positive" Economics and Policy Objectives*, 1964; Robinson, *Economic Philosophy*,

Among the eminent economists concerned with methodological problems, John Neville Keynes (1852–1949 – the father of J. Maynard Keynes) assumes a significant position. In his book on *The Scope of Method of Political Economy* (1891) he distinguished between economics as a *positive* (abstract and deductive) science and economics as an ethical (realistic and inductive) hence *normative* science – a distinction later revived and exploited by Milton Friedman (1953). According to the view of the latter "*positive economics* is in principle *independent* of any particular ethical position or normative judgement" (our italics) and deals with "what is", thus it is "an 'objective' science, in precisely the same sense as any of the physical sciences", whereas *normative economics* is a "regulative science" advising on "what ought to be" and thus "cannot be independent of positive economics". The difficulty of maintaining such a position obviously lies in the abundant evidence that the majority of *economic "facts" are not "independent" of value judgements.* The magnitude of a specific mineral deposit may be one of the facts independent of a value judgement, although the estimation of its size may already be normatively tinted. But the decision over which time span this deposit shall be exploited, certainly depends on a value judgement which in turn may influence the price of the mineral. Furthermore, the most typical economic fact, namely the shape of a person's preference order (utility function) is nothing but the result of a value judgement. And most important, the central economic principles of maximizing utility or profit or any similar entity are all value judgements. Or as Emmer (1967), p. 36, says: " . . . it is easy to see that the rule that scarce means should so be allocated as to maximize the satisfaction of ends is the equivalent of an ethical premise. It is a final goal, and it is a volition. There is nothing in man's environment that can be observed to indicate that he *ought* to be efficient." Therefore it seems that rather the *reverse* of Friedman's statement is true, namely that "positive economics cannot be independent of normative economics." This proposition is much less absurd than it appears to be at first sight. Consider an economic theory containing the premise "Mr. *X* prefers in a specific context commodity *A* over *B*." If our theory is supposed to serve

---

1962; Machlup, *Essays in Economic Semantics*, 1963; Lowe, *On Economic Knowledge*, 1965; Krupp (ed.), *The Structure of Economic Science*, 1966; Emmer, *Economic Analysis and Scientific Philosophy*, 1967; von Hayek, *Studies in Philosophy, Politics and Economics*, 1967; Tintner, *Methodology of Mathematical Economics and Econometrics*, 1968; Georgescu-Roegen, *The Entropy Law and the Economic Process*, 1971; Dasgupta (ed.), *Methodology of Economic Research*, 1968; Hunt and Schwartz (eds.), *A Critique of Economic Theory*, 1972.

Mr. *X*'s goals then the above premise implies the imperative "choose commodity *A* instead of *B*" thus yielding a normative theory. If, however, the goal of our theory is not to serve Mr. *X* but to describe the economic behavior (e.g. the price formation of commodities) manifested by a group of people including Mr. *X*, then our theory is positive, but still presupposes Mr. *X*'s value judgement or an assumption about it. Although the proposition "Mr. *X* prefers in a specific context commodity *A* over *B*" is itself not normative, it certainly is not *independent* of Mr. *X*'s value judgement. Thus we have to return to our conclusions made in Chapter 2, namely (1) that the distinction between "positive" and "normative" becomes meaningful only when referred to a fairly well bounded theory or model, but creates confusion when applied to entire disciplines or vaguely delineated subdivisions of them, and (2) the criteria for distinguishing a "positive theory" from a "normative theory" is to be found in the boundaries of this theory. If the theory comprises within its limits, an imperative requesting the fulfillment of a certain aspect (not merely containing or describing this aspect or value judgement) then one may speak of a normative theory with regard to this one aspect. If the theory does not contain or imply any such imperative one may say that this theory is positive or neutral with regard to this particular aspect (for details see Subsections 2.3 to 2.8). This result is all the more important as the long-established view that economics proper must be a positive discipline (held by J. S. Mill, Senior, Cairnes, Sidgwick, J. N. Keynes, Pareto, Max Weber, and many others) has, in the Western hemisphere, only recently been seriously challenged – indeed, by such eminent economists as Gunnar Myrdal (1954), Smithies (1954, 1955), Joan Robinson (1962), and Boulding (1969).

It is most important to realize that in economics the factual observations themselves are the result of interpretations and value judgements. Even such a conservative economist as Friedrich von Hayek stressed that the facts of economics and other social sciences "differ from the facts of the physical sciences in being . . . beliefs which are as such our data . . . and which, moreover, we cannot directly observe in the minds of the people but recognize from what they do and say"[25] and later Machlup added that "this, indeed, is the essential difference between the natural and the social sciences: that in the latter facts, the data of 'observation', are themselves results of interpretations of human actions by human actors."[26] Myrdal who in the original,

[25] Von Hayek, 'Scientism and the Study of Society', 1942, p. 279.

[26] Machlup, 'The Problem of Verification in Economics', 1955, p. 16.

Swedish version of his book *The Political Element in the Development of Economic Theory* (1930) started from a "positivistic" view, acknowledges in the Preface to the English translation of this work (1954) his conversion to the normative camp through the following words:

> By presenting the book in its original form I have abstained from making it conform to my present position. Instead, I should like to add to the references just given a few remarks of self-criticism.
>
> The book is devoted almost entirely to criticism. The suggestions in the last chapter for a positive solution of the problem, on how to introduce valuations into economic analysis and thus make it possible to draw political conclusions on a scientific basis, are very sketchy, although I still believe that they point in the right direction; these ideas have been further developed, particularly in *An American Dilemma*. I still consider the criticism correct and worth doing. But throughout the book there lurks the idea that when all metaphysical elements are radically cut away, a healthy body of positive economic theory will remain, which is altogether independent of valuations. Political conclusions can then be inferred simply by adding to the objective scientific knowledge of the facts a chosen set of value premises.
>
> This implicit belief in the existence of a body of scientific knowledge acquired independently of all valuations is, as I now see it, naive empiricism. Facts do not organize themselves into concepts and theories just by being looked at; indeed, except within the framework of concepts and theories, there are no scientific facts but only chaos. There is an inescapable *a priori* element in all scientific work. Questions must be asked before answers can be given. The questions are an expression of our interest in the world, they are at bottom valuations. Valuations are thus necessarily involved already at the stage when we observe facts and carry on theoretical analysis, and not only at the stage when we draw political inferences from facts and valuations.
>
> I have therefore arrived at the belief in the necessity of working always, from the beginning to the end, with explicit value premises. The value premises cannot be established arbitrarily: they must be relevant and significant for the society in which we live. To begin with, they must be made concrete in terms of economic interests actually pursued by groups of people, and of real human attitudes to social processes. Under no circumstances should the value premises in realistic research be represented by the sort of general and abstract principles of which the economists in

> our great tradition of natural law and utilitarianism avail themselves to bridge the gulf between objective science and politics. This is why the immanent criticism of economic doctrines, contained in the present volume, remains not only valid but relevant and useful, in spite of my philosophical naivete in the wider question of how to base objective research on subjective valuations.[27]

In a similar, though perhaps slightly less radical, vein Joan Robinson says:

> Perhaps Gunnar Myrdal is too sweeping when he says (speaking as an economist) that "our very concepts are value-loaded" and cannot be defined except in terms of political valuation (Myrdal, 1969, p. 337). It is true that economic terminology is coloured . . . All the same, taking a particular economic system as given, we can describe the technical features of its operation in an objective way. But it is not possible to describe a system without moral judgements creeping in. For to look at a system from the outside implies that it is not the only possible system; in describing it we compare it (openly or tacitly) with other actual or imagined systems. Differences imply choices, and choices imply judgement. We cannot escape from making judgements and the judgements we make arise from ethical preconceptions that have soaked into our view of life and are somehow printed in our brains. We cannot escape from our own habits of thought. The Bogy bars the way. But we can go around about. We can see what we value, and try to see why.[28]

A related point is that economics, even so-called "positive economics" is constantly imposing implicit value judgements upon businessmen, politicians, administrators and the community at large. The strongest voice defending this argument belongs to Boulding[29] whose major thesis grows out of the systems approach, and may concisely be described as follows: In some sciences, the centre of gravity by necessity is shifting from the purely cognitive to the instrumental aspect, because by improving our understanding of the world, we progressively change it. Thus the working of a "generalized Heisenberg principle" can be discerned – it gradually converts the originally cognitive process of science into an instrument of valuation and goal achieve-

[27] Myrdal, *The Political Element in the Development of Economic Theory*, English translation, 1954, pp vii–viii.

[28] Robinson, *Economic Philosophy*, 1962, quoted from the Penguin edition (1973, pp. 18–19).

[29] Boulding, 'Economics as a Moral Science', 1969.

ment by which the cognitive process itself might be changed and so on. Those who separate these two aspects by drawing a sharp but more or less arbitrary line between positive and normative science, shut their eyes to the *interaction between cognition, valuation and action*. Cybernetics, ecology, systems science and the widespread concern for environmental pollution have vividly demonstrated that we cannot understand our "social and economic reality" without studying this interaction and without incorporating normative propositions into our models. Thus, to say it bluntly, the dream of a value-free science may be dreamed at the cost of never waking up.

This warning has special bearings upon economics, as it is this discipline which is about to change the world according to its own image. Although its doctrines of "rationality" of the "*homo oeconomicus*", of "profit maximization" etc. could not fully be imposed upon real man, they undoubtedly pushed him in direction of seeking pecuniary profits at the cost of such goals as high craftmanship, artistic creativity, elimination of slums and pollution, crime reduction, spiritual, intellectual and esthetic enrichment of life, as well as other objectives, not, or not yet, subject to economic measurement. This argument by no means is restricted to the micro-level, but holds no less for macro-economics which gave the politicians such optimization concepts as "gross national product", "real per capita income" etc. which omit certain cost and benefit elements essential for the genuine well-being of individuals as well as nations.

A further argument reinforces *systems thinking* in economics; it not only facilitates the understanding of the normative character of economics but is, from the methodological view point, the most interesting among the arguments. It asserts that the choice of the appropriate economic *model*, for a specific purpose, is a subjective and not an objective matter. This argument too forms a corner stone of our book and is contained in a series of publications which might not have found the attention they deserve.[30] A methodologically and pedagogically excellent summary is given by Papandreou (1959) who deserves credit for demonstrating lucidly why theory construction in economics is such a precarious activity. According to this presentation economists are not prepared to accept universal propositions without qualifications or specification of the social space (specific context) and thus do not generate theories but models, namely constructs which are not capable of refutation but merely of confirmation and which when confirmed are *purely*

[30] Papandreou, *Economics as a Science*, 1958. *idem.*, 'Explanation and Prediction in Economics', 1959. *idem.*, 'Theory Construction and Empirical Meaning in Economics', 1963.

explanatory devices. For predictive purposes, however these models cannot be used without an additional *value judgement*. "What it does mean is that predictions based on models are necessarily dependent upon the state of mind of the economist . . . the economist about to make a choice of a model is guided by a *subjective ordering* or models with respect to the likelihood of their confirmation by reference to data relating to a given historical individual, such as, say, the U.S. economy for the period 1960–1963." Papandreou (1959, p. 1099) thus comes very close to the conclusion of Helmer and Rescher (1959) according to which the value judgement of the *expert becomes an indispensable part in the operation of management science models*.

Of course, Marxist economists have always argued that value judgements are intrinsically interwoven with economics, but this has traditionally been denigrated as a political bias, while systems analysis and our method of neutralizing (or de-neutralizing) systems demonstrate methodically and precisely under what circumstances *any* discipline is neutral or normative with regard to which aspect. It reveals that it is meaningless to say economics is positive, just as it is meaningless to assert that it is normative, as long as the basis of reference for these qualifications is omitted. Economics can be normative with regard to some aspects (e.g. the rules of logic, inductive reasoning, rational choice) and simultaneously positive with regard to others (e.g. profit maximization and "efficient" income allocation – if the pertinent rules are deliberately excluded or if certain constraints override those rules in some circumstances).

6.52 *The Modern Dispute on Methodology*[31]

Yet it was not so much Friedman's somewhat inadequate distinction between positive and normative economics, but the more fundamental issue of *hypothesis testing* that led to the *modern dispute on methodology*. According to Friedman, positive economics ought to develop a theory or hypothesis that yields valid and meaningful predictions: "The hypothesis is rejected if its predictions are contradicted ('frequently' or more often than predictions from an alternative hypothesis); it is accepted if its predictions are not

[31] Because of their relevance to this work, the major articles of this controversy were originally intended to be reproduced in an Appendix to this Chapter. As this would have exceeded the editorial limits set for this book, we can merely offer a concise survey of the main arguments. For details we refer the reader to the following literature: Nagel (1963), Simon (1963), Samuelson (1963, 64, 65).

contradicted; great confidence is attached to it if it has survived many opportunities for contradiction . . . The validity of a hypothesis in this sense is not by itself a sufficient criterion for choosing among alternative hypotheses. Observed facts are necessarily finite in number, possible hypotheses, infinite. If there is one hypothesis that is consistent with the available evidence, there are always an infinite number that are." Therefore hypotheses which are consistent with additional evidence at hand are preferred to those being less consistent with other knowledge and available evidence. "The choice among alternative hypotheses equally consistent with the available evidence must to some extent be arbitrary, though there is general agreement that relevant considerations are suggested by the criteria 'simplicity' and "fruitfulness', themselves notions that defy completely objective specification." After acknowledging the difficulty of actually testing particular predictions in the social sciences by experiment, Friedman vehemently attacks the position that, in view of these difficulties, the conformity of the "assumptions" of a hypothesis to "reality" is equally relevant to the validity of the hypothesis as the test by predictions. He argues that the relation between the significance of a theory and the 'realism' of its 'assumptions' is almost opposite of that suggested by the view under criticism, " . . . to be important . . . a hypothesis must be descriptively false in its assumptions."

This principle which Herbert Simon, in opposition to Friedman, calls the "principle of unreality" and Paul Samuelson, in no lesser opposition, refers to it as the "*F*-twist", has found some defenders. So for instance Ernest Nagel the well-known epistemologist, agrees that the adequacy of a theory must be judged, not by assessing the realism of its assumptions, but rather through "examining the concordance of a theory's logical consequences with the phenomena the theory is designed to explain." If the last phrase under quotation marks would correspond precisely to Friedman's "test by prediction" (something which might easily be doubted), then Friedman's and Nagel's *conclusions* were identical indeed. But even then Nagel (1963 – see the third section of his article) admits that Friedman's "sound conclusion is supported by erroneous arguments", offering an illustration *par excellence* of the case where economists may go astray unless guided either by sound epistemological knowledge or by a blindly fortunate coincidence.

One of the major shortcomings of Friedman's exposition was *the failure* to elucidate his meaning of the terms "realistic" and "unrealistic", thereby creating widespread confusion among responding economists. The expression "*unrealistic*" has a variety of widely divergent interpretations and may mean for example:

either

(1) "not giving exhaustive description" or

(2) "highly improbable or false" or

(3) "to hold under idealized conditions only" or

(4) "not subject to empirical testing" or

(5) "failing in an empirical test" or even

(6) "highly abstract or generalized".

The first three of these meanings are discussed in Nagel's (1963) paper, the last three in that by Lerner (1965). Without common agreement on one of these interpretations, there is little hope of clarifying the acceptance or rejection of the "principle of unreality". Nagel furthermore demonstrates that Friedman, in replacing "theoretical terms" by "non-theoretical ones", alters the meaning and function of the statements containing them, but without being aware of this epistemological *faux pas*. However, it must be pointed out that the traditional distinction between *theoretical terms*, signifying nothing actually observable, and *observational terms*, representing empirically determinable features, has been called into question by the more revolutionary of the modern epistemologists (see Subsection 7.32).

According to Samuelson, Nagel has not vindicated that which is characteristically Friedman's methodology. Samuelson denies that "unrealism in the sense of factual inaccuracy even to a tolerable degree of approximation is anything but a demerit for a theory or hypothesis." He, like Herbert Simon, is convinced that Friedman's conclusion is the result of fallacious reasoning. Samuelson (1963) demonstrates this by a step by step argument of eight points which ultimately is based on the notion that *every* conclusion (e.g. prediction or explanation) already is implied by its premises (assumptions). At this stage one might even ask whether the notion of *material implication* expounded in modern deductive logic – see the last two lines of the semantical definition of $\supset$ in the *truth table* of Table 4-2, according to which, *a false proposition may imply a true one* – could be employed to salvage, at least from a logical point of view, Friedman's principle. But Fritz Machlup (1964) tries to defend Friedman's position by reminding Samuelson that most assumptions and theories in economics represent simplifications of reality and therefore are unrealistic. "Samuelson agrees that abstract, simplified theories may be useful as an aid in understanding reality. He insists however that a theory suffers to the extent that its assumptions contain factual inaccuracies. Samuelson further insists, and Machlup denies, that if the consequences of a theory are empirically valid (realistic), then the theory as such must be empirically valid and so must its assumptions. That is, the assumptions imply the theory and the theory implies the consequences."[32] But Machlup, or anyone else, failed to point out that Samuelson (1963, item 6) seems to have confused the notion of "being a subset" with that of "implication". While the two concepts are closely related they are by no means identical as the former belongs to the logic of extension while the latter belongs to the logic of intension (of Subsections 3.25 and 4.11).

Apart from the confusion caused by the term "theory" (which in Samuelson's view comprises not only the premises but also all conclusions, while in Machlup's view conclusions are excluded – furthermore these two authors have conclusions on different levels in mind) in the course of this scuffle between Machlup and Samuelson a new issue of controversy arises through Samuelson's insistence that "Scientists never 'explain' any behavior, by theory or by any other hook. Every description that is superseded by a 'deeper explanation' turns out upon careful examination to have been replaced by still another description ...." From this statement it is not quite clear whether Samuelson wants to call "description" a process commonly addressed as "explanation" by philosophers and scientists[33] or whether he subscribes to the entire philosophy of descriptivism. In the former case we might be confronted merely with a semantical issue while in the latter the question arises as to which of the three camps of descriptionists[34] Samuelson belongs to. In this case he might open his view to such criticism as the following:

[32] Garb, 'Professor Samuelson on Theory and Realism: Comment', 1965, p. 1151.

[33] "An explanation is a group of statements or a story from which the thing to be explained can logically be inferred and whose assumptions removes or diminishes its problematic or puzzling character ... explanation and inference are very closely related. They are, in fact, the same process regarded from opposite points of view. Given certain premises, any conclusion which can logically be inferred from them can be regarded as being explained by them. And given a fact to be explained, we say that we have found our explanation for it when we have found a set of premises from which it can logically be inferred." Copi, *Introduction to Logic*, 1968, p. 376.

[34] The first camp representing *radical descriptionism* accepts data alone and claims that scientific research is, or is to be, limited to observations. The second, "black boxism" as it is called by Bunge (cf. *Scientific Research II*, 1967, pp. 54–62) accepts hypotheses limited to *observable* phenomena; such "subsumptive explanations" are then called descriptions. The third, "anti-pictorialism" accepts hypotheses, and explanations beyond observational phenomena but restricted to *iconic* rather than *symbolic* models, interpreting the former as "metaphorical or didactical tricks rather than as pictures of reality."

In conclusion, descriptivism has two harmful effects: (i) it blinds people to any new fact beyond the surface of things, thereby blocking the gathering of information suggested by the deeper theories, and (ii) it makes people miss the opportunity and the joy of new thought that every new fact affords. By virtue of (i) descriptivism is self-defeating; by virtue of (ii) it encourages superficiality and prevents the transformation of protoscience into science . . .

The dominant contemporary view is rather the following. Everything except the existence of the universe – which is presupposed by any question – is explainable to some extent even if it has not yet been explained . . . What is true is that no *perfect* – completely exhaustive and accurate – explanation is ever achieved; consequently there are no *final* explanations.[35]

The question as to the outcome of this modern dispute on methodology looms in the reader's mind. Did it result in a deadlock, as Garb[36] asserts? Was it nothing else but a semantic confusion, as Lerner[37] suggests? Was it a wasteful play of words in which some eminent economists let themselves be caught? We hesitate to affirm any of these queries, but rather believe that this spirited and passionate dispute (to which we attribute at least as great a historical significance as the *Methodenstreit* of the nineteenth century) fulfilled a most important function. Was it not high time that leading economists took off a few hours from their business of devising impressive theoretical structures – the true value of which shall by no means be discounted – to find out that many of their constructs – whether created by Friedman, Machlup, Samuelson or anyone else – rest on shaky *empirical* foundations, if not on quick-sand? A careful study of the detailed arguments of this methodological contention and the ability to read between the lines will reveal two things:

(1) that economists, including the foremost experts of the economic sciences, can draw further benefit from a solid grounding in semantics, logic and epistemology;

(2) that two fundamental issues of the economic sciences are as yet unresolved, namely (i) the "argument by analogy" which in economics seems to form the predominant mode of induction, (ii) the problem of hypothesis and theory testing, the complexity of which is greatly enhanced when arguments rest on analogies.

[35] Bunge, *Scientific Research II*, 1967, pp. 58–59.
[36] *op. cit.*, p. 1151.
[37] Lerner, 'Professor Samuelson on Theory and Realism: Comment', 1965.

The fact that these issues are unresolved, however, does not entail the deadlock of the dispute. By this time it should be obvious that Friedman's principle of unreality can neither be accepted nor rejected as long as its author keeps silent on his intended meaning of the term "unrealistic". If he settles for the meaning of "highly generalized" as suggested by Lerner, then Friedman's principle is reduced to a platitude that few scholars will question – not even Samuelson. If Friedman means "most unlikely or false", then he is likely to lose the support of Nagel, Machlup and anyone else (the argument 2 of Table 6-4 illustrates why he will lose support). However, if he were to choose any of the remaining four interpretations he might start the entire controversy over again, as in each case many subtleties would have to be resolved before a sound judgement is feasible.

The assumptions of the first argument of Table 6-4 are "realistic" while those of the second argument are "unrealistic" in the sense of "highly unlikely or false". The conclusion, however, is "realistic" in both arguments. But this does not mean that the conclusion implies the assumptions of Argument 2, although these very assumptions imply the conclusion. Although the premises of these examples can hardly be compared with full fledged theories, they vividly illustrate two things: (1) that an empirical theory is epistemologically unacceptable if it offers a true or highly likely conclusion (prediction) based on false or highly unlikely assumptions, and (2) that the "unreality" of the assumptions is hardly a positive merit of a theory. Because in Argument 1 the realistic assumptions *correctly* explain the conclusion, while in Argument 2 the unrealistic assumptions give a factually false explanation, hence do *not* explain this conclusion in spite of the analytical correctness of argument 2.

TABLE 6-4

Comparison of true and false premises leading to identical conclusions

	Argument 1	Argument 2
Assumption *A*	All flamingos are pink	All flamingos are green
Assumption *B*	All ravens are black	All ravens are white
Conclusion *C* (Prediction)	∴ Flamingos and ravens (will) differ in color.	∴ Flamingos and ravens (will) differ in color.

6.53 *Stochastic and Holistic Aspects of Economics*

Are we living in a deterministic or in a stochastic universe? Gerhard Tintner

(1968, 1973) repeatedly pointed out, that traditional as well as most of modern economics (with the exception of game and decision theory, as well as information economics) is modelled after nineteenth century deterministic physics. But this might be an old-fashioned approach, especially in view of the fact that modern quantum physics is thoroughly probabilistic. Thus Tintner suggests that economists should follow this new trend and consider economic phenomena frankly and fundamentally from a stochastic point of view, i.e. treat economic variables as random variables – see Tintner (1973, p. 74). Of course, econometricians for the last four decades or so have assumed such a probabilistic point of view, and have tried to fit statistic hypotheses into mathematical economic models, as well as to subject these hypotheses to statistical testing. Furthermore, as we have seen in Subsections 6.2 and 6.3, it cannot be denied that decision theorists and information economists are dealing predominantly, and often exclusively, with stochastic models. But usually the assumption is implied that the sample is taken from a universe with a *static* probability distribution, i.e. one permanently fixed and unchanging over time. Because of this unrealistic assumption, Tintner proposes that economists should generally accept and apply the theory of evolutionary time series, and deal with families of probability distributions that are flexible enough to change their forms. The first attempt to apply such time series to economics was made by Haavelmo (1954); but in spite of serious efforts, this theory of stochastic processes is still not yet sufficiently developed and encounters a series of difficulties.

However it is questionable whether the problem of indeterminacy can be solved by simply removing some technical or statistical obstacles. It seems that the answer to the question as to the stochastic or non-stochastic nature of the universe must be sought on a much deeper epistemic level. Above all, the question arises whether or not a strict distinction between "pure chance" and "accidental chance" should be made. Some scholars argue that only the former is incompatible with determinism while the latter is reconcilable with it. J. J. Smart, for example argues along those lines:

> If indeterminism is true, then some events occur by pure chance. Thus the emission of an alpha particle from a radioactive atom at a given moment of time is according to modern quantum mechanics a matter of pure chance: there is no previous state of the world which implies (*via* the laws of nature) that this event will occur at this time. It is important to distinguish "pure chance" from the ordinary concept of "chance" or "accident" which is quite compatible with determinism. Consider two

> events as follows. (1) At a particular time *t* a radium atom emits an alpha particle. (2) At a particular time *t* a man walking along a road is struck on the head by a falling branch. The first case is one of chance in the sense that, if modern quantum mechanics is to be believed, it is not deducible from any specification, however complete and precise, of some previous state of the universe. The second case on the other hand is one of chance in a sense which is perfectly compatible with determinism. There is no law of nature which relates walking along roads to being hit on the head by falling branches but nevertheless this particular occurrence would be deducible, if determinism were true, from a complete specification of the boundary conditions obtaining in a sufficiently large portion of the universe at some previous time. In commonsense (and less scientific) terms, an accident is the intersection of two causal chains.[38]

As strong as this trend of probability theory and statistics in economics and the applied sciences might be, there exists a further trend that will greatly influence the methodological evolution of these disciplines. It may be called the "holistic point of view" and can be traced, on one side, to Taoist Chinese philosophy, and on the other side to Leibniz as well as Hegel. In economics it was first Léon Walras (1834–1910 – not to be confused with his economist father August Walras) who in his equilibrium theory (1874) demonstrated the *interdependence* of the prices and quantities of *all* commodities traded in an economy. Although prices and quantities constitute merely a small sector of economic variables, they nevertheless cover the most important sector. Thus Léon Walras' crucial insight into the holistic nature of the economy (interdependence of economic variables) impressed Schumpeter (1883–1950) sufficiently to declare the general equilibrium approach the "Magna Carta of economic theory" – Schumpeter (1954, p. 242) – and to regard Léon Walras as the greatest among the economists. But Walras – realizing the unfeasibility of a practical macro-economic approach in which the price and quantity of each individual commodity is accounted for – was satisfied with conceptualizing his theory in form of a fairly abstract system of simultaneous equations. He certainly harbored no ambition of using this frame as a basis for a practically applicable social accounting system. Yet the seed was planted, and in our time the basic idea of Léon Walras has been practically exploited through Leontief's (1951) interindustry analysis. There the difficulty created by the great number of

[38] Smart, *Between Science and Philosophy*, 1968, pp. 297–298.

commodities traded in a modern economy is overcome by aggregating them to a limited number of industries (accepting among a series of simplifying assumptions the one that every industry produces only a single product). These advances by Léon Walras and W. Leontief offer the first, but by no means only, indications of holistic thinking in economics. On the micro-economic and management level the *ceteris paribus* approach of Alfred Marshall (1842–1924), assuming all variables, except one or two as unchanged, has been replaced to a considerable extent by the *mutatis mutandis* approach revealing the interdependence of all variables through a system of simultaneous equations. Since *matrix algebra* was devised primarily for the purpose of solving large systems of simultaneous equations, and since the latter are the vehicle *par excellence* to deal with more or less holistic systems (i.e. with the interdependence of a smaller or larger number of variables united in a specific system), matrix algebra itself can be regarded as an analytical means that greatly helped to promote a synthetic objective. In a similar vein cybernetics and the theory of feedback controls must be regarded as analytical techniques that, to a large extent, serve the holistic cause. But parts of Chapter 7 will be devoted to these matters and the systems approach in general.[39] In concluding this Chapter, and for further readings, we should like to refer the reader to a Symposium on the Notions of Model and Causality in Economics organized and reprinted by *Synthese* in Vol. 20 (1969).

[39] Of special value from our point of view is the article by Wold, 'Mergers of Economics and Philosophy of Science', 1969, and the contribution of Meissner and Wold, 'The Foundation of Science on Cognitive Mini-Models, With Applications to the German Methodenstreit and the Advent of Economics', 1974.

CHAPTER 7

PHILOSOPHY OF SCIENCE AND THE SYSTEMS APPROACH

7.1 Introduction

The Received View of the philosophy of science – in a way still dominating many physical and social sciences, yet already vigorously challenged – is not identical with positivism but emerged in its wake. This view is strongly biased toward the construction of scientific theories by means of *axiomatic calculi* to which *partial observational interpretations* are given. As F. Suppe (1974, p. 4) points out: "the positivistic analysis of scientific knowledge erected upon the Received View has been rejected . . . , but none of the alternative analyses of scientific knowledge which have been suggested enjoy widespread acceptance."

Suppe discusses in considerable detail the Received View and its criticism as well as alternatives presented by Toulmin, T. S. Kuhn, Hanson, Feyerabend and Bohm. In the following we shall not merely summarize the controversy between the traditional view and those challengers, but go beyond Suppe's presentation by drawing attention to further developments. First, we shall show that there exists a transition between the more formalistic Received View and some of its non-formalistic alternatives (especially the one presented by Thomas Kuhn). And, second, we shall indicate that the attempt of bridging the gap between the analytical and non-analytical approaches is nothing but an elegant application of systems thinking.

This "bridge" is based on a work by Sneed (1971), elaborated by Stegmüller (1973a), and brought to the attention of a wider audience by the central panel-discussion of Kuhn, Sneed and Stegmüller at the Fifth International Congress of Logic, Methodology and Philosophy of Science (London, Ont., August–Sept., 1975).

One of Stegmüller's major contributions lies in the detailed demonstration that Sneed's new, and set-theoretically carefully worked out, notion of "theory" – *theory*, not merely as a collection of statements but as a complex structure or system consisting of a fairly permanent *propositional core* as well as of a *set of intended applications*, *a set of empirical claims* etc. – fits well with the theory notion implied by Kuhn's (1962) revolutionary book. This is the more startling as Kuhn's is a historic-sociological, perhaps even psychological approach. As Stegmüller shows, Sneed's formalism permits a plausible explanation of the clash and misunderstanding between the Received View on science and the modern one of Kuhn, Hanson and others.

Such an explanation seems to be urgently needed because, as Stegmüller points out, many "young philosophers of science were driven into a sort of intellectual schizophrenia. On one hand they found the Kuhnian approach uncommonly attractive, on the other, if they took Kuhn's criticism seriously, they felt forced to regard it as in need of fundamental revision . . . It has been my firm conviction for a long time that this represents a wholly impossible situation, and that it is absolutely imperative to bridge the gap between the historically and the systematically oriented approaches."[1]

Of course, the key is found in the fact that the modern view of science implies an entirely different notion of theory than that held by the tradition camp. Whereas the conventional picture is not only *propositional-descriptive* but also purely *static*, the modern picture is *structural-holistic*, *dynamic* as well as *instrumental*, because it not only emphasizes the recorded insights of science but stresses the entire process of *doing* science, as well as the *holding* and *using* of theories, of *elaborating* and eventually of *replacing* them by better ones. Yet before discussing the *system-oriented view of science*, we have to outline concisely the essence of the traditional panorama.

7.2 Epistemology: The Received View

The emergence of what F. Suppe calls the "Received View", and what we shall occasionally address as "uncritical empiricism" (cf. our footnote 2), can be traced to the epistemological crises caused by relativity theory and quantum physics during the first two decades of this century. None of the philosophies rivalling each other around 1900 (mechanistic materialism, neo-Kantianism, Croce's neo-Hegelianism, Bergson's vitalistic irrationalism, American pragmatism and Mach's neo-positivism) was capable of coping with the breakdown of the conventional world picture brought about by modern physics. No longer could time and space be considered absolute notions, nor could one continue to base knowledge on sensations when sense experience became meaningless in the realm of nuclear particles. In the wake of this turmoil, a radical version of empiricism came to the fore under the designation of *logical positivism*. In the narrow sense it embraces Hans Reichenbach and, above all, the disciples as well as epigones of the Vienna Circle, out of which the dominant figure of

[1] Stegmüller (1975b, pp. 2–3).

Rudolf Carnap emerged. Often, however, logical positivism is taken to refer also to Bertrand Russell, Ludwig von Wittgenstein, even Karl Popper and others; although this must be considered a most inaccurate designation to which no one would have objected more than any of these philosophers, it is nevertheless true that they too contributed essentially to what is nowadays regarded as the Received View of the philosophy of science. Its early versions are found by Carnap (1923 and 1928) and may be regarded as a kind of synthesis of Mach's positivism (with its phenomenal regularities represented by means of *observational* as well as *theoretical terms*) and Poincaré's conventionalism (according to which theoretical terms are nothing but conventions) with a dash of logic added in form of a third category: *the logical terms* (e.g. sentential connectives). The result is an axiomatic framework built from:

(1) *observational terms* providing the nexus to phenomenal reality,

(2) *theoretical terms* facilitating representation as well as comprehension, and

(3) *logical terms* providing the syntactical mortar for keeping the structure together.

In addition to the axioms, theorems and definitions (see Subsection 4.14), *rules of correspondence* are required. They fulfill the important function of connecting the theoretical terms with the observational ones. Without these rules the *interpretation* of the theory (uninterpreted calculus), through specific *models*, would hardly be possible. Yet the most essential ingredients of uncritical empiricism are (in addition to the static-propositional definition of "theory") a series of more or less controversial principles.

7.21 *The Principles of Uncritical Empiricism*

The first principle or dogma, to speak in Quine's terminology, is found in the notion that there is a "fundamental cleavage between truths which are *analytic*, or grounded in meanings independent of matters of fact, and truths which are *synthetic*, or grounded in fact" (Quine 1953, p. 20). This principle is derived from Kant's philosophy and can be traced to Hume and Leibniz. It has been challenged mainly by Quine (1953) who ultimately identifies it with the reduction dogma (our second principle) as well as with our sixth principle. Quine thus employs what we must consider a systems approach (for details see our paragraph on "the sixth principle"). However, Suppe (1974, p. 72) and other authors believe that Quine has not demonstrated the untenability of the analytical–synthetical distinction, but merely has shown the fact that this distinction has not yet been fully justified. While others like Putnam (1962) argue that many scientific statements (including principles and laws) are neither analytic nor synthetic but fall into the category of *lawlike* clusters. Such cluster-statements consist of certain properties clustering to each other in such a way that most but not all of them must be present to form a specific cluster concept. G. Maxwell (1962), on the other hand, seems to accept the analytic–synthetic dichotomy in principle, but argues that *analyticity is context-dependent*. Thus an analytic sentence in one context may have to be considered as synthetic in another. This is in full accord with our own systems approach according to which we have demonstrated (in Sections 2.3 to 2.8) something similar for a different aspect; there we have shown that a system may be considered as positive or normative depending on the context, that is to say, depending on the location of the system boundary. In Chapter 2, we have hinted at the belief that a systems approach may help in revealing the relativity of many other properties assumed to be context-dependent.

The second principle is called by Quine the "dogma of reductionism", but is better known as the meaning theory of verification or, shortly, as the *verification principle*. It asserts that *a statement is cognitively meaningful if and only if it can be verified (or falsified) objectively*. This not only brands all metaphysical statements as cognitively meaningless, but also excludes any kind of value judgement or other introspective experiences.[2]

Furthermore, there was the old controversy between those who believed that verification must refer to *phenomenalistic sense data*, and the ultimately victorious group who insisted that it can refer to nothing but *physical events*. Above all, the principle *per se* cannot be verified objectively and thus itself would belong to the category of metaphysical and meaningless statements.

A third principle, which W. Salmon (1975) calls the third dogma of empiricism, consists of *the assertion that scientific explanations are logical arguments*; it is usually addressed under the name of "covering laws of explanation". This principle was introduced in two stages, first by Hempel and Oppenheim (1948) and then by Hempel (1966) at a comparatively late time. The basic idea is easy to comprehend: *A deterministic theory explains by means of a*

[2] As hinted at previously (see Section 2.1) we consider introspection as a cognitive experience (though a subjective one) and hence an empirical event – after all the word "empirical" stems ethymologically from the word "experience". This is one of our justifications for distinguishing between *uncritical* and critical *empiricism*. The latter admits subjective experiences such as value judgements, and criticizes or rejects some of the principles of the Received View as discussed here.

deductive argument (first stage); that is to say the *explanatory and predictive power* of a deterministic theory lies in the premise of its deductive argument whereby the conclusion (theory or hypothesis) is explained by the pertinent premises. The latter consists of one or more statements of antecedent conditions $C_1, C_2, \ldots C_k$ and of one or more general laws $L_1, L_2, \ldots L_r$ while the conclusion describes the phenomenon E to be explained:

Logical deduction	$C_1, C_2, \ldots, C_k$	Statements of antecedent conditions	Explanans
	$L_1, L_2, \ldots, L_r$	General Laws	
→	E	Description of the empirical phenomenon to be explained	Explanandum

Then three logical conditions (R_1 to R_3) and an empirical condition (R_4) of adequacy can be extracted:

(R_1) The explanandum must be a deductive consequence of the explanans.

(R_2) The explanans must contain general laws, which constitute a requirement for the derivation of the exlanandum.

(R_3) The content of the explanans must be empirical and testable (at least in principle) by observation.

(R_4) The explanans must consist of empirically true sentences.[3]

The principle asserts furthermore (second stage) that *a probabilistic theory explains by means of an inductive argument*; in its simplest form it would adhere to the following kind of argument:

$p(O, R)$ is close to 1
i is a case of R
――――――――― (makes highly probable)[4]
i is a case of O

Hereby R designates a random experiment, and O its outcome, while $p(O, R)$ represents the pertinent probabilistic law. The second premise corresponds to the antecedent condition (under the deterministic situation) and the inductive conclusion is the hypothesis to be explained (probabilistically) by the premises.

[3] Cf. Hempel and Oppenheim, 1948, pp. 137–139.

[4] See Hempel, 1966, p. 67.

An enormous amount of literature has accumulated on those *covering laws* and on the subject of explanation and prediction. The validity of those covering laws for the social and instrumental science has frequently been put in question. Indeed, the case of historical explanations, where general laws are hardly obvious, constituted from the very outset a stumbling block to the general acceptance of this principle; and Dray (1957, 1964) rightly criticizes Hempel by arguing that his models are not applicable in most cases of historical explanation – see also Nash (1969, pp. 75–158), and Ryan (1973).[4a]

A more general criticism of this third dogma was recently raised by Salmon (1975) who advanced three interesting points against accepting the inferential view of scientific explanation:

(1) That irrelevances in the premises (e.g. the introduction of an irrelevant premise) are harmless to logical arguments but fatal to explanations – which indicates that an explanation must be more than an argument fulfilling Hempel's conditions.

(2a) That phenomena whose probabilities are low cannot properly be explained. Assume for example a loaded die which results in a "one" in 90 out of 100 casts. Would it then not seem odd to say that the casting of a "one" can be explained, while that of any of the other surfaces cannot? (The statement that "the frequent occurrence of a "one" can be explained by the loading of the die", would not answer this query.)

(2b) Genuine scientific explanation is not possible if indeterminism holds. This is treated as a corollary to (2a). Salmon points out that in accepting this dogma we face the dilemma of either *a priori* ruling out indeterminism or of holding that events are explainable only if they are completely deterministic.

(3) There is no justification for imposing temporal asymmetry upon explanations (whereas arguments are free of this limitation). For example, "a particular lunar eclipse can be predicted accurately, using the laws of motion and a suitable set of initial conditions holding prior to the eclipse; the same eclipse can equally well be retrodicted using posterior conditions and the same laws. It is intuitively clear that, if explanations are arguments, then only the predictive argument can qualify as an explanation, and not the retrodictive one. The reason is obvious. We explain events on the basis of antecedent causes, not on the basis of subsequent effects."[5]

[4a] G. H. von Wright (1971) developed a hermeneutic theory of *teleological* explanations (instead of *causal* explanations, as demonstrated above) for human actions. See also Stegmüller (1975a, pp. 103–147).

[5] Salmon, (1975, p. 13).

Salmon therefore concludes that: "to give scientific explanation is to show how events and statistical regularities fit into the causal network of the world."[6] But he admits that this leads us directly into one of the most serious epistemological problems, "namely, to provide an explication of causality without violating Hume's strictures against hidden powers and necessary connections."[7]

A fourth principle is vital for understanding the difference between the traditional view and Sneed's new approach. This principle derives from the distinction between observational and theoretical terms and *asserts the existence of an observational language distinct from the theoretical language*. This distinction no longer holds in Sneed's theory (which is among other things an extension and refinement of Ramsey's solution to the problem of theoretical terms). For Sneed a term may well be observational in one theory and theoretical in another. Thus the criterion for distinguishing an observational from a theoretical term no longer depends on the kind of language to which they belong but *depends entirely on the boundaries of the theory* (here again a typical feature of the systems approach becomes obvious).

The fifth principle is that of *inductive inference*. It forms the central idea, not only of the Received View, but of any empirical scientific endeavor. From the view-point of uncritical empiricism it is an indispensable complement of the verification principle, because if direct verification is possible at all, it is so only for particular and existential propositions, but not for universal ones. The verification of a natural law or other generalization is possible at best in a second-hand fashion, that is to say by means of induction. This explains the great effort which positivists, and especially Carnap, put into the development of an inductive logic based on the *a priori* probability notion (see Subsections 5.24 and 5.32). If this endeavor would have proved successful, it might have even been possible to demonstrate that *the principle of inductive inference* is of analytical and not of a metaphysical nature. That this principle, in spite of its indispensability and success, is still beset by conceptual and methodological difficulties, was discussed in Chapter 5.

A sixth principle, too, is closely connected (if not identical) with the verification principle and insists that *individual statements are verifiable*. This stands in sharp contrast to the view of Quine and many system-theorists who argue that only larger entities (e.g. theories but not hypotheses) are accessible to verification or refutation. Indeed, the assertion that whole theories, but not individual hypotheses, are subject to test, is one of the crucial assertions of modern holism.

[6] *Idem.*, p. 18.
[7] *Idem.*, p. 18.

The seventh is the principle of *meaning invariance* which insists that the meaning of scientific terms is independent of the pertinent theory. It is explicitly rejected by Feyerabend (1962) and disagrees also with the theory of Sneed and Stegmüller which permit possible changes in the observational versus theoretical nature of a term (one and the same term may be observational in one theory but theoretical in another). Thus this principle is not only related to the fourth principle but overlaps with the first one, at least in as much as it might also reject the context-dependency of analyticity.

As an eighth principle one might accept the so called "*theory of development by reduction*". It regards science as "a cumulative enterprise, extending and augmenting old successes with new successes; old theories are not rejected or abandoned once they have been accepted; they are just superseded by more comprehensive theories to which they are reduced", (Suppe, 1974, p. 56). The reduction of the laws of traditional chemistry to those of nuclear physics is an excellent illustration, but only of the core of this kind of reductionism. The principle has been strongly criticized by Bohm, Feyerabend, Hanson and, above all, T. Kuhn. The revolutionary book of the latter (1962) in a way pivots on the opposite thesis, emphasizing the need for distinguishing clearly between *normal science* (elaborating, supporting and revising a well established body of knowledge) and *revolutionary science* (challenging a well established paradigm, and replacing it by a new one which in time becomes well established and the object of normal science).

Our attempt to formulate the essence of uncritical empiricism in eight principles (together with the five linguistic conditions summarized by Suppe and reprinted below) has the modest purpose of giving a rough outline of this important doctrine. However, the principles discussed might well be reducible to a smaller number (as Quine's work suggests) or supplementable by further principles of derived or secondary status.

7.22 *Refinements and Ultimate Version of Uncritical Empiricism*

Logical positivism and the Received View underwent an evolution that lasted for almost half a century. In the course of this development many subtle issues were analyzed and often solved in a more or less elegant way. Here it is not possible to go into those details, but two important issues can be hinted at. The first one refers to the positivistic requirement that theoretical terms have to be *defined explicitly* in terms of observational terms (a typical example of this requirement is to be found in *Bridgeman's operationalism* where a theoretical concept must be defined in terms of a measurable operation). But this not only involves dispositional terms (e.g. "probable", "fragile", "hard"), but makes the correspondence rule itself define a dispositional property (i.e. the rule is formulated in terms of *a would be result*). But Carnap showed that dispositional terms, although cognitively meaningful, cannot be explicitly or operationally defined in first order predicate calculus. Besides, as the critics of Bridgeman's operationalism have pointed out, alternative measurement operations for one and the same concept lead to a series of concepts, but not to unique concepts. This would destroy the required one–one correspondence between concept-meaning and measurement-operation. Two different solutions to this dilemma have been proposed: (i) to axiomatize the theory in *modal logic* which is amenable to subjunctive and contrary-to-fact conditionals, or (ii) to accept weaker requirements for connecting theoretical terms with observational ones. Indeed, the final version (see below, item 5) contains much weaker correspondence requirements than the *original version* (which *stipulated an explicit definition of the theoretical notions in terms of the observational notions*).

Although the second and easier way was chosen within the frame of the Received View, in recent times *modal logic* has been employed to clarify the problems of causality and interpretation. For a considerable time it has been realized that the formulation of scientific laws as *indicative* sentences (i.e. by means of assertorial logic) creates difficulties. Ultimately such laws express what *would* happen under circumstances that need not yet be facts. Thus it would be appropriate to formulate those laws as hypothetical statements, usually called *counterfactual conditionals* (in the broad sense comprising both subjunctive as well as contrary-to-fact conditional sentences which lend themselves to the specification of *dispositional* terms and are analyzable within modal logic). Since the appearance of two fundamental papers by Chisholm (1946) and Goodman (1947), much attention has been paid to the problem of counterfactuals – for a survey and anthology of the more important recent papers see Sosa (1975). As the problem of causality has not yet been solved satisfactorily by traditional *regularity analysis*, the hope has arisen that the *analysis of counterfactuals* might open a more promising alternative avenue. Hereby a cause is envisaged as something that makes a difference in comparison to what *would* have happened without it (this corresponds to Hume's *second* definition of causality), while a counterfactual is taken as a statement about *possible worlds*, that is to say, alternatives to actual situations. Some subtleties have indeed been clarified by this novel approach, but, needless to say, no definite solution to the problem of causality has come about. The major effect of this counterfactual analysis upon the Received View lies in the fact that its final version (item 1 – see below) has admitted a possible extension through modal logic.

In spite of all these endeavors, fundamental issues remained open, and led to the present crises in which logical positivism can no longer be considered a viable epistemological basis. But since no broad acceptable alternative has thus far emerged, it seems important to know and comprehend the end results of this process. Thus Suppe summarized the final version of the Received View in the following five linguistic conditions which a scientific theory is supposed to fulfill:

Final Version of the Received View[8] (Linguistic Conditions)

(1) There is a first-order language L (possibly augmented by modal operators) in terms of which the theory is formulated, and a logical calculus K defined in terms of L.

(2) The non-logical or descriptive primitive constants (that is, the "terms") of L are bifurcated into two disjoint classes: V_0 which contains just the observation terms; V_T which contains the non-observation or theoretical terms. V_0 must contain at least one individual constant.

(3) The language L is divided into the following sublanguages, and the calculus K is divided into the following subcalculi:

(a) The *observation language*, L_0, is a sublanguage of L which contains no quantifiers or modalities, and contains the terms of V_0 but none from V_T. The associated calculus K_0 is the restriction of K to L_0 and must be such that any non-V_0 terms (that is, non-primitive terms) in L_0 are explicitly defined in K_0; furthermore, K_0 must admit of at least one finite model.

(b) The *logically extended observation language*, L'_0, contains no V_T terms and may be regarded as being formed from L_0 by adding the quantifiers, modalities, and so on, of L. Its associated calculus K'_0 is the restriction of K to L'_0.

(c) The *theoretical language*, L_T, is that sublanguage of L which does not contain V_0 terms; its associated calculus, K_T, is the restriction of K to L_T.

These sublanguages together do not exhaust L, for L also contains

[8] From Suppe (ed.), *The Structure of Scientific Theories*, 1974, pp. 50–51.

mixed sentences – that is, those in which at least one V_T and one V_0 term occur. In addition it is assumed that each of the sub-languages above has its own stock of predicate and/or functional variables, and that L_0 and L_0' have the same stock which is distinct from that of L_T.

(4) L_0 and its associated calculi are given a *semantic interpretation* which meets the following conditions:

(a) The domain of interpretation consists of concrete observable events, things, or things-moments; the relations and properties of the interpretation must be directly observable.

(b) Every value of any variable in L_0 must be designated by an expression in L_0.

It follows that any such interpretation of L_0 and K_0, when augmented by appropriate additional rules of truth, will become an interpretation of L_0' and K_0'. We may construe interpretations of L_0 and K_0 as being *partial semantic interpretations of* L and K, and we require that L and K be given no observational semantic interpretation other than that provided by such partial semantic interpretations.

(5) A *partial interpretation* of the theoretical terms of the sentences of L containing them is provided by the following two kinds of postulates: the *theoretical postulates* T (that is, the axioms of the theory) in which only terms of V_T occur, and the *correspondence rules* or postulates C which are mixed sentences. The correspondence rules C must satisfy the following conditions:

(a) The set of rules C must be finite.

(b) The set of rules C must be logically compatible with T.

(c) C contains no extralogical term that does not belong to V_0 or V_T.

(d) Each rule in C must contain at least one V_0 term and at least one V_T term essentially or non-vacuously.

Since these conditions are not fulfilled in most existing sciences (e.g. few of them have actually been fully axiomatized) they hardly represent a realistic picture. At best one might accept them as an ideal to be approached rather than attained; but even this does not seem to be acceptable to many critics of this comparatively uncritical embracing of empiricism.

7.3 Reaction and Alternatives

Philosophy of science as a cultural manifestation cannot escape the law of dialectic. No less than any other humanistic endeavor, it is subject to forces and counterforces, actions and reactions, thesis and antithesis. We are presently witnessing a very natural reaction to an epistemological trend oversaturated with positivistic notions – notions that appear to us narrow and obsolete in the face of many revolutionary insights generated by such novel disciplines as cybernetics and automation theory, neurophysiology, bio-chemistry and bio-physics, the broad spectrum of ecological studies, nuclear and sub-nuclear physics as well as modern cosmology. To this have to be added the world-shaking achievements of the medical, engineering and administrative sciences. All this has helped to reveal that in spite of many valuable achievements, logical positivism is at bottom a very restrictive and perhaps simplistic philosophy.

It dawns upon an increasing number of scholars that the naive hope to separate completely our scientific endeavors from our *Weltanschauung* has to be abandoned. Of course, great dangers lurk in such a realization. The risk of throwing overboard the many valuable methodological tools which the Received View put at our disposal, the hazard of loosing oneself in a boundless subjectivism, or irrationalism and, above all, the peril of science becoming the volley-ball of ideologies.

Among the most vociferous critics of the Received View are the representatives of, what Suppe calls, the "*Weltanschauungen* Analyses", by us addressed as the "normativistic camp".[9] It comprises scholars with often diverse views such as Bohm, Churchman, Feyerabend, Hanson, Kuhn, Rudner, Toulmin, Singer and many others who believe that any science and any scientific outlook is fraught with value judgements. For two reasons we hesitate to add to this list the previously mentioned names of Sneed and Stegmüller. First, because their writings rarely emphasize the subjective-normative element (to which they ultimately, however, seem to submit[10]). And second, their endeavor appears to represent a further phase in the evolution of the philosophy

[9] This expression should not be confused with "normative methodology" (i.e. prescribing methodological rules for testing hypotheses etc.) because Kuhn, Feyerabend and others explicitly reject such methodology.

[10] The following passage gives proof of the normative remnant present in Stegmüller's theory:

> In these branches we have located a juncture where value judgements are unavoidable in deciding which way to proceed. Should someone regard *this* as subjectivism, the *only* correct reply is that *this is a species of subjectivism which we simply must swallow*. Stegmüller (1975b, p. 15).

of science. Their view must be regarded as a *synthesis* resulting from the clash between the positivistic thesis, on one side, and the normativistic on the other. A similar novel and linguistic-formalistic approach is that of Leinfellner (see e.g. Leinfellner and Köhler 1974) who on one side is influenced by the linguistic view of Carnap and Hempel, on the other, by the formalistic school of theory formation as practiced by Suppes and his disciple Sneed (the "Stanford School"). But Leinfellner is less interested in the essence of a theory than in the problem of creating usable models. Indeed, during the last decade he endeavoured to axiomatize various theories of the social sciences. Leinfellner (1974) rejects the metatheoretical analysis of scientific theories which is restricted to cognitive and syntactical functions. He advances instead an "epitheoretical" analysis which includes a reconstruction of the background knowledge of social theories, and takes into consideration modal, especially normative and deontic, aspects. This approach he illustrates by analyzing statistical decision theory in an epitheoretical fashion, thus opening participation for specialists from many quarters such as economists, sociologists, political scientists, historians, philosophers, mathematicians etc.

7.31 *The Normativistic Outlook*

The common bond of the normativistic camp lies in the notion that *science is an ongoing cultural activity with all its dynamical, dialectical and normative aspects*. Yet, contrary to widespread belief, we do not regard this holistic conception of science as diametrically opposed to the traditional one. Experts conversant with the systems approach will rather view the positivistic conception as a subset of the normativistic one. Where the positivists saw merely a set of propositions, the normativists see a collection containing this propositional set, as well as sets of relations, actions, applications, etc. Thus the systems approach and our method of neutralizing systems (as developed in Chapter 2) might help to explicate the arch-difference between the positivistic and the normativistic camp, because an activity (necessarily embedded in a system) presupposes some value judgements, while a collection of descriptive sentences does not. Therefore the major difference between these two camps lies in the shift of the boundaries of a system called "science". If these boundaries are kept so narrow that the system contains not much beyond descriptive sentences, the neutrality of that narrow system seems acceptable; but as soon as the boundaries are expanded far enough to embrace the entire activity of *doing* science, then the neutrality of science becomes an illusion, because many value judgements which previously were excluded and relegated to the environment of science are now part of its system. It was such a major boundary shift that was instigated by men like Hanson, Kuhn and Feyerabend. Is it then surprising that they arrive at ideas about science which are very different from those of the Received View?

Of course, there are further differences (between these camps), but they may well be closely related to the fundamental boundary-difference mentioned above. Take the divergent view about constructing, testing and accepting hypotheses. Does not a shift of boundaries also mean a shift in emphasis? A group that concentrates on a smaller system often neglects important features of the environment, while the other group concentrating on a system containing part of what otherwise constitutes the environment, is likely to obtain a more cohesive picture. Hanson's (1958) *doctrine of meaning dependence*, emphasizing that facts are "*theory-laden*", can be explained in these terms. Since facts are not sentences and since the correspondence theory between facts and sentences can no longer be maintained, facts must be explained in broader contextual terms. It requires widening one's system, and concentrating on aspects previously neglected. Hanson does this by forcing us to admit that conceptual organization influences our process of perceiving ("seeing that"). The well known vexation picture which can be interpreted as either a *pelican* or an *antelope* is merely a primitive illustration. A more subtle example is offered by comparing Tycho Brahe who, undaunted by Copernicus, "sees that" the sun rotates westwards, with his assistant Johannes Kepler who "sees that" the earth rotates eastwards.

Thus Hanson's process of *seeing that* involves a broader system than merely experiencing a visual image; it requires and includes a *conceptual organization* that is bound to be subjectively tainted by previous experience. Due to our past conditioning we are inescapably giving *preference* to one interpretation over others. It is in this sense that "facts" (which seem to be inseparable from the process of "perceiving facts") are loaded with values. This leads to Hanson's central concern, the process and logic of scientific discovery and the theories resulting from it. He regards *theories as being or providing patterns of conceptual organization that render data intelligible.* But those theories, he contends, are discovered not by inductive but by retroductive inferences[11] (pattern recognition).

[11] The term "retroductive inference" is taken from Peirce who interprets Aristotle's third inference not as "practical" inference (as we did in Section 4.4 and as it is usually done) but as *retroduction* (also reduction or abduction). Peirce seems to have referred to those inferences which involve a kind of pattern recognition. Whether the set of retroductive inferences is or is not a sub-set of the set at all inductive inferences in the broad sense is for us an open question.

Such views not only deny the existence of *neutral* facts, but also lead Hanson to reject the notion of a neutral observation language. On the contrary, he insists that patterns of our scientific conceptual organization always contain a linguistic component and bias. He also points at the difference between representing (arranging) and referring (characterizing) and asserts that sense-data, like pictures, *represent*, while sentences *refer*. But above all "there is a corresponding gap between visual pictures and what we know. Seeing bridges this, for while seeing is at the least a 'visual copying' of objects, it is also more than that. It is a certain sort of seeing objects: seeing that if *x* were done to them *y* would follow. This fact got lost in all the talk about knowledge arising from sense experience, memory, association and correlation."[12] Although some scholars criticized Hanson, and tried to demonstrate that not all seeing is "seeing that", Suppe (1974) agrees that Hanson made a plausible, though not a conclusive, point that at least all observation involves "seeing that", but that Hanson's cannot be considered a detailed analysis of the scientific process.

Thomas Kuhn's (1962) very different work comes closer to such a task, and in a way supplements that of Hanson. Taken together, they furnish a fair outline of the modern normativistic view of science. Kuhn as an historiographer of science envisages every scientific discipline as consisting of a succession of revolutionary discontinuities and non-revolutionary periods. The jump caused by the *revolutionary* scientist brings forth what Kuhn called the "paradigm" – a term that created much confusion among Kuhn's critics – while the non-revolutionary periods enable the *normal* scientists, the so-called "puzzle-solvers", to articulate, elaborate and support the paradigm in vogue until overthrown by a new paradigmatic revolution. "Paradigm" is an extremely broad and vague notion, comprising a network of conceptual, theoretical, instrumental, metaphysical and quasi-metaphysical commitments; it was later divided by T. Kuhn (1974) into sub-concepts (the "exemplar" and the "disciplinary matrix"). It may be compared to Hanson's conceptual pattern but may have even wider normative implications; it comprises the scientific *Weltanschauung* (the "disciplinary matrix" acquired by scientists during their training process) as well as the applications (the "exemplars" which pose questions and lead to solutions by means of which scientists learn their crafts). It is the *disciplinary matrix* which forms the common ground of a discipline during a given period and which is undermined and ultimately rejected during a revolutionary episode. Thus it is the notion of *discontinuity*, so strongly stressed in Kuhn's work, which is the actual powder keg. Toulmin

[12] Hanson, *Patterns of Discovery*, 1958, pp. 29–30.

(1953), long before Kuhn, launched a similar view but without asserting this *discontinuity* of the scientific process that became so crucial. But is it not a matter of degree and a matter of interpretation to envisage the scientific process as either continuous or as discontinuous? Does not any academic discipline possess some continuous as well as some discontinuous aspects? Does Kuhn's assertion not resemble the pseudo-contradiction of saying "the cup is half empty" after someone else asserted that "it is half full"? We agree with Kuhn's thesis of discontinuity, but for a reason that becomes obvious only after considering some of the consequences. Discontinuity in science always involves a dramatic shift in paradigm, a fundamental change in the way one sees reality. Indeed, it cannot be denied that the revolutions of Copernicus and Kepler, Galileo and Newton, Lavoisier and Priestley, Medeleev and J. L. Meyer, Darwin and Wallace, Einstein and Michelson, Plank and Heisenberg, to name only the most obvious ones, brought about drastic modifications in the scientific world view. Not merely because they added new bits of knowledge, but because they relegated to the realm of myth crucial elements that until then were regarded as legitimate truths. Similarly, we may be certain that there are elements in our present body of scientific knowledge which are justifiable by nothing but our present paradigms or, to speak with Hanson, by the momentary fashion of organizing data into a conceptual pattern. Kuhn's belief that the conflict between competing paradigms cannot be solved by logic but merely by persuasion, is one of the most contended of his pronouncements. It seems to be related to his denying that there is a difference between the *discovery* and the justification of a theory – with which for one, Hanson would not agree. The ultimate merit of Kuhn's work, apart from his rich and subtle historical documentation, is drawing attention to the fact that a theory consists of several diverse parts which differe widely as to their nature, significance and permanence. However, it was not Kuhn but Sneed (1971) who pointed at a rigorous way to distinguish, systematize and integrate these various parts of a theory.

The third main pillar of the normativistic camp, Paul Feyerabend, takes Popper's neo-rationalism as his point of departure and carries it to its ultimate consequence, that is to say, to an extreme relativistic position which McEvoy (1975) calls "sceptical fallibilism".[13] Feyerabend (e.g. 1958, 1962, 1965,

[13] "Thus on the Popperian model of growth, the outcome of evaluation of competing theories depends ultimately on the acceptance or rejection of 'basic statements'. Such a decision is a matter of convention. It can never be conclusively justified and is always open to revision. In the light of this epistemological vertigo, Feyerabend sees only one possible consequence – sceptical fallibilism." McEvoy (1975, p. 63).

1970a, 1970b, 1975), like Hanson and Kuhn, denies the neutrality of the observation language, as well as the principle of meaning invariance and simultaneously that of consistency. For him, too, factual observations are context-dependent; he even eliminates the empirical vestiges in Popper's doctrine by claiming that no (higher level) theory can be *tested* against reality but merely *against other, incompatible theories*. This *theory pluralism* is the core of Feyerabend's theory, and ultimately rests on the Hegelian idea of dialectical criticism; this theory also bears some affinity to works of E. A. Singer (1924, 1959) and C. W. Churchman (e.g. 1968, 1971) who tend toward a *discipline pluralism* according to which the solution of a scientific problem requires a multi-disciplinary approach. Feyerabend also believes that statements cannot be derived from facts (hence the latter cannot justify the former) but can only be derived from other statements. Hence the acceptance or rejection of a hypothesis must be a matter of convention. Yet the testing is ultimately not a comparison of statements but one of human reaction to such statements, hence is not in need of a common observation language. This anthropocentric view is called by McEvoy (1975, p. 59) "the watershed in Feyerabend's decline from the confident heights of critical rationalism to the despairing depths of sceptical fallibilism." McEvoy continues by critically pointing out (p. 64) that "Feyerabend attempts to buttress his philosophy of 'anything goes' with a hodge-podge of diverse philosophical doctrines" while Stegmüller (1973a, p. 305) calls Feyerabend's epistemology "*anarchistic*", and says: "It seems that Feyerabend is not so much concerned to attain *greater clarity about the phenomenon of science* than *to enhance the pleasure in and with science* (translated)".

7.32 *The Sneed–Stegmüller Synthesis*

It seems that in Feyerabend's later publications, the *Weltanschauungen* analysis reached its limit. Thus it is hardly surprising that the new synthesis is found not in a continuation of this extreme subjectivism and philosophical nihilism, but in the quest for a balanced view about the interplay between the subjective and the objective.

One starting point of the synthesizers is the normativistic notion that the static *statement view* of the theory of science is inadequate. Thus they too accept the proposed dynamization materialized in the *structuralistic conception of theories* (this terminology is used by Stegmüller, based on Bar-Hillel – it even reveals a subconscious influence of systems thinking). Their other starting point is the need for a rigorous set-theoretical presentation – especially promoted by the axiomatization attempts of Patrick Suppes (1957, 1969).

It must be emphasized that Sneed has developed his view on the basis of particle mechanics only, and it will require further effort to generalize this view and extend it to other scientific disciplines, especially also to the social sciences. Furthermore it must be borne in mind that Sneed's (1971) presentation – and also Stegmüller's (1973a) pedagogically excellent elaboration – is lengthy and fairly complex, and cannot be presented with a few strokes. For these reasons we can merely attempt to sketch, in a highly simplified fashion, the basic idea behind Sneed's novel approach.

First of all he rejects the positivistic idea of a unique universal and thus unbounded application of a theory. Instead he recognizes that a *theory* T consists of a *fairly permanent core* K and *a set of intended applications* I (such that $I \in$ /A(K) and /A designates the application operation – the sets of applications may intersect with each other). Thus we may present the theory T as an ordered pair of the core K and the intended applications I:

$$T = \langle K, I \rangle.$$

But the core K itself consists of a set of models M (e.g. *classical* particle mechanics), a set of possible models M_p (e.g. particle mechanics in general), a set of possible partial models M_{pp} (e.g. particle *kinetics*)[14] and a set of constraints C on those models, as well as a set of functions or variables ν:

$$K = \langle M, M_p, M_{pp}, C, \nu \rangle \quad \text{and}$$

$$T = \langle M, M_p, M_{pp}, C, \nu, I \rangle.$$

Hereby the following holds $M \subseteq M_p \subseteq M_{pp}$. The relation between these model categories is best understood when bearing in mind that (as Kuhn points out) the student of a scientific theory, physics in particular, who is familiar with equations in form of elements of M_{pp} usually searches during his home or laboratory work for solutions in terms of M_p. Similarly Kuhn says, "the creative imagination required to find an M_p corresponding to a non-standard M_{pp} (say a vibrating membrane or string before these were normal applications of Newtonian mechanics) is one of the criteria by which great scientists may sometimes be distinguished from mediocre (ones)" (Kuhn, 1975, p. 4). Thus

[14] To avoid confusion, some variance in terminology must be pointed out: Sneed (1971) and Stegmüller (1975b) speak of *possible models* and *possible partial models*, while Stegmüller (1973a) and Kuhn (1975) use the expressions *potential models* and *partial potential models* respectively.

getting acquainted with a newly encountered theory means, among other things, learning a series of pertinent applications; while *applying* a theory means devising further applications. In cases where the theory core K has been extended (by research within *normal* science), the *extended core* E goes beyond K by containing a set of additional laws L and a set of additional constraints C_a and a set of additional functions or variables v_a:

$$E = \langle M, M_p, M_{pp}, C, v, L, C_a, v_a \rangle$$

then the *extended structure* of theory T_e becomes:

$$T_e = \langle M, M_p, M_{pp}, C, v, L, C_a, v_a, I \rangle.$$

In the cases of a scientific revolution (in Kuhn's sense), the core would not be expanded, but would be exchanged for a new one, and a new theory would emerge. In this way Sneed's structuralistic, or in our terminology, "system theoretic", approach permits a formalistic representation of the notion of revolutionary progress as well as of Kuhn's distinction between *normal* versus *revolutionary* progress. As Stegmüller (1975b, p.8) points out, it also "permits an elegant simplification of what Lakatos' *theory or research programmes* intended to achieve while avoiding the difficulties and vagueness attached to this theory."[15] Yet Stegmüller also emphasizes that the purpose of this theory-dynamics was by no means developed for the sake of supporting or defending Kuhn's theory. This concordance with the elucidation of Kuhn's theory must be regarded as a kind of windfall arising from the consideration of fundamental problems in a novel and rigorous way.

In addition to the preceding remarks, the Sneed–Stegmüller approach is characterized by the following features. Above all, it operates simultaneously with *three different notions of theory*: first, theory in the purely *conceptual-structural* (but non-propositional) sense, as represented by $T = \langle K, I \rangle$; second, theory in the *propositional* sense of *making empirical claims* expressed by $I \in A$ or $I \in /\!A(N)$ or $I \in /\!A(K^r)$ – whereby A represents the class of all intended applications and /A the application-operator on a *theory net* N based on *core refinements* K^r; third, in the *behavioral* sense of *holding a theory*. The latter could be interpreted in the *weak* sense in which a person, at a specific time, possesses supporting evidence for believing that N is the optional, available theory net. But in order to accommodate this approach better to that of Kuhn, the *strong* version is chosen. It admits that "the set I of intended applications of a theory is not completely specified from the very beginning

[15] Cf. Lakatos (1970 and 1972).

by means of a list or a strict definition; it is an *open* set for which the theory's creator has stipulated a sub-set I_0 of paradigmatic examples, and which can be changed (through additions and cuts) in the course of working with the theory, provided the condition $I_0 \subseteq I$ is met," (Stegmüller, 1975b, p.12). With this formulation the set I becomes the set of Kuhnian paradigms for the set I_0, and holding a theory in this strong sense becomes an explication of Kuhn's notion of *normal* science, because it means the holding of a theory by *a group of scientists sharing a common scientific paradigm*. A clear distinction between the immutable core or paradigm, and the "accidental" changes or core refinements, constitutes a most essential feature of this approach.

Furthermore, the distinction between the models of M and the possible (or potential) models of M_p, on one side, and *possible partial models of* M_{pp}, on the other, is crucial, because the T-theoretical terms are envisaged as being contained in the former but not in the latter. Thus, as Kuhn says, the models of M_{pp}, are "the entities to which a given theory might apply by virtue of their description *in the bare basic vocabulary of the theory*" Kuhn (1975, p. 3), (our italics). That this *elimination of the theoretical terms* is a possible, and in many cases permissible, procedure was pointed out by Ramsey half a century ago.[16] But after accepting this, one ceases to speak of a partially interpreted theoretical language connected by rules of correspondence to an observation language. Instead, one merely distinguishes between T-theoretical and T-non-theoretical terms (i.e. quantities or functions which are theoretical, or non-theoretical respectively, *within* theory T). And *a term is T-theoretical if and only if it cannot be measured without reference to theory T*. If the term can be measured independently of theory T, it is called T-non-theoretical (e.g. *in particle mechanics*, "space" is a non-theoretical notion while "mass" or "force" are theoretical notions within this particular theory). Sneed improved upon the notion of Ramsey-eliminability in several ways.[17] Above all, his differentiation between *laws* (contained in M, M_p, M_{pp}, and L)[18] and *constraints* (contained in C and C_a) puts a limit to certain combinations of

[16] Where theoretical terms are dispensable for the essential formulation of the theory, one speaks of *Ramsey-eliminability*. In these cases the merit of theoretical terms lies mainly in simplifying a theory and in making it more precise as well as economical.

> Where Ramsey-eliminability is not feasible there . . . one speaks of a second type of merit of theoretical terms: the T-theoretical terms enable prediction as well as explanation and supply methods of hypothesis testing that were not possible without them (Stegmüller, 1973a, p.94, translated).

[17] For details and thorough explanations see Stegmüller (1973a, pp. 75–106).

[18] Laws hold in some or all applications.

theoretical magnitudes, and generates relations and cross-references between specific applications. Indeed, isolated applications have little meaning while those tied to each other by common constraints greatly gain in meaning. Kuhn even refers to Sneed's notion of *constraint* as his *central novelty*, and regards it as more fundamental than Sneed himself might have thought.

A further crucial feature of this approach grows out of other previously mentioned issues; it is the distinction between the *basic law* contained in the original *core* and valid for *all* applications, and the *special laws* contained only in the *expanded core* and valid merely for *some* applications.

Finally, there are Kuhn's ideas of *revolutionary science, irrefutability of a theory, scientific progress*, and *theory dislodgement* (without falsification) with all of which Stegmüller tries to cope. But merely some hints can here be offered: "We can, by paralleling Popper's argument proving the non-verifiability of strict universal quantifications, obtain the following proof for the unrefutability of a theory on the basis of a finite number of refuted empirical claims: *since the number of possible refinements of a core is potentially infinite, no number, be it ever so large, of unsuccessful attempts to refine a given core can be considered conclusive proof that a successful refinement of this core is impossible*. Thus, we are not forced to give up the theory; there might just be a still undiscovered refinement which would prove successful when discovered" (Stegmüller, 1975b, p. 22). *Thus theories are viewed as instruments for making empirical claims about reality*, and this seems to agree with Kuhn's assertion that in normal science persons but not theories are put to test, because the responsibility for an eventual "refutation" is no longer sought in the theory but in its user. It is he who succeeds or fails in strengthening the empirical claims advanced with the aid of this very instrument. Two possibilities (i.e. two notions of ordinary progress) are at his disposal: either extending the set of intended applications ($I_t \subset I_{t+1}$; t . . . time index) or the refinements of the core; if he fails in one or the other or in both, it is now deemed to be due to a lack of personal acumen, rather than a deficiency of the theory as an instrument. As to the third notion, that of revolutionary progress, Stegmüller thinks that Kuhn has not provided "*an adequate concept of revolutionary progress for the case of theory dislodgement*". He even regards the provision of a rigorous formulation of such a concept as the "missing link" in Kuhn's presentation, and the only possibility to escape from teleological metaphysics, on one side, and "relativism", on the other. Sneed's *reduction concept* and Ludwig's (1970) work on '*blurred*' functions are mentioned as steps in direction to a way out of this dilemma, but no definite solution seems to be presently available.

What is now Kuhn's reaction to the Sneed–Stegmüller approach? Kuhn admits that for him set theory was until recently "an unknown and altogether forbidding language". But he did not shirk the effort to acquire a rudimentary knowledge, and continues with the following words: "nevertheless, I have learned enough to embrace with enthusiasm the two major conclusions of Professor Stegmüller's (1973a) book. First, though still at an early stage of its development, Dr. Sneed's new formalism makes important new territory accessible to analytic philosophy of science. Second, though sketched with a pen I can scarcely hold, Sneed's first chart of the terrain displays remarkable resemblances to a map I had previously sketched from scattered travellers' reports brought back by itinerant historians of science" (Kuhn, 1975, p. 1) – he furthermore asserts emphatically that Stegmüller understood his (Kuhn's) own work "better than any other philosopher." Although there are minor points of disagreement between them,[19] Kuhn's general tenor is most enthusiastic.

[19] The areas of disagreement between Thomas Kuhn, on one side, and the Sneed–Stegmüller formalism, on the other side, concerns several technical details. For example, in Kuhn's view it is not necessarily the theory, but may well be *the application* of this theory, which *determines whether a specific concept or function is theoretical or not*. He also points out that in order to determine what belongs to a *theory core* and what to an *expanded core* will require much more specification than Sneed and Stegmüller have so far supplied. Kuhn, therefore, concludes "that before the Sneed formalism can be used effectively to identify and, analyse episodes in which theory-change occurs by replacement, rather than simply by growth, some other technique must be found to distinguish, the elements in a core from those in its expansion. What is needed, I take it, is an explicit and general articulation, within the formalism, of some widely shared intuitions, two of which were expressed above. Why is Newton's second law clearly constitutive of mechanics, his law of gravitation not? (Footnote omitted.) What underlies our conviction that relativistic mechanics differs conceptually from Newtonian in a way that, say, Lagrangian and Hamiltonian mechanics do not?" (Kuhn, 1975, pp. 13–14). Furthermore, Kuhn considers Stegmüller's use of the *reduction relation* (for reducing one theory core etc. to another) as dangerously circular. Stegmüller, on the other hand, takes issue with Kuhn's notion of progress and writes: "It certainly is unsatisfactory, to introduce the concept of scientific progress in such a way that one slips into sociology, declaring always those researchers as the more progressive ones, who in the end proved themselves successful in fighting out a 'paradigm conflict'. This would virtually mean making no essential distinction between political and scientific revolution. In some of his formulations Kuhn does create the impression of actually assuming this point of view. Thus the polemic directed against him on this score is comprehensible and, in as far as it rests on a valid interpretation, is fully justified." Translated from Stegmüller (1975a, p.525). Stegmüller calls Kuhn's notions of progress "teleologically infected" and suggests to solve the problem of scientific progress in the following way: "*Elimination of a theory under 'scientific*

Let us summarize the advantages of this radically new and dynamic view of a scientific theory. First of all, *a theory thus becomes an instrument*; and instruments, unlike propositions, have no truth values, hence *cannot be refuted* but can merely be substituted by other theories. The failure of a theory to explain a certain phenomenon may not at all lie with the theory, but might have to be sought in the inadequacy of the scientist who, among the *open set of extensions and applications*, might not have been skillful enough to discover the appropriate ones for the explanation of this particular phenomenon. This would close the first rationality gap in Kuhn's epistemic-historical account. If theories cannot be refuted, then scientists do not necessarily behave irrationally (as the opponents of Kuhn reproached him for asserting, and as Kuhn might indeed have thought before having become acquainted with the Sneed–Stegmüller formulation) if acting contrary to the falsification procedures of Popper.

Furthermore, Carnap's distinction between theoretical and observational languages receives a major blow, because in the light of this novel view (which also includes an improved and extended version of Ramsey's elimination procedure for reducing theoretical terms to their observational constituents) *the distinction between theoretical and observational terms becomes "context-dependent"*. Hence no longer is one able to distinguish between two different kinds of languages, because *a term* may now be considered *theoretical in one theory* (e.g. "utility" in accounting theory where market prices but not utilities are being directly observed) *but observational in another theory* (e.g. in certain behavioral theories where "utilities" may be observable by introspection or the manifestation of indifference attitudes, etc.).

Another advantage, particularly of Stegmüller's (1973a/76) formulation, lies in closing the second rationality gap which is rooted in Kuhn's original assertion that progress in science is not cumulative hence not different from that of the fine arts, literature, philosophy and other humanistic endeavors – hence Kuhn does not regard the transition from an old to a new paradigm as a cumulative progress, since for him the two paradigms are incommensurable. Stegmüller, however, shows that wherever a new theory is capable of explaining all phenomena explained by the old theory and, beyond that, capable of explaining additional phenomena, not explainable by the old one; we are dealing with cumulative hence genuine progress.

---

progress' is present whenever the old theory is structurally reducible to the new theory. Elimination of a theory without progress, however, is present when such a reduction is not possible." Translated from Stegmüller (1975a, p. 529).

The most profound contribution however lies, as already hinted at, in Sneed's (1971) revelation that there does not exist a single intended application of a theory but many (e.g. the double-classification theory of accounting is not only applicable to the business enterprise but also to other micro- and even many macro-economic entities) which overlap and are connected by the set (C) of constraints (e.g. an increment of "wealth" is not only *assumed to be additive* in business accounting but also in input-output analysis). These various applications all obey the fundamental assumptions, but beyond them each application may have additional specific assumptions which solve the problem of *change within constancy*, as long as one remains within the boundaries of "normal science".

Thus the Sneed–Stegmüller formulation offers all the advantages of a dynamic viewpoint encountered in Thomas Kuhn's informal and historical presentation, without the shortcomings of the latter. The activity of "ordinary science" is now expressed by an *extension of the structural core (from K to E) and the discovery of new intended applications (from I_0 to I) while* the upheaval of "*revolutionary science*" finds its expression in the *substitution of the old theory core (K) by a new one (K′).*

7.4 The Systems Approach, Its Criticism, and Its Potential

7.41 *Normativists and System Theorists*

There exists a remarkable affinity between the view of the normativists and those of many proponents of the systems approach. As we have seen, the *Weltanschauung*-philosophers have adopted a holistic point of view (which is also the hallmark of the system experts), and thus are looking at science from the vantage point of a structural perspective. Many system theorists, in turn, have adopted the subjectivistic attitude which characterizes the *Weltanschauung*-philosophers. This is well manifested in the systems literature, but may shortly be illustrated by a few quotations starting with some of the last words from von Bertalanffy, the founder of General System Theory (GST), who wrote shortly before his death in 1972:

> Having been educated in the philosophical tradition later called the Vienna Circle, I may perhaps hint at the change that has taken place in this regard. The epistemology (and metaphysics) of logical positivism was determined by the ideas of physicalism, atomism, and the "camera theory" of knowledge. These, in view of present-day knowledge, are quite simply obsolete.

Instead of physicalism and reductionism, the problems and modes of thought occurring in the biological, behavioral and social sciences should equally be taken into account. Compared to the analytical procedure of classical science, with linear causality connecting two variables as the basic category, the investigation of organized wholes of many variables requires new categories of interaction, transaction, teleology, etc., with many problems arising in epistemology, mathematical models and techniques. Furthermore, knowledge is not a simple approximation to "truth" or "reality"; it is an interaction between knower and known, thus depending on a multiplicity of factors of a biological, cultural, linguistic, etc., nature. This leads to a "perspective philosophy" for which physics, fully acknowledging its achievements in its own and related fields, is not a monopolistic way of knowledge. Against reductionism and theories declaring that reality is "nothing but" a heap of physical particles, genes, reflexes, drives or whatever the case may be, we see science as one of the "perspectives" that man, with his biological, cultural and linguistic endowment and bondage, has created to deal with the universe, he is "thrown into," or rather to which he is adapted owing to evolution and history (von Bertalanffy, 1972, p. xix).[19a]

A similar tune is heard from other general system theorists: "the new theories of perception and cognition recognize the active role of the knowing subject in the process of knowledge" (Laszlo, 1972, p. 197); "An epistemology that interprets human experience as an 'objective' representation, independent of the experiencer, is not only delusive but tends to avert considerations of the peculiar powers of the experiencer in interacting with the world" (A. Wilson, 1973, p. 121). "A new way of looking at the world has evolved in which individual phenomena are viewed as interrelated rather than isolated, and complexity has become a subject of 'interest'" (Klir, 1972, p. 16); "In fact, as we previously suggested, the general system theorist . . . might only ask that they consider . . . that the only real truth about any phenomenon will be that found . . . at the point where percept and concept collapse and where logical and empirical, and inductive and deductive conclusions become indistinguishable" (Sutherland, 1973, p. 189).

Looking at such quotes, the reader might wonder why general system theorists, in spite of their affinity with the *Weltanschauung*-philosophers, are treated by them as outsiders. It seems that it is not so much the sometime radical attitude, but rather their overambition and occasional lack of rigor

[19a] Reprinted from Laszlo, *Introduction to Systems Philosophy*, 1972.

which cast GST into the role of a philosophic stepchild. Indeed, the quality of its philosophic research rarely matches the originality or rigor encountered in the publications of Feyerabend, Hanson, T. Kuhn, Sneed or Stegmüller. Indeed, it seems that for this reason some philosophers and scientists, such as Ackoff, Churchman, H. Simon, who are very active in systems research would reject the label of "general system theorists" and have distanced themselves from the pertinent association. Thus it might be important to draw a line between different camps within the systems approach and to avoid any identification of a proponent of systems thinking with the organized core of the movement. There are, however, several serious philosophers associated with the latter, and there is genuine hope that one day the significance of this movement will gain appreciation in the quarters of professional philosophy.

In spite of many differences and divergencies within the systems camp, the following basic notion, on one side form a common bond, on the other, enable to distinguish this camp from other groups. Apart from the *system definition* and the distinction between *system versus environment* as well as the notion of *systems hierarchy* (all discussed in Section 2.2), there is the theoretically important distinction between an *open system*, permitting *inputs* (matter, energy, information) from the environment and *outputs* (transformed matter, energy, information) to the environment, and a *closed system* which is self-contained, permitting neither inputs from, nor outputs to, the environment. In practice the entire universe seems to be the only true closed system, hence the predominant interest, of systems research, in open systems. But occasionally, especially in the physical sciences, one may treat, for the sake of analytical convenience, an actually open system as though it were closed.

Still more important system notions are those of *entropy* (the degree of physical or informational disorder) and *negentropy* (the degree of order, organization or information). Whoever believes that these concepts are but transmutations from the physical sciences, is gravely mistaken. Of course, the *principle of increasing entropy* is nothing but the second law of thermodynamics. But it is by no means certain that this latter area belongs solely to physics. Attention has been drawn repeatedly to the fact that *thermodynamics is either the physics of economic value or even the economics of physics* – cf. G. Helm (1887, p. 72ff); L. Winiarski (1900, pp. 265, 287); Georgescu-Roegen (1971, p. 276ff). The latter author even hails N. L. Sadi Carnot (1796–1832), the father of thermodynamics, as "the first econometrician", and points out that "*our whole economic life feeds on low entropy*, to wit, cloth, lumber, china, copper, etc., all of which are highly ordered structures ....

We may then take it as a brute fact that low entropy is a *necessary* condition for being useful" (Georgescu-Roegen, 1971, pp. 277–278). If this sounds surprising, it is only because one forgets that thermodynamics arose out of the economic problem of making steam engines and similar devices more efficient. Analogously, it is no coincidence that the term negentropy is not only used to designate physical order, but also informational order (unfortunately often identified with information or even knowledge). Indeed, often the distinction between a physical and an informational medium is difficult to make (e.g. nerve impulses are usually considered purely informational while the transmission of hormones seem to be not only informational but to some degree also performative).

The resulting *input–conversion–output cycle*, characteristic for every system, leads directly to the problem of control and feedback. Systems research has greatly benefited from cybernetics, the mathematical theory of control mechanisms, made widely popular by Norbert Wiener (1894–1964) and elaborated by many others. "*Negative feedback* is informational input looping back to the system in such a way as to decrease the deviation of output from a steady state" (F. Baker, 1973, p. 8). *Positive feedback* which increases this deviation and may lead to the destruction of a system, is therefore much less significant for the purpose of control and viability. Feedback processes are not only complicated by an often enormous number and a complex structure of cybernetic loops, but also by problems of *growth*, *differentiation*, *duplication* (propagation), *integration*, and *fusion* of systems. In this connection various boundary and interface problems emerge – according to Katz and Kahn (1966, pp. 60–61), a *system boundary* is understood as "the demarcation lines or regions for the definition of appropriate systems activity, for admission of members into the system, and for other imports into the system", while an *interface* is the area of contact or interdependency between systems. Finally there is the notion or principle of *equifinality*, suggested by von Bertalanffy, according to which an open system, but not a closed one, may reach the same *final state*, in different ways, *from different initial conditions*. This final state is characterized not by a static but a dynamic equilibrium, usually called a *steady state* – originally addressed by von Bertalanffy as a "Fliessgleichgewicht".

Beyond all this common ground lies von Bertalanffy's controversial attempt "to explain" why organisms (i.e. low entropy states) are at all possible in a universe dominated by the law of increasing entropy. As he believes "this apparent riddle disappears by the consideration that the classic second principle (i.e. the entropy law) by definition pertains only to closed systems" (von Bertalanffy, 1968, p. 159). But if this were so, open systems would not be subject to the second law of thermodynamics and hence, once established, would never disintegrate. Hence it seems that this law holds for open no less than for closed systems, but that, under some circumstances, this law can locally be overruled by some other principle. Von Bertalanffy also is mistaken if he believes that this riddle applies only to biological entities. The creation of heavy atoms in the nuclear furnace of stars is obviously the creation of low entropy systems from a higher entropy environment. First of all, one must realize that such events are, according to the entropy law, not impossible but merely improbable. And second, one must assume the existence of some *organizing forces*, as postulated in our *principle of concrescence* together with Bronowski's notion of *stratified stability* (for both see Subsection 7.53) which shows the emergence of such highly organized systems as plants, animals, and humans, as much less unlikely than one might suppose on the basis of the entropy law alone (see also Eigen, 1971).

7.42 *Systems Research versus General System Theory*

The term "system", though by no means new, has come into high vogue during the last two decades. It can be encountered in the physical sciences no less than in biology, and assumes special importance in the social, engineering and administrative disciplines. An impressive amount of literature has recently accumulated on this subject and continues to grow by spreading into many disciplines. The vigor of the systems movement and the wide stimulus which it created may indicate that systems thinking is more than a whim of the time. Nevertheless, the systems approach has still to shake off a faddish flavour, and has hardly yet matured into a generally accepted methodological paradigm. General acceptance has certainly not yet been achieved, and the reaction against a certain branch of this approach, namely against General System Theory (GST), ranges from silent disregard by most philosophers to fiery attack by scholars from other areas.[20] For this reason it may be advisable to distinguish between GST on one side and the systems approach or systems research in general on the other.

[20] See for example the "devastating" criticism of General Systems Theory by Buck, 'On the Logic of General Behaviour Systems Theory', 1956; the more moderate criticism by Lektorsky and Sadovosky, 'On Principles of System Research', 1961; and the somewhat misdirected wholesale rejection of systems theory by Phillips, 'Systems Theory – A Discredited Philosophy', 1969.

As outlined in our Chapter 2, the systems approach is based on the insight that the interrelations of certain components may result in an entity (system) with its very own properties. Hence, this approach looks at systems holistically, emphasizing the *interrelations* of the system's components as well as the *properties* and *boundaries* of the system *vis-a-vis* its *environment*. It ultimately focuses on the function or *purpose* of the system, and pays special attention to the *hierarchy of systems* as well as to the *reconciliation of the goals* of the super-system with those of the embedded subsystems. Finally it aims at the formulation of those features and laws that underlie systems in general.

General Systems Theory (GST) is a movement founded and led by Ludwig von Bertalanffy and promoted by the Society for General Systems Research; it may share all those endeavors outlined in the preceding paragraph, but *it goes far beyond them*. Above all, GST aims at a unification and peculiar reconstitution of most, if not all, sciences. Furthermore, it seems to *imply* a fairly *radical* holistic notion, not identical with, but close to vitalism. GST can best be understood as a reaction, perhaps over-reaction, to the dominant position of physics within modern science, to its methodology and its lack of teleological concepts. In view of this, it is less surprising if von Bertalanffy, as a biologist, has sought to replace the "lifeless" positivistic foundations of science by a kind of holistic vision, laying claim to the fact that "General System Theory, therefore, is a general science of 'wholeness' which up till now was considered a vague, hazy, and semi-metaphysical concept. In elaborate form it would be a logico-mathematical discipline, in itself purely formal but applicable to the various science. For sciences concerned with 'organized wholes', it would be of similar significance to that which probability theory has [been] for sciences concerned with 'chance events'.[21] But von Bertalanffy's deeds belie his words, because his own research bears hardly any similarity to that of a mathematico-logical discipline." This is acknowledged by Ashby, one of the most faithful disciples of GST:

> Two main lines are readily distinguished. One, already well developed in the hands of von Bertalanffy and his co-workers, takes the world as we find it, examines the various systems that occur in it – zoological, physiological, and so on – and then draws up statements about the regularities that have been observed to hold. This method is essentially empirical. The second method is to start at the other end. Instead of studying first one

[21] Ashby, 'General Systems Theory as a New Discipline', 1958, p. 2. The above quote from Ashby is acknowledged by von Bertalanffy (1962, p. 4).

system, then a second, then a third, and so on, it goes to the other extreme, considers the set of "all conceivable system" and then reduces the set to a more reasonable size. This is the method I have recently followed.[22]

Thus GST is burdened with a kind of dualism (some are malicious enough to call it a "schizophrenia") with regard to its very nature. One possible way out of the dilemma is to deny the distinction between analytical and empirical discipline, as the passage quoted in the preceding Subsection from Sutherland (1973, p. 189), seems to imply. But this will satisfy few philosophers unless arguments are presented that exceed in strength the argument of Quine (1953) – see our Subsection 7.21. Our personal preference is to regard the systems approach as a methodology, and thus as a part of philosophy (see our Section 7.5).

If GST were the new super-science that could replace traditional science, as the earlier writings of general system theorists suggested[23], a major prerequisite would have to be fulfilled. It is the demonstration that GST can explain better than traditional science, the phenomena of integration or concrescence (as we called them in Section 3.1). The integration of certain components into a system creates new qualities and appearances which are not encountered with the components above. In some instances traditional science did show that some entities can be reduced to other more basic entities; in other instances the properties of a system of higher order were, indeed, predicted on the basis of some components (e.g. Mendeleev did in fact predict the properties of the first element discovered by Lecoq de Boisbaudran and called by him "gallium"). But such reductions and predictions are only the first steps, not the last, toward a genuine explanation of wholeness. GST, however, has so far not been able to improve upon traditional science in this regard. One cannot even consider GST as a highly formalized, but ultimately empirical, framework as is, for example, the general relativity theory. Because the notions and principles of GST (such as centralization, competition, constitutivity, differentiation, equifinality, finality, growth, hierarchical order, progressive mechanization, system, wholeness, etc.) are in no way close to the significance of the concepts, premises and conclusions of relativity theory, or the mathematical presentation of any other part of an empirical science.

Any high-flying endeavor to reconstruct the entire realm of science, to become a new super-science, is in danger of losing itself in verbosity, ambiguities

22 L. von Bertalanffy, *General System Theory*, 1968, p. 37.

23 Cf. L. von Bertalanffy, 'An Outline of General System Theory', 1950.

and contradictions, at worst even in mysticism. Indeed, it is not so much its program as the ambiguity of some of its publications which endangers GST. Although von Bertalanffy and other proponents made serious contributions to systems thinking, and may ultimately have moderated their original ambitions, much criticism raised against GST seems to be well founded and may be summarized as follows:

(1) General Systems Theory suffers from definitional, conceptual and methodological ambiguities. Apart from much vagueness of presentation,[24] concepts are often generally illustrated rather than defined or defined in an insufficient and non-quantifiable way. Furthermore, methodology and scientific status (empirical science versus analytical science, and the ability to explain and predict, etc.) of this "new discipline" leaves much to be desired.

(2) The undeniable fact that the traditional scientific approach (the mechanistic-analytical approach as general system theorists like to call it) lacks certain teleological and other concepts desirable for a full development of the biological, social and applied sciences, is insufficient to reject the traditional approach;[25] the latter cannot be substituted by a mere "sectarian program". The systems approach should be regarded as a supplement, but not a substitute for traditional science.

(3) A generalized *theory* of systems has inherent difficulties which have not yet been fully assessed.[26] A basis for systems of diverse kinds runs the risk that the properties common to all systems may not be significant enough to afford economy of science and thus to warrant utmost abstraction. Logic and pure mathematics so far are the only disciplines where an *extreme* degree of abstraction has proved rewarding. Empirical sciences seem to have a natural limit beyond which little is gained by further generalization or analogy. Let

[24] Young, 'A Survey of General Systems Theory', 1965, offers an interesting review of scholars concerned with systems and analyzes the conformity and diversity of their concepts.

[25] Cf. Nagel, 'Teleological Explanations and Teleological Systems', 1953, reprinted in *Readings in the Philosophy of Science*, ed. by Brody, pp. 106–120.

[26] During the last 15 years the present author has been instrumental in developing a general theory of accounting or management information systems. Even this comparatively "low" degree of abstraction proved to be such a formidable task that the ultimate solution is still to be sought. See Mattessich, 'Towards a General and Axiomatic Foundation of Accountancy', *idem.*, *Accounting and Analytical Methods*,1964a; *idem.*, *Die Wissenschaftlichen Grundlagen des Rechungswesens* – Eine analytische und erkenntniskritische Darstellung doppischer Informationssysteme fuer Betriebs- und Volkswirtschaft, 1970; *idem.*, 'Methodological Preconditions and Problems of a General Theory of Accounting', 1972.

us bear in mind the slogan that "all one can say about everything, is nothing". For this reason the present popularity of systems study, as Herbert A. Simon remarks, "is more a response to pressing needs for synthesizing and analyzing than it is for any larger development of a body of knowledge . . ."

(4) As an empirical discipline, GST has neither supplied significant hypotheses subject to testing procedures, nor provided pertinent testing criteria. In general, it is criticized for its dogmatism and lack of self-critique.

Many of the quotations presented below indicate that even scholars most sympathetic to systems thinking have expressed doubts about the premises of GST and the direction in which it has been moving. Ackoff, who is heavily engaged in systems research and who himself is an occasional contributor to *General Systems*, suggests making a distinction between GST and Systems Research:

> In this paper I would like to contrast General Systems Theory and Systems Research with respect to several of their important characteristics. My assertions about General Systems Theory are based primarily on the writings of Bertalanffy, and my assertions about Systems Research are based on my own assertions about Operations Research. Systems Research includes a host of activities other than Operations Research, but I do think that Operations Research is typical of these with respect to the characteristics that I will consider . . .
>
> . . . my evaluative remarks about methodological implications of the two approaches do not imply that all the work falling in one camp is good and in the other is bad. Good and bad work has been done in both camps. I am evaluating the methodological implications of "movements" taken holistically, not the individual researchers of which these movements are made up.
>
> Although I have deep respect for much of the work done under the name of General Systems Theory, I am apprehensive about certain implications which Bertalanffy's concept of this theory has on possible unification of science. It will be recalled that he was largely motivated by a desire to unify science through General Systems Theory.
>
> I am going to try to show that Bertalanffy tried to unify science by reassembling aspects of nature into which science had already disassembled it. I shall argue that science can be unified without going through an initial disunification. Secondly, I shall try to show that Bertalanffy's method of unifying science would result in the further separation of both the

theoretical and applied aspects of nonformal science, and of the formal and non-formal sciences.[27]

Further doubts, mainly as regards the high degree of generality, are raised by Herbert Simon:

> A number of proposals have been advanced in recent years for the development of "general systems theory" that, abstracting from properties peculiar to physical, biological, or social systems, would be applicable to all of them (footnote omitted). We might well feel that, while the goal is laudable, systems of such diverse kinds could hardly be expected to have any nontrivial properties in common. Metaphor and analogy can be helpful, or they can be misleading. All depends on whether the similarities the metaphor captures are significant or superficial . . . (pp. 84–85).
>
> In both science and engineering, the study of "systems" is an increasingly popular activity. Its popularity is more a response to a pressing need for synthesizing and analyzing complexity than it is to any large development of a body of knowledge and technique for dealing with complexity. If this popularity is to be more than a fad, necessity will have to mother invention and provide substance to go with the name (p. 118).[28]

More recently Melcher (1975) criticized GST along the following lines:

> General systems theory has offered great promise to those who would look through the lens of the general systems perspective. The approach is attractive to both theoreticians and practitioners in all fields. It directs attention to complex interrelationships, particularly the interaction among components through time. The systems theorist's orientation is to describe and predict complex elements and relationships in the real world. This is the promise of systems theory. We all support this goal; however, it has been easier to specify than to achieve. A critical examination of the area reveals some achievements, many problems, and continuing promise in the social sciences.
>
> Systems theory provides a wholistic perspective by focusing attention on the dynamics of relationships. It puts in bold relief that traditional

[27] Ackoff, 'General Systems Theory and Systems Research Contrasting Conceptions of Systems Science', 1963, p. 117.

[28] Simon, *The Sciences of the Artificial*, 1969. Further evidence of this more sceptical approach can be found in Simon and Newell, 'Models: Their Uses and Limitations', 1956, while other administrative scientists embrace General Systems Theory less critically, e.g. Johnson, Kast and Rosenzweig, 'Systems Theory and Management', 1964.

analyses, using comparative statics, often lead to partial analyses and misleading conclusions. Yet when one closes in on the systems concepts and attempts to apply them, their meaning and usefulness seem to evaporate. New promises lead us on; but new insights and perspectives in the social sciences remain mostly just beyond the horizon.

Katz and Kahn (1966) attempted to examine organizations by using the systems perspective. After an initial chapter reviewing systems concepts, they largely abandoned this approach in developing their view of social organizations. (A.) Kahn (1966) also provided an initial discussion of systems theory in his eclectic book, but he, too, abandoned reference to systems concepts in the rest of the volume. Others use systems terminology to describe organizations, but the traditional elements are simply relabeled using systems terms.[29]

After all that has been said about GST, it is not surprising if many philosophers ignore GST, if D. C. Phillips calls it a "discredited philosophy", if Herbert Simon expresses scepticism about it, and if Russel Ackoff and others try to distance themselves from it by emphasizing the distinction between GST, on one side, and systems research or systems thinking, on the other. The major distinction between the movement of GST and the loosely organized and undogmatic endeavor called the systems approach, or *systems research* in the broadest sense, lies not only in the much lesser degree of ambition, but above all in the acceptance of the traditional empirical and analytic methods provided by current science. Without any preconceived theory, systems researchers, depending on their own inclination, emphasize either the study of the behavior and properties of *actual* systems (e.g. Herbert Simon[30] or Russel Ackoff[31]) or the construction of mathematical models of

[29] Reprinted from Melcher, 'Theory and Application of Systems Theory: Its Promises, Problems, and Realizations', 1975, p. 1.

[30] "The research that has been done over the past five years on the design of computer time-sharing systems is a good example of the study of computer behavior as an empirical phenomenon . . . To understand them, systems had to be constructed, and their behavior observed." (pp. 20–21).

"In this essay I should like to report on some things we have been learning about particular kinds of complex systems encountered in the behavioral sciences." (p. 85), Simon, *The Sciences of the Artificial*.

[31] "It seems to me that Systems Research is on sounder grounds than General Systems Theory because it takes systems as it finds them: holistically, in all their multidisciplinary glory. It unifies the disciplines in the conduct of research and hence it produces facts, laws, and theories, which are multidisciplinary in character. The theories produced by Operations Research, for example, do more than summarize a set of available theories in

systems (e.g. Oskar Lange[32]), or the methodological and other philosophical implications of systems (e.g. West Churchman[33]), or any other aspects concerning systems. Similar to GST, their objective is (1) to learn more about the common features of phenomena which man or nature aggregates into perceptible, factual entities, (2) to develop a conceptual apparatus for studying those phenomena, and possibly (3) to develop a methodological tool, applicable beyond purely conceptual systems to empirical ones.

7.43 *The Father of Systems Theory: Bogdanov or von Bertalanffy?*

A further complaint brought forth, not so much against GST, than against von Bertalanffy (1901–1972), is his persistent silence about the originator of a truly generalized systems theory, Alexander A. Bogdanov (1873–1928). The fundamental and highly original work of the latter appeared in Russia under the title *Tektologia*, Vols. 1 to 3 (1912–1927), hence many years before von Bertalanffy's first system-theoretic notions – which then were restricted to biology – were published (1928). Above all, a German version of the decisive first two volumes of Bogdanov's much more comprehensive presentation of systems organization was published, as early as 1926–1928, in von Bertalanffy's very own mother tongue. It furthermore was reviewed in the pertinent German literature.[34] We are far from accusing von Bertalanffy, whose many genuine contributions remain undisputed, of plagiarism; the history of science has shown repeatedly that ideas, at their time of maturity,

---

a cross-disciplinary language because these theories come out of the study of systems, rather than the study of theories of systems." Ackoff, 'General Systems Theory and Systems Research – Contrasting Conceptions of Systems Science', 1963, p. 119.

[32] See *Wholes and Parts* (1962/1965).

[33] "Well, then, what is the systems approach? On the one hand, we must recognize it to be the most critical problem we face today, the understanding of the systems in which we live. On the other hand, however, we must admit that the problem – the appropriate approach to systems – is not solved, but this is a very mild way of putting the matter. This is not an unsolved problem in the sense in which certain famous mathematical problems are unsolved. It's not as though we can expect that next year or a decade from now someone will find the correct systems approach and all deception will disappear. This, in my opinion, is not in the nature of systems. What is in the nature of systems is a continuing perception and deception, a continuing re-viewing of the world, of the whole system, and of its components." Churchman, *The Systems Approach*, 1968, p. 230.

[34] The first volume of *Tektologia's* German translation, *Allgemeine Organisationslehre* (1926), was reviewed by J. Pregel under the title 'Um die allgemeine Organisationslehre' in *Weltwirtschaftliches Archiv*, **25**, July 1972, p. 18 ff.

frequently emerge in the minds of two or more scholars simultaneously. Thus von Bertalanffy may well have conceived his system ideas without any influence from Bogdanov's work. But it seems most unlikely that such a widely read scholar as von Bertalanffy who concerned himself for almost four decades with research in the general systems field, producing over fifty publications in this area, never came across the German translation of *Tektologia*, nor encountered the name of its author – a name known widely enough to occupy a separate section in the *Encyclopedia of Philosophy* (1967), just twenty-five pages after the section devoted to von Bertalanffy. It is vain to speculate whether von Bertalanffy remained throughout his lifetime unaware of his predecessor. We can merely state the fact that in none of von Bertalanffy's publications on this subject does Bogdanov's name appear. It is true that Bogdanov's books were for some time disregarded in Soviet Russia, in spite of the author's intimate acquaintance with Lenin; but during the last two decades, however, Bogdanov's ideas have been vindicated and accepted in the USSR.[35] In von Bertalanffy's defense, it must be pointed out that on the American continent neither the Russian original nor the German translation of *Tektologia* was hardly ever heard of (the *Encyclopedia of Philosophy*, for instance, mentions Bogdanov's interest in organization theory, but does not list his *Tektologia*), nor has as yet an English translation of it appeared. To our knowledge, the first English article on this fundamental work was published as recently as 1975.[36]

Von Bertalanffy's first major work (1928) aimed at, what we would consider, a *synthesis* between the two opposing biological theories. Out of the clash between "*biological mechanism*" and "*vitalism*" emerged his own system-theoretic view, which he christened "*organismic biology*".[37] At this time von Bertalanffy was far from generalizing his system ideas, and it took more than a decade before his first article on general systems theory was published (1945). Bogdanov, however, developed his theory from the very outset (1912) as a *general* theory of systems organization, and provides a broad gamut of illustrations ranging from atomic, chemical, and biological

[35] Gorelik, 'Re-emergence of Bogdanov's *Tektology* in Soviet Studies of Organization', 1973.

[36] *idem.*, 'Principal Ideas of Bogdanov's "Tektology": the Universal Science of Organization', 1975.

[37] Its main feature is "the establishment of laws of biological systems" in contrast to mechanism which "neither saw or wished to see this fundamental characteristic of life", and vitalism which "put a philosophical construction in the place of natural scientific investigation". Bertalanffy (1933/1962, p. 188).

"complexes" (a term he uses interchangeably with "systems") to man and human organizations. Above all, Bogdanov develops a fairly comprehensive conceptual apparatus for dealing with the very problems later explored by the disciples of GST and cybernetics. Thus Bogdanov's main concern is a clarification and generalization of organizational modes encountered in nature and society. He asserts that "Tektology deals with organizational experiences not of this or that specialized field, but of all these fields together. In other words, tektology embraces the subject matter of all the other sciences and of all the human experience giving rise to these sciences, but only from the aspect of method, that is, it is interested only in the modes of organization of this subject matter" (Bogdanov, 1922, p. 82).[38]

The vocabulary used in *Tektologia*, and even many of its notions, are, of course different from those used in GST; but the basic thrust of both is surprisingly similar. For Bogdanov is concerned with the organizing and disorganizing forces of systems, with their differentiation, growth and duplication, with the interdependencies between system and environment, with the control and variances, types of stability, the selection, vulnerability and crisis of systems, etc. It even seems that "many generally theoretical problems of the system approach are elaborated by A. Bogdanov more fully and rigorously than it is the case in the contemporary theory of systems and cybernetics," as Setrov (1970, p. 59), claims.

At this stage one might point at the endeavours of other scholars or groups of scholars aiming relatively early at goals similar to those pursued by Bogdanov and von Bertalanffy. A holistic world view was developed in the first decades of our century by the Austrian sociologist, economist and philosopher Othmar Spann (1878–1950). His neo-romantic universalism (later called "Ganzheitstheorie") not only gives priority to wholes (e.g. institutions of art, education, the state, the family) over their constituent parts, but even attributes, in a typically idealist–universalist fashion, a higher degree of reality, as well as higher values, to those wholes. Although the major application of Spann's universalism, and its hierarchic tendencies, are found in his sociological-economic works (recommending a normative study of social institutions), he also wrote a holistic logic under the title *Ganzheitliche Logik* (republished in 1971). Nowadays his holistic influence lingers on in the *Zeitschrift für Ganzheitsforschung* edited by his disciple W. Heinrich.

But even before the beginning of this century the Austrian psychologist and philosopher Christian Ehrenfels (1859–1932) published thoughts "Über

[38] Quoted from Gorelik (1975, p. 3).

Gestaltsqualitäten" (1890) and thus initiated a holistic movement of psychology which was carried on and further developed by Max Wertheimer (1880–1943), Kurt Koffka (1886–1941) and Wolfgang Köhler (born 1887). The basic idea of this influential movement goes back to Aristotle and Kant, and manifests itself in the assertion that *every experience is organized in wholes* that are greater than the sum of their parts. But Ehrenfels did not limit himself to psychology, and applied the notion of Gestalt (structured entity or system) also to areas of logic, ethics, as well as metaphysical cosmology. More recently (since the forties) have French scholars, like the anthropologist Lévi-Strauss, (1949, 1958), the literary critic Roland Barthes (1963, 1966, 1967) and many others, attempted to apply Gestalt or system-thinking under the term of "structuralism" to such areas as linguistics, ethnology, anthropology and sociology – cf. Schiwy (1969).

The movement of structuralism can be traced to Ferdinand de Saussure (1857–1913) who, in opposition to the traditional historical linguistic school of William Jones and Friedrich Schlegel, introduced a study of language in which the *structural questions dominate* the evolutionary ones. But just as structuralism has spread to other areas beyond linguistics, it is not an exclusively French domain – although in the fifties and sixties it has become a typical Parisian fashion. Beside the Paris school of structuralism there is the even older Swiss school of Geneva (at the university of which de Saussure held his last chair) and where the renowned epistemologist and child psychologist Jean Piaget (1968) regards himself as an enthusiastic structuralist. Furthermore there is the American school of linguistic structuralism to which no lesser than Noam Chomsky must be counted.

7.44 *Ackoff's and Churchman's Contributions*

During the last two decades the systems approach has assumed a stunning variety of aspects manifested under such expressions as systems analysis, systems engineering, systems methodology, systems philosophy, systems science, systems theory, systems thinking, etc. It cannot be the task of this Chapter to deal with the voluminous literature accumulated in all these areas; only the most important *methodological* aspects of the systems approach will here be discussed and related to philosophy of science. Apart from GST[39]

[39] Other major representatives of GST, beside L. von Bertalanffy, and Ashby (see e.g. his 'General Systems Theory as a New Discipline', 1958), Boulding (e.g. 'General Systems Theory – The Skeleton of Science', 1956), and Rapoport (e.g. 'Remarks on General Systems Theory', 1963); Laszlo (e.g. *Introduction to Systems Philosophy*, 1972).

and the more empirical–technical areas summarized under the threefold headings of "systems analysis, systems engineering, and systems science",[40] there are many, more independent authors who deserve mentioning.[41] However, from the viewpoint of epistemology of the administrative sciences, three scholars, previously quoted, deserve special attention: Russell L. Ackoff, C. West Churchman and Herbert A. Simon. They contributed significantly towards methodological or other philosophic insights of systems thinking, and we deem their ideas highly relevant to the central topic of this book.

Russell Ackoff manifests the rare combination of a pragmatic attitude with a clear vision for the need of sound methodological research. For many years he has been one of the most perceptive contributors to General Systems Research, and his long-standing experience in the research, teaching and application of systems has significantly helped to shape modern systems thinking. Of special significance are his paper "Towards a System of Systems Concepts"[42] and his book on *Scientific Method*.[42a] The paper (see also our Subsection 2.22) from the very outset makes a distinction between an *abstract system* (all the elements of which are *concepts*) and a *concrete system* (at least two elements of which are factual *objects*), and emphasizes its exclusive concern for the latter. This is a clear indication that, for Ackoff, systems research is an *empirical* discipline or at least part of one. However, this disregard of abstract systems could easily be misinterpreted. It is not likely to mean that the *conceptual picture* of an empirical system (which itself can be regarded as a system, but an *abstract* one) does not fall within Ackoff's range of interest. It may merely indicate that his brand of Systems Research is not

[40] Research and publications of RAND-Corporation, Santa Monica were of decisive influence in this area. Other relevant publications for instance are: David O. Ellis and Fred J. Ludwig, *Systems Philosophy*, 1962; Eckman (ed.), *Systems: Research and Design* 1961; Hall and Fagen, *A Methodology for Systems Engineering*, 1962; Hare, *Systems Analysis: A Diagnostic Approach*, 1967; Mesarovic, *The Control of Multivariable Systems*, 1960; Iberall, *Toward a General Science of Viable Systems*, 1972.

[41] E.g.: Johnson, Kast and Rosenzweig, *The Theory and Management of Systems*, 1963; Buckley (e.g. *Sociology and Modern Systems Theory*, 1967; Seiler, *Systems Analysis in Organizational Behavior*, 1967; Kuhn's *The Logic of Social Systems*, 1974. Among the many anthologies in this field are some especially well known: Buckley (ed.), *Modern Systems Research for the Behavioral Scientist*, 1968; Emery (ed.), *Systems Thinking*, 1969; Laszlo (ed.), *The Relevance of General Systems Theory*, 1972b; *idem.*, (ed.), *The World System*, 1973; Baker (ed.), *Organizational Systems*, 1973; Optner (ed.), *Systems Analysis*, 1973.

[42] In *Management Science*, 1971.

[42a] 1962 and Ackoff and Emery, *On Purposeful Systems*, 1972.

concerned with systems encountered in pure logic and mathematics. A further question arises as to the nature of information systems which are occasionally regarded as conceptual systems. In Ackoff's framework, however, it seems rather that they would be treated as "concrete" systems, since the creation, transmission and reception of information are empirical phenomena. Another decisive feature of this scheme is the classification of systems according to their goal-oriented behavior (see our Table 2-1) into *state-maintaining, goal-seeking*, *purposive* and *purposeful systems*. While the first merely *reacts* (e.g. a simple thermostat system), the second already *responds* by exercising choices of strategies but not of goals (e.g. an automatic pilot); the third can *pursue different goals*, without however selecting the goal to be pursued (e.g. a computer programmed to play checkers); finally the fourth displays *will*, and thus selects his own goal (e.g. an organization). Ackoff adds a fifth type, the *ideal-seeking system*, which after attaining its goal, proceeds selecting another goal, one even closer to its standard of perfection. These distinctions seem to be important for understanding systems and their evolution. Ackoff makes similar distinctions for the components or elements of the system, and finally concludes with the *conceptual* difference between an *organism* and an *organization*: while both are purposeful systems, organisms do not possess "purposeful" elements.

The fundamental work by Ackoff and Emery (1972) pivots on the task of *deriving the notions of function and purpose from the mechanistic notions of traditional science* (without falling back on behavioral positivism). This exciting attempt begins with a set of generic mathematical and physical concepts from which, step by step, a long series of further concepts are constructed. Among these the *producer-product* concept (x is a producer of y) is regarded by the authors as most critical, because from there the step to the notion of *functional class* – and various structural and functional relations between actions and outcomes (uni-uni, uni-multi, multi-multi) – is made. We, however, regard as the most crucial steps the ones from functional sets to *goal seeking* and *purposeful* systems. These big leaps, however, leave several questions open; above all they do not reveal clearly enough, what we consider, the crucial point in the relation between mechanistic and teleological concepts. While Ackoff and Emery (1972) seem to represent the notions of "goal" and "purpose" as fairly unproblematic *extensions* of physical concepts, we believe that *mentalistic aspects* (e.g., beliefs, intentions, norms, goals, purposes) and *materialistic aspects* (e.g., events, properties, points of location and time, mass, acceleration) *belong to different epistemic categories*. Although these two sets of notions are inevitably bound to each other by constituting two facets of one and the same coin, they nevertheless *represent two different aspects of experience* which must not be confused with each other. To see the connection between them, for example, between purpose and event, the "coin" must be flipped – and it is this flipping of the coin (i.e., the revelation that a leap to a different epistemic category has been made) which leaves something to be desired in Ackoff's and Emery's otherwise excellent presentation. This does not mean that these authors neglect to deal with such notions as awareness, consciousness, mental states, etc. On the contrary, they assure us that the "definition of mental states is the preoccupation of this book" (p. 72), yet they pay insufficient attention to the distinction between inner and outer experience. *For us a system has a goal or purpose either* (1) *because the inner or mentalistic aspect of the system is developed highly enough so that norms emerge out of this very system* (e.g., in form of new holistic properties) or (2) *because some norms are imposed, in one form or the other, from outside upon the system*. In the latter case the pertinent system becomes an instrumental extension of some other system, and the goal of the former is reducible to the purpose of the latter. For Ackoff and Emery (1972), however, the major criterion of purposeful action seems to be rather the proper (*active multifunctional* and, of course, environmentally independent) *relationship between structure of action and function of outcome.*

Although Churchman shares many interests and views with Ackoff, his temperament and his contributions to systems thinking are of an entirely different nature. Churchman's philosophic training and natural inclination lead him to focus his attention on the existence or non-existence of a hierarchy of systems, and their interdependencies, above all, on the *reconciliation between the goals of the sub-systems with the goal of the super-system*. This inevitably leads him to the intricate problem of *systems improvement*. The following passages are most characteristic of Churchman's outlook and aim:

> Now, the management scientist's argument against "efficiency" is that it is always conceived in relation to a small segment of the social organization. Mere attention to cost reduction by itself, he says, may do the very opposite of what the manager intends. In fact, cost reduction in many instances may actually *increase* the system's total cost.[43]

Or in a broader context:

> Now of course the discussion of individual behavior does properly belong under the theme described here as the ethics of large-scale systems. It is

[43] Churchman, *The Systems Approach*, 1968b, p. 20.

perfectly proper to talk about a given person within a system in terms of the quality of his behavior, just as we have talked about the quality of behavior of education and health. We could therefore sensibly ask whether an individual might have lived his life in a better way than he did, given the resources made available to him by the whole system. The point, however, is that we cannot judge improvement in an individual unless we have some understanding of the nature of the whole system in which this individual lives. The theme we are exploring is one that claims that a concept of ethical conduct depends at least in part on the concept of system improvement. The ethics of whole systems incorporates the concepts of the ethics of individual behavior and places the problem of the ethics of individual behavior within the context of the whole system.[44]

But to answer the question of how to improve a system, one needs criteria for and measures of effectiveness. Once such measures are conceived one might proceed to explore the more difficult question: Which system or system-structure is satisfactory, or even optimal, for a given purpose? But this modest question conceals a highly complex issue for which no fundamental or general solution can be expected overnight.[45] All one can do at this stage is to analyse the problem on several levels. To have begun with this task of clarification is one of Churchman's merits. His major concern pivots on the question whether the scientist charged with the design or improvement of a system can or should accept the goals and value judgements of his client.[46] This question is Churchman's Thread of Ariadne, it is the recurrent theme of most of his writings:

[44] Churchman, *Challenge to Reason*, 1968a, p. 5.

[45] Emery, *Organizational Planning and Control Systems*, 1969, hints at the difficulties here involved:

> With three identical elementary tasks there are two different structures, and with four such tasks there are five alternatives. The number grows to a total of 2,312 alternative structures in the case of ten elementary tasks . . . In an actual system most of the elementary tasks are, of course, distinct rather than identical. This enormously expands the number of alternatives . . . With ten such tasks there are over 28 million alternatives . . .
>
> We need not be intimidated by this numbers game. A count of the alternative structures perhaps provides an interesting and impressive index of the impossible complexity of the systems problem facing a designer but on finding an "optimal" structure. Paradoxically, the very vastness of the numbers simplifies the task of choosing the structure in practice. (pp. 7–8).

[46] Cf. Mattessich, 'Philosophie der Unternehmensforschung', 1962.

> In the past the economist or engineer could say to himself: "These are the goals that my client wishes to attain, and I will study how he can best attain them. It is none of my business whether these goals are the correct ones." But when the scientist begins to work hand in hand with the top administrator, he can no longer take such a detached viewpoint toward his client's goal. He must ask himself whether the goals specified by the client are the correct ones in terms of the client's interests, and he often discovers that they are incorrectly stated or dangerously narrow from the point of view of the improvement of the entire system.[47]

Here the problems of "sub-optimization versus over-all optimization" converge with the question whether science can be free of values. But Churchman does not simply suggest substituting the management scientist's value judgements for those of the manager or imposing them upon him; he rather suggests that the scientist's task is to help the manager in clarifying his own goals. But is it not likely that in this process of advice and "purification", the manager may, at least to some extent, be influenced by the value judgements of the scientist? Such questions may conceal a more fundamental problem: *To what extent can broad value judgements be "substituted" by scientific analysis or, rather, reduced to value judgements of a more basic or narrow type?*

Most decisive, however, is Churchman's view about the essence of the systems approach:

> All along, our effort will be to expand our capability of thinking about systems. Consequently, this is not a book on the subject of how each individual should learn to think; it is more concerned with the resources that a society has at its disposal for thinking better about its systems . . . A book of this sort is an extension of the old-fashioned logic and rhetoric in which the student is trained adequately to think about the world . . . today our expanding technology provides us with all kinds of additional resources beyond the basic types of logic which were taught by Aristotle, Spinoza, Dewey and others. There is a plethora of additional resources that we will want to explore as we develop some basic idea on how to think in our century.[48]

[47] *Challenge to Reason*, 1968a, pp. 11–12. Passages with a similar ring are found in other works of Churchman: cf. *Prediction and Optimal Decision*, 1961 and *The Systems Approach*, 1968b.

[48] Churchman, *The Systems Approach*, 1968b, pp. 10–11.

Here, too, we encounter the conviction that systems thinking may represent the indispensable methodological tool for our era. In Churchman's view this approach will overcome the chasm between the extreme realist, who thinks in terms of the short-run and narrow sub-systems, and the extreme idealist, who might choose the entire universe and the infinite long-run as his bases of vision. The essence of systems thinking lies in constantly relating subsystems back and forth to the pertinent super-system or environment, and in trying to synchronize their often conflicting goals. He points at the many difficulties to be encountered in this endeavor, but warns the reader *not* to expect "like in a detective story, that in the end we will propose solutions to the perplexing problems . . ." (Churchman, 1968a, p. 82).

At some earlier time Churchman (1964) presented nine "axioms" for a general systems theory which are reprinted here as a mere summary, hence without the comments he attached to them:

(1) Systems are designed and developed (evaluation).

(2) Systems are component designed.

(3) The components of systems are also systems.

(4) A system is "closed" if its evaluation does not depend on the design of its environment within a specific class of environments.

(5) A general system is a system that is closed and remains closed for all possible environments.

(6) There exists one and only one general system (monism).

(7) The general system is optimal (optimism).

(8) General system theory is the methodology of searching for the general system.

(9) The search becomes more difficult with time and is never completed (realism); cf. Churchman (1964, pp. 173–175).

From a purely epistemological standpoint, Churchman's major contribution to the systems area is his book on *The Design of Inquiring Systems* (1971). There he made the fascinating attempt to illuminate, *from a systems point of view*, the epistemic theories of such major philosophers as Leibniz (together with Descartes and Spinoza), Locke (together with Hume and Bishop Berkeley), Kant, and Hegel – as well as that of E. A. Singer to which Churchman, as a former student of Singer, feels particularly attached. The idea to interpret science and knowledge-creation as a kind of information system, has far-reaching consequences. Not only does it impart a novel perspective to epistemology, it also invites the reader to contemplate the relationships between various information systems. In the light of such a thought we suggest that it is no longer absurd to speak of a common ground between, for example, such a venerable and exalted area as *epistemology*, on one side, and such a prosaic and applied field as *accountancy*, on the other. Both are important information systems which have more in common with each other than either philosophers or accountants might suspect. Here we cannot discuss Churchman's (1971) book, but refer the reader to the original source, as well as to such review articles as those of Mitroff (1973) and Mason (1969).

7.45 *Herbert Simon's Science of Design and Artificial Intelligence*

Herbert A. Simon's approach to systems, in contrast to Churchman's has a strongly positivistic slant, and is less geared toward the loosely knit macro-systems of society, than toward the much tighter micro-systems of administration with their sub-systems. His approach may be encountered in many of Simon's writings, but is best summarized in *The Sciences of the Artificial* (1969). For him system thinking pivots on the problem of how to develop a *science of design*, i.e. a scientific basis for designing and testing systems. Thus, in contrast to von Bertalanffy, he does not stress biological organisms and naturally grown social systems (e.g. a society of ants), but is concerned predominantly with artificial, or man-made systems (as regards human behavior, Simon would remark that as long as this behavior is adapted to goals, it also is artificial[49]). This obviously implies a strong teleological emphasis:

> If science is to encompass these objects and phenomena in which human purpose as well as natural law are embodied, it must have means for relating these two disparate components. The character of these means and their implications for certain areas of knowledge – psychology and engineering in particular – are the central concern of the first three chapters . . . (p. 4). The engineer is concerned with how things *ought* to be – ought to be, that is, in order to *attain* goals, and to *function*. Hence, a science of the artificial will be closely akin to a science of engineering – but very differ-

[49] Cf. *The Sciences of the Artificial*, p. 52. The above remark reveals the semantical trap into which Simon might step if he identified "adaptation" of a system as an artificial process; then the natural sciences, too, especially biology, become sciences of the artificial.

ent, as we shall see in my third chapter, from what goes currently by the name of "engineering science" . . . (p. 5).[50]

While Simon, in accord with other authors, emphasizes the relation among purpose, elements, and environment of the system, he distinguishes between *inner* and *outer environment*. This terminology is only occasionally recognized in systems literature and might need some explanation. It appears that Simon's "inner environment" corresponds to what is usually addressed as the system's structure (i.e. the *elements* of the system proper together with the *relations* between them), and his "outer environment" corresponds to the environment beyond the system's boundaries. Whether these expressions are fortunate or confusing ones may be a controversial issue, but they do put emphasis on the interrelation between structure and environment – underlining the fact that a system is a meeting place between inner and outer environment:

Central to their (the artifacts) description are the goals that link the inner to the outer system. The inner system is an organization of natural phenomena capable of attaining goals in some range of environments; but ordinarily there will be many functionally equivalent natural systems capable of doing this.

The outer environment determines the conditions for goal attainment. If the inner system is properly designed, it will be adapted to the outer environment, so that its behavior will be determined in large part by the behavior of the latter . . . (p. 11) . . . the behavior of the system will only partly respond to the task environment; partly it will respond to the limiting properties of the inner system (p. 13).[51]

Since it is often difficult to predict in advance the behavior of a complex system, Simon recommends system experimentation through *simulation*, declaring that this technique, indeed, may *create* new *knowledge* about system behavior. He is especially interested in demonstrating that system behavior can be predicted even under ignorance, or with a minimal knowledge of the system's structure. In connection with this, he speaks in favor of what is called *black box* theories:[52]

[50] Simon, *The Sciences of the Artificial*, 1969, pp. 4 and 5.

[51] *The Sciences of the Artificial*, p. 11, 13.

[52] "A black box theory treats its object or subject matter as if it were a system devoid of internal structure; it focuses on the system's behavior and handles the system as a single unit." Bunge, *Scientific Research*, Vol. 1, p. 509.

> We knew a great deal about the gross physical and chemical behavior of matter before we had a knowledge of molecules, a great deal about molecular physics before we had any theory of elementary particles – if, indeed we have such a theory today.
>
> This skyhook-skyscraper construction of science from the roof down to the yet unconstructed foundations was possible because the behavior of the system at each level depended on only a very approximate, simplified, abstracted characterization of the system at the level next beneath.[53]

He also refers to John von Neumann's research in computer reliability and the question of organizing a system in such a way that, as a whole, it becomes relatively reliable in spite of the possible unreliability of its components. This research he takes as evidence that it is possible to construct a *mathematical* theory of systems independent of a corresponding factual micro-theory of the pertinent system. But the reader must not misinterpret this as Simon's rejection of empirical research in computer science; it merely helps him to emphasize that a distinction has to be made between the factual knowledge about individual system components (e.g. the solid-state physics of transistors) and *behavioral research of the entire system*. This kind of research forms the core of what Simon envisions as systems research in a truly empirical sense. In this connection Simon advances *an idea that might turn out to be one of the major insights of modern systems research*:[54]

> As we succeed in broadening and deepening our knowledge – theoretical and empirical – about computers, we shall discover that in large part their behavior is governed by simple general laws, that what appeared as complexity in the computer program was, to a considerable extent, complexity of the environment to which the program was seeking to adapt its behavior.
>
> To the extent that this prospect can be realized, it opens up an exceedingly important role for computer simulation as a tool for achieving a deeper understanding of human behavior. For if it is the organization of components, and not their physical properties, that largely determines behavior, and if computers are organized somewhat in the image of man, then the computer becomes an obvious device for exploring the consequences of alternative organizational assumptions for human behavior. Psychology can move forward without awaiting the solutions by neurology

[53] *The Sciences of the Artificial*, p. 17.
[54] Further details on this insight were elaborated previously by Simon (1962).

> of the problems of component design – however interesting and significant these components turn out to be.[55]

Reflections of this nature and a series of experiments lead Simon to postulate the hypothesis that even man, as a behavioral system, is structured simply, and that the apparent complexity stems rather from the complexity of his environment. His brain operates serially, limited not only as to memory capacity but also with regard to digesting not more than a few signals simultaneously. If sufficiently confirmed, such a hypothesis could become of far-reaching consequence for psychology as well as systems science. But of more immediate consequences for our theme are Simon's views on the relationship between professional schools and the science of design:

> Schools of engineering, as well as schools of architecture, business, education, law, and medicine, are all centrally concerned with the process of design.
>
> In view of the key role of design in professional activity, it is ironic that in this century the natural sciences have almost driven the sciences of the artificial from professional school curricula. Engineering schools have become schools of physics and mathematics; medical schools have become schools of biological science; business schools have become schools of finite mathematics . . . (p. 56).
>
> In the past, much, if not most, of what we knew about design and about the artificial sciences was intellectually soft, intuitive, informal, and cookbooky . . . (pp. 56–57).
>
> The older kind of professional school did not know how to educate for professional design at an intellectual level appropriate to a university; the newer kind of school has nearly abdicated responsibility for training in the core professional skill. Thus we are faced with a problem of devising a professional school that can attain two objectives simultaneously education in both artificial and natural science at a high intellectual level. This too is a problem of design – organizational design. (p. 57).
>
> . . . The professional schools will reassume their professional responsibilities just to the degree that they can discover a science of design, a body of intellectually tough, analytic, partly formalizable, partly empirical, teachable doctrine about the design process.
>
> It is the thesis of this chapter that such a science of design not only is possible but is actually emerging at the present time. It has already begun

[55] Simon, *The Sciences of the Artificial*, 1969, p. 22.

to penetrate the engineering schools, particularly through programs in computer science and "systems engineering", and business schools through management science (p. 58).[56]

Indeed, the present book, too, is evidence of such endeavor. *Instrumental reasoning* and a *theory of design* are two facets of the same coin. Whether simple decision models or complex systems are contemplated, whether they are short-term manifestations of a brain and formalized nowhere else, or whether they are the results of a long process of design, one cannot escape the fact that their generation and operation requires instrumental reasoning. The failure of the traditional professional schools, complained about by Simon, may lie in the very neglect of a rigorous approach toward instrumental reasoning.[57]

As far as the hierarchy of systems is concerned, Herbert Simon approaches the problem from the viewpoint of decomposition. Hence, unlike Churchman who rather looks passionately at specific existing systems, noticing their inadequacy or goal-conflict with their super-system, Simon regards, quite generally, first the main or super-system and considers its possible and alternative decompositions into sub-systems. Furthermore, he is less concerned with an analysis of the philosophic intricacy of the interrelation of sub-system and super-system but submits concrete suggestions for a curriculum in design. This he summarizes under the following headings:[58]

The Evaluation of Designs

(1) Theory of evaluation: utility theory, statistical theory.

(2) Computational methods:

(a) Algorithms for choosing *optimal* alternatives such as linear programming computations, control theory, dynamic programming.

(b) Algorithms and heuristic for choosing *satisfactory* alternatives.

(3) *The formal logic of design:* Imperative and declarative logics.

[56] Simon, *The Sciences of the Artificial*, 1969, pp. 56–58.

[57] In this connection the question may arise why Simon, in spite of his concern for a science of designing *goal-oriented* entities, denies the normative character of such a science (cf. our Section 2.5).

[58] See *The Sciences of the Artificial*, pp. 79–80.

The Search for Alternatives

(4) Heuristic search: factorization and means-end analysis.

(5) Allocation of resources for search.

(6) *Theory of structure and design organization:* hierarchic systems.

(7) *Representation of design problems.*

A more recent work edited by Herbert A. Simon and Laurent Siklossy (1972) is concerned with another topic closely related to epistemology. Its title is *Representation and Meaning – Experiments with Information Processing Systems* and its content is related to such topics as "representation, semantics, natural language processing, pattern recognition, and learning", but it presents experimental results and studies of a more empirical nature. Therefore this book covers those parts of artificial and cognitive intelligence which may well supply the raw material for new epistemological insights.

Yet H. Simon and other proponents of artificial intelligence overextended themselves by making predictions or promises that could not be fulfilled.[59] One of their severest philosophic critics is Dreyfuss (1972), who questions some basic assumptions of artificial intelligence, and rejects the positivistic–atomistic attitude toward "intelligent" systems. He argues that reality is not explicable in terms of atomistic concepts, and argues that severe limitations are set to a *mechanical* robot. The latter by its very nature is lacking a *biological body* in which consciousness or reasoning in the broadest sense is not a localized affair of the brain but is a matter of the *entire* organism who

[59] "It is fitting to begin with a prediction made by Simon in 1957 as his General Problem Solver seemed to be opening up the area of artificial intelligence . . . Simon then predicts among other things,

(1) That within ten years a digital computer will be the world's chess champion, unless the rules bar it from competition.

(2) That within ten years a digital computer will discover and prove an important new mathematical theorem.

(3) That within ten years most theories in psychology will take the form of computer programs, or the qualitative statements about the characteristics of computer programs." Simon and Newell (1958), p. 6.

"Unfortunately, the tenth anniversary of this historic talk went unnoticed, and workers in artificial intelligence did not, at any of their many national or international meetings, take time out from their progress reports to confront these predictions with the actual achievements. Now fourteen years have passed, and we are being warned that it may soon be difficult to control our robots. It is certainly high time to measure this original prophecy against reality." Dreyfus, *What Computers Can't Do,* 1972, pp. xxix–xxx.

experiences whole entities. The perception of atomic phenomena does not precede those holistic experiences but succeeds them, and is a result of analysis. As long as man is not capable of constructing biological robots pliable enough to separate the relevant from the irrelevant – to a similar extent and in an approximately large variety of situations as human beings are capable of – the ultimate secret of consciousness and intelligence remains a door with seven seals.

7.5 Systems Approach as a Methodology

Methodology in general is regarded as a branch of philosophy, and might be deemed to comprise all philosophic, mathematical, and scientific methods. In contrast to this sum-total of all rational ways of pursuing knowledge there are *special methodologies* which emerge either out of the needs of specific disciplines or out of a specific attitude towards reality. The systems approach seems to be such a special methodology rather than a new science or super-science. In particular it is a methodology which *grows out of a holistic view*, and thus is not bound to a single discipline or a limited number of them. The holistic world view is no novelty but requires the acceptance of certain basic assumptions. It can be encountered in the philosophies of Gianbattista Vico (1668–1744), G. W. F. Hegel (1770–1831), Karl Marx (1818–1883), A. N. Whitehead (1861–1947) and many other philosophers (perhaps going back as far as Heraclitus and Lao Tse), and is necessarily accompanied by a strong emphasis on history; because to look at something holistically commits a person to an over-all vision as regards time no less than space. But the systems approach is not a mere revival of an abandoned philosophy, nor a revision of any existing one; it does offer something strikingly new. This novelty becomes most obvious in a comparison between Hegelianism and Systemism. Hegel presented an entire philosophic system, and thus also a methodology (his peculiar brand of dialectics), but his methodology is not capable of setting boundaries to the infinity and eternity enforced by a naive or unadulterated holism. The systems approach aspires less to a global philosophic structure, but is adaptable to a variety of philosophies and, mainly, or even merely, wants to provide a methodology which – in spite of its holistic foundation – remains undefeated by the problem of temporal and spatial infinity. This latter problem was the very stumbling block of Hegel's philosophy. For how can a philosophic system give guidance to the discovery of truth, and to that of the right action, if its ultimate yard-stick is a globally unknowable, infinite and eternal universe? It is that yard-stick which must be changed or adapted to systems of smaller scale, to systems which seem comprehensible enough to discern values and goals.

The peculiar feature of the systems approach, as was repeatedly emphasized throughout this book, is the flexibility of forming more or less arbitrary systems for specific purposes *without losing sight of the super-system or environment in which the system is embedded*. The insight that we cannot infer values from an infinite universe has been known to man for millenia. It is for this reason that he created religions, setting values for the benefit of his communities or for mankind in general. But most religions, in one form or another, take heed of man's environment and impose laws and taboos to maintain a harmony between man and nature. Thus the question arises whether the so-called novelty of the systems approach is something new at all. We still think it is; perhaps not new in a religious or even generally philosophic sense, but certainly new in a methodologic and scientific sense. It is only in the last few decades that a methodology emerged, and was applied to a series of scientific disciplines, which systematically facilitates the interrelating of the focal object, back and forth, with the embedding matrix.

Of course, sub-consciously the systems approach has been applied previously in many disciplines. Indeed, one purpose of this book was to give illustrations of such applications. So, for example, it was pointed out in Subsection 3.33 that Russell's paradox was solved ultimately by the systems notion of distinguishing clearly between object- and meta-language, or that Gödel's indeterminability theorem could lead to the notion of a hierarchy of systems in which the characteristics of some variables (truth value of certain propositions) can be determined only by looking at pertinent meta-systems. Another example is the development of matrix algebra, which enabled the solution of large systems of simultaneous equations, thus revealing the interdependences of variables so characteristic of systems thinking. Applications of this idea to economics and management science are found in Léon Walras' (1837–1910) equilibrium theory, Wassily Leontief's interindustry analysis, and in what W. W. Cooper called, the *mutatis mutandis* approach in operations research.

The strong analytical trend in philosophy and science during this century has inevitably led to a more synthetically oriented reaction. As pointed out in our Section 7.3, philosophic trends, like artistic ones, can be fully understood only in terms of reactions to immediately preceding or present, but vanishing, ideas. How could one ever hope of comprehending the revolutionary art of a Beethoven and Berlioz, the romantic poetry of a Byron and Wordsworth, the paintings of a Gericault and Delacroix, if not in terms of a reaction to classicism? How can anyone grasp the music of Stravinsky and Schoenberg, the literature of Proust and Joyce, the art of Klee and Picasso, if not as a reaction to a worn-out romanticism? Similarly, the present happenings in philosophy and methodology must be seen in the dialectical light of a counter-movement to the once vigorous and pervading influences of logical positivism and analytical methodologies.

7.51 *Georgescu-Roegen's New Version of Dialectics*

Dialectics is too often identified with what is popularly and unfortunately called the "muddle-headed" reasoning of Hegel. We have no intention of defending this frequently misunderstood "logic" of one of the most influential thinkers of modern times. Nor do we believe that Hegelian dialectics is an appropriate methodology for modern science or philosophy. And if dialectics itself was once swept away by the dialectical process, no one should be surprised if it is being reincarnated in a somewhat different image.

An example of such reincarnation is revealed in the writings of Georgescu-Roegen (1971). The dialectics proposed by this highly original economist-philosopher is rooted in the observation that a vast number of essential concepts are "*surrounded by a penumbra within which they overlap with their opposites*." So for example a photon is a particle and simultaneously a wave, a virus is a crystal and yet it is in a way a living matter, a person may be considered young by his seniors and yet old by his juniors, a certain government system may have socialistic and, at the same time, capitalistic aspects. Other concepts of this kind are "good", "justice", "likelihood", "want", etc. In contrast to such *dialectical concepts* are the *arithmomorphic concepts*[60] which have sharp boundaries, do not overlap and hence account for the tremendous efficiency of mathematics and traditional logic.

The major difference between these two kinds of concepts lies in the crucial principle of contradiction "*B* cannot be both *A* and non-*A*". It holds for the arithmomorphic concept but does not hold for dialectical concepts.

In order to make it clear what we understand by dialectical concept, two points need special emphasis.

First, the impossibility mentioned earlier of deciding whether a concrete quadrangle is "square" has its roots in the imperfection of our senses and

[60] The expression "arithmomorphic" was coined by Georgescu-Roegen to designate symbols and concepts which "are as directly distinct as a single number in relation to the infinity of all other" (1971, p. 14).

of their extensions, the measuring instruments. A *perfect* instrument would remove it. On the other hand, the difficulty of deciding whether a particular country is a democracy has nothing to do . . . with the imperfection of our sensory organs. It arises from another "imperfection", namely that of our thought, which cannot always reduce an apprehended notion to an arithmomorphic concept . . .

The second point is that a dialectical concept – in my sense – does not overlap with its opposite *throughout the entire range of denotations*. To wit, in most cases we can decide whether a thing, or a particular concept, represents a living organism or lifeless matter. If this were not so, then certainly dialectical concepts would be not only useless but also harmful. Though they are not *discretely distinct*, dialectical concepts are nevertheless *distinct*. The difference is this. A penumbra separates a dialectical concept from its opposite. In the case of an arithmomorphic concept the separation consists of a void: *tertium non datur* – there is no third case. The extremely important point is that the separating penumbra itself is a dialectical concept. Indeed, if the penumbra of *A* had arithmomorphic boundaries, then we could readily construct an arithmomorphic structure consisting of three discretely distinct notions: "proper *A*", "proper non-*A*", and "indifferent *A*". The procedure is most familiar to the student of consumer's choice where we take it for granted that between "preference" and "nonpreference" there *must* be "indifference".[61]

The attentive reader of our Section 4.3 on Multivalued and Modal Logic will notice that these new areas of logic move into the direction of Georgescu-Roegen's dialectical notions – indeed it is surprising that this economist so broadly versed in philosophic literature does not refer to those novel areas. Yet he hits not far from it by providing a section under the heading "Probability: An Illustration of Hegelian Dialectics". But there is a major difference between the modern dialectics and that of Hegelians. The latter would assert that "*A* is non-*A*" (e.g., "pure Being and Not-Being are the same") holds always, not only for certain concepts in certain situations. This must seem muddle-headed – not only to the uninitiated but to all philosophers who reject Hegel's premise that truth can be found only in the universe taken as a whole. Hegel in disregarding the gulf between finite and infinite conceptual thought reduces one to the other, affirming the unity of both but denying their distinction. In contrast to *Plato*, who tried to solve the riddle of the

[61] From Georgescu-Roegen, *The Entropy Law and the Economic Process*, 1971, pp. 46–47.

Many versus the One (e.g. the many factual approximations to a square versus the one ideal hence true notion of a square not attainable by empirical means) by postulating *a separate world of incorruptible ideas and ideals, Hegel's solution attributes truth to nothing but the entire universe* which for him is identical to the Absolute, the pure Being, the Rational, the Real, the total process of Self-Reflection, the infinite Spirit, Substance and Subject, as well as the Totality all wrapped into one. Thus the practical need for clear-cut or arithmomorphic concepts is deliberately suppressed by Hegel in favor of a dialectical comprehension of the identity-in-difference. Only Hegel's conviction that speculative reasoning can fathom the essence of the universe, allowed him to operate with a truth notion which has become meaningless for an age that is rapidly awakening to the limitations set to every kind of knowledge.

Furthermore, it must be noted that Hegel's "logic" is an examination of the concepts and categories of reasoning, not of its inferential methods. This makes it so very different from modern logic. But in its strong emphasis on *relations* Hegelian logic may be said to have anticipated our modern view; yet even here the accent is on a different aspect. As Durant (1926/52, p. 295) pointed out:

> Idea without relations of any kind is empty; this is all that is meant by (Hegel's) saying that "Pure Being and Nothing are the same": Being absolutely devoid of relations or qualities does not exist, and has no meaning whatever . . . Of all relations, the most universal is that of contrast or opposition. Every condition of thought or of things – every idea and every situation in the world – leads irresistibly to its opposite, and then unites with it to form a higher or more complex whole. This "dialectical movement" runs through everything that Hegel wrote. It is an old thought, of course, foreshadowed by Empedocles, and embodied in the "golden mean" of Aristotle, who wrote that "the knowledge of opposites is one". The truth (like an electron) is an organic unity of opposite parts.[62]

It seems to us that Hegelian dialectics aimed at something which modern cybernetics attained in a much better, more proper and far more accurate way. Dialectics is concerned with change and its feedbacks, but paradoxically enough the Hegelian version tried to solve a dynamic problem in a static fashion. By asserting that two opposites are the same, Hegel obviously meant

[62] From Durant, *The Story of Philosophy*, 1926. Quoted from the Cardinal Edition, 1952, p. 295.

to say that an event *in time* reverts to its opposite (e.g. the master becomes the slave), but the way he presented it was static and thus was too easily misinterpreted as saying that an event is, *at the same time*, its opposite. Of course if one looks at the universe as a whole, as Hegel claimed to do (though always being forced to deal with parts) time may be irrelevant. But such a viewpoint presupposes the fallacious assumption that the whole is comprehensible or even fully comprehended. Thus our methodological reflections might lead us into the realm of speculation. Indeed we feel apologetic about the next Subsection which is indeed a short excursion into the realm of metaphysics. However, it is not only one guided by empirical clues of modern cosmology but also one that should lead to some basic principles of systems methodology.

7.52 *A Modern Version of the Conflagration Hypothesis*

To deal with the problem of change without due consideration of time, is not unlike the attempt to see without light, to hear without sound, or to smell without chemical reactions. Whether one assumes that things happen in time or that time is a dimension of things (as the Stoics asserted and as modern physics seems to confirm) makes little difference to the fact that time is the other facet of change, or, to express it antropomorphically, *time is related to a sixth sense enabling us to "smell" change*. This makes time and change inseparable from each other. But change has many aspects and the systematic concern with this phenomenon goes back to Heraclitus (born between 504 and 501 B.C.) whose philosophy is popularly summarized by his saying that "all things are in flux"; above all he is Hegel's precursor in regarding *reality as one* and conceiving *unity in diversity*. Thus Heraclitus emphasized change or Becoming, but not at the total exclusion of Being, as is commonly supposed. Whereas Parmenides (born *ca*. 515 B.C.) is more radical – he opposed Heraclitus' viewpoint so vehemently as to reject all Becoming as illusionary – recognizing nothing but that which "is", namely Being, the one and only reality that neither arises out of Being nor out of not-Being, but is eternally unchanging. Plato and even more so, Aristotle synthesized those views by regarding the immaterial reality as changeless, but its material aspects as subject to change. An interesting extension of Heraclitus' view was introduced by the Stoic school which regarded the eternal course of the universe as cyclical. Each period passes through the creation of all the elements etc. (whereas it makes little difference for our purpose whether these are four, as the Stoics believed, or *at least* 106 elements, as modern chemistry tells us) and ends with a conflagration or immense explosion. From there on everything starts anew exactly as before. This not only resembles the "big-bang theory" of modern cosmology (opposed by the theory of continuing creation), but gives us opportunity to formulate a not quite unsupported assumption perhaps capable of overruling the crucial law of entropy. Each period of the cosmic cycle constitutes, from our modern point of view, a period of increasing entropy (spatial equalization of energy) the end of which is the greatly lamented energy- or heat-death of the universe: since not only caloric but any kind of energy can move merely from a higher to a lower energy level (but neither *vice versa* nor within indifferent energy levels), cosmic energy undergoes in time a distribution process which ultimately results in a state of such complete equalization, that is to say, *disorder*, that any further energy exchange becomes impossible. But as *every change involves a transfer of energy-matter*, the entropy law seems to ennunciate not merely the energy- or heat-death but the general death of the universe, because then *change*, whatever kind one may think of, is no longer a possibility – and something incapable of change hardly can be called anything else but "dead". Is not the discovery of anti-particles (positrons, anti-neutrinos, anti-protons, etc.), during the last forty years or so, a first clue to the behavior of the universe at the extreme stage of the energy death? Might not occur at such a moment a breakdown of the barrier between matter and the anti-matter that may lure behind the mysterious black holes? Would then not, through some kind of mega-explosive conflagration, the entire universe swing into the realm of a low-entropy state of anti-matter with a fresh start on the other side of the cosmic mirror?[62a]

[62a] Layzer (1975) presents a cosmological theory which describes the various stages of cosmic evolution as follows:

> In a model devised by the author (Layzer) and his students the initial state of the universe is assumed to be devoid of all information and structure. In the period immediately following the "big bang" (a) the universe is in the thermodynamic equilibrium, maintained by the rapid interaction of particles of radiation. After expanding for about 15 minutes, the universe crystallizes, or freezes, into an alloy of metallic hydrogen and helium (b). Because of the continuing cosmic expansion this solid universe shatters into fragments of approximately planetary mass (c), which forms a "gas" in the sense that they interact frequently and randomly much like the molecules of an ordinary gas. In the planetary gas density fluctuations eventually develop (d) as groups of several fragments adhere; the fluctuations grow at larger and larger scales as groups of fragments themselves aggregate (e). Eventually a hierarchy of structures is formed, corresponding to stars, galaxies and clusters of galaxies seen today (f). Layzer (1975, p. 66). The letters (a) to (f) refer to illustrations (p. 67) here not reproduced.

An excellent, fairly up-to-date survey of cosmological evolution, as based on scientific evidence and hypotheses, is offered by Stegmüller (1975a, pp. 255–375).

Or might perhaps the conflagration come about through the release of all the tension between two halves of the universe both saturated with high entropy, the realms of matter and anti-matter, resulting in a new episode of the universe beginning with two new halves of extremely low entropy? Such speculations seem far-fetched but are hardly less meaningful than the heat-death of the universe. In spite of its scientific support through the entropy law, it seems to be no more plausible than a periodically reverting, yet continuing universe. Only one major aspect of the Stoics' hypothesis of periodic conflagration seems to us objectionable: the perfect identity of the various episodes with one another. The suggestion of a conflagration possessing the peculiarity of converting high-entropy matter into low-entropy anti-matter might be the first step to an amendment of the original hypothesis. The Stoics had no hunch about such a peculiar possibility, but a defender of their unamended theory could argue that at some time in the next episode of the universe, I would again be sitting at the same desk, and writing the very same words for the same book – only that all the protons would have negative charges, the electrons positive ones, the spins might also be reversed etc. Since most of our experience with change, confirms that no two events are perfectly identical (even the physicists' assumption that all "elementary" particles of a certain kind are identical to each other, is beginning to crumble), the new or revised conflagration hypothesis might more realistically be regarded as expressing a *helical* rather than cyclical periodicity. In this case the *dimension of simple recurrence* is enhanced by a *dimension of variation or novelty*, such that time itself becomes a reflection of more than mere repetitious change.

7.53 *Five Ontological Assumptions of Systems Methodology*

But quite independent of the above speculations, it is possible to postulate the following five ontological hypotheses, which might be regarded as the most basic principles of systems methodology. As with most postulate statements, they sound either obscure or trivial or both. Besides, their high degree of generality does not promise any immediate practical application or usefulness. Nevertheless, a systems approach without them resembles a plant without roots, and their explicit formulation seems to complement rather than duplicate past efforts in systems research. Their dual nature tempts us to a double formulation, in such a way that the *ontological hypotheses* are listed on the *left hand side*, while the corresponding *systems principles* are listed on the *right hand side*.

1. Polarity Principle

(1a) Being (i.e. any kind of existing entity) presupposes another "being" of opposite polarity. This results in a tension, the release of which tends to annihilate (fully or partly) one or both of these entities, or to create a new one with its own opposite.

(1b) To any system belongs a counter-system (e.g. the environment). A removal of the boundary between these systems tends to dissolve one or both of them and possibly creates a new or changed system with its own counter-system.

The polarity principle is abundantly manifested in nature. We remind the reader of the polarities between matter and anti-matter, between the positive and negative charges of elementary and not-so-elementary particles, the release of tensions in such electrical discharges as thunderstorms, the action and reaction in mechanics and thermo-dynamics, etc. In biology and sociology the existence of cells, plants, animals, human beings and organizations in an environment, or the destruction of some cells, animals, men, organizations by others or each other may further count as examples of this principle. Its apparent triteness vanishes as soon as it jolts us out of the conventional belief that we can analyze an entity without heed to its counter-entity, and as soon as it dawns upon us that *polarity* and *tension* are the most fundamental notions underlying the phenomenon of Being. One might even regard this principle, together with the next one, as the key to the phenomenon of existence.

2. Periodicity Principle

(2a) Becoming, the dynamic aspect of Being, presupposes (cyclical, helical or similar) *periodic* changes.

(2b) Any system is subject to change, obeying some kind of *periodicity* (originating within or outside of the system).

On the micro-level the example *par excellence* of the periodicity principle is the atom with its *pulsating and rotating* electron shells or fields around the nucleus. But any atom is more than mere being, it is subject to changes and thus is becoming. The quantum jumps of electrons from an outer shell to an inner shell, the consequent release of radiation – made visible in the spectral lines characteristic for each atom – and the energy loss due to this radiation, are evidence that even the pre-uranium atoms are *not* eternally self-contained and permanently stable units.[63] Thus one gets to the next level of change in which again a kind of periodicity manifests itself: the decay of atoms and the transfer of energy lead in time to the birth, evolution, and death of stars with all the nuclear transformations described by modern astro-physics and cosmology. The latter, too, operate with periodicity assumptions not only of stellar but also of galactic and super-galactic life-cycles. In biology and the social sciences the periodicity ranges from the life-cycles of primitive plants and animals over the periodicity of the four seasons to the business cycles of the economy. Every phase of "dead" and "living" existence appears to be penetrated by periodicity. The cycle of day to night alone has induced a myriad of organic cycles in biological creatures of all kinds. The struggle for survival induced another sequence that cannot be regarded as anything but periodic. The necessity for periodicity lies ultimately in the previously postulated *polarity*, which apparently *can be sustained only by a constantly recurring change*. Thus being cannot be sustained in a purely static or linear fashion, and seems to need *the support of an inner coil* – as though nature was forced to invent a tectonic device, capable of maintaining relatively stable yet flexible structures in the simplest way possible. Indeed, there exist illustrations from every-day life that show the efficiency of periodicity as a truly tectonic device of nature: take the invention of torsion steel (twisted steel rods, often with helical reinforcements around their main body); it was one of the major achievements in further strengthening reinforced concrete. In other words, it was the *twisting* (the imparting of a helical periodicity) of the steel rods that made possible a much stronger structure.[64] Was this idea of a bright nineteenth-century engineer perhaps anticipated by nature in form of a periodic twisting of events in a dialectical fashion? Furthermore, it should be obvious that the periodicity principle constitutes the foundation to any kind of dialectic or cybernetic mechanism. Since cybernetics is an integral part of much systems research, the reader should be less surprised to encounter a discussion on "Becoming", "change", and "periodicity" in a section about systems methodology.

[63] As regards the atomic nucleous and its hypothesized components (quarks,gluons etc.), too little is known today to present any illustrations, but there is no counter-evidence to doubt the validity of the periodicity principle in this sub-nuclear realm.

[64] The steel spirals, in spring mattresses, are perhaps an even better known example of this very same periodicity principle. If one compares the strength and resilience of a spiral spring with that of a flat spring, one gets a hint of the workings of this principle.

3. *Principle of Concrescence*

(3a) Beside the general process of increasing disorder (entropy), there exist localized processes which integrate individual (component) entities into an entity of higher order with properties of its own.	(3b) There exist processes of organization, affecting (component) systems in such a way that the emerging super-system reveals an order and some properties not manifested by any of its individual components.

This principle of concrescence[65] (or assemblage, or co-ordination, or organization) forms the foundation or pre-condition to a wide variety of notions that extend from what Bronowski calls "stratified stability" to the central idea behind Lewis Thomas best seller, *The Lives of a Cell*. In this book, Thomas, a renowned pathologist with a poetic bent, illustrates in a unique way that in the biological sphere, our conventional view of what is an organism .and what is not, needs revision in the light of modern research. Thus he points out, for example, that such typical cell components as mitochondrias (the well-known power stations of biological cells in which respiration and energy production occurs by converting adenosine-diphosphate into adenosine-triphosphate) "are in a strict sense not ours. They turn out to be little separate creatures, the colonial posterity of migrant prokaryocytes, probably primitive bacteria that swam into ancestral precursors of our enkaryotic cells and stayed there. Ever since, they have maintained themselves and their ways, replicating in their own fashion, privately, with their own DNA and RNA quite different from ours. They are as much symbionts as the rhizobial bacteria in the roots of beans. Without them, we would not move a muscle, drum a finger, think a thought."[66] On the other hand he makes us aware that such an obvious individual entity as that of a "solitary ant, afield, cannot be considered to have much of anything on his mind; indeed, with only a few neurons strung together by fibers, he can't be imagined to have a mind at all, much less a thought. He is more like a ganglion on legs. Four ants together, or ten, encircling a dead moth on a path, begin to look more like an idea. They fumble and shove, gradually moving the food toward the hill, but as though

[65] Our principle of concrescence must not be confused with Whitehead's "principle of concretion", which asserts the "initial aim" or final cause of each concrescence, and thus is identified by him with God. Cf. Whitehead (1929, p. 345). But in many respects Whitehead's "philosophy of organism" (1929, pp. 342–343), is closely related to the systems approach.

[66] Thomas, *The Lives of a Cell*, 1974, p. 4.

by blind chance. It is only when you watch the dense mass of thousands of ants, crowded together around the hill, blackening the ground, that you begin to see the whole beast, and now you observe it thinking, planning, calculating. It is an intelligence, a kind of live computer with crawling bits for its wits."[67] This example vividly shows that an entire aggregate of ants or other social creatures can be envisaged as possessing a mind of higher order than does an individual creature. Thus *consciousness defined broadly enough* may be attributable not only to individual men or animals, but, on one side, to aggregates such as communities, economies, nations, perhaps the universe. If one combines this view with that of Whitehead's (1929) on "feeling",[68] consciousness in our sense, may also be attributed to such "dead" matter as machines, toys, molecules, atoms, atomic nuclei, etc. Hence consciousness spans a wide spectrum and is a matter of degree; it may be thought of as *the introspective facet of any kind of entity or system*.

Thus apart of mere boundary fluctuations of apparently very well-defined entities, there emerge organizing or concrescent tendencies in the universe that assemble systems of higher order out of systems of lower order. The former are no less organisms or organizations, and they exhibit characteristics not revealed in their component parts. Above all, this happens in spite of the dominant law of entropy (the second law of thermo-dynamics) which proclaims the inevitable growth of disorder and thus the vanishing of available energy in the universe or one half of it. The reason why, in a sea of ever-increasing disorder, some localized units of order (at the cost of accelerated disorder in other units) can emerge, lies in a variety of stepwise concrescent selection and evolution processes. "The atoms form molecules, the molecules form bases, the bases direct the formation of amino acids, the amino acids form proteins, and proteins work in cells. The cells make up first of all the simple animals, and then the sophisticated ones, climbing step by step. The stable units that compose one level or stratum are the raw material for random encounters which produce higher configurations, some of which will chance to be stable. So long as there remains a potential of stability which has not become actual, there is no other way for change to go."[69] This reflection is expanded by Bronowski in the area of physical evolution when he explains that it is virtually impossible for a star to build from hydrogen, in a single

[67] *Ibid.*, p. 12.

[68] For Whitehead *feeling* is "the basic generic operation of passing from the objectivity of the data to the subjectivity of the actual entity in question." *Process and Reality*, 1929, p. 55.

[69] Bronowski, *The Ascent of Man*, 1973, p. 348.

step, heavy and super-heavy elements. Here, too, a long and time-consuming sequence of many steps is required before all chemical elements are assembled.[69a]

4. Principle of Formative Preference

(4a) Every existing entity is (or can be interpreted as) the result of a *selection process* within this or some other entity, manifesting a norm or preference.

(4b) The formation of a system implies a *selection* among alternatives which, by necessity, is bound to some norm or preference wherever it may reside.

The principle of formative preference is intricately interwoven with the holistic outlook of the systems approach. Preferences, norms and value judgements can perhaps be neglected as long as one deals with a collection of descriptive sentences, (e.g. science in the positivistic sense). But the moment the system boundaries are broadened to include the dynamic aspects of creating these sentences, preferences inevitably enter the picture. Of course, seen from a general point of view, these preferences need not express those of human beings. The process of natural selection in biology is, from a systems point of view, no less the expression of a norm than the selection of a Wienerschnitzel over a Cordon Bleu at the dinner table of the Waldorf-Astoria. Since the preceding principle of concrescence has laid the foundation for attributing some kind of consciousness to any kind of system, it is hardly surprising to learn that an impersonal consciousness may entail an equally impersonal preference. Of course, *neither the word "consciousness" nor the word "preference" is here used in the narrow customary sense*, but in a very broad sense which spans a wide spectrum. With such a meaning in mind, it is even legitimate to say that a positively charged particle "prefers" a negatively charged one, since it is attracted by the latter but repulsed by another positive particle. Similarly, one would have to accept the stochastic or accidental formation of an entity as a preference or value judgement of nature. Thus preference in this sense has little to do with the notion of free will.

[69a] A most exciting and rigorous, statistical analysis of the early stages of biological evolution (i.e. from dead to living "matter") has been offered by the German Nobel-laureate Eigen (1971), while a somewhat competing view was presented by Hans Kuhn (1973). For a more popular, but excellent discussion of both views, as well as of Monod's less profound best seller (1970), see Stegmüller (1975a, pp. 376–482). A more detailed popular presentation of Eigen's approach is presented by Eigen and Winkler (1975).

Of course for a positivistically indoctrinated proponent of the Received View, the expression "non-personalistic value judgement" is likely to be a contradiction in terms. For him a value judgement is either personalistic or it is no value judgement at all. He is prone to define consciousness (i.e. the capacity to make value judgements and exhibit other mentalistic qualities) in so narrow a sense as to attribute it only to human beings and groups of them. This, however, means that he draws an arbitrary line between man and other entities of nature. Surely, our linguistic habits are tolerant enough and, above all, our behavioral sciences are advanced enough, to attribute to higher animals some kind of consciousness including the exercise of preferential choices. But if this is acceptable for higher animals why not for lower ones? Neither biology nor psychology offers the least clue where in the animal or plant kingdom the demarcation between consciousness and non-consciousness must be drawn, or for that matter that it must be drawn in form of a single line and not in form of a gradual, stepwise scale. On the contrary, it seems that modern science denies the existence of such a clear-cut demarcation. The fact that evolution makes innumerable jumps – from electrical fields and sub-nuclear particles to nuclear particles and light atoms, to heavy atoms, to molecules, to amino acids, to proteins, to plants and lower animals, to higher animals and finally to man and his institutions – is no reason for declaring any of those discontinuities as a line of demarcation, on the threshold of which consciousness, or mind, or spirit would suddenly emerge. The *rationalistic dualism*, postulating mind and matter as two separate and independent entities, seems to have been one of the most unfortunate ideas of philosophy, fueling confusion and a destructive strife between idealists and materialists. We, on our part, cannot accept any other distinction between mind and matter than that between two Janus-faces of one and the same entity. Accordingly, any entity, be it as small as a sub-nuclear particle, is supposed to have an *internal* or *mentalistic* and an *external* or *materialistic aspect*. Of course the internal aspect can only be "felt" by the pertinent entity and eludes direct observation from outside – by this we do not claim that, for example, a flower "feels" the same way as a human being does. But is there not the possibility that at the bottom of the scale, i.e. at the level of elementary particles, a bit of this *inner tension escapes* in form of an electrical field? If this were so, the double nature of elementary particles exhibiting field and wave properties, on one side, and corpuscular properties, on the other, would become the most basic evidence for supporting a *holistic*, and not a rationalistic, kind of *dualism*.

Of course, the norms of nature are nothing but the laws of nature. Thus the normative and the positive aspects of nature are in perfect unison – only in the realm of man do we notice an apparent split between these two aspects. And the reason is that we ourselves are human beings and not mere atoms, molecules or animals. But why then introduce this dichotomy already at the physical instead of the human level where present usage seems to put it? But does present usage always do so? Certainly not; since Darwin and Wallace we speak of "natural *selection*," and this indicates clearly that biologists and scientists in general, as well as philosophers and laymen, consciously or subconsciously envisage *a process of choice* in which nature sets norms and exercises preferences. Thus to speak of norms of nature, is not as absurd as it may sound to someone grown up in a positivistically saturated atmosphere. The justification of this somewhat unaccustomed usage lies in the above-mentioned fact that a consistent system-oriented analysis does not reveal any discontinuity in the hierarchy of nature's entities which is decisive enough to warrant making the distinction between *mind* and *matter* at a higher level than the most basic one. In our view, *this dichotomy, and others following in its wake, should not be conceived as one between man and nature but as one between two facets of nature, between a broad spectrum of inner aspects and an equally broad spectrum of outer aspects*. An answer to the pregnant question posed above, might be found in comparative analogies between entities at various steps of the entire gamut of existence known to us – i.e. by descending from human beings (and their institutions) down the entire scale until sub-nuclear elements and electro-magnetic fields are reached. The first steps appear to be relatively easy, because there is enough zoological and behavioral evidence to suppose that chimpanzees and other higher animals have, indeed, inner experiences analogous, though not identical, to ours. But the further we step down the scale the more problematic the matter becomes. As Whitehead (1933, p. 208), says, "it seems that, in bodies that are obviously living, a coordination has been achieved that raises into prominence some functions inherent in the ultimate occasions. For lifeless matter these functions thwart each other, and average out so as to produce a negligible total effect." It is because of this "averaging out" that one has difficulties in establishing the analogies mentioned previously. But whatever kind of support we are able to muster, it will always be based on *mere circumstantial evidence*. If we cannot even be sure that my friend's toothache feels the same as the one I had some time ago, how can we hope to establish better than circumstantial evidence for the analogies of inner experiences between entities so diverse as a human being, on one side, and, let us say, a fish or a tree, on the other? Nevertheless, circumstantial evidence does exist in favor of such analogies over a wide range of the animal kingdom and, to some extent, for particular instances of the plant kingdom.

Our preöccupation with preferences, norms, value judgements, utility and thus apparently with usefulness, in this book, may tempt the reader to interpret our opposition to pragmatism (expressed in Subsections 1.4 and 6.41) as hypocritical. On one side we harshly criticize pragmatic philosophy, on the other we plead for the recognition of preferences that seem to lead to a utilitarian and instrumentalistic approach. The source of this possible confusion is easily disclosed, and the confusion removed. The main difference between classical pragmatism (especially as promulgated by William James) and our notion of instrumental reasoning, lies in the juxtaposition of personal with impersonal norms. Pragmatism (unfortunately often also addressed as "instrumentalism") tried to elevate personal preference or usefulness to the truth criterion of science, whereas *we suggest to employ the postulated preferences or norms of nature as the criteria for discerning truth from falsehood*. Thus science has two options: it can choose the narrow sentential or propositional path, pursued in the past, which excludes value judgements as far as possible; or alternatively, the structuralistic path which reveals all the activity and dynamics involved in scientific research, and which is bound to admit impersonal as well as personal preferences and value judgements into its realm of discourse.

If the second alternative is chosen, the principle of formative preference becomes a generalization of the biological principle of natural selection no less than of the Marxian idea of history's judgement. But preference of nature and judgement of history are complex notions that must be seen in a broad context. The fact that the life span of a dragon fly is only a single day, does not mean that nature's preference for the dragon fly is less than for the brontosaurus, whose individual life span surely was much longer. The fact that the species of dragon flies are still populating the earth while those of the brontosaurus are not, reveals the judgement of biological history (from the angle of our momentary point of view) in a very different light.

The most important reason for introducing the principle of formative preference lies, of course, in its significance for the contentions made in our Sections 2.3 to 2.8. The postulation of this principle is a precondition and ultimate justification for the conclusions reached in earlier sections, on the basis of much vaguer notions.

5. *Information Principle*

(5a) Entities possess qualities and tendencies which can be interpreted as *due to norms and*

(5b) The *norms incorporated* in a system become *a fixed source* of information for this system, *similar sources of information*. Such information may be permanently incorporated in the entity or temporarily imposed from outside.

whereas the norms *temporarily imposed* upon the system by the environment, constitute *a variable information source* for this system. Such informations determine the characteristics and the behavior of the system.

The specific formulation of this *principle of information* was greatly influenced by the reading of Konrad Lorenz' book *Die Rückseite des Spiegels* (1973). This work constitutes the highly original attempt of an *empirical* approach to epistemology or, more accurately, a biological examination of the evolution of information- and knowledge-creating systems and sub-systems. Lorenz shows that there exists an empirical answer to Kant's inquiry concerning the "thing-in-itself". The latter is not, as Kant and his disciples thought, something completely separate from human or animal perception, but something intricately connected with it – i.e., that we are capable only of grasping merely those aspects of the thing-in-itself for which we were endowed by the evolution of our most utilitaristic knowledge apparatus. Thus we obtain a true but highly simplified picture of reality in its fullest sense:

> For Kant's transcendental idealism there does not exist a *correspondence* between the thing-in-itself – usually mentioned in the singular – and the way in which our forms of perception and categories of thought make it appear in our experience. For him the experience is *not a picture* of reality, not even a grossly distorted or crudely approximated one. Kant well recognizes that the forms of all perceptions available to us are determined by structures of experiencing subjects and not by those of the object to be experienced, but (he recognizes) not that the structure of the "perceiving apparatus" could have something to do with reality . . .
>
> Obviously Kant was of the opinion that an empirical-scientific (naturwissenschaftliche) answer to this question is impossible in principle. The fact that the forms of perception and the categories of thought were not – as the empiricists, e.g. Hume and others, believed – created by individual experience, must, for Kant, have supplied the evidence that they are "logically necessary" ("denknotwendig") and thus are not at all "acquired" ("entstanden") but given *a priori*.
>
> The self-evident answer of the biologist, familiar with the facts of evolution, to the above-quoted question was inaccessible to this great thinker.

It says: the organization of the sense organs and nerves enabling living beings to orient themselves in the world, emerged by phylogenesis ("stammesgeschichtliche") interaction with, and adaptation to, reality which permits us to experience it (reality) as phenomenal space. Thus it is "*a priori*" for the individual in as much as it is, and must be, prior to any experience in order to make experience possible. But its function is historically conditioned and not by logical necessity; other solutions are also possible: the *paramecium*, for example, gets along with a so-called one-dimensional "apperception of space". How many dimensions "space-in-itself" has we cannot know." K. Lorenz, *Die Rückseite des Spiegels*, 1973, pp. 19–20.[69b] Translation.

Consequently Lorenz shows that some cognitive phenomena are gained by a process of pattern matching *adaptation*, and that these processes are, at least in principle, the same for the most primitive as well as the most sophisticated living beings. But he points out that the cognitive "hypotheses" incorporated into the systems by those ancient processes of adaptation are only one part, namely the rigid or "dogmatic" part, of the systems' knowledge mechanism. There also exist processes of acquiring *short-term* knowledge lending greater flexibility to the pertinent system. "Behavior resting on functions of those mechanisms is characterized by responding to an environmental situation in a meaningful way, though it (the situation) has, in its particular form, been previously encountered neither by the species nor the individual" (Lorenz, 1973, pp. 40–41, translated). We believe that what Lorenz calls the *dogmatic kind of knowledge* corresponds in our research (Mattessich 1974a – see also Sections 2.3 to 2.8 of the present book), at least partly, to the norms permanently incorporated in systems while the ability of organisms to acquire *"short-run" knowledge*, in Lorenz' terminology, corresponds, at least in part, to our system's capability of receiving temporary commands from the environment. Lorenz also emphasizes that both kinds of knowledge, the dogmatic as well as the short-run knowledge are required to secure the success of the system and its species.

The relation between information theory (in the broadest sense, going far beyond the restricted information notion of Shannon and Weaver 1949) to epistemology as well as systems theory is dealt with by Oeser (1976) in an elaborate work of four volumes (the fourth one still to appear); somewhat older works by Brillouin on *Science and Information* (1962) and *Scientific Uncertainty and Information* (1964) are also highly commendable.

[69b] For a related but somewhat different view see Piaget (1971), pp. 268–305.

7.54 *Relevance to Instrumental Reasoning*

In concluding this book we should like to summarize the reasons why a systems methodology (ultimately based on the five principles listed in the preceding Subsection) is relevant, perhaps even essential, for instrumental reasoning and the instrumental sciences alike. As previously pointed out, such a methodology offers a special way of looking at reality but, in contrast to traditional scientific methodologies, it provides a dynamic rather than a static point of view. This new methodology is supposed to help reveal not only the world as it is, but as it becomes. And in order to achieve the latter, the forces of change ought to be illuminated. The major conceptual tools for such a pursuit are the *norms* manifested in the systems to be investigated, as well as the *actions*, *reactions*, and *reconciliations* following from the clash of those norms. Thus the task is to investigate the *behavior* of systems. To use an even stronger antropomorphically biased term, one could say, the concern is with *doing*, the analysis of which is the prerogative of the applied sciences as taught in the professional schools of agriculture, business administration, education, engineering, forestry, health sciences, law, etc. Hence an epistemology of the applied sciences will have to put instrumental reasoning and therefore systems methodology into the very center of its conceptual apparatus.

The close connection between a discipline concerned with the evolution and the design of systems, on one side, and a goal-directed process of reasoning, on the other, seems obvious. Thus the expression "*instrumental reasoning*" conveys to us a process of reasoning which includes deductive and inductive logic, as well as preference criteria, and, in consequence, the *explication and reduction of value judgements, the "rational" pursuit of goals, and the adaptation of models or systems to the goal attainment* as far as environmental or other constraints permit. Therefore, the *ultimate* concern of instrumental reasoning is neither the forming and proving of analytical propositions, nor the formulation and verification of natural laws, but the examination of a process leading to the acceptance of conceptual or factual systems for attaining preconceived goals. If a sane person accepts or recommends, in good faith, a certain system for a specific purpose, he usually has reasons for doing so. These reasons are assumed to be the result of a process, the very *foundations* of which were here at issue. To comprehend the foundations of this process of instrumental reasoning, an understanding of traditional logic (deductive and inductive) is a necessary but not a sufficient condition; it will require further insights which hopefully may be acquired by modern economics and systems methodology in cooperation with such branches as axiology and deontology, as well as statistics, set theory, and the behavioral sciences in the broadest sense. Instrumental reasoning need be conceived neither as a separate nor as a novel area; to our mind it is mainly a methodological component of systems research. Perhaps it should be envisaged as an extension or complement of analytical and empirical reasoning. It might also be destined to become, on one side, a mediator between the administrative sciences and other disciplines; on the other side, a safeguard protecting the systems approach from either of two extremes: becoming an area of mere "philosophastering", or becoming another technical or, to use Simon's expression, intellectually soft area of professional studies. After such high-flying programmatic words, one should quickly add that most of these ambitions still have to materialize in due course, probably simultaneously with the growth of the systems approach. But in as far as systems research is a serious current affair, and in as much as the components of teleologic and normative reasoning are presently being integrated into the systems approach, in so far a basis for instrumental reasoning already does exist.

Yet, obviously, this does not mean that instrumental reasoning is relevant to nothing but the applied sciences. The reader who faithfully followed us to this very end will have noticed our preference for viewing science in the broad and dynamic sense. Thus even the pure sciences require much "doing" and many value judgements during this process of doing. This, however, need not tempt us to subscribe to the tenets of pragmatic philosophy, which proclaims that all sciences are nothing but instruments for creating the useful. As previously hinted at, if *the useful* would be derivable from the norms of nature, the above proposition might be more palatable to us – but this is not the case. The term "useful" in classical pragmatism has a purely personalistic connotation; and it is here where the line between pure and applied science could be drawn. The consequences of nature's norms are more a matter of the pure science, while those of human norms are closer to the applied ones. For this very reason we believe that it would be advantageous to regard a good deal of the social sciences as applied rather than pure fields. From all this also follows that – although both, natural as well as social sciences are amenable to the systems approach – this methodology seems to offer more to the social than to the natural sciences. When looking at nature through the spectacles of traditional scientific methodology, the distortions created by the lack of a value-perspective may be less dangerous than when looking through the same spectacles at the fabrics of society. For this latter task one had better don the spectacles of systems methodology, permitting us to penetrate the fog of value judgements looming in every corner – and this even if the grinding of the lenses has not yet reached perfection. Whether GST and its official philosophy, sanctioned by von Bertalanffy and presently developed by Ervin Laszlo (e.g. 1972), will be able to grind better lenses and procure the necessary tools, is difficult to conjecture. It seems, however, that the new *synthetic* implements cannot supplant the old *analytical* ones,[70] but *must complement* them. Thus a rigorous approach, exploiting the powerful analytical arsenal at our disposal, as attempted by Sneed and Stegmüller, recently also by Bunge (1973), as well as by staff-members of the International Institute for Applied Systems Analysis (in Schloss Laxenburg near Vienna)[71] and others, seems to us most promising for a systemic or structuralistic reconstruction of the philosophy of science. In this connection, the new area of *system simulation* may deserve the attention of philosophers; not so much because of its analytical prerequisites, but because of its *opening up the mysterious realm of "possible worlds"*. Although this term is frequently invoked by philosophers (especially in modal logic), until recently there was little chance to explore the realm behind this term on a broad, practical front. This has changed dramatically through the application of system computer simulation to industrial problems[72] and to ecological, military, meteorological as well as many other situations. The recent excitement over such works as Forrester's *World Dynamics* (1971). Meadows' *et al.*, *The Limits to Growth* (1972), Mesarovic and Pestel's *Mankind at the Turning Point* (1974), etc., reflects the wide interest in simulation on a *global* scale. It might also suggest that *the future of the applied and social sciences lies less in precise scientific predictions than in the exploration of possible worlds*, and thus perhaps in the *choice* of a better world than would otherwise be feasible. Such a shift of emphasis would by no means render irrelevant the problems of belief, knowledge and truth for the applied and social sciences, because a possible world is not an arbitrary one, but one that is potentially true. *Only if the projection of such a world would turn out to be false in spite of the full materialization of all underlying assumptions, would the corresponding system be not realistic enough, and thus not reflect a potentially true world or state of nature.*

There is a further advantage in *system simulation: it offers not only the*

[70] Many adherents of GST, like Wilson, seem to share Lewis' (1944) view that "the analytical process of scientific epistemology . . . is by its nature 'a basilisk which kills what it sees and only sees by killing'." (Wilson, 1973, p. 123.)

[71] E.g. See Walters and Clark (1975) and Linstone and Turoff (1975).

[72] E.g. Forrester (1961), Mattessich (1961 and 1964b), Balderston and Hoggat (1962). For a comprehensive survey see Naylor (1971).

imitation of possible factual worlds but also that of possible moral worlds. As Bunge (1973, p. 128), points out: "The concept of simulation . . . depends on the value concept: indeed, simulation is valuable – hence often deliberate – analogy. The concept of simulation is as pragmatic as the value concept – on a non-platonic axiology, that is, on one according to which there are not values but rather valuable objects, and according to which valuation is performed by organisms." Thus it is possible to experiment *in abstracto* with limited universes, under varying factual as well as moral conditions. This not only is something fairly novel, but also something highly desirable at a time when the consequences of our value judgements ought to receive as much doubt and careful consideration as do our positive theories and their consequences.

As to *value judgements* in science, we have repeatedly asserted the inevitability to take them into consideration. But this does not mean that the pronunciation of a value judgement ought to be regarded as a scientific statement. In our view the objectivity of science is guaranteed only by a clear revelation of the norms that might have influenced directly or indirectly a theory or hypothesis. We have no objection to regard the pronunciation of a value judgement as a philosophic instead of a scientific activity (cf. Chmielewicz, 1970, p. 72), but then *it is doubtful whether a philosophically undiluted science is possible at all.* The best one can do is to separate the philosophical statements and value judgements as clearly as possible within each theory and scientific context.[73] Because even if one would succeed in eliminating value judgements by drawing tight boundaries around a discipline, we would not do justice to the modern dynamic-structuralistic view of science, as presented by Thomas Kuhn, Sneed, Stegmüller, and adopted by our systems methodology. Every systemic structure is inextricably connected to internal (incorporated) as well as external (environmental) norms. And every person looking at science, technology, or branches of them, from a holistic point of view, is forced to take into consideration norms and value judgements, in one way or the other. This does not mean that we believe in the possibility of deriving prescriptive sentences from descriptive sentences. This, indeed, would be falling into the trap of the *naturalistic fallacy*. We, however, regard science as a system which by its very existence is endowed with certain norms, and the activities and results of which are influenced by these norms. Yet some of the norms of science are not mere *holistic properties* of this specific system but

[73] A useful discussion about value judgements in science, philosophy and technology and a classification of different types of value judgements is found by Chmielewicz (1970).

can be traced even farther. According to the structuralistic view, a scientific theory is a simplified structural analogue of part of reality. But the latter too is envisaged as a system endowed by the evolutionary process with some basic norms. Thus some norms of science are a result of norms incorporated in a system addressed variously as reality, the universe, or the cosmos.

While our *structuralistic* methodology is in a position to illuminate and explain the transition from positive to normative aspects of a system (and vice versa), no methodology that regards theories as a collection of propositions, seems to be able to reconcile normative with positive (or subjective with objective) aspects. We believe that even such recent attempts of the *Constructivistic School* of Erlangen[74] are bound to fail in this regard. But valuable contributions of this school could easily be utilized by regarding their *"community of consensus" as a system endowed with "transsubjective" norms*. Such a marriage between our method of neutralizing (and de-neutralizing) systems and the thoughts of the School of Erlangen might explain more satisfactorily the connection between positive and normative aspects than without the aid of systems methodology. But this puts a special burden on the shoulders of future system methodologists. Above all, it will be their task to further examine and illuminate such relations as those between sentences and mathematical structures, between mathematical structures and systems in general, and thus between sentences and systems. They must continue the search for a comprehensive logico-mathematical framework capable of mastering not only assertoric but also normative (deontic as well as imperative) arguments. Furthermore the search must be directed toward means of formalizing systems in such a way that the *holistic aspects*, characteristic of a specific system but not of any of its components, can be represented explicitly and can be integrated elegantly with the components of the system.

[74] The so-called "Erlangen-model" – e.g. see Lorenzen (1974), Lorenzen and Schwemmer (1975), Schwemmer (1976), Steinmann *et al.* (1976) – may be regarded as a reaction to critical rationalism, and grows out of Schwemmer's *constructivism* which manifests a broad influence by such authors as Brower, Gentzen, Kant, Poincaré, Dilthey as well as the Hegelian–Marxian dialectic. It is thus not unrelated to the Frankfurt school of Habermas and his precursors. The Erlangen-model resembles in some features the Delphi-method as developed by Helmer (1967) and others (see Linstone and Turoff 1975). Similar to the latter, it presupposes a community of experts or "reasonable" people, tends towards a community consensus (transsubjectivity and reasonable consent) and emphasises practice-oriented thinking (the rules of *open connections* and normative genesis), the basis of which are the cultural and, above all, natural needs of people.

That neither formal nor informal languages can be brought into a one–one correspondence with the world of facts, was discovered by Wittgenstein in a long and wearysome process of philosophic re-examination. After such revelation there is not much left but to hope that scientific theories are more than *sentential pictures* of reality, that they are perhaps *structural analogues* which depict reality, more accurately than purely linguistic configurations are able to do. Perhaps this is the ultimate reason for the immense success of modern mathematics: it keeps up the hope for tools of replicating the systemic structure of reality. And here is *the reason why our five methodological principles are actually ontological postulates: it is found in the belief that the most reliable method to represent existing entities, is still by means of isomorphic structures*. Of course this isomorphism refers to nothing but "essential structuralistic features", and often enough affords merely a crude replication. Yet it leads to the structure of that system which in the *lingua franca* of science and philosophy goes under the name of "empirical theory" – and this in spite of the fact that the latter is usually believed to be a body of propositions. Nevertheless the idea of essentialistic isomorphism is not bound to lead to an uncompromising correspondence theory of truth. As long as one admits the imperfections of this correspondence and as long as one searches for means of improving them by seeing the world in a more holistic way, there exists *a solid bridge between the systemic (but not the linguistic) correspondence theory and the coherence theory of truth*. Furthermore if every systemic entity is presumed to possess an *internal or reflective* aspect as well as an *external or material* one, then such an entity may be looked at from two different but related angles. We might call these two viewpoints of seeing or representing a system, the *normative-teleologic mode*, depicting the reflective or even personalistic aspects of a system, and the *positive-mechanistic mode*, referring to the material and mechanistic aspect, and depicting a system in the way natural science is accustomed to represent reality and its bits and pieces. To what extent it is then possible to translate one aspect into the other still has to be explored in detail, but it seems safe to say that *a norm or value judgement* in the normative-teleological mode corresponds to *a datum, a fact, an occurrence, or a constraint*, in the positive-mechanistic mode. Thus the perplexing split between normative versus positive representation has found its explanation in the *two Janus-faces of human reality* which we are trying to mirror. And the quintessence of this view can be summarized in the simple insight that the *difference between a fact and a norm hinges on the point of view* from which a system is looked at. If the teleological aspects are abstracted, that is to say if the system is viewed as non-teleological, a certain system relation may emerge as a fact. When, however, the goal is taken into consideration, that is to say, if the system is viewed as teleological, the same system relation may emerge as a norm. This view together with other novel system aspects (e.g. the structuralistic theory interpretation of Sneed and Stegmüller as well as insights found by Nicolis and Prigogine (1977), Jantsch and Waddington (1975), and others) may hopefully bring us closer toward a truly *dynamic systems theory and methodology* which puts less emphasis on the permanency than on the variability of a system structure.

The crucial question is whether one of these two aspects dominates the other or whether they possess equivalent significance. From a universal point of view the equivalence seems to be implied by our *holistic dualism* (see 7.53); but from a human and instrumental point of view, there can be little doubt that the *internal aspect* (with its mental, preferential and teleologic notions) *dominates.* But this too promotes a kind of holism, because goals and norms hardly can be comprehended without tracing their reasons or "causes" and their effects through at least some stages of the system's hierarchy. This *moderate holistic point of view* would neither aim at the comprehension of the entire universe, nor would it be discouraged by the impossibility of such an undertaking, it would rather rest on the belief that *a part viewed in isolation cannot be understood as well, than when viewed (1) in its environmental setting and (2) under consideration of essential interdependences with other parts.* Yet this *neo-holism* is more than a convenient methodology: Relativity theory considers matter, energy, space, time, and gravitational force as nothing but different aspects of *one and the same process*; quantum mechanics offers experimental evidence that "*matter*" merely *seems* to be localized in the area of its highest concentration whereas it is an electromagnetic field that *penetrates the entire universe*; finally, physicists admit that it is "not possible to formulate the laws of [quantum theory] in a fully consistent way without reference to consciousness: (Wigner 1970); biological and behavioral sciences too hypothesize the *unity* of the two-dimensional aspect of mind and matter, and the social sciences reveal the *interdependencies* of human ecological systems. Under such circumstances *the representation of reality makes sense only if all of it, also the realm of value judgements, is taken into account,* and if atomistic philosophies, like logical positivism and critical rationalism, are abandoned in favour of a more holistic outlook.

BIBLIOGRAPHY

Achinstein, P., 'Models, Analogies, and Theories', *Philosophy of Science*, **31**, October 1964, pp. 328–349.

Ackoff, R. L. (with collaboration of Gupta, S. R. and Minas, J. S.), *Scientific Method – Optimizing Applied Research Decisions*, J. Wiley & Sons, Inc., New York, 1962.

Ackoff, R. L., 'General System Theory and Systems Research Contrasting Conceptions of Systems Science', *General Systems*, **8**, 1963, pp. 117–124.

Ackoff, R. L., 'Towards a System of Systems Concepts', *Management Science*, **17**, July 1971, pp. 661–671.

Ackoff, R. L. and Emery, F. E., *On Purposeful Systems*. Chicago: Aldine–Atherton Press, 1972.

Adam, A., Helten, E. and Scholl, F., *Kybernetische Modelle und Methoden*, Westdeutscher Verlag, Opladen, 1970.

Adams, E. M., *Ethical Naturalism and the Modern World View*, Chapel Hill, N.C., 1960.

Adorno, T. W. *et al.*, *Der Positivismusstreit in der deutschen Soziologie*, Luchterhand, Berlin, 1969.

Agassi, J., 'The Confusion Between Science and Technology in the Standard Philosophies of Science', *Technology and Culture*, **VII**, 1966, pp. 348–366.

Ahmavaar, A. Y., *The Cybernetic Methodology of Social Science* (in Finnish), Helsinki 1969 – an English formalization and abbreviation appeared under the title 'Cybernetics as the Foundational Science of Action', in *Cybernetica*, **3**, 1975, pp. 171–200.

Albert, H., 'Wissenschaft und Politik', *Probleme der Wissenschaftstheorie*. Festschrift *für Victor Kraft* (ed. by E. Topitsch), Vienna, 1960, pp. 201–232.

Albert, H. (ed.), *Theorie und Realität*, J. C. B. Mohr, Tübingen, 1964.

Albin, P. S., *The Analysis of Complex Socioeconomic Systems.* Lexington: D.C. Heath & Co., 1975.

Alston, W. P., 'Meaning', in P. Edwards (ed.), *Encyclopedia of Philosophy*, **5**, MacMillan and Free Press, New York, 1967 pp. 233–241.

Anderson, G. and Radnitzky, G. 'Wissenschaftlicher Fortschritt: umstritten auch in der Wissenschaft', in *Wirtschaft und Wissenschaft*, No. 4/1975, pp. 9–11.

Anderson, G. and Radnitzky, G. (eds.), *Progress in Science and Methodology*, Proceedings of the Conference 'Wissenschaftstheorie – Förderungsprogramm der Fritz Thyssen Stiftung', forthcoming.

Aristotle, *Metaphysics*.

Aristotle, *Nichomachaean Ethics*.

Arrow, K. J., *Social Choice and Individual Values*, (2nd. ed.), J. Wiley & Sons, Inc., New York, 1951.

Ashby, W. R., *An Introduction to Cybernetics*, Chapman and Hall, London, 1956.

Ashby, W. R., 'General Systems Theory as a New Discipline', *General Systems*, **3**, 1958, pp. 1–6.

Ashby, W. R., *Design for a Brain*, J. Wiley & Sons, Inc., New York, 1960.

Ashby, W. R., 'Principles of Self-Organizing Systems', in H. V. Förster and G. W. Zopf (eds.), *Principles of Self-Organization*, Pergamon Press, New York, 1962.

Ashby, W. R., 'Induction, Prediction and Decision-making in Cybernetic Systems', in E. Kyburg and E. Nagel (eds.), *Induction: Some Current Issues*, Wesleyan University Press, Middletown, Conn., 1963, pp. 55–73.

Ashby, W. R., 'The Set Theory of Mechanism and Homeostasis', *General Systems Yearbook*, 9, 1964, pp. 83–97.

Ashby, W. R., 'Principles of the Self-Organizing Systems', *Modern Systems Research for the Behavioral Scientist*, (ed. by W. Buckley), Aldine Publ. Co., Chicago, 1968, pp. 108–118.

Assimov, I., *Biogr. Encyclopedia of Science and Technology*, Doubleday, N.Y., 1964.

Austin, J. L., *How to Do Things with Words*, Oxford, 1962.

Ayer, A. J., *The Problem of Knowledge*, Penguin, Harmondsworth, U.K., 1956.

Bacon, F., *Novum Organum*, 1620.

Baetge, J., *Betriebswirtschaftlich Systemtheorie*, Westdeutscher Verlag, Opladen, 1974.

Baetge, J. (ed.), *Grundlagen der Wirtschafts- und Sozialkybernetik – Betriebswirtschaftliche Kontrolltheorie*, Westdeutscher Verlag, Oplanden, 1975.

Baker, F. (ed.), *Organizational Systems – General Systems Approaches to Complex Organizations*, R. D. Irwin, Inc., Homewood, Ill., 1973.

Balderston, F. E. and Hoggatt, A., *Simulation of Market Processes*, Institute of Business and Economic Research, Berkeley, 1962.

Barker, S. F., *Induction and Hypothesis: A Study of the Logic of Confirmation*, Cornell University Press, Ithaca, N.Y., 1957.

Barthes, R., *Sur Racine*, Paris, 1963, Paris, Ed. du seuil 1969, Coll. Pierres vives.

Barthes, R., *Critique et verité*, Paris, 1966.

Barthes, R., *Système de la Mode*, Paris, 1967.

Beer, S., 'Below the Twilight Arch - A Mythology of Systems' in Eckman (1961).

Belnap, N. D., Jr., 'B. Comments on H. Simon's 'The Logic of Heuristic Decision Making', in N. Rescher (ed.), *The Logic of Decision and Action*, University of Pittsburgh Press, Pittsburgh, 1966, pp. 27–35.

Bernal, J. D., *Science in History*, Vols. 1–4, C. A. Watts & Co., London, 1954. Quotes from the third edition, Penguin & Co., Harmondsworth, 1965.

Bernoulli, J., *Ars Conjectandi*, 1713.

Bertalanffy, L. von, *Kritische Theorie der Formbildung*, Bornträger, Berlin, 1928.

Bertalanffy, L. von, *Modern Theories of Development – An Introduction to Theoretical Biology*, (English version of Kritische Theorie der Formbildung), Oxford University Press, Oxford, 1933. Quotations from Harper Torchbook edition, 1962.

Bertalanffy, L. von, 'Zu einer allgemeinen Systemlehre', *Blätter für deutsche Philosophie*, 3, 4, 1945.

Bertalanffy, L. von, 'An Outline of General System Theory', *British Journal for the Philosophy of Science*, 1, 1950, pp. 134–165.

Bertalanffy, L. von, *General System Theory*, George Braziller, New York, 1968.

Bertalanffy, L. von, 'Foreword' to *Introduction to Systems Philosophy* by E. Laszlo, 1972, pp. xvii–xxi.

Binkley, R., 'A. Comments on H. Simon's "The Logic of Heuristic Decision-Making" ', in N. Rescher (ed.), *The Logic of Decision and Action*, University of Pittsburgh Press, Pittsburgh, 1966, pp. 21–26.

Black, D., *The Theory of Committees and Elections*, Cambridge University Press, Cambridge, 1958.

Black, M., *Problems of Analysis*, Cornell University Press, Ithaca, N.Y., 1954.

Black, M., 'Induction', in P. Edwards (ed.), *Encyclopedia of Philosophy*, **4**, pp. 169–181, MacMillan and Free Press, New York, 1967.

Blalock, H. M. and Blalock, A. B., *Methodology in Social Research*, McGraw-Hill, New York, 1968.

Blaug, M. (ed.), *Economics of Education*, (2nd ed.), Pergamon Press, New York, 1970.

Blumberg, A. E., 'Logic, Modern', in P. Edwards (ed.), *Encyclopedia of Philosophy*, **5**, pp. 12–34, MacMillan and Free Press, New York, 1967.

Bochenski, I. M., *The Methods of Contemporary Thought*, translated by P. Caws, D. Reidel Publ. Co., Dordrecht-Holland, 1965.

Bochenski, I. M., *A History of Formal Logic*, translated by I. Thomas, (2nd ed.), Chelsea Publishing, New York, 1970.

Bogdanov, A., *Tektologia: Vseobshchaya Organizationnaya Nauka*. (*Tektology: The Universal Science of Organization*), Izdatelstvo Z. I. "Nauka", Moscow, 1922 edition. (1912).

Bogdanov, A., *Allgemeine Organisations Lehre – Tektologie*, Vols. I and II, Organisation Verlagsgesellschaft m.b.H. Berlin, (S. Hirzel), 1926–1928.

Bohm, David, *Quantum Theory*, Prentice Hall, Englewood Cliffs, N.J., 1951.

Bohm, David, *Causality and Chance in Modern Physics*, Routlege and Kegan Paul, London, 1957.

Bohm, David, *The Special Theory of Relativity*, Benjamin, New York, 1965.

Boland, L. A., 'Discussion: Methodology as an Exercise in Economic Analysis', *Philosophy of Science*, **38**, March 1971, pp. 105–117.

Boole, G., *The Mathematical Analysis of Logic*, B. Blackwell, Oxford, 1948 (1847).

Bossel, H., S. Klaczko, and N. Müller (eds.), *Systems Theory in the Social Sciences*, Birkhäuser, Basel, 1976.

Boulding, K., 'General Systems Theory – The Skeleton of Science', *General Systems*, **1**, 1956, pp. 11–17.

Boulding, K. E., 'Economics as a Moral Science', *American Economic Review*, **59**, March 1969, pp. 1–12.

Braithwaite, R. B. (ed.), *The Foundations of Mathematics and other Logical Essays*, Kegan Paul, Trench, Trubner, London, 1931.

Braithwaite, R. B., *Scientific Explanation, a Study of the Function of Theory, Probability and Law in Science*, Harper, New York, 1960.

Breuer, J., *Introduction to the Theory of Sets*, Prentice-Hall, Englewood Cliffs, N.J., 1958.

Brillouin, L., *Science and Information Theory*, Academic Press, New York, 1962.

Brillouin, L., *Scientific Uncertainty and Information*, Academic Press, New York, 1964.

Brody, B. A., 'Logical Terms, Glossary of', in P. Edwards (ed.), *Encyclopedia of Philosophy*, **5**, pp. 57–77, MacMillan and Free Press, New York, 1967.

Brody, B. A. (ed.), *Readings in the Philosophy of Science*, Prentice-Hall, Englewood Cliffs, N.J., 1970.

Bronowski, J., *Science and Human Values*, Hutchinson, London, 1958 and 1961.

Bronowski, J., *The Identity of Man*, The National History Press, New York, 1965, 1971 edition.

Bronowski, J., *Nature and Knowledge: The Philosophy of Contemporary Science*, Oregon State System of Higher Education, Eugene, 1969.

Bronowski, J., *The Ascent of Man*, Little, Brown and Co., Boston, 1973.

Buck, R. C., 'On the Logic of General Behaviour Systems Theory', *Minnesota Studies in the Philosophy of Science*, **I**, 1956, pp. 223–228.

Buckley, W. F., *Sociology and Modern Systems Theory*, Prentice Hall, Englewood Cliffs, 1967.

Buckley, W. F. (ed.), *Modern Systems Research for Behavioral Scientists*, Aldine Publ. Co., Chicago, 1968.

Bunge, M. (ed.), *The Critical Approach to Science and Philosophy*, Free Press, New York, 1964.

Bunge, M., 'Technology as Applied Science', *Technology and Culture*, **VII**, 1966, pp. 329–347.

Bunge, M., *Scientific Research*, Vols. I & II, Springer-Verlag, New York, 1967.

Bunge, M., *Method, Model and Matter*, D. Reidel Co., Dordrecht, Holland, 1973.

Burks, A. W., 'The Presupposition Theory of Induction', *Philosophy of Science*, **20**, 1953, pp. 177–197.

Burks, A. W., 'On the Presuppositions of Induction', *Review of Metaphysics*, **8**, 1954–55, pp. 574–611.

Busse von Colbe, W., and Mattessich, R. (eds.), *Der Computer im Dienst der Unternehmungsführung*, Bertelsmann Universitätsverlag, Bielefeld, 1968.

Cantillon, R., *Essai sur la Nature du Commerce en Géneral*, 1755.

Carnap, R., 'Über die Aufgabe der Physik und die Anwendung des Grundsatzes der Einfachheit', *Kant-Studien*, **28**, 1923, pp. 90–107.

Carnap, R., *Der logische Aufbau der Welt*, Weltkreis Verlag, Berlin, 1928.

Carnap, R., *The Logical Syntax of Language*, Kegan Paul, Trench, Trubner, London, 1937 (1934).

Carnap, R., *Foundations of Logic and Mathematics*, University of Chicago Press, Chicago, 1939.

Carnap, R., *Introduction to Semantics*, Harvard University Press, Cambridge, Mass., 1942.

Carnap, R., *Formalization of Logic*, Harvard University Press, Cambridge, Mass., 1943.

Carnap, R., *Meaning and Necessity; a Study in Semantics and Modal Logic*, University of Chicago Press, Chicago, 1947. Enlarged ed., 1956.

Carnap, R., 'Empiricism, Semantics, and Ontology', *Revue Internationale de Philosophie*, **40**, 1950, pp. 20–40.

Carnap, R., *The Continuum of Inductive Methods*, University of Chicago Press, Chicago, 1952.

Carnap, R., *Logical Foundations of Probability*, (2nd ed.), University of Chicago Press, Chicago, 1962. (1950).

Carnap, R. and Jeffrey, R. C. (eds.), *Studies in Inductive Logic and Probability*, Vol. I., University of California Press, Berkeley, 1971.

Carnap, R., 'A Basic System of Inductive Logic, Part I,' in R. Carnap and R. C. Jeffrey (eds.), *Studies in Inductive Logic and Probability*, Vol. I. University of California Press, Berkeley, 1971, pp. 33–67.

Carrel, A., *Man the Unknown*, Harper, New York, 1944.

Castañeda, H. N., 'Ought, Value, and Utilitarianism', *American Philosophical Quarterly*, **6**, October 1969, pp. 257–275.

Chappell, V. C., *The Philosophy of David Hume*, Modern Library, New York, 1963.

Chisholm, R. M., 'The Contrary-to-fact Conditional', *Mind,* **55**, 1946, pp. 289–307.

Chmielewicz, K., *Forschungskonzeption der Wirtschaftswissenschaft*, C. E. Poeschel Verlag, Stuttgart, 1970.

Chomsky, N., *Syntactic Structures*, Janua Linguarum, ser.min.4 Mouton, Den Haag, 1957.

Chomsky, N., *Topics in the Theory of Generative Grammar*, Janua Linguarum, ser.min., Mouton, Den Haag, 1966.

Chomsky, N., *Language and Mind*, Harcourt, Brace & World, New York, 1968.

Churchman, C. W., *Theory of Experimental Inference*, MacMillan, New York, 1948.

Churchman, C. W., *Prediction and Optimal Decision – Philosophic Issues of a Science of Values,* Prentice-Hall, Englewood Cliffs, N.J., 1961.

Churchman, C. W., 'On Rational Decision Making', *Management Technology*, **2**. December 1962, pp. 71–76.

Churchman, C. W., 'The *X* of *X*', *Management Science*, **9**. April 1963, pp. 351–357.

Churchman, C. W., 'An Approach to General Systems Theory', in M. D. Mesarovic (ed.), *Views on General Systems Theory,* Chapter 14, Wiley, N.Y., 1964, pp. 173–175.

Churchman, C. W., *A Challenge to Reason,* McGraw-Hill, New York, 1968a.

Churchman, C. W., *The Systems Approach,* Dell Publ. Co., New York, 1968b.

Churchman, C. W., *The Design of Inquiring Systems*, Basic Books, New York, 1971.

Churchman, C. W., and Buchanan, B. G., 'On the Design of Inductive Systems: Some Philosophical Problems', *British Journal for the Philosophy of Science*, **20**, 1969, pp. 311–323.

Churchman, C. W. and Ratoosh, P. (eds.), *Measurement,* Wiley, New York, 1959.

Chwistek, L., 'The Theory of Constructive Types', *Annales de la Société Polonaise de Mathématique*, **2**, 1924, pp. 9–48, and **3**, 1925, pp. 92–141.

Clarke, D. S., Jr., *Deductive Logic. An Introduction to Evaluation Techniques and Logical Theory*, Southern Illinois University Press, Carbondale, 1973.

Copi, I. M., *Introduction to Logic*, (3rd ed.), MacMillan, New York, 1968.

Copi, I. M. and Gould, J. A. (eds.), *Readings in Logic*, MacMillan, New York, 1964.

Copi, I. M. and Gould, J. A., (eds.), *Contemporary Readings in Logical Theory*, MacMillan, New York, 1967.

Danilov, V. J. (ed.), *The Future of Science and Technology*, Museum of Science and Industry, Chicago, 1975.

Dasgupta, A. K. (ed.), *Methodology of Economic Research*, Asia Publishing, N.Y., 1968.

Debreu, G., *Theory of Value – An Axiomatic Analysis of Economic Equilibrium*, Wiley, New York, 1959.

Dlugos, G., Eberlein, G., and Steinmann, H. (eds.), *Wissenschaftstheorie und Betriebswirtschaftslehre*, Bertelsmann, Düsseldorf, 1972.

Dobb, J. L., 'Probability and Statistics', *Transactions of the American Mathematical Society*, **36**, 1934, pp. 759–775.

Dray, W. H., *Laws and Explanations in History*, Oxford University Press, London, 1957.

Dray, W. H., *Philosophy of History*, McGraw-Hill, New York, 1964.

Dreyfus, H. L., *What Computers Can't Do – A Critique of Artificial Reason*, Harper & Row, New York, 1972.

Durant, W., *The Story of Philosophy,* 1926; Cardinal Ed., New York, 1952.

Eckman, D. P., (ed.), *Systems: Research and Design*, Wiley, New York, 1961.

Ehrenfels, C., 'Über Gestaltqualitäten', *Vierteljahresschrift für wissenschaftliche Philosophie*, Vol. 14, 1890, pp. 249–292.

Eigen, M., 'Selforganization of Matter and the Evolution of Biological Macromolecules', *Die Naturwissenschaften* 58, 10, 1971, pp. 465–528.

Eigen, M. and Winkler R., *Das Spiel – Naturgesetze steuern den Zufall*, R. Piper & Co., Munich, 1975.

Ellis, O. and Ludwig, F. J., *Systems Philosophy*, J. Wiley & Sons, Inc., New York, 1962.

Emery, F. E. (ed.), *Systems Thinking*, Penguin Books Ltd., Harmondsworth, 1969.

Emery, J. C., *Organizational Planning and Control Systems*, Macmillan, London, 1969.

Emmer, R. E., *Economic Analysis and Scientific Philosophy*, Allen & Unwin, London, 1967.

Feigl, H., 'De Principiis Non Disputandum . . . ?', in M. Black (ed.), *Philosophical Analysis*, Prentice-Hall, Englewood Cliffs, N.J., 1950, pp. 113–147.

Feigl, H. and Brodbeck, M. (eds.), *Readings in the Philosophy of Science*, Appleton-Century-Crofts, New York, 1953.

Feigl, H. and Maxwell, G., *Minnesota Studies of the Philosophy of Science*, Vol. III, University of Minnesota Press, Minneapolis, 1962.

Felix, L., *The Modern Aspect of Mathematics*, Basic Books, New York, 1960.

Fellner, W., *Probability and Profit*, R. D. Irwin, Homewood, Ill., 1965.

Feltham, G. A., *Information Evaluation*, American Accounting Association, 1972.

Ferber, R. and Verdoorn, P. J., *Research Methods in Economics and Business*, MacMillan, New York, 1962.

Feyerabend, P. K., 'An Attempt at a Realistic Interpretation of Experience', *Proceedings of the Aristotelian Society*, (New Series), 58, 1958, pp. 143–170.

Feyerabend, P. K., 'Explanation, Reduction and Empiricism', in H. Feigl and G. Maxwell (eds.), *Minnesota Studies in the Philosophy of Science*, Vol. III, University of Minnesota Press, Minneapolis, 1962, pp. 28–97.

Feyerabend, P. K., 'Problems of Empiricism', in R. Colodny (ed.), *Beyond the Edge of Certainty*, Prentice-Hall, Englewood Cliffs, N.J., 1965, pp. 145–150.

Feyerabend, P. K., 'Problems of Empiricism II', in R. Coldony (ed.), *The Nature and Function of Scientific Theories*, University of Pittsburgh, Pittsburgh Press, 1970a, pp. 275–353.

Feyerabend, P. K., 'Against Method', in M. Radner and S. Winokur (eds.), *Minnesota Studies in the Philosophy of Science*, Vol. IV, University of Minnesota Press, Minneapolis, 1970b, pp. 17–130.

Feyerabend, P., *Against Method*, New Left Books, London, 1975.

Fishburn, P. C., *Decision and Value Theory*, Wiley, New York, 1964.

Fishburn, P. C., *Utility Theory for Decision Making*, Wiley, New York, 1970.

Fischer-Winkelmann, W. F., 'Plädoyer gegen die Einbeziehung krypto-normativer Aussagen in die Betriebswirtschaftslehre', *Zeitschrift für Betriebswirtschaftliche Forschung*, I, January 1974, pp. 53–62.

Fisher, R. A., 'On the Mathematical Foundations of Theoretical Statistics', *Philosophical Transactions of the Royal Society*, Series A, **222**, 1921, pp. 309–368.

Forrester, J. W., *Industrial Dynamics*, J. Wiley & Sons and M.I.T. Press, New York, 1961.

Forrester, J. W., *World Dynamics*, Wright-Allen Press, Cambridge, Mass., 1971.

Frank, H. G., *Kybernetik und Philosophie,* Duncker und Humbolt, Berlin, 1966.

Frege, G., *Grundgesetze der Arithmetik*, 1893.

Friedman, M., *Essays in Positive Economics*, University of Chicago Press, Chicago, 1953.

Garb, G., 'Professor Samuelson on Theory and Realism: Comment', *American Economic Review*, **55**, December 1965, pp. 1151–1153.

Geach, P. T. and Black, M. (eds.), *Translations from the Philosophical Writings of Gottlob Frege*, Oxford University Press, Oxford, 1952.

Gellner, E., *Words and Things*, Victor Gollancz, London, 1959.

Georgescu-Roegen, N., *The Entropy Law and the Economic Process*, Harvard University Press, Cambridge, Mass., 1971.

Glöckner, P. -H., *Das Finden von Begriffen*, Poeschel Verlag, Stuttgart, 1963.

Gödel, K., (see p. 88), *Monatshefte für Mathematik und Physik,* 1931, 173–198.

Goguen, J. A., '*L*-Fuzzy Sets', *Journal of Mathematical Analysis and Applications*, **23**, 1967, pp. 145–174.

Goldman, A. I., *A Theory of Human Action*, Prentice-Hall, Englewood Cliffs, N.J., 1970.

Goode, W. J. and Hatt, P. K., *Methods in Social Research*, McGraw-Hill, New York, 1952.

Goodman, N., 'The Problem of Counterfactual Conditionals', *Journal of Philosophy*, **44**, 1947, pp. 13–34; reprinted in his *Fact, Fiction and Forecast.*

Goodman, N., *Fact, Fiction and Forecast*, Harvard University Press, Cambridge, Mass., 1955.

Gorelik, G., 'Re-emergence of Bogdanov's *Tektology* in Soviet Studies of Organization', Working Paper No. 226, Faculty of Commerce and Business Administration, University of British Columbia, 1973.

Gorelik, G., 'Principal Ideas of Bogdanov's "Tektology": The Universal Science of Organization', *General Systems*, **20**, 1975, pp. 3–13.

Griffiths, A. P. (ed.), *Knowledge and Belief*, Oxford University Press, Oxford, 1967.

Grochla, E., 'Polarität in betriebswirtschaftlicher Forschung und Lehre', *Zeitschrift für Betriebswirtschaft*, **29**, February 1959, pp. 65–76.

Grochla, E. (ed.), *Handwörterbuch der Organisation*, Poeschel Verlag, Stuttgart, 1969.

Grochla, E., Fuchs, M., and Lehmann, H. (eds.), *Systemtheorie und Betrieb,* Sonderheft 3/74 of *Zeitschrift für betriebswirtschaftliche Forschung*, 1974.

Grümm, H. R. (ed.), *Analysis and Computation of Equilibria and Regions of Stability*, International Institute for Applied Systems Analysis, Laxenburg (Austria), 1975.

Haavelmo, T., *A Study in the Theory of Economic Evolution*, North-Holland, Amsterdam, 1954.

Habermas, J., 'Analytische Wissenschaftstheorie und Dialektik', in *Der Positivismusstreit* by Adorno, T. W. *et al.*, 1969a.

Habermas, J., 'Gegen einen positivistisch halbierten Rationalismus', in *Der Positivismusstreit* by Adorno, T. W. *et al*., 1969b.

Hacking, I., *Logic of Statistical Inference*, Cambridge University Press, Cambridge, 1965.

Hall, A. D. and Fagen, R. E., *A Methodology for Systems Engineering,* Van Nostrand, Princeton, N.J., 1962.

Hanson, N. R., *Patterns of Discovery*, Cambridge University Press, Cambridge, 1958.

Hare, Van C., *Systems Analysis: A Diagnostic Approach*, Harcourt, Brace & World, Inc., New York, 1967.

Harsanyi, J. C., 'Popper's Improbability Criterion for the Choice of Scientific Hypotheses', *Philosophy*, **35**, 1960, pp. 332–340.

Hatfield, H.S., *The Inventor and His World*, Paul, Trench, Trubner, London, 1933.

Hayek, F. A. von, 'Scientism and the Study of Society', *Economica*, **5**, August 1942, pp. 267–291.

Hayek, F. A. von, *Studies in Philosophy, Politics and Economics*, University of Chicago Press, Chicago, 1967.

Heijenoort, J. van, *From Frege to Gödel, Source Book on Mathematical Logic*, Cambridge, Mass., 1966.

Heinen, E., *Das Zielsystem der Unternehmung*, Gabler, Wiesbaden, 1966.

Heinen, E., 'Zum Wissenschaftsprogramm der entscheidungsorientierten Betriebswirtschaftslehre', *Zeitschrift für Betriebswirtschaft*, **39** (1969), pp. 207–220.

Heinen, E., *Grundfragen der Entscheidungsorientierten Betriebswirtschaftslehre*, Goldmann Verlag, Munich, 1976.

Heller, H., *Staatslehre*, 3 vols., Leyden 1934.

Helm, G., *Die Lehre von der Energie*, Leipzig, 1887.

Helmer, O., *The Systematic Use of Expert Judgement in Operations Research*. Rand Corporation, Santa Monica, Calif., 1963.

Helmer, O., *A Use of Simulation for the Study of Future Values*, Rand Corporation, Santa Monica, Calif., 1966.

Helmer, O., *Social Technology*, Basic Books, New York, 1966.

Helmer, O., *Analysis of the Future: The Delphi Method*, Rand Corporation, Santa Monica, Calif., 1967.

Helmer, O. and Rescher, N., 'On the Epistemology of the Inexact Sciences', *Management Science*, **6**, October 1959, pp. 25–52.

Hempel, C. G., 'On The Nature of Mathematical Truth', in J. R. Newman (ed.), *The World of Mathematics*, Vol. III, Simon and Schuster, N.Y., 1956, pp. 1619–1634.

Hempel, C. G., *Aspects of Scientific Explanations and Other Essays*, Free Press, New York, 1965.

Hempel, C., *Philosophy of Natural Science*, Prentice-Hall, Englewood Cliffs, 1966.

Hempel, C. G. and Oppenheim, P., 'Studies in the Logic of Explanation', *Philosophy of Science*, **15**, 1948, pp. 135–175.

Henkin, L., Suppes, P., and Tarski, A. (eds.), *The Axiomatic Method with Special Reference to Geometry and Physics*, North-Holland, Amsterdam, 1959.

Herschel, J. F. W., *A Preliminary Discourse on the Study of Natural Philosophy*, London, 1830.

Hesse, M. B., *Models and Analogies in Science*, University of Notre Dame Press, Notre Dame, Ind., 1966.

Hesse, M. B., 'Models and Analogy in Science', in P. Edwards (ed.), *Encyclopedia of Philosophy*, **5**, pp. 354–359, MacMillan and Free Press, New York, 1967.

Hinterhuber, H. H., *Innovationsdynamik und Unternehmensführung*, Springer Verlag, Vienna, 1975.

Hintikka, J., 'A Two-Dimensional Continuum of Inductive Methods', in J. Hintikka and P. Suppes (eds.), *Aspects of Inductive Logic*, North-Holland Publishing, Amsterdam, 1966, pp. 113–132.

Hintikka, J. and Hilpinen, R., 'Knowledge, Acceptance, and Inductive Logic', in J. Hintikka and P. Suppes (eds.), *Aspects of Inductive Logic*, North-Holland Publishing, Amsterdam, 1966, pp. 1–20.

Hintikka, J. (ed.), *The Philosophy of Mathematics*, Oxford University Press, Oxford, 1969.

Hitch, C. J., 'On the Choice of Objectives in Systems Studies', in D. P. Eckman (ed.), *Systems: Research & Design*, Wiley, New York, 1961, pp. 43–51.

Hoel, P. G., *Introduction to Mathematical Statistics*, (2nd ed.), Wiley, New York, 1954.

Hoffmann, F., *Entwicklung der Organisationsforschung*, 2. ed. Gabler, Wiesbaden, 1976.

Hood, W. C. and Koopmans, T. C. (eds.), *Studies in Econometric Method*, Wiley, New York, 1953.

Hostelet, G., *L'Investigation Scientifique des Faits d'Activité Humaine avec Application aux Sciences et aux Techniques Sociales*, M. Rivierè, Paris, 1960.

Hotelling, H., 'The Consistency and Ultimate Distribution of Optimum Statistics', *Transactions of the American Mathematical Society*, **32**, 1930, pp. 847–859.

Houffer, S. A. *et al.*, *Measurement and Prediction*, Princeton University Press, Princeton, 1950.

Hugger, W., *Weltmodelle auf dem Prüfstand*, Birkhäuser, Basel, 1974.

Hughes, G. E. and Cresswell, M. J., *An Introduction to Modal Logic*, Methuen, London, 1968.

Hume, D., *A Treatise of Human Nature*, 1738.

Hume, D., *An Enquiry Concerning Human Understanding*, 1748.

Hunt, E. K. and Schwartz, J. G. (eds.), *A Critique of Economic Theory*, Penguin, Harmondsworth, U.K., 1972.

Hutchison, T. W., *The Significance and Basic Postulates of Economic Theory*, A. M. Kelley, New York, 1960.

Hutchison, T. W., *"Positive" Economics and Policy Objectives*, Harvard University Press, Cambridge, Mass., 1964.

Iberall A. S., *Toward a General Science of Viable Systems*, McGraw-Hill, New York, 1972.

Jantsch E. and Waddington, C. H. (eds.) *Evolution and Consciousness: Human Systems in Transition*, Addison Wesley, Reading, Mass, 1976.

Jeffrey, R. C., *The Logic of Decision*, McGraw-Hill, New York, 1965.

Jeffreys, H., *Essays in Biography*, MacMillan, London, 1933.

Jeffreys, H., *Theory of Probability*, Clarendon Press, Oxford, 1939.

Johnson, R. A., Kast, F. E., and Rosenzweig, J. E., *The Theory and Management of Systems*, McGraw-Hill, Co., New York, 1963; 2nd. ed., 1967.

Jones, R., *Essay on the Distribution of Wealth and on the Sources of Taxation,* 1831.

Kant, I., *Kritik der reinen Vernunft* (Critique of Pure Reason), 1781.

Kant, I., *Kritik der praktischen Vernunft* (Critique of Practical Reason), 1788.

Kant, I., *Kritik der Urteilskraft* (Critique of Judgement), 1790.

Kasner, E., and Newman, J. R., 'Paradox Lost and Paradox Regained', in J. R. Newman (ed.), *The World of Mathematics*, Vol. III, Simon and Schuster, New York, 1956 pp. 1936–1955.

Kast, F. E. and Rosenzweig, J. E., 'Systems Theory and Management', *Management Science*, **10**, 1964, pp. 367–384.

Kast, F. E. and Rosenzweig, J. E., *Organization and Management*, McGraw-Hill, New York, 1970.

Katz, D. and Kahn, R. L. *The Social Psychology of Organizations*, Wiley & Sons, Inc., New York, 1966.

Kershner, R. B. and Wilcox, L. R., *The Anatomy of Mathematics*, Ronald Press, New York, 1950.

Keynes, J. Maynard, *A Treatise on Probability*, MacMillan, London, 1921.

Keynes, J. Neville, *The Scope and Method of Political Economy*, (3rd Rev. ed.), MacMillan, London, 1930. (1891).

Kirschmann, P. K., *Information and Reflection on Some Problems of Cybernetics and How Contemporary Dialectica Materialism Copes with Them*, D. Reidel Publ. Co., Dordrecht, 1970.

Klaczko, S., *Systemanalyse der Selbstreflexion*, Birkhäuser, Basel, 1974.

Klir, G. (ed.), *Trends in General Systems*, Wiley & Sons, New York, 1972.

Kneale, W. and Kneale, M., *The Development of Logic*, Clarendon Press, Oxford, 1962.

Knight, F. H., On the History and Method of Economics, University of Chicago Press, Chicago, 1956.

Knight, F. H., *Risk, Uncertainty, and Profit*, London, 1957.

Knight, F. H., 'Methodology in Economics – Part II', *Southern Economics Journal*, 27, April 1961, pp. 273–281.

Köhler, R., *Theoretische Systeme der Betriebswirtschaftslehre im Lichte der neueren Wissenschaftslogik*, C. E. Poeschel, Stuttgart, 1966.

Kolmogorov, A. N., *Foundations of the Theory of Probability*, Chelsea Publishing, New York, 1950 (1933).

Koopman, B. O., 'The Bases of Probability', *Bulletin of the American Mathematical Society*, **46**, 1940, pp. 763–774.

Koopmans, T. C., *Three Essays on the State of Economic Science*, McGraw-Hill, New York, 1957.

Kosiol, E., 'Erkenntnisgegenstand und methodologischer Standort der Betriebswirtschaftslehre', *Zeitschrift für Betriebswirtschaft*, **31**, 1961, pp. 129–136.

Kosiol, E., Szyperski, N., and Chmielewicz, K. 'Zum Standort der Systemforschung im Rahmen der Wissenschaften', *Zeitschrift für betriebswirtschaftliche Forschung* (N.F.) **17**, 1965, pp. 337–378.

Kotarbinski, T., *Praxiology – An Introduction to the Science of Efficient Action*, Pergamon Press, New York, 1965.

Krelle, W., *Präferenz- und Entscheidungstheorie*, J. C. B. Mohr, Tubingen, 1968.

Krelle, W., Müller, H., and Neumark, F. (eds), *Systeme und Methoden in den Wirtschafts- und Sozialwissenschaften*, J. C. B. Mohr, Tubingen, 1964.

Kretzmann, N., 'Semantics, History of', in P. Edwards (ed.), *Encyclopedia of Philosophy*, 7, pp. 358–406, MacMillan and Free Press, New York, 1967.

Krimerman, L. I. (ed.), *The Nature and Scope of Social Sciences: A Critical Anthology*, Appleton-Century-Crofts, New York, 1969.

Kripke, S. A., 'Naming and Necessity', in *Semantics of Natural Language*, (ed. by

D. Davidson and G. Harman), Reidel & Co., Dordrecht, 1972, pp. 253–255, 763–769.

Krupp, S. (ed.), *The Structure of Economic Science*, Englewood Cliffs, Prentice-Hall, N.J., 1966.

Kuhn, A., *The Logic of Social Systems*, Jossey-Bass, San Francisco, 1974.

Kuhn, A., 'Boundaries, Kinds of Systems, and Kinds of Interactions', *Organization and Administrative Sciences*, **6**, No. 1, Spring 1975, pp. 39–46.

Kuhn, H., 'Entstehung des Lebens: Bildung von Molekülgesellschaften', *Forschung 74*, Frankfurt a.M., Vol. **W11**, 9, 1973, pp. 42–46.

Kuhn, T. S., *The Structure of Scientific Revolutions*, University of Chicago Press, Chicago, 1962.

Kuhn, T. S., 'Second Thoughts on Paradigms', in F. Suppe (ed.) *The Structure of Scientific Theories*, University of Illinois Press, Urbana, 1974, pp. 459–482.

Kuhn, T. S., 'A Formalism for Scientific Change', Manuscript of a paper presented at the 5th International Congress of Logic, Methodology and the Philosophy of Science, 1975 (to be reprinted in the Proceedings).

Kyburg, H. E. Jr., *Probability and the Logic of Rational Belief*, Wesleyan University Press, Middletown Conn., 1961.

Kyburg, H. E. Jr., *Probability and Inductive Logic*, MacMillan, New York, 1970.

Lakatos, I., 'Falsification and the Methodology of Scientific Research Programmes', in *Criticism and the Growth of Knowledge*, by I. Lakatos and A. Musgrave (eds.), Cambridge University Press, Cambridge, 1970, pp. 91–182.

Lakatos, I., 'History of Science and its Rational Reconstruction', *Boston Studies in the Philosophy of Science*, **VIII**, 1972, pp. 91–182.

Lamberton, D. M. (ed.), *Economics of Information and Knowledge*, Penguin, Harmondsworth, U.K., 1971.

Lange, O., *Wholes and Parts*, translated by E. Lepa, Pergamon Press, Oxford, 1965.

Langer, S. K., *An Introduction to Symbolic Logic*, (3rd rev. ed.), Dover, New York, 1967.

Laszlo, E., *Introduction to Systems Philosophy*, Gordon and Breach, New York, 1972a.

Laszlo, E., (ed.), *The Relevance of General Systems Theory*, George Braziller, New York, 1972b.

Laszlo, E., *The Systems View of the World*, George Braziller, New York, 1972c.

Laszlo, E., (ed.), *The World System-Models, Norms, Variations*. George Braziller, New York, 1973.

Lawrence, N., *Alfred North Whitehead*, Twayne Publishers, Inc., New York, 1974.

Layzer, D. 'The Arrow of Time', *Scientific American*, December 1975, pp. 56–60.

Leach, J. J., Butts, R. E., and Pearce, G. (eds.), *Science, Decision and Value*, D. Reidel Publ. Co., Dordrecht, 1973.

Lektorsky, V. A. and Sadovky, V. B., 'On Principles of System Research', *General Systems*, **5**, 1961, pp. 171–179.

Leiner, B., 'Notes on Etiality, the Adaptation Criterion, and the "Inference-Decision" Problems', *Information, Inference and Decision*, ed. by G. Menges, D. Reidel Publishing Co. Dordrecht-Holland, 1974.

Leinfellner, W., 'A New Epitheoretical Analysis of Social Theories', in W. Leinfellner and E. Köhler (eds.), *Developments in the Methodology of Social Science*, D. Reidel Publ. Co., Dordrecht, 1974, pp. 3–4.

Leinfellner, W. and Köhler, E. (eds.), *Developments in the Methodology of Social Science*, D. Reidel Publ. Co., Dordrecht, 1974.

Leplin, J., 'Contextual Falsification and Scientific Methodology', *Philosophy of Science*, 39, December 1972, pp. 476–490.

Lerner, A. P., 'Professor Samuelson on Theory and Realism: Comment', *American Economic Review*, 55, December 1965, pp. 1155–1164.

Levi, I., Gambling with Truth: *An Essay on Induction and the Aims of Science*, Knopt, New York, 1967.

Lévi-Strauss, C., *Les structures élémentaires de la parenté*, 1.ed. Pr. universitaires de France, Paris, 1949.

Lévi-Strauss, C., *Anthropologie structurale*, Plon, Paris, 1958.

Lewis, C. I. and Langford, C. H., *Symbolic Logic*, New York, 1932.

Lewis, C. I. and Langford, C. H., 'History of Symbolic Logic', in J. R. Newman (ed.), *The World of Mathematics*, Vol. III, Simon and Schuster, New York, 1956, pp. 1859–1877.

Lewis, C. S., *The Abolition of Man*, MacMillan, New York, 1944.

Linsky, L., "Referring," in P. Edwards (ed.), *Encyclopedia of Philosophy*, 8, pp. 95–99, MacMillan and Free Press, New York, 1967.

Linsky, L., (ed.), *Reference and Modality*, Oxford University Press, Oxford, 1971.

Linstone, H. A. and Turoff, M., (eds.), *The Delphi Method – Techniques and Applications*, Addison-Wesley Publ. Co., Reading, Mass., 1975.

Lorenz, K., *Die Rückseite des Spiegels*, R. Piper, München, 1973.

Lorenzen, P., *Konstruktive Wissenschaftstheorie*, Suhrkamp Verlag, Frankfurt, 1974.

Lorenzen, P., and Schwemmer, O., *Logik, Ethik und Wissenschaftstheorie*, 2.ed. Mannheim 1975, Bibliographisches Institut Mannheim/Wien/Zürich, B.I.-Wissenschaftsverlag.

Lowe, A., *On Economic Knowledge*, Harper, New York, 1965.

Luce, R. D., and Raiffa, H., *Games and Decisions: Introduction and Critical Survey*, Wiley, New York, 1957.

Ludwig, G., *Deutung des Begriffs 'physikalische Theorie' und axiomatische Grundlegung der Hilbertraumstruktur der Quantenmechanik durch Hauptsätze des Messens*, Springer Verlag, Berlin, 1970.

Mace, C. A. (ed.), *British Philosophy in the Mid-Century: A Cambridge Symposium*, (2nd ed.), Allen & Unwin, London, 1966.

Machlup, F., 'The Problem of Verification in Economics', *Southern Economic Journal*, 22, July 1955, pp. 1–21.

Machlup, F., 'Are the Social Sciences Really Inferior?', *Southern Economic Journal*, 27, January 1961. pp. 173–193.

Machlup, F., *The Production and Distribution of Knowledge in the United States*, Princeton University Press, Princeton, 1962.

Machlup, F., *Essays in Economic Semantics*, Prentice-Hall, Englewood Cl., N.J., 1963.

Machlup, F., 'Professor Samuelson on Theory and Realism', *American Economic Review*, 54, 1964, pp. 733–736.

Malcolm, N., 'Wittgenstein, Ludwig Josef Johann', in P. Edwards (ed.), *Encyclopedia of Philosophy*, 8, pp. 327–340, MacMillan and Free Press, New York, 1967.

Mally, E., *Logische Schriften*, ed. by K. Wolf and P. Weingartner, D. Reidel Publ. Co., Dordrecht-Holland: 1971.

Malthus, T. R., *Principles of Political Economy*, 1820.

Markoff, A., *Calculus of Probability*, Academy of Sciences, St. Petersburg, 1913.

Markowitz, H. M., *Portfolio Selection: Efficient Diversification of Investment*, Wiley, New York, 1959.

Marschak, J., *Econ. Information, Decision and Prediction*, Reidel, Dordrecht, 1974.

Marschak, J. and Miyasawa, K., 'Economic Comparability of Information Systems', *International Economic Review*, 9, 1968, pp. 137–174.

Marschak, J. and Radner, R., *Economic Theory of Teams*, Yale University Press, New Haven, Conn., 1972.

Maslow, A. (ed.), *New Knowledge in Human Values*, Harper and Row, New York, 1959.

Mason, R. O., 'A Dialectical Approach to Strategic Planning', *Management Science*, **15**, April 1969, pp. B403–B414.

Massey, G. J., 'Professor Samuelson on Theory and Realism: Comment', *American Economic Review*, **55**, 1965, pp. 1155–1164.

Mates, B., *Elementary Logic*, Oxford University Press, New York, 1965.

Mattessich, R., 'Towards a General and Axiomatic Foundation of Accountancy', *Accounting Research*, **8**, October 1957, pp. 328–355.

Mattessich, R., 'Budgeting Models and System Simulation', *The Accounting Review*, **36**, No. 3, July 1961, pp. 384–397.

Mattessich, R., 'Philosophie der Unternehmungsforschung', *Zeitschrift für handelswissenschaftliche Forschung*, (now *Zeitschrift für betriebswirtschaftliche Forschung*), **14**, May 1962, pp. 249–258.

Mattessich, R., *Accounting and Analytical Methods*, R. D. Irwin, Homewood, Ill., 1964a. Reprinted in 'Accounting Classics', Scholars Book Co., Houston, 1978.

Mattessich, R., *Simulation of the Firm Through a Budget Computer Program*, R. D. Irwin, Homewood, Ill., 1964b.

Mattessich, R., 'The Impact of Electronic Data Processing and Management Science upon Accounting Theory', in M. Backer (ed.), *Modern Accounting Theory*, Prentice-Hall, Englewood Cliffs, N.J., 1966, pp. 511–534.

Mattessich, R. and Busse von Colbe, W. (eds.), *Der Computer in Dienste der Unternehmungsführung*, Bertelsmann, Guetersloh, 1968, pp. 171–191.

Mattessich, R., 'Neue erkenntnistheoretische Probleme der Betriebswirtschaftslehre', in H. Kloidt (ed.), *Betriebswirtschaftliche Forschung in internationaler Sicht*, Duncker und Humblot, Berlin, 1969, pp. 17–32.

Mattessich, R., *Die wissentschaftlichen Grundlagen' des Rechnungswesens*, Bertelsmann, Düsseldorf, 1970.

Mattessich, R., 'Messung und Bewertung', in E. Kosiol (ed.), *Handwörterbuch der Rechnungswesens*, C. E. Poeschel Verlag, Stuttgart, 1970, pp. 1105–1110.

Mattessich, R., 'Methodological Preconditions and Problems of a General Theory of Accounting', *The Accounting Review*, **47**, 3, July 1972, pp. 469–487.

Mattessich, R., 'The Incorporation and Reduction of Value Judgements in Systems', *Management Science*, **21**, September 1974a, pp. 1–9.

Mattessich, R., 'Informations- und Erkenntnisökonomik: Treffpunkt von Philosophie und Wirtschaftswissenschaft', *Zeitschrift für betriebswirtschaftliche Forschung*, **26**, December 1974b, pp. 777–784.

Mattessich, R., 'Zur Klärung des Problems der "Wertefreiheit von Wissenschaften": Ein Lösungsversuch im Wege der Systemanalyse', *Zeitschrift für betriebswirtschaftliche Forschung*, **27**, March 1975a, pp. 6–22.

Mattessich, R., 'Information Economics and the Notion of "Management Information System"', in E. Grochla and N. Szyperski (eds.), *Information Systems and Organizational Structure*, Walter de Gruyter, New York, 1975b, pp. 342–354.

Mattessich, R., 'Epistemological Consequences of Artificial Intelligence and Systems Research', *Contributed Papers, 5th International Congress of Logic, Methodology and Philosophy of Science*, London, Ont.,1975c,pp. V-85 to V-86.

Mattessich, R., 'Normative vs. Positive Systems: On the Relation between Normativity, Teleology, and Mentalistic Aspects', *Proceed. of 8th Internat. Congr. of Cybernetics*, Namur, 1976.

Maxwell, G., 'The Necessary and the Contingent', in H. Feigl and G. Maxwell (eds.), *Minnesota Studies of the Philosophy of Science*, Vol. III, pp. 398–404. 1962.

Maxwell, N., 'A Critique of Popper's Views on Scientific Method', *Philosophy of Science*, **30**, June 1972, pp. 131–152.

McEvoy, J. G., 'A "Revolutionary" Philosophy of Science: Feyerabend and the Degeneration of Critical Rationalism into Sceptical Fallibilism', *Philosophy of Science*, **42**, January 1975, pp. 49–66.

Meadows, D. H., Meadows, D. L., Randers, J., and Behrens, W. W., *The Limits to Growth*, The New American Library Inc., New York, 1972.

Meissner, W. and Wold, H., 'The Foundation of Science on Cognitive Mini-Models, with Applications to the German Methodenstreit and the Advent of Econometrics', in W. Leinfellner and E. Köhler, Developments in the Methodology of Social Science, D. Reidel Publ. Co., Dordrecht, 1974, pp. 111–146.

Melcher, A. J., 'Theory and Application of Systems Theory: Its Promises, Problems, and Realizations', *Organization and Administrative Sciences*, **6**, No. 1, Spring 1975, pp. 3–9.

Menger, K., 'A Logic of the Doubtful: On Optative and Imperative Logic', in K. Menger (ed.), *Reports of a Mathematical Colloquium*, Notre Dame University Press, Notre Dame, Ind., 1939, pp. 53–64.

Menger, K., *Morality, Decision and Social Organisation:* Toward a Logic *of Ethics*, D. Reidel Publ. Co., Dordrecht-Holland, 1974 (1934).

Menges, G., 'Die Überwindung der Ungewissheit', in *Wissenschaft und Praxis*, Köln-Opladen, 1967, pp. 357–387.

Menges, G., *Grundmodelle wirtschaftlicher Entscheidungen*, (1st ed.), Köln-Opladen, 1969.

Menges, G., 'On Subjective Probability and Related Problems', *Theory and Decision*, **1**, 1970, pp. 40–60.

Menges, G. (ed.), *Information, Inference and Decision*, D. Reidel Publ. Co., Dordrecht-Holland, 1974.

Menges, G. and Skala, H. S., 'On the problem of Vagueness in the Social Sciences', in G. Menges (ed.), *Information, Inference and Decision*, D. Reidel Publ. Co., Dordrecht-Holland, 1974, pp. 51–61.

Mensch, G., *Das technologische Patt*, Umschauverlag, Frankfurt a.M., 1975.

Mesarović, M. D., *The Control of Multivariable Systems*, J. Wiley & Sons, Inc., New York, 1960.

Mesarović, M. D. (ed.), Views on General Systems, J. Wiley & Sons Inc., New York, 1964.

Mesarović, M. D., 'Foundations for a General Systems Theory', in Mesarović, M. D., (ed.), Views on General Systems Theory, Wiley, New York, 1964, pp. 1–24.

Mesarović, M. D. and Pestel, E., *Mankind at the Turning Point*, E. P. Dutton/Reader's Digest Press, New York, 1974.

Michajlov, A. I., Cernyi, A. I., and Giljarevskij, R. S., *Osnowy Informatiki*. Moscow: Nauka, 1968, German translation, *Grundlagen der wissenschaftlichen Dokumentation und Information* Vol. 1, Westdeutscher Verlag, Köln-Opladen, 1970.

Milburn, T. W., Negandhi, A. R., and Robey, D., 'Evaluating Systems Theory Concepts: Comments', *Organization and Administrative Sciences*, **6**, No. 1, Spring 1975, pp. 11–13.

Mill, J. S., *A System of Logic*, 1843.

Milnor, J., 'Games against Nature', in R. M. Thrall, C. H. Coombs, and R. L. Davis (eds.), *Decision Processes*, Wiley, New York, 1954, pp. 49–59.

Minsky, M. (ed.), *Semantic Information Processing*, MIT-Press, Cambridge, Mass., 1968.

Mises, R. von, *Positivism*, Harvard University Press, Cambridge, Mass., 1951.

Mises, R. von, *Probability, Statistics and Truth*, Allen & Unwin, London, 1957 (1928).

Mittelstrass, J., (ed.), *Methodologische Probleme einer normativ-kritischen Gesellschaftstheorie*, Suhrkamp Verlag, Frankfurt a.M., 1975.

Mitroff, I. I., 'Systems, Inquiry and the Meanings of Falsification', *Philosophy of Science*, **40**, June 1973, pp. 255–276.

Monod, J., *Le Hasard et la Necessité*, Ed. du seuil, Paris, 1970.

Montague, R., 'On the Nature of Certain Philosophical Entities', *Monist*, **53**, 1969, pp. 159–194.

Montague, R., 'Pragmatics and Intensional Logic', *Synthese*, **22**, 1970, pp. 68–94.

Montague, R., 'English as a Formal Language', Chapter 6 of *Linguage nella Società e nella Tecnica* (ed. by B. Visentini *et al.*), Milan, 1970.

Montague, R., 'Universal Grammar', *Theorie*, **36**. 1970, pp. 373–398.

Morgenbesser, S., Suppes, P., and White, M. (eds.), *Philosophy, Science and Method*, St. Martin's Press, New York, 1969.

Morgenstern, O., *Der theoretische Unterbau der Wirtschaftspolitik*, Cologne, 1957.

Morgenstern, O., *On the Accuracy of Economic Observations*, (2nd ed.), Princeton University Press, Princeton, 1963.

Mostowski, A., 'Tarski, Alfred', in P. Edwards (ed.), *Encyclopedia of Philosophy*, **8**, pp. 77–81, MacMillan and Free Press, New York, 1967.

Moxter, A., Methodologische Grundfragen der Betriebswirtschaftslehre, Cologne, 1957.

Myrdal, G., *The Political Element in the Development of Economic Theory*, translated by P. Streeten, Harvard University Press, Cambridge, Mass., 1954.

Myrdal, G., *An International Economy, Problems and Prospects*, Harper, New York, 1956.

Myrdal, G., *Objectivity in Social Research*, Pantheon Books, New York, 1969.

Nagel, E., 'Teleological Explanation and Teleological Systems', *Vision and Action*, ed. by S. Ratner, Rudgers Univ. Press, New Brunswick, N.J., 1953, reprinted in *Readings in the Philosophy of Science*, ed. by B. A. Brody, pp. 192–222.

Nagel, E., *The Structure of Science*, Harcourt, Brace & World, New York, 1961.

Nagel, E., 'Assumptions in Economic Theory', *American Economic Review*, **53**, 1963, pp. 211–219.

Nagel, E. and Newman, J. R., *Goedel's Proof*, New York Univ. Press, New York, 1958.

Nash, R. (ed.), *Ideas of History Vol. II: The Critical Philosophies of History*, Dutton & Co., Inc., New York, 1969.

Nauta, D., *The Meaning of Information*, Mouton, The Hague, 1970.

Naylor, T. H., *Computer Simulation Experiments with Models of Economic Systems*, J. Wiley & Sons, Inc., New York, 1971.

Nemmers, E. E. and Meyers, J. H., *Business Research*, McGraw-Hill, New York, 1966.

Neumann, J. von, and Morgenstern, O., *Theory of Games and Economic Behaviour*, Princeton University Press, Princeton, 1944. rev. ed. 1947.

Newman, J. R. (ed.), *The World of Mathematics*, Vol. III, Simon and Schuster, New York, 1956.

Neyman, J., *First Course in Probability and Statistics*, Holt Rinehart and Winston, New York, 1950.

Neyman, J., 'Outline of a Theory of Statistical Estimation based on the Classical Theory of Probability', *Philosophical Transactions of the Royal Society*, Series A, **236**, 1937, pp. 333–380.

Neyman, J. and Pearson, E. S., 'On the Use and Interpretation of Certain Test Criteria for Purposes of Statistical Inference', *Biometrica*, **20-A**, 1928, pp. 175–240, 263–294.

Neyman, J. and Pearson, E. S., 'On the Problem of the Most Efficient Tests of Statistical Hypotheses', *Philosophical Transactions of the Royal Society*, Series A, **231**, 1933, pp. 289–337.

Nicolis, G. and Prigogine, I., *Self-Organization in Nonequilibrium Systems: From Dissipative Structures to Order through Fluctuations*, New York, 1977.

Nidditch, P. H. (ed.), *The Philosophy of Science*, Oxford Univ. Press, Oxford, 1968.

Oeser, E., Wissenschaft und Information, 3. Vol, Vienna–Munich–Oldenbourg 1976.

Oldenquist, A., 'Choosing, ...' *Encyclop. of Philosophy*, Vol. II, 1967, pp. 96–104.

Operations Research Society of America Ad Hoc Committee on Professional Standards, 'Guidelines for the Practice of Operations Research', *Operations Research*, **19**, September 1971.

Opp. K. D., *Methodologie der Sozialwissenschaften*, Rowohlt, Hamburg, 1970, revised version 1976.

Optner, S. L. (ed.), *Systems Analysis*, Penguin Books, Ltd., Harmondsworth, 1973.

Organization and Administrative Sciences (Kent State University), **6**, No. 1, Spring 1975 (devoted to System Theory and Organization).

Papandreou, A. G., *Economics as a Science*, Lippincott, Chicago, 1958.

Papandreou, A. G., 'Explanation and Prediction in Economics', *Science*, **129**, April 24, 1959, pp. 1096–1100.

Papandreou, A. G., 'Theory Construction and Empirical Meaning in Economics', *American Economic Review*, **53**, May 1963, pp. 205–210.

Parkinson, G. H. R. (ed.), *The Theory of Meaning*, Oxford University Press, Oxford, 1968.

Patzak, G., *Grundlagen, Methoden und Techniken systemorientierter Planung*, Habilitationsschrift, Techn. Universität, Vienna, 1976.

Peirce, C. S., *Collected Papers*, ed. by C. Hartshorne and P. Weiss, Harvard University Press, Cambridge, Mass., 1932–33.

Pfanzagl, J., *Theory of Measurement*, Physica-Verlag, Wurzburg, 1968.

Phillips, D. C., 'System Theory – A Discredited Philosophy', *Abacus*, **5**, September 1969, pp. 3–15.

Piaget, J., *Le Structuralisme,* Paris, 1968. Engl. transl.: Basic Books, N.Y., 1970.

Piaget, J., *Biology and Knowledge*, Chicago: Univ. Pr., 1971.

Piron, R., 'On "The Methodology of Positive Economics": Comment', *Quarterly Journal of Economics*, **76**, 1962, pp. 664–668.

Popper, K. R., *Logik der Forschung*, J. C. B. Mohr, Tübingen, 1935.

Popper, K. R., *The Logic of Scientific Discovery*, Basic Books, New York, 1959.

Popper, K. R., 'The Propensity Interpretation of Probability', *British Journal for the Philosophy of Science*, **10**, 1959–60, pp. 25–42.

Popper, K. R., *Conjectures and Refutations* Basic Books, New York, 1962.

Pregel, J., 'Um die allgemeine Organisationslehre', *Weltwirtschaftliches Archiv*, **25**, July 1972, p. 18 ff.

Prior A. N., 'Correspondence Theory of Truth', in P. Edwards (ed.), *Encyclopedia of Philosophy*, **2**, pp. 223–232, MacMillan & Free Press, New York, 1967.

Putnam, H., 'The Analytic and the Synthetic', in H. Feigl and G. Maxwell (eds.), *Minnesota Studies in the Philosophy of Science*, Vol. III, 1962, pp. 350–397.

Putnam, H., 'The Compleat Conversationalist: A "Systems Approach" to the Philosophy of Language', in M. D. Mesarović (ed.), *Views on General Systems Theory*, Wiley, New York, 1964, pp. 89–105.

Quine, W. V. O., 'Symbolic Logic', *Encyclopedia Americana*, **17**, p. 690. New York, 1970.

Quine, W. V. O., *From a Logical Point of View*, (2nd rev. ed.), Harper & Row, New York, 1963. (1953).

Quinton A., 'Popper, Karl Raimund', in P. Edwards (ed.), *Encyclopedia of Philosophy*, **6**, pp. 398–401, MacMillan & Free Press, New York, 1967.

Radnitzky, G., 'From Logic of Science to Theory of Research', in *Communication and Cognition*, 7., No. 1, 1974, pp. 61–124.

Radnitzky, G., 'Popperian Philosophy of Science as an Antidot against Relativism', in *Boston Studies in the Philosophy of Science* (ed. by R. S. Cohen, P. Feyerabend and M. Wartofsky), Vol. 39, Reidel, Dordrecht, 1976, pp. 465–506.

Raiffa, H., *Decision Analysis: Introductory Lectures on Choices under Uncertainty*, Addison-Wesley, Reading, Mass., 1968.

Raiffa, H. and Schlaifer, R., *Applied Statistical Decision Theory*, Division of Research, Harvard Business School, Cambridge, Mass., 1961.

Ralescu, D. A., *Applications of Fuzzy Sets to System Analysis*, Birkhäuser, Basel, 1975.

Ramsey, F. P., 'Truth and Probability', in R. B. Braithwaite (ed.), *The Foundations of Mathematics and other Logical Essays*, Kegan Paul, Trench, Trubner, London, 1931, pp. 156–198.

Rapoport, A., 'What is Information?', *Synthese*, **9**, 1959, pp. 157–173.

Rapoport, A., 'Remarks on General Systems Theory', *General Systems*, **8**, 1963, pp. 123–124.

Rapoport, A., *Operational Philosophy. Integrating Knowledge and Action*, Wiley, New York, 1965.

Rapoport, A., 'Mathematical Aspects of General Systems Analysis', *General Systems Yearbook*, 11, 1966, pp. 3–11.

Rapoport, A. and Horvath, W. J., 'Thoughts and Organization Theory', *General Systems Yearbook*, **4**, 1959, pp. 87–91. *Reprinted in Modern Systems Research for the Behavioral Scientist*, ed. by W. Buckley, Aldine Publ. Co., Chicago, 1968, pp. 71–75.

Rapp, F. (ed.), *Contributions to a Philosophy of Technology*, D. Reidel, Dordrecht-Holland, 1974.

Reichenbach, H., *The Theory of Probability*, University of California Press, Berkeley, 1949 (1934).

Reichenbach, H., *Experience and Prediction*, University of Chicago Press, Chicago, 1938.

Rescher, N., *The Logic of Commands*, Routledge & Kegan Paul, London, 1966a.

Rescher, N. (ed.), *The Logic of Decision and Action*, Univ. of Pittsburgh Press, Pittsburgh, 1966b.

Rescher, N., 'Practical Reasoning and Values', *Philosophical Quarterly*, **16**, 1966c, pp. 121–136.

Rescher, N., *Introduction to Value Theory*, Prentice-Hall, Englewood Cliffs, N.J., 1969.

Rieber, A., *Vom Positivismus zum Universalismus*, Duncker und Humblot, Berlin, 1971.

Robinson, J., *Economic Philosophy*, Watts, London, 1962.

Rorty, R., 'Intuition', in P. Edwards (ed.), *Encyclopedia of Philosophy*, **4**, pp. 204–212, MacMillan and Free Press, New York, 1967.

Rose, J., (ed.), *Advances in Cybernetics and Systems*, 3. Vol, Gordon and Breach, London, 1975.

Rosenberg, A., 'Partial Interpretation and Microeconomics', in W. Leinfellner and E. Köhler (eds.), *Developments in the Methodology of Social Science*, D. Reidel Publ. Co., Dordrecht, 1974, pp. 93–109.

Ross, A., 'Imperatives and Logic', *Philosophy of Science*, **11**, April 1944, pp. 30–46.

Rothstein, J., *Communication, Organization and Science*, The Falcon's Wing Press, Indian Hills, Colo., 1958.

Rubenstein, A. H. and Barth, R. T. (eds.), *A Directory of European Research*, Northwestern University, Evanston, Ill., 1971.

Rubenstein, A. H. and Sullivan, E. M. (eds.), *A Directory of Research-on-Research*, (2nd ed.), Northwestern University, Evanston, Ill., 1968.

Rudner, R., 'The Scientist Qua Scientist Makes Value Judgements', *Philosophy of Science*, **20**, January 1953, pp. 1–6.

Runes D. D. (ed.), *Dictionary of Philosophy*, 15th ed., Philosophical Library, New York, 1960.

Russell, B., *Our Knowledge of the External World*, Allen & Unwin, London, 1914; quotations from the 1949 edition.

Russell, B., *Introduction to Mathematical Philosophy*, Allen & Unwin, London, 1920.

Russell, B., *Mysticism and Logic*, London, 1929, quotations from the Doubleday, Inc., 1957 edition.

Russell, B., *An Inquiry into Meaning and Truth*, Allen & Unwin, London, 1940.

Russell, B., *A History of Western Philosophy*, Simon and Schuster, New York, 1945.

Russell, B., *Human Knowledge, its Scope and Limits*, Simon and Schuster, New York, 1948.

Russell, B., 'Mathematics and the Metaphysicians', in J. R. Newman (ed.), *The World of Mathematics*, Vol. III, Simon and Schuster, New York, 1956, pp. 1576–1590.

Russell, B., *Autobiography of Bertrand Russell*, Bantam, Toronto, 1968.

Ryan, A. (ed.), *The Philosophy of Social Explanation*, Oxford University Press, London, 1973.

Ryle, G., *The Concept of Mind*, Hutchinson, London, 1949.

Salmon, W., *The Foundations of Scientific Inference*, University of Pittsburgh Press, Pittsburgh, 1966.

Salmon, W., 'A Third Dogma of Empiricism', Manuscript of an Invited Paper at the 5th International Congress of Logic, Methodology and Philosophy of Science, London, Ont., Aug.–Sept. 1975 (To be reprinted in the Proceedings of this Conference.)

Samuelson, P. A., *Foundations of Economic Analysis*, Harvard University Press, Cambridge, Mass., 1947.

Samuelson, P. A., 'Problems of Methodology – Discussions', *American Economic Review*, **53**, 1963, pp. 231–236.

Samuelson, P. A., 'Theory and Realism: A Reply'. *American Economic Review*, **54**, 1964, pp. 736–739.

Samuelson, P. A., 'Professor Samuelson on Theory and Realism: Reply', *American Economic Review*, **55**, 1965, pp. 1164–1172.

Savage, L. J., *The Foundations of Statistics*, Wiley, New York, 1954.

Schanz, G., 'Zum Prinzip der Wertfreiheit in der Betriebswirtschaftslehre: Wissenschaftstheoretische Anmerkungen zu Erich Loitlsbergers Playdoyer fur eine normative Wissenschaft', *Zeitschrift für Betriebswirtschaftliche Forschung*, **6**, June 1972, pp. 379–392.

Schanz, G., 'Stellungnahme zu Staehles Pladoyer fur die Einbeziehung normativer Aussagen in die Betriebswirtschaftslehre', *Zeitschrift für Betriebswirtschaftliche Forschung*, **1**, January 1974, pp. 47–52.

Schackle, G. L. S., *Epistemics and Economics*, Cambridge University Press, 1972.

Schilpp, P. A., (ed.), *The Philosophy of Bertrand Russell*, Vol. 1, Northwestern University, Evanston, Ill., 1944.

Schilpp, P. A., *The Philosophy of Rudolph Carnap*, Open Court, La Salle, Ill., 1963.

Schiwy, G., *Der französische Structuralismus*, Rowohlt, Hamburg, 1969.

Schlaifer, R., *Probability and Statistics for Business Decisions*, McGraw-Hill, New York, 1959.

Schlesinger, G., 'On Irrelevant Criteria of Confirmation', *British Journal for the Philosophy of Science*, **21**, 1970, pp. 282–287.

Schneider, D. J. G., *Grundfragen zur Problematik der Ableitbarkeit von Zielen und Mitteln in der Betriebswirtschaftslehre*, Habilitationsschrift, Graz, 1976.

Schneider, D. J. G., 'Zur tautologischen Transformation empirischer Sätze in Handlungsempfehlungen', *Proceedings*, Arbeitskreis Wissenschaftstheorie des Verbandes der Hochschullehrer für Betriebswirtschaft e.V., Nürnberg, 1977.

Schumacher, E. F., *Small Is Beautiful: A Study of Economics as if People Mattered*, Blond and Briggs, London, 1973.

Schweitzer, M., 'Methodologische und entscheidungstheoretische Grundfragen der Prozeßstrukturierung', *Zeitschrift für betriebswirtschaftliche Forschung* (N.F.), 19, 1967, pp. 279–296.

Schwemmer, O., *Theorie der rationalen Erklärung – Zu den methodischen Grundlagen der Kulturwissenschaften*, Beck-Verlag, Munchen, 1976.

Searle, J. R., How to Derive 'Ought from "Is"', *Philosophical Review*, **73**, 1964, pp. 43–58.

Searle, J. R., *Speech Acts – An Essay in the Philosophy of Language*, Cambridge University Press, London, 1969.

Searle, J. R., (ed.), *The Philosophy of Language*, Oxford University Press, Oxford, 1971.

Seiler, J. A., *Systems Analysis in Organizational Behavior*, Homewood, Ill., 1967.

Sen, A. K., *Choice of Techniques*, B. Blackwell, Oxford, 1960; 3rd. ed, 1968.

Sen, A. K., *Collective Choice and Social Welfare*, Holden-Day, San Francisco, 1970.

Sen, A. K., *On Economic Inequality*, Clarendon Press, Oxford, 1973.

Setrov, U. I., 'Princyp Sistemnosti i Yeho Osnovnye Poniatiya', (Systemic Principle and its Basic Concepts), *Problem y Metodologii Systemnaho Issledovaniya* (Problems of Methodology in Systemic Research), Moscow, 1970.

Settle, T. W., 'Confirmation as a Probability: Dead, but it Won't Lie Down', *British Journal for the Philosophy of Science*, **21**, 1970, pp. 200–201.

Shannon, C. E. and Weaver, W., *The Mathematical Theory of Communication*, University of Illinois Press Urbana, 1949.

Sheffer, H. M., 'A Set of Five Independent Postulates for Boolean Algebras, with Application to Logical Constants', *Transactions of the American Mathematical Society*, **14**, 1913, pp. 481–488.

Simon, H. A. *Administrative Behavior*, (2nd ed.), MacMillan, New York, 1957a.

Simon, H. A., *Models of Man*, Wiley, New York, 1957b.

Simon, H. A., 'The Architecture of Complexity', *Proceedings of the American Philosophical Society*, **106**, 6, December 1962, pp. 467–482.

Simon, H. A., 'Problems of Methodology – Discussions', *American Economic Review*, **53**, 1963, pp. 229–231.

Simon, H. A., 'The Logic of Rational Decision', *British Journal for the Philosophy of Science*, **16**, 1965, pp. 169–186.

Simon, H. A. 'The Logic of Heuristic Decision Making', in N. Rescher (ed.) *The Logic of Decision and Action*. Pittsburgh: University of Pittsburgh, 1966, pp. 1–20.

Simon, H. A., *The Science of the Artificial*, MIT Press, Cambridge, Mass., 1969.

Simon, H. A. and Newell, A., 'Heuristic Problem Solving: The Next Advance in Operations Research', *Operations Research*, **6**, Jan.–Feb. 1958, p. 6.

Simon, H. A. and Newell, A., 'Models: Their Uses and Limitations', *The State of the Social Sciences*, (ed. by L. D. White), Univ. of Chicago Press, Chicago, 1959, pp. 66–83.

Simon, H. A. and Siklóssy, L. (eds.), *Representation and Meaning*, Prentice-Hall, Englewood Cliffs, N.J., 1972.

Singer, E. A., *Mind as Behavior: Studies in Empirical Idealism*, R. G. Adams & Co., Columbus 1924.

Singer, E. A., *Experience and Reflection* (C. W. Churchman, ed.), University of Pennsylvania Press, Philadelphia, 1959.

Skolimowski, H., 'The Structure of Thinking in Technology', *Technology and Culture*, **VII**, 1966, pp. 371–383.

Skyrms, B., *Choice and Chance: An Introduction to Inductive Logic*, Dickenson Publishing, Belmont, California, 1966.

Smart, J. J. C. *Between Science and Philosophy*, Random House, New York, 1968.

Smithies, A. et al., Economic and Public Policy; Brookings Lecture 1954, Brookings Institute, Washington, D.C., 1955.

Sneed, J. D., *The Logical Structure of Mathematical Physics*, Reidel, Dordrecht, 1971.

Snyder, P. D., *Modal Logic and Its Applications*, Van Nostrand, New York, 1971.

Spann, O., *Gesamtausgabe der Werke*, ed. by W. Heinrich, H. Riehl, R. Spann and F. A. Westphalen (22 Vols.), Akademische Druck und Verlagsanstalt, Graz, 1963–70.

Sosa, Ernst (ed.), *Causation and Conditionals*, Univ. Pr., Oxford, 1975.

Staehle, W. H., 'Plädoyer für die Einbeziehung normativer Aussagen in die Betriebswirtschaftslehre', *Zeitschrift für Betriebswirtschaftliche Forschung*, 3, March 1973, pp. 184–197.

Staehle, W. H., 'Zur normativen Kritik erkenntnislogischer Theorienbildung – Erwiderung auf die Stellungnahmen von Fischer-Winkelmann und Schanz', *Zeitschrift fur Betriebswirtschaftliche Forschung*, 1, January 1974, pp. 63–70.

Stählin, W., *Theoretische und technologische Forschung in der Betriebswirtschaftslehre*, Poeschel, Stuttgart, 1973.

Stegmüller, W., *Main Currents in Contemporary German, British and American* Philosophy, Reidel, Dordrecht, 1969a.

Stegmüller, W., *Wissenschaftliche Erklärung und Begründung*, Springer, Berlin, 1969b.

Stegmüller, W., *Theorie und Erfahrung*, Vol. I, Springer-Verlag, Berlin, 1970.

Stegmüller, W., *Theorie und Erfahrung*, Vol. II, Springer-Verlag, Berlin, 1973a.

Stegmüller, W., *Personelle und Statistische Wahrscheinlichkeit*, Vol. I, Springer-Verlag, Berlin, 1973b.

Stegmüller, W., *Personelle und Statistische Wahrscheinlichkeit*, Vol. II, Springer-Verlag, Berlin 1973c.

Stegmüller, W., *Hauptströmungen der Gegenwartsphilosophie*, Kröner, Stuttgart, Vol. I, 1965: Vol. II, 1975a.

Stegmüller, W., 'Accidental ('Non-Substantial') Theory Change and Theory Dislodgment', contribution to the Kuhn–Sneed–Stegmüller Panel Discussion of the 5th International Congress of Logic Methodology and Philosophy of Science (London, Ont., Aug.–Sept., 1975b). Quotations are from a manuscript reprinted (in revised form) in the Proceedings of this Conference, Part 4, Reidel, Dordrecht, 1977, pp. 269–88.

Stegmüller, W., *The Structure and Dynamics of Theories*, Springer-Verlag, N.Y., 1976.

Steinbuch, K., *Automat und Mensch über menschliche und maschinelle Intelligenz*, Springer-Verlag, Heidelberg, 1961.

Steinmann, H., Böhm, H., Braun, W., Gerum, E., and Schreyögg, G. 'Zur Wertfreiheit in der Betriebswirtschaftslehre', *Zeitschrift für Betriebswirtschaft*, 1976, S.821–831.

Stevens, S. S., 'Measurement, Psychophysics, and Utility', in C. W. Churchman and P. Ratoosh (eds.), *Measurement, Definitions and Theories*, Wiley, N.Y., 1959, pp. 18ff.

Stravenhagen, G., *Geschichte der Wirtschaftstheorie*, (4th ed.), Vandenhoek und Ruprecht, Goettingen, 1969.

Strawson, P. F. (ed.), *Philosophical Logic*, Oxford University Press, Oxford, 1967.

Sueren, P. A. M. (ed.), *Semantic Syntax*, Oxford University Press, Oxford, 1975.

Suppe, F. (ed.), *The Structure of Scientific Theory*, University of Illinois Press, Urbana, 1974.

Suppes, P., *Introduction to Logic*, Van Nostrand, Princeton, 1957.

Suppes, P., 'The Philosophical Relevance of Decision Theory', *Journal of Philosophy*, **58**, 1961, pp. 605–614.

Suppes, P., 'A Comparison of the Meaning and Uses of Models in Mathematics and the Empirical Sciences'. *Studies in the Methodology and Foundations of Science*, ed. by P. Suppes, D. Reidel Publ. Co., Dordrecht, 1969.

Suppes, P., 'Decision Theory', in P. Edwards (ed.), *Encyclopedia of Philosophy*, **2**, pp. 310–314, MacMillan and Free Press, New York, 1967.

Sutherland, J. W., *A General Systems Philosophy for the Social and Behavioral Sciences*, George Braziller, New York, 1973.

Swinburne, R. (ed.), *The Justification of Induction*, Oxford University Press, Oxford, 1974.

Tarascio, V. J., 'Value Judgements and Economic Science', *Journal of Economic Issues*, **5**, March 1971, pp. 98–102.

Tarski, A. 'Der Wahrheitsbegriff in den formalisierten Sprachen', *Studia Philosophica*, **1** 1935–36, pp. 261–405.

Tarski, A. *Logic, Semantics, Metamathematics*, Clarendon Press, Oxford, 1956.

Tarski, A., *Introduction to Logic and to the Methodology of Deductive Sciences*, (34d rev. ed.), Oxford University Press, New York, 1965.

Taylor, R., *Action and Purpose*, Prentice-Hall, Englewood Cliffs, N.J., 1966.

Technology and Culture: 'Toward a Philosophy of Technology', **VII**, 1966, pp. 301–340.

Teilhard de Chardin, P., *Le Phenomène Humain*. Paris, Ed. du Seuil, 1955.

Thomas, L., *The Lives of a Cell*, Viking Press, New York, 1974.

Tintner G., 'Foundations of Probability and Statistical Inference', *Journal of the Royal Statistical Society*, Series A, **112**, 1949, pp. 251–286.

Tintner, G., *Methodology of Mathematical Economics and Econometrics*, University of Chicago Press, Chicago, 1968.

Tintner, G., 'Some Aspects of Stochastic Economics', *Stochastics*, **1**, 1973, pp. 71–86.

Topitsch, E. (ed.) *Logik der Sozialwissenschaften*, Kiepenheuer & Witsch, Cologne, 1965.

Toulmin, S., *The Philosophy of Science*, Hutchinson, London, 1953.

Trappl R. and Pichler, F. R., (eds.) *Progress in Cybernetics and Systems Research*, Volume I, Hemisphere Publishing Corporation, Washington D.C., 1974.

Trappl, R. and Hanika, F. de Paul, (Eds.) *Progress of Cybernetics and Systems Research*, Volume II, Hemisphere Publishing Corporation, Washington D.C., 1974.

Turquette, A. R., 'Modality, Minimality and Many-Valuedness', in *Proceedings of a Colloquium on Modal and Many Valued Logics*, Acta Philosophica Fennica Fasc, Helsinki, XVI, 1963, pp. 261–276.

Wald, A. 'Contributions to the Theory of Statistical Estimation and Testing Hypotheses', *Annals of Mathematics and Statistics*, **10**, 1939, pp. 299–326.

Wald, A., *Statistical Decision Functions*, Wiley, New York, 1950.

Walras, Léon, *Eléments d'Economie Pure*, Paris, 1974.

Walters, C. and Clark, W., 'Methodological Problems in the Modeling and Analysis of Ecological Systems', in H. R. Grumm (ed.), *Analysis and Computation of Equilibria and Regions of Stability*, International Institute for Applied Systems Analysis, Laxenburg, 1975, pp. 24–39.

Warnock, G. J. (ed.), *The Philosophy of Perception*, Oxford University Press, Oxford, 1967.

Weber, M., *Gesammelte Aufsätze zur Wissenschaftslehre*, Winckelmann, Tübingen, 1922.

Weber, M., *The Methodology of the Social Sciences*, Free Press, New York, 1949.

Wellmer, A., *Methodologie als Erkenntnisproblem- zur Wissenschaftslehre Karl R. Poppers*, Suhrkamp Verlag, Frankfurt a.M., 1967.

Wendt, D. and Vlek, C. A. J. (eds.), *Utility, Probability, and Human Decision Making*, D. Reidel Publ. Co., Dordrecht, 1973.

Whewell, W., *History of Inductive Science*, 1837.

Whewell, W., *Philosophy of the Inductive Sciences*, 1840.

White, A. R. (ed.) *The Philosophy of Action*, Oxford University Press, Oxford, 1975.

Whitehead, A. N., *Science in the Modern World*, McMillan, New York, 1925.

Whitehead, A. N., *Process and Reality*, McMillan, New York, 1929; quotations from the 1952 edition.

Whitehead, A. N., *Adventures of Ideas*, MacMillan, New York, 1933; quotations from Mentor-edition, 1955.

Whitehead, A. N., *Modes of Thought*, Cambridge University Press, Cambridge, Mass., 1938.

Whitehead, A. N. and Russell, B., *Principia Mathematica*, Cambridge University Press, Cambridge, 1910–13.

Whyte, L. L., Wilson, A. G., and Wilson, D., (eds.), *Hierarchical Structures*, Elsevier, New York, 1969.

Wiener, N., *Cybernetics – Or Control and Communication in the Animal and the Machine*, MIT-Press, Cambridge, Mass., 1948; second edition, 1961.

Wiener, N., *The Human Use of Human Beings – Cybernetics and Society*, Houghton Mifflin, New York, 1950.

Wigner, E. P., *Symmetries and Reflections*, MIT-Press, Cambridge, 1970.

Wilder, R. L., *Introduction to the Foundations of Mathematics*, Wiley, N.Y., 1952.

Wilson, A., 'Systems Epistemology', *The World System*, ed. by E. Laszlo, G. Braziller, New York, 1973, pp. 119–140.

Wilson, E. B., *An Introduction to Scientific Research*, McGraw-Hill, New York, 1952.

Winiarski, L., 'Essai sur la mécanique Sociale: L'Energie Sociale et ses Mensurations', Part II Revue, *Philosophique*, **XLIX**, 1900.

Wisdom, John, *Foundations of Inference in Natural Science*, Methuen, London, 1952.

Wisdom, John, 'The Need for Corroboration, Comments on Agassi's Paper', *Technology and Culture*, **VII**, 1966, pp. 367–370.

Wittgenstein, L. von, *Tractatus Logico-Philosophicus*, Routledge and Kegan Paul, London, 1961 (1922).

Wittgenstein, L. von, *Philosophical Investigations*, Blackwell, Oxford, 1953.

Wold, H. O., 'Mergers of Economics and Philosophy of Science', *Synthese*, **20**, 1969, pp. 427–482.

Wright, G. H. von, *A Treatise on Induction and Probability*, Routledge and Kegan Paul, London, 1951.

Wright, G. H. von, 'Deontic Logic', *Mind*, **60**, 1951, pp. 1–15.

Wright, G. H. von, *The Logical Problem of Induction*, (2nd rev. ed.), Macmillan, New York, 1957.

Wright, G. H. von, 'Practical Inference', *Philosophical Review*, 72, 1963, pp. 159–179.
Wright, G. H. von, *An Essay in Deontic Logic and the General Theory of Action*, North-Holland Publishing, Amsterdam, 1968.
Wright, G. H. von, *Explanation and Understanding*, London, 1971.
Young, O. R., 'A Survey of General Systems Theory', *General Systems*, 9, 1965 pp. 61–80.
Young, Y. Z. and Margerison, T. (eds.), *The Explosion of Science*, Crown Publishers, New York, 1968 (Vol. I), 1969 (Vol. II).
Zadeh, L. H., 'Fuzzy Sets', *Information and Control*, 8, 1965, pp. 338–353.

DICTIONARIES, ENCYCLOPEDIAS, AND INDICES

Chambers' Encyclopedia (new revised ed.), Vols. 1–15, ed. by M. D. Law and M. V. Dixon, International Learning Systems Corporation Ltd., London, 1968.

The Concise Encyclopedia of Western Philosophy and Philosophers, ed. by J. O. Urmson, Hutchinson, London, 1960.

Dictionary of the History of Ideas. 4 vols. and Index, ed. by P. P. Wiener, Charles Scribner's Sons, New York, 1968 and 1973.

Encyclopedia of Philosophy, Vols. 1–8., ed. by P. Edwards, MacMillan Co. and Free Press, New York, 1967.

Encyclopedia of the Social Sciences, 25 vols., ed. by E. R. A. Seligman, MacMillan, New York, 1930.

Index of Economic Journals, Vols. I to VII, American Economic Association, R. D. Irwin, Homewood, Ill., 1961–1967.

International Directory of Philosophy and Philosophers., ed. by G. Varet and P. Kurz, Humanities Press, Inc., New York, 1965.

International Encyclopedia of the Social Sciences, 17 vols., ed. by D. L. Sills, MacMillan and Free Press, New York, 1968.

The Philosopher's Index, ed. by R. H. Lineback, D. Reidel Publishing Co, Dordrecht.

Vocabulaire *Technique et Critique de la Philosophie*, by A. Lalande, Presses Universitaires de France, Paris.

SOME JOURNALS OF PHILOSOPHY, APPLIED AND SOCIAL SCIENCES

The Accounting Review, Quarterly Publication of the American Accounting Association, ed. by S. A. Zeff.

Acta Informatica. Springer Verlag, Berlin.

Advances in Cybernetics and Systems, ed. by J. Rose, Gordon and Breach, London.

American Economic Review, Journal of the American Economic Association, ed. by G. H. Borts.

American Philosophical Quarterly, ed. by N. Rescher, B. Blackwell, Oxford.

Analysis, ed. by C. J. F. Williams, B. Blackwell, Oxford.

Annals of Systems Research (Yearbook of the Netherland Society for Systems Research), ed. by R. van Rootselar.

The Aristotelian Society: Proceedings and Supplementary Volumes, ed. by A. A. Kassman, London.

Behavioral Science, Journal of the Society for General Systems Research, ed. by J. G. Miller, Louisville, Kentucky.

Biological Cybernetics, ed. by H. B. Barlow, B. Hassenstein, I. Kohler, D. M. MacKay, W. Reichardt, and I. F. Schouten, Springer-Verlag, Berlin.

Bibliography of Philosophy, a Quarterly Bulletin, ed. by R. Klibansky and L. Jerphagnon, International Institute of Philosophy, Paris.

British Journal for the Philosophy of Science, Cambridge Univ. Press, Cambridge.

Canadian Journal of Philosophy, ed. by J. King-Farlow *et al*, Canadian Association for Publishing in Philosophy, Edmonton.

Cultural Hermeneutics, Dordrecht, D. Reidel.

Cybernetica, Journal of the International Association for Cybernetics, Namur.

Cybernetica, Vols. 1 (1958) to 18 (1975), Namur.

Dialectica, an International Quarterly Review of Philosophy of Knowledge, ed. by P. Bernay *et al.*, Bienne, Switzerland.

Dialog, Canadian Philosophical Review, ed. by V. Cauchy and H. M. Estall, Montreal.

The Economic Journal, the Quarterly Journal of the Royal Economic Society, ed. by J. S. Fleming, Oxford.

Economy and Society, Routledge & Kegan Paul, Oxford.

The Engineering Economist, ed. by R. P. Lutz, American Society for Engineering Education.

Erkenntnis, an International Journal of Analytical Philosophy, ed. by K. Hempel, W. Stegmüller and W. K. Essler, D. Reidel Publishing Co, Dordrecht.

Foundations of Language, an International Journal of Language and Philosophy, ed. by W. Abraham *et al.*, D. Reidel Publishing Co, Dordrecht.

Futures, IPC Science and Technology Press, England.

General Systems, Annual Yearbook of the Society for Systems Research, ed. by A. Rapoport, Washington, D.C.

Harvard Business Review, ed. by R. F. Lewis, Boston.

IBM Systems Journal, ed. by A. G. Davis, International Business Machines, New York.

Information and Control, ed. by M. Eden, Academic Press, New York.

Interfaces, ed. by L. S. Simon, Institute of Management Sciences, New York.

International Congress of Cybernetics – Proceedings 1st (1956) to 8th (1976), Namur.

International Logical Review, Rassegna Internazionale di Logica, ed. by F. Spisani, Bologna.

Journal of Accounting Research, ed. by N. Dopuch, The Institute of Professional Accounting.

The Journal of Business, ed. by I. Schweiger, Faculty of Graduate School of Business, Univ. of Chicago, Chicago.

Journal of Cybernetics, Transactions of the American Society for Cybernetics, ed. by L. J. Fogel, Scripta Publ. Co, Washington, D.C.

Journal of Economic Literature, ed. by M. Perlman, American Economic Association.

The Journal of Finance, ed. by J. M. Guttentag, The Wharton School, Philadelphia.

The Journal of Industrial Economics, ed. by J. A. Menge, Basil Blackwell, Oxford.

The Journal of Law and Economics, ed. by R. H. Coase and W. M. Landes, University of Chicago Law School, Chicago.

Journal of Medicine and Philosophy.

Journal of Philosophical Logic, ed. by B. C. van Fraassen, D. Reidel Publishing Co., Dordrecht.

The Journal of Philosophy, ed. by B. Berofsky *et al.*, New York.

The Journal of Political Economy, ed. by J. A. Frenkel, H. G. Johnson, S. Peltzman, and G. Stigler, Univ. of Chicago Press, Chicago.

Journal of the Association of Computing Machinery, ed. by R. E. Miller, New York.

Journal for the Theory of Social Behavior, ed. by P. F. Secord and T. Mischel, assisted by R. Harré, B. Blackwell, Oxford.

Land Economics, a quarterly journal devoted to the study of economic and social institutions, ed. by M. Atterbury, University of Wisconsin, Madison.

Management Science, Journal of the Institute of Management Sciences, ed. by M. K. Starr, New York.

Mathematical Programming, Journal of the Mathematical Programming Society, ed. by M. L. Balinski (International Institute for Applied Systems Analysis, Laxenburg, Austria), North Holland Publ. Co.

Mathematical Systems Theory, Springer Verlag, Berlin.

Mind, a Quarterly Review of Psychology and Philosophy, ed. by D. Hamlyn, B. Blackwell, Oxford.

The Monist, an International Quarterly Journal of General Philosophical Inquiry, ed. by E. Freeman, La Salle, Illinois.

Noûs, ed. by N. Castañeda, Indiana University, Bloomington.

Operations Research, Journal of the Operations Research Society of America, ed. by G. L. Memhauser.

Operational Research Quarterly, ed. by K. B. Haley, Operations Research Society Ltd, London.

Organizational Behavior and Human Performance, Academic Press, Inc., New York.

Organization and Administrative Sciences, ed. by A. R. Negandhi, Comparative Administration Research Institute, Kent State University.

Origins of Life, ed. by C. Ponnamperuma, D. Reidel Publ. Co., Dordrecht.

Personnel Psychology, a Journal of Applied Research, ed. by F. Kuder, Durham, North Carolina.

Philosophia, Philosophical Quarterly of Israel, ed. by A. Blum and A. Kasher, Bar-Ilan University, Tel Aviv.

The Philosophical Forum, Boston University, Boston.

The Philosophical Quarterly, ed. by B. Mayo, University of St. Andrews, U.K.

Philosophical Review, ed. by the Faculty of the Sage School of Philosophy, Cornell University, Ithaca, N.Y.

Philosophical Studies, an International Journal for Philosophy in the Analytical Tradition, ed. by K. Lehrer, D. Reidel Publishing Co., Dordrecht.

Philosophy, ed. by R. Bambrough, MacMillan Journals Ltd, London.

Philosophy and Public Affairs, ed. by M. Cohen, Princeton Univ. Press, Princeton.

Philosophy of Science, official Journal of the Philosophy of Science Association, ed. by R. S. Rudner.

Philosophy of Social Sciences, an International Journal, York Univ., Toronto.

Problems of the Science of Science, ed. by J. Kaczmarek, D. Reidel Publishing Co., Dordrecht.

Proceedings: 1st to 8th International Congress on Cybernetics, International Association of Cybernetics, Namur.

Ratio, ed. by S. Körner, B. Blackwell, Oxford.

The Review of Economics and Statistics, ed. by H. S. Houtakker and J. F. Kain, Harvard Univ. Press, Boston.

The Review of Economic Studies, Journal of the Society for Economic Analysis Ltd., ed. by P. J. Hammond and S. Nickel, Dept. of Economics, Univ. of Essex, Colchester.

Scientia, International Review of Scientific Synthesis, ed. by N. Bonetti and A. De Murtas, Milano, Italy.

Social Indicators Research, an International and Interdisciplinary Journal for Quality-of-life Measurement, ed. by A. C. Michalos, D. Reidel Publishing Co., Dordrecht.

Social Theory and Practice, an International and Interdisciplinary Journal of Social Philosophy, Tallahassee, Florida, U.S.A.

Soviet Cybernetics Review, ed. by W. B. Holland, Santa Monica: Rand Corporation.

Studies in History and Philosophy of Science, ed. by G. Buchdahl and L. L. Laudan, MacMillan Journals Ltd, London.

Synthese, an International Journal for Epistemology, Methodology and Philosophy of Science, ed. by J. Hintikka, D. Reidel Publishing Co., Dordrecht.

Systems Theory Research, (Translation of *Problemy Kibernetiki*) ed. by A. A. Lyapunov, Nauka Press, Moscow; Consultants Bureau, New York.

Technology and Culture, the International Quarterly of the Society for the History of Technology, University of Chicago Press, Chicago.

Theoria, A Swedish Journal of Philosophy, ed. by G. Hermerén and K. Segerberg, Lund, Sweden.

Theory and Decision, an International Journal for Philosophy and Methodology of the Social Sciences, ed by G. L. Eberlein, W. Kroeber-Riel, W. Leinfellner, and F. Schick, D. Reidel Publishing Co., Dordrecht.

Teaching Philosophy, ed. by A. Wilson and W. Todd, University of Cincinnati, Ohio, Cincinnati.

Zeitschfit für betriebswirtschaftliche Forschung (formerly: Z.f. handelswissenschaftliche F.), ed. by K. Hax, W. Busse von Colbe, E. Grochla, R. Guembel, H. Hax, G. Lassmann, D. Schneider, and K. von Wysocki, Schmalenbach Gesellschaft, Cologne.

Zeitschrift für Allgemeine Wissenschaftstheorie, Journal for General Philosophy of Science, ed. by A. Diemer, L. Geldsetzer and G. König, Steiner Verlag, G.m.b.H. Wiesbaden.

Zeitschrift für Ganzheitsforschung (Neue Folge), ed. by W. Heinrich, Vienna.

For further references see Gerber, W., 'Philosophical Journals', *Encyclopedia of Philosophy*, Vol. 6, ed. by P. Edwards, pp. 199–216.

INDEX OF NAMES

INDEX OF SUBJECTS

THEORY AND DECISION LIBRARY

An International Series in the Philosophy and Methodology of the Social and Behavioral Sciences

1. Günther Menges (ed.), *Information, Inference, and Decision*. 1974, viii + 195 pp.
2. Anatol Rapoport (ed.), *Game Theory as a Theory of Conflict Resolution*. 1974, v + 283 pp.
3. Mario Bunge (ed.), *The Methodological Unity of Science*. 1973, viii + 264 pp.
4. Colin Cherry (ed.), *Pragmatic Aspects of Human Communication*. 1974, ix + 178 pp.
5. Friedrich Rapp (ed.), *Contributions to a Philosophy of Technology. Studies in the Structure of Thinking in the Technological Sciences*. 1974, xv + 228 pp.
6. Werner Leinfellner and Eckehart Köhler (eds.), *Developments in the Methodology of Social Science*. 1974, x + 430 pp.
7. Jacob Marschak, *Economic Information, Decision and Prediction. Selected Essays*. 1974, three volumes, xviii + 389 pp.; xii + 362 pp; x + 399 pp.
8. Carl-Axel S. Staël von Holstein (ed.), *The Concept of Probability in Psychological Experiments*. 1974, xi + 153 pp.
9. Heinz J. Skala, *Non-Archimedean Utility Theory*. 1975, xii + 138 pp.
10. Karin D. Knorr, Hermann Strasser, and Hans Georg Zilian (eds.), *Determinants and Controls of Scientific Developments*. 1975, ix + 460 pp.
11. Dirk Wendt, and Charles Vlek (eds.), *Utility, Probability, and Human Decision Making. Selected Proceedings of an Interdisciplinary Research Conference, Rome, 3–6 September, 1973*. 1975, viii + 418 pp.
12. John C. Harsanyi, *Essays on Ethics, Social Behavior, and Scientific Explanation*. 1976, xvi + 262 pp.
13. Gerhard Schwödiauer (ed.), *Equilibrium and Disequilibrium in Economic Theory. Proceedings of a Conference Organized by the Institute for Advanced Studies, Vienna, Austria, July 3–5, 1974*. 1978, 1 + 736.
14. V. V. Kolbin, *Stochastic Programming*. 1977, xii + 195.